D1065434

Russia's Steppe Frontier

RUSSIA'S STEPPE FRONTIER

The Making of a Colonial Empire, 1500–1800

Michael Khodarkovsky

INDIANA
University Press

Bloomington & Indianapolis

THIS BOOK IS A PUBLICATION OF

INDIANA UNIVERSITY PRESS
601 NORTH MORTON STREET
BLOOMINGTON, IN 47404-3797 USA

HTTP://IUPRESS.INDIANA.EDU

Telephone orders 800-842-6796
Fax orders 812-855-7931
Orders by e-mail IUPORDER@INDIANA.EDU

THE PAPER USED IN THIS PUBLICATION MEETS THE MINIMUM
REQUIREMENTS OF AMERICAN NATIONAL STANDARD FOR INFORMATION
SCIENCES—PERMANENCE OF PAPER FOR PRINTED LIBRARY
MATERIALS, ANSI Z39.48-1984.

MANUFACTURED IN THE UNITED STATES OF AMERICA

LIBRARY OF CONGRESS CATALOGING-IN-PUBLICATION DATA

Khodarkovsky, Michael, date
RUSSIA'S STEPPE FRONTIER : THE MAKING OF A COLONIAL EMPIRE, 1500–1800 /
MICHAEL KHODARKOVSKY.
P. CM. — (INDIANA-MICHIGAN SERIES IN RUSSIAN AND
EAST EUROPEAN STUDIES)
INCLUDES BIBLIOGRAPHICAL REFERENCES AND INDEX.
ISBN 0-253-33989-8 (CLOTH : ALK. PAPER)
1. RUSSIA—TERRITORIAL EXPANSION. 2. RUSSIA—BOUNDARIES.
3. RUSSIA—HISTORY—PERIOD OF CONSOLIDATION, 1462–1605.
4. RUSSIA—HISTORY—1613–1689. 5. RUSSIA—HISTORY—1689–1801.
6. IMPERIALISM. I. TITLE. II. SERIES.
DK43 .K485 2002
947.04—DC21   2001003581

1 2 3 4 5   07 06 05 04 03 02

Wäre ich ein Schmetterling . . .

Out of the three possible governments—democracy, aristocracy, and monarchy—it is hard to say which one is the best; instead one needs to consider the circumstances of each society, its geography, territorial size, and the state of the people, to decide which government is most appropriate. Thus, politics and *democracy* are the best ways to secure prosperity and order in individual cities and small countries. *Aristocracy* might be fine for large countries, which are safe from invasion because they are surrounded by the sea or impassable mountains, and particularly where the people are well educated, as is evident from the examples of England and Sweden. But where there are huge territories, open frontiers, and, most of all, an illiterate and unenlightened public ruled more by fear than its own interests, there the first two are unsuitable; there *monarchy* is required.

—V. N. Tatishchev, *Istoriia rossiiskaia*

CONTENTS

CONTENTS

Migration of the Native Elite and Commoners
Colonial Contest I: Law and Administration
Colonial Contest II: Land

ACKNOWLEDGMENTS

This book is the product of a decade of research and writing, and it would have certainly taken much longer without the timely and generous support of various foundations. In 1992–93 a fellowship from the Kennan Institute for Advanced Russian Studies of the Woodrow Wilson Center allowed me to initiate the project at the Library of Congress, and a grant from the International Research and Exchange Board provided me with an opportunity to continue the research in the Russian archives. From 1995 to 1997 fellowships from the National Endowment for the Humanities and the National Council for Russian and East European Research provided critical support for an interrupted two-year leave to complete research both in U.S. libraries and in the archives of Russia, Ukraine, and Turkey.

I would be amiss not to express my thanks to the dedicated staffs of the archives in Moscow, St. Petersburg, Astrakhan, Elista, Kazan, and Orenburg in Russia as well as those in Kiev, Ukraine, and Istanbul, Turkey. My speical thanks go to the staff of the Russian Archive of Ancient Documents, where I was kindly invited to join the traditional tea breaks, which made a long day in the often unheated reading room seem much shorter.

I am particularly grateful to those of my colleagues who read the entire manuscript and offered their constructive criticisms and detailed comments: Charles Halperin, Richard Hellie, Valerie Kivelson, Alfred Rieber, and Barbara Rosenwein. My thanks go also to those who read and commented on various parts of the manuscript: John Alexander, Thomas Barfield, Yuri Slezkine, and Lisa Vollendorf.

I am obliged to the publishers of *Comparative Studies in Society and History, The Journal of Modern History,* and *Russian History* for their consent to use the material which I previously published in the form of articles.

Throughout my tenure at Loyola University of Chicago, the university and my colleagues have offered their unwavering support. My special thanks go to Loyola's Office of Research Services; to the Center for Instructional Design, where Monica Salinas-Liening taught me the high-tech miracles of preparing maps and illustrations; and to my colleagues in the department, who greeted each new leave of mine with a handshake and a smile.

Last but not least I owe much to my wife Insa, who understood my self-imposed burden of writing; to my parents, who were happy to spend as much time with their grandson as I needed for my work; and to Loïc, who will soon understand why papa had to go to the library.

Russia's Steppe Frontier

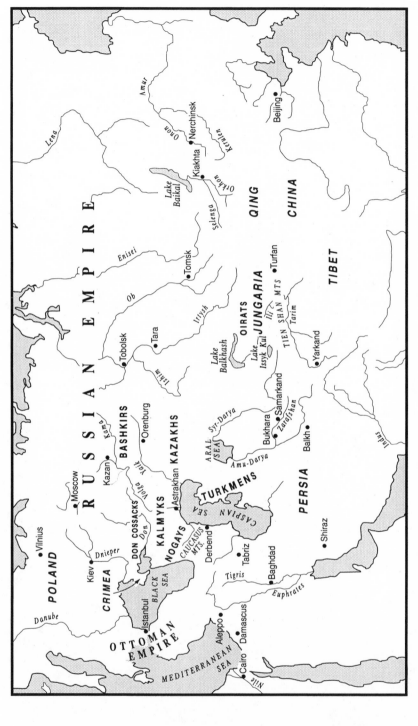

MAP 1.   Eurasia in the eighteenth century.

INTRODUCTION

The two largest Christian empires, the Roman and the Byzantine, shared the same destiny: their messengers of death arrived from across their frontiers. These facts were well known in sixteenth-century Moscow: that the Roman empire collapsed in the fifth century C.E., drained of its resources and exhausted by a long and ultimately unsuccessful resistance to Germanic "barbarians," and that a thousand years later the Byzantine empire, unable to prevent the advance of various nomadic tribes, similarly succumbed to the Ottoman Turks. Moscow was determined to avert the fortunes of Rome and Constantinople and spared no effort to preserve and defend its empire against successive waves of Turkic and Mongol nomads emerging from the Eurasian steppe. Of course, Moscow first had to build an empire.

Having emerged "on the Slavic *limes* of the Turkic steppe,"[1] the history of Russia, like that of its predecessor, Kievan Rus, was intimately bound up with the history of its steppe neighbors. While Kievan Rus had quickly and irreversibly succumbed to the Mongol invaders, Moscow patiently and successfully labored to prevail over the "wild steppe" and its nomadic inhabitants. How did Moscow succeed in transforming its dangerous southern frontier into a part of the Russian Empire and the steppe peoples into imperial subjects? What impact did the rapidly changing fortunes of various steppe confederations have on Russia—its ideologies, policies, and institutions? This book is an inquiry into the history of the steppe and its inhabitants and the making of the Russian Empire in the southern and southeastern frontier regions.

Most studies of the southern frontier focus on Russia's military fortifications, the construction of forts and towns, the expansion of agricultural settlements, and the role of the Cossacks.[2] By contrast, this book is about the Russian government's attitudes toward the peoples across the frontier, its ideologies of expansion, objectives and policies in the region, methods of developing dependency, changing perceptions and colonization of the newly vanquished peoples and territories, and their eventual incorporation into the imperial domain. It is also, of course, about the natives and their views of the Russian government and its policies, their choices between resistance and cooperation, and the inevitable and profound transformation of their societies under the impact of Russia's imposing presence.

The reader will see that Russia's expansion to the south and east was anything but haphazard, spontaneous, and uncontrolled, as is commonly believed. Rather, it was a deliberate process with varying motives and policies, to be sure, but consistent in its objectives of expansion and colonization of the new regions and peoples. By the late eighteenth century, the borders of the Russian Empire in the south and southeast had become contiguous with those of the Ottoman, Persian, and Chinese empires. Until that time, Russia was a frontier society par excellence, where porous frontiers and poorly defined political and territorial boundaries served as an invitation to continuous expansion.

Between the late fifteenth and the late eighteenth centuries, Russia's policies evolved from defending its vulnerable steppe frontiers by repulsing nomadic invasions to a deliberate aggrandizement and conscious transformation of the new territories and subjects. Cultivating the new lands and pacifying, settling, and converting its new subjects to Orthodox Christianity became an imperial *raison d'état* in the eighteenth century and Russia's own *mission civilisatrice*.

To be sure, most societies at some point were frontier societies. It was not until the mid-fourteenth century that Europe succeeded in establishing the relatively stable borders of Latin Christendom. First, Europe's Christian rulers had to engage in defensive measures against Viking raiders from the north and Magyar horsemen from the southeast, and only later to embark upon successful expansion through the establishment of settlements (*Ostsiedlungen*) among the Slavs in the east and the *Reconquista* of the Iberian peninsula from the Muslims in the southwest.[3]

By the sixteenth century, Spain, "whose existence had been one long Crusade,"[4] and Muscovy, which was rapidly emerging from obscurity with a "manifest destiny" of its own, had risen as colossi to stand guard on Europe's eastern and western flanks against the world of Islam. Separated by the unbridgeable gulf in their interpretations of Christian dogma, the rulers in both Moscow and Toledo arrogated to themselves the notion of being protectors of all Christians. The two imperial ideologies portrayed their respective empires as defenders of Christian civilization, and later as missionaries bearing Light to the non-Christians.

In a complex and substantial way, the identities of both Muscovy and Spain were shaped by their encounter with the Muslim world. But Muscovy's southern frontier was more than an ideological divide between Christianity and Islam. It also separated a sedentary population from a nomadic one, agricultural activity from pastoral herding, and a sovereign state under one monarch from the tribal confederations with weak central authority.

Situated on the easternmost fringes of Europe, Moscow faced the world geographically and culturally far removed from the cities of the European monarchs, the castles of their knights, the towns of the merchants, and the farming villages of the peasants. South and southeast of Moscow across the uncertain divide lay the vast expanses of the Eurasian steppe, populated at different times by various nomadic peoples: from the Scythian and Sarmatian tribes in the eighth century B.C. to the Mongol and Turkic peoples by the time our story begins in the late fifteenth century.

Moscow's neighbors in the steppe were mostly Muslim confederations of nomadic tribes, whose lifestyle, military organization, economy, culture, and religion differed markedly from those of the Muscovites. The difference between Moscow and its nomadic neighbors was further accentuated by the fact that the latter were Asiatic, and thus racially distinct from Europeans. The Russians, however, appear to have been largely oblivious to the category of racial identity until the eighteenth century, when they began to identify themselves more closely with Europe and European civilization.

Traditional western historiography, which was formed during the heyday of nation-states, deemed the history of the steppe peoples to be of no visible significance because the nomadic tribes were not state-organized societies. The steppe was simply regarded as a no-man's-land which separated one state from another. It is a measure of this remarkable neglect that William McNeill's celebrated book *Europe's Steppe Frontier* (Chicago, 1964) does not contain a single reference to any of the numerous steppe peoples. Instead, it leaves the reader with a clear impression that steppe lands lay vacant and waiting to be divided and settled by the Russian, Habsburg, and Ottoman empires. As the reader will see, the colonization of the steppe in the eighteenth century was not a function of the technological innovations in agriculture, as McNeill had argued, but rather a measure of Russia's success in providing security for the settled communities from the devastating nomadic raids.

Russian historians before 1917 had paid considerable attention to the issues of the steppe frontier. But theirs was a black-and-white picture of Russia's affirmed right and duty to expand the boundaries of Christianity and Civilization. They presented a detailed story of Moscow's struggle against Mongol domination and later against other, no less villainous, steppe nomads. Consequently Russia's expansion in the south was seen as a natural process intended to curb Crimean and Nogay raids and colonize the newly conquered lands. Because these lands were contiguous, Russian historians and the public in general made no clear distinction between conquest and colonization. In fact, the notion of conquest became subsumed by the notion of colonization, which was presumed to be in the interests of the Russian Empire and, by extension, of all the imperial subjects.[5]

It was this prevailing nationalist view that early Soviet historians were instructed to reject and reverse. After 1917, "colonization" and "colonial policies" became negative concepts condemning in one broad sweep the previous imperial regime and its policies toward national and religious minorities. Throughout the 1920s and 1930s, references to "the colonial policies of the tsarist regime" proliferated, but this was not the time for serious academic studies, as the Soviet leadership had other priorities.

Fostering a separate national consciousness and a sense of historical injustice among the non-Russian peoples of the Soviet Union was typical of the 1930s. But with the outbreak of World War II, the new demands for patriotic unity required consolidation of the country's diverse population, and the notion of "the Russian Empire as the prison of peoples" was slowly deemphasized. In its stead, the Soviet ideological machine began to stress "Russia's civilizing role" and introduced the notion of "fraternal friendship among the peoples of the USSR" led by the great Russian people. By the early 1990s, the "unbreakable union of the republics" proved to be anything but, and the sudden demise of the Soviet Union along national lines put national, ethnic, and religious identities at the center of renewed historical inquiry unconstrained by Soviet ideological dogma. The result was a fragmented representation of the historical process, with each interest group claiming its own separate, highly politicized, and nationalistic past.

While nationalist and ideological concerns of Russian-Soviet historiography may explain the absence of a systematic study of the southern frontier, Russian and Soviet historians did explore various aspects of steppe history. In the nineteenth century, at a time when some Russian writers and composers, such as Alexander Pushkin and Alexander Borodin, began to romanticize the nomads and their past, most historians continued to dwell on the traumatic experience of the Mongol conquest and its impact on Russia's destiny. Although historians' interpretation of the Mongol period often served to validate contemporary views of Russia's present and future, the net result was the publication of hundreds of valuable documents concerning the history of Russia's relations with the steppe peoples. Soviet historians continued this tradition, assembling thousands of documents into volumes intended to illustrate the history of Russia's relations with other peoples. It is these numerous published collections, together with the unpublished materials from the central and regional archives, that serve as the documentary basis for this book.

4

This book spans three hundred years of history, during which the Eurasian steppe, from the Don River in the west to Lake Balkhash in the east, was transformed from a distant frontier into an integral part of the Russian Empire. The story begins in the late fifteenth century, when the demise of the Golden Horde turned Muscovy into a rapidly expanding frontier society. By the late eighteenth century, Russia's huge territorial acquisitions in the south and east had made it one of the largest empires in the world.

Chapter 1 argues that the conflict between the Russian state and the steppe societies was an intractable frontier antagonism deeply ingrained in the fundamental structural incompatibilities of the two entities. To the extent that raiding activity underpinned the foundation of the steppe societies, Moscow's survival and prosperity demanded an end to the endemic guerrilla warfare along its southern frontier. The chapter underlines the differences between the two societies by discussing the political, economic, and military organization among the indigenous peoples and the role of religion and ideology in Moscow's relations with the peoples of the steppe.

Chapter 2 discusses mutual structural misconceptions which characterized the relationship between the Russian government and its steppe neighbors. Moscow considered all the newly encountered peoples to be the tsar's subjects and demanded their oath of allegiance (*shert'*), surrender of hostages (*amanat*), and payment of tax (*yasak*), while promising in return rewards and annuities (*zhalovan'e*). However, to the steppe peoples, who perceived their relationship with Russia through their own politico-cultural system, the terms of engagement looked remarkably different. Russia was only one of several regional powers with whom they chose to sign an advantageous peace treaty, in return for which Moscow agreed to deliver presents and payments. This chapter discusses each of the above concepts and argues that the Russian government's policies in the southern borderlands were also a function of the contested vocabularies and identities that Russia would finally succeed in imposing on the peoples and landscape of the region.

Chapters 3 and 4 present a chronological narrative of Russia's continuing expansion into the steppe. Chapter 3 discusses the history of Moscow's relations with the successors to the Golden Horde: the Crimean, Kazan, and Astrakhan khanates, as well as the Nogays throughout the sixteenth century. Chapter 4 addresses the history of Russia's relations with the newly encountered peoples in the lower Volga basin, the North Caucasus, and the Kazakh steppe in the following centuries.

Finally, Chapter 5 examines the patterns of the Russian government's policies in the southern frontier regions, which were rapidly evolving into imperial borderlands throughout the latter part of the seventeenth century and into the eighteenth. This chapter illustrates how the new policies and objectives marked a clear shift from previous frontier concepts, which were closely intertwined with the legacy of the Golden Horde, to the more modern and more European concerns of settling, colonizing, civilizing, and evangelizing the new lands.

The book is organized along two lines: thematic (chapters 1, 2, 5) and chronological (chapters 3 and 4). The risk of occasional repetition notwithstanding, such an approach presents a chronological narrative of Russia's relations with the steppe, and at the same time places their symbiotic relationship into a conceptual and analytical framework. The thematic chapters are intended to provide a new lens through which one can view the traditional historical narrative.

In the end, I hope to demonstrate that Russia was no less a colonial empire than any of the other Western European powers, even though Russia's colonial possessions lay not overseas, but within its ever-expanding contiguous boundaries; that the empire-building process in Russia was as much a product of the metropolis and its various ideologies of expansion as it was a result of the interaction between Russia and the indigenous societies along its frontiers; and that the complexity of the economic, political, and cultural interactions between these two very different worlds accounted for specific dynamics of Russia's expansion and its eventual transformation from a vulnerable frontier society into a colonial empire.

[1]

THE SOCIOLOGY OF THE FRONTIER,
OR WHY PEACE WAS IMPOSSIBLE

A party of 120 Russians arrived at the Yaik River to trade their grain for salt and fish with the Yaik Cossacks. They were returning to their village in the central Volga region when they were surprised by a war party of 600 Kazakhs and Karakalpaks. All were seized and taken away to become slaves and laborers. One of them, Mikhail Andreev, was able to escape from his Kazakh captor with two horses. Five days later he reached the Ufa District. There, in the steppe near the Yaik River, he was captured again, this time by a group of twenty Bashkirs, who took him to their village. For two months he was a slave of one of the Bashkirs until a Russian official, who arrived to collect *yasak* (a tribute or tax from the non-Christian population) among the Bashkirs, ransomed him for a silver-trimmed bridle, a pair of boots, and a fur hat. Later Andreev reported to the Russian officials that the Bashkirs were preparing to raid the Russian towns and that many Russians and Chuvash were still lingering in captivity there.[1] The year was 1720.

This story raises several issues at once : the extent of Russia's control over its purported subjects, the hostility of the non-Christian population of the empire toward the government, and the latter's dubious ability to collect taxes in such circumstances. But above all this story exemplifies the porous and indefensible nature of the steppe frontier, which, long after the government's initial undertakings to secure it, continued to subvert any attempts at expanding trade and settling the region. Such stories were typical. Mikhail Andreev was luckier than most of his compatriots, who usually endured far longer times in captivity and did not always find their way home.

Throughout the period discussed here, Russia's southern frontier remained a zone of uncertainty, a huge expanse of open steppe, with ever-present danger for those who ventured into it or lived nearby. Even in the mid-eighteenth century, when the Russian government acquired a much fuller control of its borderlands, the Russian peasants in the frontier regions continued to farm their land fully armed and were often indistinguishable from the Cossacks.[2]

For centuries Russia was engaged in the struggle to wrest control over the steppe from its nomadic inhabitants. What we know is the Russian version of this long-lasting conflict. What we also need to know is the story from the other side—the numerous nomadic and seminomadic peoples for whom the steppe was a homeland. Only when their story, which remained dormant for so long, is told can we fully understand the dynamics of Russia's imperial expansion and its final conquest and colonization of the steppe and its inhabitants.

In this chapter I argue that the interests of the two sides were fundamentally irreconcilable and that confrontation between them was unavoidable. This confrontation was a function of the ever-present and growing incompatibility between two very different societies. On the one side was Christian Russia, a military-bureaucratic state, with urban centers and a dynamic agricultural-industrial economy. On the other were various non-Christian societies with kinship-based social organizations and static, overwhelmingly nomadic-pastoral economies. We shall see how these structural differences, deeply ingrained in the social, economic, political, and religious character of the societies on both sides of the frontier, led to persistent and intractable conflicts throughout the period.

SOCIAL AND POLITICAL ORGANIZATION IN THE STEPPE

The peoples and societies that Russia faced along its southern frontier had much in common. Most of them emerged from the ruins of the Mongol Empire and one of its subsequent political successors, the Golden Horde, a steppe-based Turko-Mongol society that dominated the vast territory from the Danube River to the Aral Sea. The Golden Horde ruled over the Russian princes for more than two centuries before its ultimate demise in the early sixteenth century made way for Moscow's unstoppable expansion into the steppe.

During the three centuries of Moscow's expansion, the Russians encountered peoples with different degrees of social and political organization. Some were based in urban centers and had a relatively sophisticated sociopolitical organization (Kazan, Astrakhan, the Crimea), others were seminomadic societies (Kabardinians, Kumyks), and some were nomads par excellence (Nogays, Kalmyks, Kazakhs). At the same time, all of Russia's

8

steppe neighbors shared a common feature that set them sharply apart from Russia: none of them was a monarchy of the European type, that is, a sovereign, agricultural, state-organized society with clearly delineated territorial boundaries. Rather, they were tribal groups primarily bound by ties of kinship and military alliance and with a predominantly pastoral economy.[3]

The highest level of political organization among the steppe nomads was a confederation, usually short-lived and loosely knit. The constituent groups within a confederation remained economically and politically independent. The steppe societies had no sovereignty over a specific territory in a traditional sense. Instead, they proceeded along the migration routes toward their seasonal pastures. Like the sovereign states, nomadic peoples also had to defend their pastureland against the invasions of their steppe neighbors. But unlike the sedentary states, the pastures of the steppe peoples frequently changed because of the adverse weather, famine, or wars.

The absence of urban centers among the steppe peoples allowed for the formation of only rudimentary forms of government and bureaucracy. Even the Crimean and Kazan khanates, whose economy and politico-administrative systems were quite sophisticated, could not compare with Russia in this regard. In order to understand the basic terminology and structures of the societies discussed in this book, a closer look at their sociopolitical organization is necessary.

The Nogays

From ancient times, when Strabo and Herodotus described the nomadic lifestyle of the peoples in the steppe around the Black Sea, to the middle of the eighteenth century, when the steppe pastures were rapidly becoming agricultural lands, the enormous expanse of the Eurasian steppe served as a natural habitat for various nomadic peoples. During the three centuries discussed in this book, the western part of the Eurasian steppe was dominated by several nomadic confederations: Nogays in the sixteenth century, Kalmyks in the seventeenth, and Kazakhs in the eighteenth.

When and how the Nogays emerged as a distinct tribal confederation and what particular tribes they comprised are questions that cannot be answered with certainty. It is generally believed that the Mongol tribe called the Mangits constituted a core of the Nogay Horde. In the thirteenth century, the Mangits were joined by numerous Turkic tribes to form an army of the Golden Horde commander and later coruler, Nogay. A century later, as the ties between different parts of the Golden Horde weakened, the Nogays emerged from obscurity under a military commander of Mangit origin, Edige, the founder of the Nogay ruling dynasty. With ever-changing tribal boundaries in the nomadic confederation, the Nogay Horde included eighteen Turkic and Mongol tribes by the mid-sixteenth century. The Mangits, even though they were thoroughly Turkicized, remained the dominant tribe among the Nogays, and many neighboring peoples referred to the Nogays as the Mangit Horde.[4]

The beginning of this study finds the Nogays as an established tribal confederation distinct from both their Turkic (Kazakhs, Bashkirs, Tatars) and their Mongol (Kalmyks) neighbors. The most distinct marker was neither their language, a Turkic dialect that the Nogays shared with their many neighbors, nor a different ethos, a notion not easily applied to the nomadic confederations with frequently changing tribal membership. Rather, it was the ruling dynasty, whose descendants derived their origin from the dynasty's founder, Edige. In unwritten but clearly understood rules throughout the Turko-Mongol world, only the descendants of Chinggis khan were considered the heirs to the Golden Horde or other parts of the Chinggisid Empire. A prominent military commander, Edige was not of Chinggisid origin. This meant that the Nogay rulers, unlike their more noble brethren in the Crimea, Kazan, Astrakhan, and Siberia, were ineligible to claim the heritage of the Golden Horde.

This difference was clearly reflected in political nomenclature. A careful observer of early-sixteenth-century Muscovy, Baron Sigismund Herberstein, noted that the Nogays had no tsar (i.e., a khan), but only a princely chief (i.e., a *beg*).[5] The beg (referred to in Russian as a grand prince, *bol'shoi kniaz'*) was the ruler of the Nogays. The next in line of succession was the *nureddin* (a personal name of Edige's eldest son which evolved into a title), an heir apparent and the second highest title, followed by the *keikuvat* (a title derived from the name of Edige's younger son) and the *toibuga*.[6]

Tradition demanded that each specific title correspond to a specific territory. Thus, in the sixteenth century the beg's residence was in Saraychik, and his pastures were on the Yaik River; the nureddin was allotted the pastures to the west, along the Volga; and the keikuvat had those to the east along the Emba. The title of toibuga, first mentioned in the second half of the sixteenth century, probably emerged as a consequence of Kazan's fall into Muscovite hands in 1552, an event in which the Nogays played a significant role. While there is no clear indication of what the toibuga's responsibilities were, it is possible that the toibuga was in charge of a certain territory and people of the former Kazan khanate, thus controlling the northern and northeastern Nogay pastures.[7]

The candidates for the four princely titles had to be confirmed in the Nogay Grand Council, known as the *körünüsh* (*korniush* in Russian transliteration), which consisted of the members of the ruling house (*mirzas*), tribal aristocracy (*karachis*), distinguished warriors (*bahadurs*), the beg's retinue (*imeldeshes*), and Muslim clergy (*mullahs*). The beg had his own administration (a treasurer, a secretary, scribes, tax collectors) and a council comprising the best and most trusted people. Yet his authority as projected

10

through this rudimentary official apparatus was greatly circumscribed by the powerful and independent mirzas and karachis.[8]

It was the weakness of central authority that led to the interminable wars among the Nogays. The first serious division occurred in the late 1550s, when the Nogay nureddin, Kazy, abandoned his pastures along the Volga and moved to the steppe of the North Caucasus. His Nogays became known as the Kazy Nogays or the Lesser Nogay Horde. The remaining Nogays on the Volga and Yaik rivers under Ismail beg and his sons were referred to as the Greater Nogay Horde. In the early seventeenth century, the Greater Nogay Horde would break down further under the onslaught of the Kalmyks.

The Crimea and Kazan

The dissolution of the Golden Horde produced not only fully nomadic steppe societies such as the Nogays, but also khanates, rudimentary city-states with a peculiar combination of sedentary and nomadic lifestyles. The Crimea and Kazan, the two most important such khanates to emerge in the 1430s from the decaying Golden Horde, had much in common. While Kazan's ruling house was founded by Ulu Muhammed, the grandson of the famous khan of the Golden Horde, Tokhtamysh, the Crimean dynasty was founded by another descendant of Chinggis khan, Haji Giray. The Girays far outlasted Ulu Muhammed's dynasty in Kazan, and shortly after the latter became extinct in 1517, Sahip Giray arrived from the Crimea to claim the Girays' right to the throne in Kazan. Both before and after this event, the Crimean khans continuously laid claims to be heirs to the entire Golden Horde territory, which, of course, included Kazan.

In the Crimea, an heir apparent to a khan bore the title *kalgay* (*kalga*) and could be either a khan's brother or a son. The kalgay usually received pastures along the Dnieper River, northwest of the Crimea. Next in line of succession was the nureddin, who was given pastures along the Kuban River east of the Crimea. It is not apparent whether a similar system existed in Kazan.[9]

The power of a Crimean khan rested to a large extent on the support of the karachis, the chiefs of the four major tribes: the Shirins, Baryns, Argyns, and Kipchaks. After the early sixteenth century, the Mangit tribe also occupied an important position in both the Crimea and Kazan, yet the Shirins and the Baryns always retained their preeminence. In 1508 the chief of the Shirin tribe, Agish, wrote to the Grand Prince Vasilii III, pointing out among other things the significance of his position in Crimean politics. He compared the Crimea with a cart, where his sovereign, the khan, was the right shaft and he, Agish, with his people and an army of 20,000, was the left one.[10]

In both the Crimea and Kazan, major decisions were made at the khan's council (*divan*), or, if necessary, at a larger gathering (*kurultay*), which included nobles, clergy, and the "best" people. Members of the nobility in

11

descending order of prestige were chiefs of the karachis (*emirs*), other chiefs (*biks*), and the biks' younger sons (*mirzas*). While emirs were few, the biks and mirzas numbered several hundred. In contrast to the Nogays, the Crimean and Kazan khans relied on a larger and more sophisticated administration. For instance, in the 1520s the Kazan administration included at least thirteen different official ranks. Both the Crimea and Kazan inherited their administrative apparatus from the Golden Horde and maintained it to control and collect taxes from the agricultural communities on their territories.[11]

Much less is known about two other khanates that emerged from the wreckage of the Golden Horde: Astrakhan and Siberia. They had the same basic sociopolitical organization as the Crimea and Kazan. Yet their economic bases and geographic locations accounted for some differences. Astrakhan khans, for instance, derived much of their income from trade, since there was little agriculture in the lower Volga steppe. Kazan khans, by contrast, relied heavily on the taxes paid by the numerous peasants of the region. The Crimea, ultimately the most powerful political entity, drew upon several resources: trade, agriculture, and the profits from military campaigns.

The Kazakhs

The Golden Horde was not the only political entity of the former Mongol Empire to fall apart in the mid-fifteenth century. To the southeast of the Golden Horde, another part of the former Mongol Empire, the Chagatay khanate, which occupied much of Central Asia, was also in turmoil. Out of its ruins emerged the Uzbek khanate of Khorezm, with its prosperous urban centers of Urgench, Khiva, Bukhara, and Kokand in the desert south of the Aral Sea. At the same time, several Uzbek tribes fled Khorezm to the steppe north of the Aral. There they formed a nomadic confederation and became known as the Uzbek-Kazakhs (*kazak* or *kazakh* literally means a fugitive, freebooter), then simply as Kazakhs, and in the eighteenth century also as Kirgiz-Kazakhs (Kirgiz-Kaisaks).

This confederation included various Turkic and Turkified Mongol tribes: the Mangits, Kipchaks, Naimans, Kongrats, and others. Many of the tribes were the same ones that constituted parts of other nomadic confederations. But if the Mangits were the dominant tribe among the Nogays, the Kongrats played the same role among the Uzbeks and Kazakhs. Yet the overlapping of the tribes within various confederations, which later became different ethnic groups, was significant. It is not accidental that the Uzbeks, Kazakhs, and Karakalpaks all derive their historical and literary tradition from the same source, the epic of Alpamysh.[12]

After a series of internal wars between the members of the Chinggisid dynasty, Kasim khan and his son Khak-Nazar forged a Kazakh confederation, which lasted through most of the sixteenth century. The Kazakhs occu-

FIGURE 1.   Kazakh camp. From *Aziatskaia Rossiia* (St. Petersburg: Izdanie Pereselencheskogo Upravleniia, 1914), vol. 1, p. 157.

pied enormous pasturelands from the Yaik in the west to the Irtysh in the east. By the late sixteenth century, the Kazakhs were already divided into three distinct entities: the Lesser, Middle, and Greater Hordes (*juz*).[13]

Each Horde was ruled by a khan, with other members of the ruling dynasty known as sultans. Non-Chinggisid nobility consisted of *biis* (called begs or *biks* among other Turkic peoples) and *batyrs* (or *bahadurs*). Lower in the social hierarchy were the notables (mostly elected local leaders referred to in Russian as *starshiny*), who exercised significant influence over various matters. While the fundamental features of the political organization among the Kazakhs were quite similar to those of other steppe societies, the Kazakhs seemed to lack the more differentiated hierarchical structure of the Nogays, let alone the Crimea or Kazan. The authority of a khan was severely circumscribed by the members of the nobility, who preserved their influence and an independent power base.

The Kalmyks

The Kalmyks were the nemesis of all the Turkic peoples in the Eurasian steppe. They were a western branch of the Mongols known as the Oirats or

Dörben-Oirats, in reference to an alliance of four Mongol tribes: the Torguts, Derbets, Khoshuts, and Jungars. To their Muslim Turkic neighbors they were known as Kalmyks (from the Turkic, literally meaning to leave behind), perhaps in reference to the fact that they remained perpetual outsiders, incorporated into neither the Chinggis Mongol Empire nor its successor states, the Chagatay khanate and Yuan China.

In the 1440s, when the new khanates and nomadic confederations were emerging throughout the Turko-Mongol world, the Oirats also became united under Esen *tayiji* (the title of a ruler). Successful and bloody campaigns waged by Esen and his successors left a deep imprint in the historical memory of the region's various peoples. In the Turkic epos of Alpamysh, shared by many peoples of Central Asia, the Kalmyks invariably appear as the most powerful and dangerous villains.

The Kalmyks were different from Muslim Turkic peoples in more than one regard. Their confederation consisted exclusively of Mongol tribes not found among the Turkic nomadic confederations, they spoke a Mongol language, and their rulers did not belong to the Chinggisid dynasty. In a region that indisputably belonged to the world of Islam, their differences with their Muslim neighbors were accentuated even further by their adherence to Lamaism or Tibetan Buddhism, brought from Tibet in the late sixteenth century.

The social and political hierarchy of the Kalmyks had much in common with other Turko-Mongol societies, although certain titles and names were influenced by the Chinese tradition. The members of the ruling dynasty bore the title of *tayishi* and were divided into three categories according to their status and wealth. Members of the lesser nobility were known as *zayisangs*. A chief tayishi, who later was called a khan, was to be agreed upon by consensus among the tayishis and influential zayisangs. There was a hierarchy of court and administrative officials as well as a large ecclesiastical hierarchy headed by the Lama, a regent of the Dalai Lama in Tibet.[14]

The first known reference to the Kalmyks in Russian sources is dated 1535 and mentions their submission to the Kazakhs. Throughout much of the sixteenth century, the Kalmyks indeed found themselves overwhelmed by the Kazakhs.[15] But by the early 1600s, the Kalmyks once again rose to prominence among the Turko-Mongol steppe societies. It was at this time that pressure from the Mongols in the east and the lure of the vacant Nogay pastures in the west compelled some Kalmyks to depart from Jungaria. Most of these Kalmyks were Torguts, which remained a dominant tribe among the Volga Kalmyks. The Kalmyks' chief tayishis and khans continued to derive their dynastic tradition from their ancestor, the chief tayishi of the Torguts, Kho-Urlük, who led their migration from Jungaria to the Caspian steppe.[16]

The North Caucasus

Similar to Jungaria, much of the North Caucasus remained outside the control of the successor states to Chinggis khan's vast empire. Dozens of peoples inhabited the region, which was a frontier area between the Golden Horde and Il-Khanid Persia. When the Russians arrived in the 1560s to build a fort near the Terek River, they encountered the Kumyks and the Kabardinians, two peoples who dominated this northeastern corner of the Caucasus and through whom the Russians learned about other peoples in the area.

By far the most powerful and numerous people in the North Caucasus were the Adygs, better known as Circassians to their neighbors on both sides of the frontier. The Adygs populated almost the entire North Caucasus range from the Black to the Caspian seas. Their language was unrelated to the Turko-Mongol languages of their neighbors and belonged to a distinct Adyg-Abkhasian branch of the Caucasian language group. The predominant group among the various subdivisions of the Adyg people was the Kabardinians. The territory of Kabarda, split into Lesser and Greater Kabarda, was south of the Terek River and occupied most of the central and northeastern parts of the North Caucasus. To the southeast were numerous clusters of village societies, later known as Chechens; to the south were Ingushes, Ossetians, and Balkars.

Tucked in the northeastern corner of the Caucasus were the Kumyks, a Turkic people of northern Daghestan. The Kumyks, together with a number of other peoples whom they dominated, were organized into the largest principality in the North Caucasus under their ruler, the *shamkhal* (*shevkal*). The shamkhal had a residence in the town of Tarki (presently Makhachkala, the capital of Daghestan) together with his court and officials. The shamkhal was to be succeeded by an heir apparent, the *krim-shamkhal*. Long under Islamic influence, Tarki was also a residence of the sheikh-ül-Islam, the leader of the Muslim clergy among the shamkhal's subjects. The circumscribed power of the shamkhal notwithstanding, his principality exhibited a more complicated and centralized political organization than did most other societies of the North Caucasus.

Southern Daghestan was the site of another notably powerful principality ruled by the *utsmii* of Kaitag, where the Kaitags (today known as Dargins) were the predominant ethnic group. The utsmii was a hereditary ruler with residence in Majalis. Because of Kaitag's proximity to the Persian borderlands, the utsmiis traditionally found themselves under the sway of the Persian shahs, whereas most other peoples of the North Caucasus had closer ties to the Crimean khans and Ottoman sultans.[17]

Apart from the principalities of the shamkhals and utsmiis, most other peoples of the North Caucasus were organized into societies with highly fragmented political structures. Among the Kabardinians, for instance, the nobles were divided into the *pshi,* whom the Russian referred to as princes, and the *uorki,* the lesser nobility, whom the Russians called *uzden.* Princes were held in great esteem, but none was elected to a superior position to rule others. The use of the term "uzden," which the Russians applied to the Kabardinians, was indicative of Moscow's initial ignorance of the newly encountered peoples. This was a term of Turkic origin applied to lesser nobility among the Kumyks and other Turkic peoples of the Caucasus (Karachis, Balkars), but not among Kabardinians or other Adygs. Other nobles among the Kumyks and some of their neighbors bore titles similar to those in other Turko-Mongol societies: khan, beg, and mirza.

The nobles lived off tribute paid by conquered neighboring peoples, taxes paid by the peasants, and booty. While the nobles lived in fortified villages upland, where their serfs grazed their sheep and horses, the free peasants lived and farmed in the fertile valleys and plains of the North Caucasus. These peasant settlements (*kabaks*) were essentially independent and were left alone, except for the payment of taxes from their farming lands and fisheries in exchange for the nobles' protection.[18]

Other peoples of the region were organized into democratic societies or brotherhoods with no social differentiation. The Chechens, for example, lived in free societies, a cluster of villages or clans united by kinship, territory, and a mutual oath; the elders decided common matters in the councils, and the best warriors led raids and ambushes. Like many other ethnonyms in the Caucasus, the Russians learned the word Chechen from the Kabardinians, to whom they were known as Shashans or Chechens (by the name of the village). The Kumyks called them Michiks or Mischiks (from the name of the river), and to the Georgians they were known as Kistys. The Chechens called themselves Nakhchi or "people."

Adding to the confusion of changing names and unfamiliar concepts was the difficulty that Russians had imagining a people without a state and single ruler. It was almost a revelation to the governor-general of the Caucasus, P. S. Potemkin, who observed in the late eighteenth century that "the peoples referred to as the Chechens and Kumyks do not comprise real nations [*natsiia*] under such names, but every village has its own chief [*vladelets*] and is governed by its own laws."[19]

[ ]

The emergence of the new steppe societies in the fifteenth and sixteenth centuries was first and foremost a process of political formation and did not coincide with the ethnic boundaries. Members of the same tribe often found themselves part of different confederations founded and distinguished by a ruling dynasty. Given the geography of the area, the wide open steppe of

16

southern Eurasia, most of the societies of this region were either nomadic or seminomadic. Even those societies that were based in urban centers (the Crimea, Kazan, and Astrakhan), imposed taxes on the agricultural communities, and collected customs from trade retained a nomadic lifestyle, economy, and military.

All of the societies facing the Russian state in the south were decentralized and fragmented. On the one end of this broad spectrum were the societies with virtually no political hierarchy, such as the Chechen brotherhoods of the North Caucasus. On the other end were complex political confederations, such as that of the Kalmyks. From the Caucasus to Jungaria, these were societies organized for war. Prestige, valor, leadership, and booty all were earned and obtained in war. Lasting peace was antithetical to the very existence of the peoples that Russia confronted along its southern frontier.

RAIDING AND WARFARE

War not only reinforced the nomads' martial and social values, it provided a more significant source of income than did trade. Naturally Russia found itself in a state of constant warfare and its southern borderlands a target of endless nomadic predation, in the form of either military campaigns or raids. The large-scale campaigns were usually led personally by the khan or one of his sons. In the seventeenth century, the Kalmyk khan could assemble an army of 40,000 horsemen, and the Crimean khan 80,000.[20] Small-scale raids usually involved several hundred horsemen, and sometimes as many as 2,000 or 3,000.

Armed mostly with sabers, spears, and bows and arrows, the nomadic armies were a self-equipped militia. For instance, in preparation for his campaign against Kiev in 1501, the Crimean khan, Mengli Giray, ordered every man over the age of fifteen to show up with three horses for each person and one cart for every five people. If they lacked horses or weapons, they could lease them from others and repay the debt at the end of the campaign. High speed and mobility were always great advantages. Carrying few supplies, the nomadic cavalry depended solely on the availability of fodder in the steppe, so its range and effectiveness were severely limited by seasonal and weather conditions. Winter campaigns took place occasionally, but only when the horses were well enough fed to endure a short campaign. Mindful that the nomadic armies had no baggage trains, the Russians made every effort to take grain into towns and burn hay in the fields if they heard of approaching raiding parties.[21]

Moscow was well aware of the limitations of the nomadic lifestyle. In 1560 Ivan IV advised the Nogay mirza Ismail: "In the fall, you should attack the Crimea, because as you know, the Crimeans with their horses and herds

FIGURE 2. Turkmens at war. From George N. Curzon, *Russia in Central Asia in 1889 and the Anglo-Russian Question,* 2nd ed. (London: Longmans, Green, and Co., 1889).

FIGURE 3. Turkmens at peace. From *Aziatskaia Rossiia,* compiled by A. Kruber et al., 4th ed. (Moscow: Tip. T-va I. N. Kushnerev, 1915), p. 175.

cannot survive on fodder in both the summer and fall at the same place, at Perekop. Then they leave Perekop and cross the Dnieper River, come to the Chernyi Les, and there they graze their herds. So at this time you should send your sons to raid the Crimea."[22]

By the late fifteenth century, the introduction of gunpowder rendered the nomadic armies incapable of seizing towns surrounded by new types of fortifications and backed by cannon. In 1500 the Crimean troops burned the suburbs of several Polish towns but could not capture them, just as the large Crimean army that reached Moscow in 1571 failed to take the city.[23] Instead of capturing urban centers, the Crimean Tatars preferred to lay siege to them and effectively lock the garrison in. While some Crimeans blockaded the city, others had a free hand in rounding up and capturing local residents. The blockade continued until the party carrying booty away was beyond the garrison's reach.[24]

Yet small-scale raids, not large military campaigns, had been most typical of frontier encounters. Along its southern and southeastern frontier, Russia had to face an interminable armed conflict: a guerrilla warfare aimed at capturing people, seizing property, enforcing privileged trade conditions, and extracting tribute. Even when the Russian government was prepared to buy the cooperation of tribal leaders and pay those who took part in its military campaigns, the traditional values of the warrior society worked against Russian efforts to stabilize the frontier. Successful raids, not a marginal participation on the side of Russia's regular military, were the main means of exhibiting valor and achieving renown.

The economics of raiding served only to reinforce the traditional militaristic values of nomadic society and militated against the interests of the Russian government. Consider one typical raid in 1500, in which a war party of 1,000 Crimeans returned with 5,000 Lithuanian captives. The high price that slaves fetched in the Ottoman and Central Asian markets, as well as the high price of ransom, made it hard for the Russian government to provide incentives sufficiently attractive to discourage this sort of raiding. Not every raid was as successful, but, in general, profits from an average small-scale raid, involving several hundred horsemen and resulting in the seizure of a dozen captives and several hundred horses, far outweighed the payments offered by the Russian government.

Of course, there was one other alternative, namely, redirecting the thrust of the raiding activity. Thus, in 1516, the Crimean khan, Muhammed Giray, intent on maintaining peace with Moscow, paid his son Alp to prevent him and his thousand-strong war party from raiding Muscovite borderlands. Instead, Alp launched a raid into the Lithuanian lands. But this strategy worked only until the other side, Poland-Lithuania in this case, offered a stronger incentive to the khan and his son.[25]

Guerrilla warfare was also driven by immediate and opportunistic needs. Geopolitical considerations mattered little in the world of steppe politics, and even when peace agreements were concluded, small-scale raids persisted unabated. Time and again the Russian envoys in the Crimea reported that Crimean raiding parties were about to set out for Muscovy, and "the khan and his sons were unable to restrain their people because they were impoverished and starved."[26] No wonder that small-scale raids were usually impossible to prevent.

By the early sixteenth century, Moscow had grown into the most formidable military power in the region. Its treasury was full, and its military was reorganized and equipped with firepower. When in 1532 news reached Moscow of an impending Crimean invasion, Muscovite troops armed with cannon and arquebuses were deployed near the fords along the Oka River. The firepower of the Muscovite armies was so impressive that the Crimean khan, seeking to discredit Moscow in the eyes of the Ottoman sultan, informed him that Moscow had armed the sultan's enemies, the Persians, with 30,000 arquebuses.[27]

Some nomadic leaders learned to appreciate such firepower early on. In the early 1500s, while the Crimea and Moscow were still allies, Mengli Giray continually requested that Moscow send boats with troops armed with cannon and arquebuses down the Don River to attack the Horde. He later asked Grand Prince Vasilii III to order the boats to sail against Astrakhan with five men in each boat and with one cannon and two arquebuses for every three

FIGURE 4. Muscovite small cannon of the late fifteenth century. The inscription indicates that it was cast in September 1485 by someone named Iakov, on the order of the Grand Prince Ivan III. From Nikolai Borisov, *Ivan III* (Moscow: Molodaia Gvardiia, 2000).

boats. He assured Vasilii that Astrakhan would fall if the Russians attacked from the river and the Crimeans by land. Moscow deliberately procrastinated, and the Crimeans eventually received cannon and gunners from the Ottomans.[28]

Several decades later, the Nogays besieged Moscow with similar pleas for firearms. In 1553, on the eve of Astrakhan's takeover by Moscow, the appeal of the Nogay mirza Ismail to Ivan IV was a clear testimony to Moscow's growing military advantage: "We would have fought against Astrakhan, but we have no river vessels; we would have laid siege to Astrakhan, but we have no firearms."[29] Other Nogays also attributed the rapid military gains by Moscow to its use of gunners but predicted that the Russians would soon try to move beyond the Caspian Sea and Volga toward the Yaik River, Derbent, and Shemakha, "and our books say that all Muslim rulers would be enslaved by the Russian tsar."[30]

While nomadic horsemen remained mostly armed with traditional weapons, recognition of the devastating power of firearms triggered an arms race in the steppe. By the eighteenth century, spheres of arms distribution were well established. Russia, even though it maintained a ban on the sale of firearms to its non-Christian subjects and neighbors, had occasionally and reluctantly armed the Kalmyks. The Ottomans provided arms for the Crimeans and Kuban Nogays, and the Kazakhs obtained muskets from Bukhara and Khiva.[31] Nomadic armies, however, were slow to adapt to modern warfare, change tactics, or deploy and use firearms efficiently.

By the late eighteenth century, the nomadic military proved to be completely helpless against Russia's fortification lines and the devastating firepower of its modern military. As Russian forts and settlements approached and Russian irregular military armed with light, mobile cannon reached deeper into nomadic territory, even remote corners of the steppe were no longer safe. Faced with increasingly harsh imperial demands, the inhabitants of the steppe were eventually forced to give up their traditional independence.

CAPTIVES AND SLAVES

While military campaigns and raids by the nomadic armies conjure up images of burning Russian towns and villages, neither large-scale military efforts nor small-scale war parties were engaged in indiscriminate burning and plunder. Rather, their goal was to seize captives who, whether they were later sold in the markets of Kaffa, Azov, Bukhara, and Khiva or handed back in return for a ransom, had always fetched a handsome price and were the most desirable prize in the raids and wars.

Loss of population to the nomadic raiders was a chronic and debilitating problem along the southern frontier. During their campaign in Lithuania in 1501, the Crimeans were reported to have seized 50,000 captives. When the

Nogays signed a peace treaty with Moscow in 1618, they released 15,000 Russian captives.[32] By some estimates 150,000 to 200,000 Russians were captured in the first half of the seventeenth century.[33] These are only some of the most striking examples involving large numbers of captives. Throughout the centuries, thousands of anonymous Russian peasants, laborers, craftsmen, and soldiers ended up as slaves in foreign lands. They were captured near their villages and towns while working in the fields, fishing in the rivers, laboring in the salt mines, and making journeys to the markets, and they were, of course, taken prisoner in battles.[34] After West Africa, Eastern Europe—and Russia in particular—was the second largest supplier of slaves in the world.

Moscow's growing concern for captives in the sixteenth century came from its newly crystallized self-consciousness as a Russian Orthodox state with a divine duty to save Orthodox Christians from infidel captivity. One of the first efforts to change the status quo concerning captives was made in 1517 by Vasilii III, who instructed his envoy to the Crimea to insist that the Russian captives be released without ransom. The envoy's efforts were to no avail.[35] Moscow was more successful in imposing its conditions on Kazan in 1551, when it demanded the release of Christian prisoners and under the threat of capital punishment banned Muslims from keeping Christian slaves. Moscow warned that Kazan's failure to accept this condition would mean another war.[36] Almost a century later, when other measures to prevent raiding failed, Moscow embarked on the construction of extensive fortification lines in the south, in an effort "to stop blood-spilling and enslavement of Christians."[37]

The extent of the problem is most apparent from the introduction of a special tax in Muscovy for ransoming Christian captives. This ransom tax (*polonianichnyi sbor*) lasted from 1551 until 1679. Muscovy's comprehensive legal code of 1649 devoted one of its twenty-five chapters exclusively to the issue of ransoming Russian captives. All Muscovite taxpayers were to pay an annual sum collected by the Foreign Office, because "God commanded through a prophet not to spare gold and silver for your brother, but ransom him, and God will reward manifold the pious tsar and all Orthodox Christians." The ransom was stipulated in accordance with captives' social status: the highest ransom was based on the size of captive noblemen's estates. In one particularly striking example, after three years of captivity in the Crimea, the ransom for a high-ranking Russian nobleman, B. V. Sheremet'ev, was estimated at 60,000 silver talers. At the bottom of the ransom scale were the serfs and slaves, with a stipulated ransom of fifteen rubles per person.[38]

Freeing Christian captives was not only a matter of divine duty for any good Christian, but also a matter of compassion for the captives' plight. The Muscovite government, usually implacable when concerned with its own interests and sources of revenue, expressed through the legislation its unambiguous sympathy for the captives. Upon their release from captivity, taxpaying townsmen were free to settle wherever they wished, and the slaves and their families were no longer bound to their masters "because of their suffering in captivity."[39]

The government made every effort to gain freedom for Russian captives. Typically a Russian envoy to the Crimea was provided with a list of Russian captives. The list was then submitted to the Crimean khan, who was expected to release them in exchange for payments.[40] Where the government officials could not tread, itinerant merchants bought the captives and brought them to Moscow in exchange for handsome compensation from the government or individuals.

Moscow encouraged everyone—government officials, merchants, foreign envoys, and native rulers—to purchase the freedom of Russian captives. Eager to exhibit their loyalty to Moscow and to profit from a transaction, nomadic chiefs and nobles often did so. Sometimes, of course, their plans went astray, as happened in 1551 with the Nogay beg, Yusuf. A certain Russian captive named Iurii was about to be sold into slavery to Bukhara when Yusuf decided to ransom him in exchange for two of his own people, three good horses, a camel, and a piece of fur. Iurii promised to compensate Yusuf with 200 rubles but fled instead. Embittered, Yusuf wrote to Ivan IV demanding that he find Iurii and pay the promised amount.[41]

For the captors, a prisoner was simply an item of trade that fetched a certain price. In one example in 1538, the Nogay captors deemed inadequate a ransom offered by Ivan IV for a captured Russian prince, Semen Bel'skii. One Nogay, well disposed to Ivan, explained that the Polish king, the Crimean khan, and the *pasha* (the Ottoman military governor) of Azov all wanted to buy Bel'skii, and that Ivan could have Bel'skii only if he matched an offer from the Polish king. He then proceeded to detail the king's offer. The Nogays were obviously bidding up the price, waiting for the best offer. Despite Ivan's desire to get hold of his enemy Bel'skii, who had previously defected to Poland-Lithuania, he rejected one of the Nogay demands to exchange Bel'skii for eleven Russian men. He explained that "it was against our custom to give Christians in ransom." In the end, Bel'skii was sold to the Crimean khan and joined the khan in military campaigns against Moscow.[42]

The supply of Christian captives was responsible for the bulk of the slave trade in the region in the sixteenth century. In 1529 half of all the slaves in the Ottoman Crimea were identified as coming from Ukraine (*Rus*) and Muscovy (*Moskoflu*). The other half were the Circassians.[43] The Ottoman port of Kaffa was at the center of the regional slave trade. The Ottoman regulations on the slave trade there distinguished between those slaves who were brought from the Tatar and Circassian areas and those from Ottoman territories, such as the forts of Azak (Azov) and Taman. The former were considered to be coming from outside the Ottoman Empire and were fully taxed, while the tax on the latter was lower by half. In the late sixteenth century, Ottoman revenues from the slave tax constituted almost one-third of the total revenue of the Ottoman possessions in the Crimea.[44]

The pervasive incentives of turning captives into a source of substantial profit through either enslavement or ransom reached almost comic proportions on another contested frontier, the Habsburg-Ottoman borderlands in Hungary. Apparently some men acted as "professional prisoners," allowing themselves to be captured and then volunteering to raise the ransom money from the families of other prisoners, making a profit in the process.[45]

Those who were not ransomed became slaves and were assigned various duties. In the Crimea, some were employed in agriculture or used as interpreters and guides to lead war parties into the Russian territory. Those sold on the slave markets of the Ottoman Empire or Central Asian khanates were employed as craftsmen, laborers, or domestics. After a certain number of years, slaves could be set free by their owners. Judging by a group of Russian slaves who found their way to freedom from the khanates of Central Asia in the 1670s, their average stay in captivity was about twelve years, after which they were either given freedom by their masters or ransomed by the Russian officials and merchants.[46]

The government's efforts to prevent Orthodox Christians from becoming slaves in the Islamic lands stand in sharp contrast to its complicity in selling non-Orthodox Christians into slavery. The Nogays, who joined the Muscovite forces in the military campaigns in Livonia, met no objections from the government to purchasing German and Polish prisoners in Moscow. At the same time, Moscow took pains to instruct local *voevodas* (Russian military governors) along the route of the Nogays' return to make sure that there were no Russians among the captives traveling with the Nogays.[47]

By the second half of the sixteenth century, the seizure of captives was no longer a one-way street. Some Nogay chiefs complained that the Russian voevodas assisted their rivals who raided, captured, and sold into slavery many Nogays. The Crimeans and Ottomans also found themselves to be a target of the increasing raids by the Don Cossacks, and they demanded that Moscow rein in the Cossacks and return captured Ottoman subjects without ransom.[48]

One other issue that eventually led to numerous and consequential disputes was the flight of native fugitives to Russia. In the 1580s the Nogays continually complained about their runaways who fled to Astrakhan and were harbored there by the Russian authorities. They demanded that Moscow return German and Lithuanian fugitives and pay compensation for the Russian ones (*rusak*). Moscow stubbornly rejected the latter demand because "the Russian captives were fleeing from captivity, and many of them joined the Cossacks and could not be returned." Such refrains were familiar to both sides; in the past the Nogays had rejected Russian demands to return captured Russians under the pretext that the latter had already been sold to Bukhara. Now it was Moscow's turn to reciprocate.[49]

Until the late eighteenth century, ransom remained the most common way to redeem captive Christians. Although the construction of fortification lines succeeded in reducing the number of Russians falling into captivity, it did not stop the raids altogether. Both large-scale campaigns and small war parties continued to devastate the expanding Russian settlements. In one such campaign in 1717, the Kalmyks, together with their temporary allies, the Kuban Nogays, brought back 12,107 captives seized in the middle Volga provinces. To be sure, smaller war parties and smaller numbers of captives were more typical examples of successful raiding activity, such as a party of 400 Crimean Tatars who returned with 174 Russians in 1673, or 800 Karakalpaks who captured 1,000 Russian children and women in Siberia in 1742.[50]

In the 1740s, many Russians continued to linger in captivity in the Crimea, the North Caucasus, and Central Asia. More than 3,000 prisoners, mostly Russians and some Kalmyks who had taken part in a disastrous expedition led by Prince Bekovich-Cherkasskii in 1717, remained captives in Khiva. Another 500 Russians were held by the Turkmens near the Aral Sea, 3,000 to 4,000 by the Karakalpaks, and an unknown number by the Kazakhs. The government's attempts to convince the Kazakhs that they should free the captives, or at least exchange them for Kazakh captives, failed. The Kazakhs insisted that, in accordance with their custom, captives could only be sold or ransomed.[51]

Customs, however, were not necessarily written in stone, and the refusal to release the Russians was driven by an opportunity for ransom just as much as it was by custom.[52] Likewise, religious explanations of why the Russian captives could not be set free often merely cloaked opportunism. In 1517 the Crimean khan, Muhammed Giray, wrote to Grand Prince Vasilii III that his mullahs had warned him that it was a sin to release captured children between the ages of six and sixteen.[53] Yet, not infrequently, Muslims were captured and offered for ransom by other Muslims, and occasionally they were sold into slavery in direct violation of Islamic law.[54]

When it emerged in the sixteenth century, the issue of redeeming Russian Orthodox captives from the suffering and profanity of infidel captivity was a sign of both the vulnerability of Muscovy's frontiers and the government's newly conceived role as protector of Russian Orthodox Christians. But by the late eighteenth century, the roles of the captors and captives were decidedly reversed. While the Russians found themselves in relative safety behind a chain of fortification lines, increasing numbers of Muslims and pagans across the frontier became captives of Russia. Some were captured by force, many were purchased through intermediaries, but most came of their own volition in search of better opportunities in Russian towns. All were expected to convert to Orthodox Christianity in order to stay in Russia and to receive financial and other rewards.[55]

In the mid-eighteenth century, some government officials began to conceive of Russia as a multireligious and multiethnic empire. They proposed that the government extend its protection "not only to the Russian captives, but also to other Russian subjects [*rossiiskie poddannye*] regardless of their ethnicity [*natsiia*] and faith."[56] Yet the government's relentless missionary spirit dictated the fate of most of the non-Christian captives, who had been ransomed by the Russian government; they were converted to Christianity and sent to the interior regions of the empire.

TRADE AND ECONOMY

The traditional economy of Russia's steppe neighbors was static, undiversified, and extensive. It was based on grazing herds of sheep and horses, the latter being the most valued item offered by various nomadic peoples on the Russian markets. If the horse trade was important for Moscow in order to outfit its cavalry, it was absolutely essential for the steppe societies. The nomads' desperate need for trade and their dependence on foreign markets were best expressed by Ismail, whose brother, the Nogay beg Yusuf, asked his help in attacking Moscow in 1533. Ismail explained to Yusuf why he could not join him: "Your people trade in Bukhara, mine in Moscow, and if I begin war against Moscow, I and my people will be completely impoverished."[57]

In the sixteenth and seventeenth centuries, the horse trade with the nomads was strictly controlled by the Russian authorities and took place at a designated place near Moscow or in several Russian towns along the Volga. The horses were brought by nomadic merchant parties known as *ordobazarnaia stanitsa* (literally, the traveling bazaar of the Horde). Such merchant parties could be quite large; one party dispatched by the Nogays to Moscow in 1555 comprised 1,000 merchants with 20,000 horses. In 1688 the Kalmyk khan Ayuki dispatched more than 9,000 horses to be sold in Moscow, and seven years later more than 20,000 horses to the Crimea. Still, such large numbers were exceptional. From 1551 to 1564, the time of the most active trade between the Nogays and Muscovy, the Nogays brought for sale an average of 7,400 horses a year, but usually the numbers were far lower.[58]

A typical Nogay horse-merchant party arrived in Moscow in 1579. The Foreign Office, which was also responsible for the horse trade, directed the Nogay party to stay outside the city walls across the Moscow and Yauza rivers. The horses were fenced off, and the first hundred horses were counted. After collecting 4 percent customs duties for the cities of Moscow, Vladimir, and Gorodok (Kasimov)—two adult horses and two stallions for every hundred horses—the first hundred horses were taken to the market and the next hundred were counted. Several Russian military commanders were assigned to keep order and to see that all the horses were registered and that there were no fights between the Russians and Nogays. The Russian commanders faced severe punishment if they allowed nonmilitary service people, merchants, or churchmen to purchase horses. Only military service people were permitted to purchase horses, and only after the best horses had been taken for the tsar. Items allowed for trade were various types of woolens and other cloth, but items of any military significance whatsoever were banned: copper, tin, lead, iron, saltpeter, sulfur, gunpowder, bullets, firearms, spears, sabers, and other ironware. Violators were to be arrested and brought to the head of the Foreign Office, the *diak* Andrei Shchelkalov, where their merchandise would be confiscated into the tsar's treasury.[59]

The Russian market held enormous lure for the nomads. In the sixteenth century, the Nogays sought to obtain from Moscow a wide variety of products: furs, woolens, hats, armor, paper, dyes, tin pots, nails, saddles, falcons, and gold and silver in thin sheets. Even such traditional items as armor, saddles, bridles, and quivers were prized more highly if they came from Muscovite craftsmen. In the late seventeenth century, the Kalmyks increasingly sold their horses for cash to buy many of these items on the Russian markets. At the same time, in the North Caucasus, the government allowed only barter with local or Persian merchants and expanded the list of banned merchandise to include gold, silver, cash, slaves, and hunting birds.[60] Banned items varied slightly from region to region, except for a continuous and overarching ban on the trade in arms.

The horse trade was important for the local Muscovite economy and its military, but it was the trade with the Muslim states in the south that connected Muscovy to world markets. Merchants from the Central Asian khanates, Crimea, Persia, and the Ottoman Empire brought merchandise highly valued in Moscow—rich silk brocades, cottons, and spices—and in return acquired different kinds of furs, walrus tasks, falcons, armor, silver utensils, and clothing. Russian merchants traveled to the Crimea and the Ottoman cities of Istanbul, Bursa, Tokat, Amasya, and Samsun, while the Crimean and Ottoman merchants carried Russian merchandise to Egypt and Syria. Azov and Kaffa were the most important trade centers along a well-established trade route connecting Moscow and Kiev with Tokat. The trade was profitable, the volume was large, and the customs duties brought high revenues. In the early 1500s, the grand princes of Moscow seemed to have an almost endless supply of cash, and more than once the Crimean khans resorted to borrowing money from the Jewish and Armenian merchants in Kaffa, only to ask Moscow later for help in paying their debts.[61]

By the middle of the sixteenth century, Moscow's expansion in the south and changes in regional geopolitics brought the trade with the Crimea and

FIGURE 5. Bazaar in Bukhara. From *Aziatskaia Rossiia* (St. Petersburg: Izdanie
Pereselencheskogo Upravleniia, 1914), vol. 1, p. 188.

the Ottoman Empire to a halt. Moscow began to seek other routes, via newly
conquered Astrakhan, to Persia and Central Asia. United against the Ottoman interests in the region, the Russian tsars and Persian shahs had been
engaged in lively diplomatic and trade relations. In the 1620s, to encourage
trade in the region and to develop the local peoples' dependency on Russia,
Moscow temporarily exempted from customs duties Persian and local merchants trading in Tersk and Astrakhan. A century later, a Russian official,
Ivan Kirilov, described a brisk commerce in Astrakhan, where foreign and
Russian woolens, furs, leather, and linens exchanged hands to be taken to
Persia, and Persian silks and brocades went to Russia. Kirilov also noted that
most of the merchants in Astrakhan were not Russian, but Armenian, In-
dian, Persian, Bukharan, and Nogay.[62]

In the eighteenth century, the Russian government increasingly set its
sights on Central Asia, whose khanates of Bukhara, Khiva, Kokand, Tashkent, Kashgar, and Balkh were not only worthy trade partners in themselves,
but also critical links in the growing attraction of the "oriental" trade route
to India and China. A first forceful attempt to assert Russian interests in
Central Asia was made in 1717, when Peter I dispatched a well-equipped
expeditionary force led by Prince Alexander Bekovich-Cherkasskii to Khiva.

The campaign ended disastrously, with many, including the prince, slaughtered and the rest enslaved.[63]

Russia's ambitions in Central Asia, however, were not abandoned but merely delayed. In the 1730s, preferring an incremental expansion to a quick military conquest, the government resolved to build a fort halfway between Ufa and Khiva. The fort, initially built on the Or River and then moved to the Yaik, was named Orenburg and was meant to safeguard trade in the region. Ivan Kirilov, the main architect of Russian policy in the region, conceived of Orenburg as more than just another military fort. In time, Orenburg was to provide access to the natural resources of the region, become the center of trade, and lay the foundation for the Russian annexation of Central Asia.[64]

By the late eighteenth century, Orenburg surpassed Astrakhan and became the largest market on the steppe, bartering products of the steppe economy, particularly horses and sheep, and trading luxury items from the east. Traditionally, the government employed "stick and carrot" policies in using trade and access to the markets as a means of control over the peoples along the frontier. In the eighteenth century such an approach was further modified and more consciously articulated. Now various government officials insisted that using trade as a "carrot" was essential in pacifying the Kazakhs. In the 1770s a Russian envoy to the Kazakh khan Nuraly plainly stated: "The Yaik steppe for you is like a land sea with ports; the largest port is Orenburg, and [others are] Yaik town and all the Yaik River up to Gur'ev, and Astrakhan too, and you can trade in all these places and profit from it greatly, if only you learn to be more obedient and peaceful."[65]

Until Russia's military conquest of Central Asia in the 1860s, Orenburg remained the advanced military and commercial outpost of the empire. Huge caravans of 500 or more camels loaded with merchandise and silver traversed the Kazakh steppe between Orenburg, Khiva, and Bukhara. The safe passage of these caravans depended on their protection by local Kazakh and Karakalpak leaders, some of whom exacted a safe passage fee, while others preferred to rely on presents and access to Russian markets as a reward. Various government officials suggested that pacifying the Kazakhs and making them abandon their nomadic lifestyle would ensure the safety of trade in the region and would be critical for the opening of a direct land route to India, a dream of more than one Russian ruler.[66]

Just as concern over the safety of trade caravans crossing the vast spaces of the Asian steppe and desert prompted the Russian government to seek cooperation and pacification of the region's nomadic inhabitants, so were the latter pushed in the same direction by their growing dependence on trade with Russia. If the steppe was akin to the sea and the Russian towns to ports, the nomads were the seamen, who eventually had to visit the ports to replenish their supplies. Many of the seamen were pirates living off raids against the "ports" or looting the passing ship convoys (caravans). Others came to trade in peace. This indeed was the principal goal of the Russian government: to turn the pirates into merchants and caravan guards.

Throughout this period, the nomadic economies were inseparable from the economies of the neighboring sedentary societies and gravitated toward various regional trade centers, where goods and people could be seized by war or obtained by trade. The opportunities of gaining access to the markets often prompted nomadic migrations and were the cause of many wars between different nomadic peoples or their factions. Since the early sixteenth century, the Nogays had found themselves divided into those in the west, with pastures along the Volga and dependent on the Russian markets, and those occupying pastures east of the Yaik River and relying on trade with the Central Asian khanates. In the 1570s, defeated by the Kazakhs and cut off from the markets in Central Asia, the Nogays had little choice but to move farther west to become even more dependent on trade with Russian towns. A similar defeat inflicted on the Kazakhs by the Oirats in the early eighteenth century set in motion a westward movement by the Kazakhs and renewed the Kazakhs' clashes with the Kalmyks over pastures and access to Russian markets. By the late eighteenth century, Russia's relentless expansion of its territorial and trade frontiers accelerated the nomadic peoples' dependence on trade with the Russian Empire and their further inclusion into the imperial sphere of interests.

A KHAN, OR A SEARCH FOR CENTRAL AUTHORITY

One of the most distinct features of the steppe societies was the weakness of central political authority. Initially the strengthening of the authority of the khans and other local rulers was a cornerstone of Russian policies in the region. After all, Moscow itself had been subject to similar policies by the Mongols several centuries earlier. The rise of the princes of Moscow to the position of grand princes of Muscovy, and later the tsars of all Russia, was in no small measure a result of policies pursued by the khans of the Golden Horde. While the Russian lands continued to be divided into disparate principalities under numerous rival princes and the Golden Horde administration exhibited signs of decay, the khans found it more expedient to rely on the services of a single Russian prince to mobilize a loyal military force and to deliver taxes and tributes to the khans' capital, Saray. Moscow's rulers did so obligingly, in return soliciting the khans' help against recalcitrant princes. By the early sixteenth century, when the Golden Horde ceased to exist, the princes of Moscow had achieved undisputed control over the Russian principalities, now integrated into a single Muscovite state.

In the reversal of fortunes, it was Moscow's turn to face the distinctly different remnants of the Golden Horde, a variety of nomadic and seminomadic societies with rudimentary central authority. In the following centuries, Moscow's priorities would be to stop the incessant predations against its towns and villages and to provide peace and security along its southern frontier. In doing so, Moscow chose to rely on policies that had once been applied to Russia by its Mongol overlords, namely, buttressing the authority of a single ruler capable of curbing his people's raids and acting as a reliable military ally.

Nominally such a ruler with supreme authority existed in both the Crimean and Kazan khanates as well as among the steppe societies—the Nogays, Kalmyks, and Kazakhs. But even in the Crimean khanate, one of the most sophisticated polities among the successors of the Golden Horde, the authority of a khan was limited by the powerful and economically independent nobles.[67] The power of a khan was even more limited among the nomadic confederations. Considering a successor to the Kalmyk khan Ayuki in 1722, one influential Kalmyk noble explained to a Russian official: "Whoever becomes a khan would not matter. All he gains is a title and prominence, but his income comes only from his own *ulus* [an appanage consisting of people and herds]. Other tayishis have their own uluses and they govern them independently, and the khan is not supposed to interfere; and if he does, no one will obey."[68]

In the eighteenth century, successive Russian officials who were charged with implementing government policies toward the Kazakhs reported, in continual bemusement, how little power the Kazakh khans had over their people. The title of khan among the Kazakhs was not hereditary. Instead, the successor was chosen from among the sultans: the khan's sons, nephews, or brothers. In accordance with an ancient custom, the newly elected khan was lifted on a piece of white felt (*koshma*), and thus both symbolically and literally elevated. When he was lowered to the ground, his clothing, except for underwear, was stripped away. Some of the clothing was taken by the sultans, while the rest was cut into pieces and taken by the commoners. The khan was then given attire appropriate for his new position. Yet the title itself ensured neither prestige nor respect from other Kazakhs, and often various Kazakh nobles commanded far more power and authority than did their khans.[69]

Moscow, loyal to the legacy of the Golden Horde, reserved the title of khan for the members of the Chinggisid dynasty, with the status of an independent ruler equal to the Russian tsar. Thus, for instance, the town of Kasimov, granted by Moscow to one of the Chinggisid clans in the fifteenth century, was ruled exclusively by Muslim khans. Long after Kasimov became a part of the Muscovite state, Moscow continued to refer to the Kasimov rulers as tsars (khans) and *tsarevichi* (princes). Only in the 1650s, when Kasimov's last Muslim ruler, Seyyid-Burhan, converted to Christianity, was his successor and son, Vasilii, no longer mentioned as a tsar or khan.[70]

The issue arose again in 1690, when a Kalmyk ruler, Ayuki, received a diploma from the Dalai Lama of Tibet investing him with the title of khan. Shortly thereafter, recognizing Ayuki's power and influence, the Crimean khan began to refer to Ayuki as a khan. Moscow, while continuing to insist that the Kalmyks were Russian subjects, was finally compelled to follow suit. In 1708, for the sake of political expediency in securing a military alliance with the Kalmyks at a critical time, the government recognized Ayuki as a khan. This seemed a small price to pay in exchange for support from one of the most powerful nomadic armies in the region.[71]

After Ayuki khan's death in 1724, the Russian government attempted to abolish the title of khan among the Kalmyks and to replace it with that of viceroy (*namestnik*). But seven years later, after the government learned that an official embassy from China was on the way to the Kalmyk ruler to bestow the title of khan from the Qing emperor, it ordered the Chinese embassy delayed and hastily dispatched a Russian envoy to be the first to grant the title.[72]

Throughout the eighteenth century, the Russian government came to see the figure of a khan as one of the major vehicles for asserting control over its nomadic neighbors. The politics of bestowing the title and its evolution into one of the most important tools of Russian imperial policies are particularly visible in the case of the Kazakhs. The government's strategies in the Kazakh steppe were vigorously articulated in the 1740s and 1750s by Orenburg's first governor, Ivan Nepliuev, and by Russia's indispensable negotiator with the Kazakhs, Muhammed Tevkelev, who after his baptism in 1734 became known as Aleksei Tevkelev. The two disagreed on the best policy for pursuing Russian interests in the region. While Tevkelev advised strengthening the khan's authority as the best way to control the Kazakhs, Nepliuev warned that this would be damaging to Russian interests and, at any rate, impossible to achieve. His recommendation was to keep the Kazakhs in their present state, weak and divided.[73]

Other reports from local government officials suggested that Russian interests in the region would be best served by having an obedient and submissive Kazakh khan directly appointed by the Russian government. They warned that the government had to proceed cautiously in this direction. It should initially insist that an already elected khan seek confirmation of his title by an imperial decree, thus leaving no doubt as to his status as a Russian subject. The government also might begin cultivating the loyalty of one or several Kazakh sultans in advance. These sultans were to be publicly praised and given money and presents to buy the support of other Kazakhs. Upon the khan's death, one of these sultans might be appointed a viceroy, and later, if he proved loyal to Russia, he might be declared khan. Such was the advice of two seasoned officials charged with governing the Orenburg region, Tevkelev and Petr Rychkov, in a 1759 memorandum to the Foreign Office.[74]

These were, in essence, the ideas expounded by Tevkelev in the 1740s and then further elaborated and supported by Rychkov. Both Tevkelev and Rychkov believed that it was paramount to Russian interests to deprive the Kazakhs of the ability to elect their own khans. Their strategy was to endow the position of khan with stronger authority by elevating him over the influence of his own people and forging direct links between a khan and Russian authorities. At the same time, to prevent a khan from becoming too powerful and independent, they urged that the position not become hereditary.[75] Their views proved to be popular in St. Petersburg and became the foundation of Russian policies in the following decades.

While confirmation of a khan required only nominal Russian involvement, appointing a khan meant entanglement in local Kazakh politics. Russian officials understood this well and requested that a detailed description of Kazakh khans and their heirs, clans, and pastures be submitted for the government's consideration. But because the Kazakhs had no strict rules of succession and the government had no intention of creating one, the choice of a new khan was almost always fraught with rivalries and wars between Kazakh groups pitted against each other. Now that the Russian government had to side with one group or another, hostilities inevitably spilled over against the Russian authorities. The government's choice of a khan was not based on his eligibility or popularity among the Kazakhs, but only on his loyalty to Russia. Most of the time other heirs refused to accept a Russian candidate, and they tried to engineer their own election by the loyal biis, claiming that they belonged to a more senior clan or higher rank.[76]

St. Petersburg rewarded a loyal khan by building forts in which he could reside or take refuge and by bestowing gifts and payments. The government also sought to create pomp and circumstance around the position of a khan. It intended to make such a position more attractive to a candidate and at the same time to put the process of coronation entirely in government hands. In 1792 the senate decreed a minutely prescribed procedure for the inauguration of a Kazakh khan. The Kazakh nobles and notables were to gather near Orenburg. There they were to be met and greeted by Russian military commanders and an artillery salute. Two carriages were to be sent from Orenburg to bring a newly elected khan to the governor. A sumptuous feast for all those present was to follow, and gifts were to be distributed to the sultans. In a camp built especially for this purpose, the khan was to kneel on a carpet in the presence of his nobles and notables and repeat an oath delivered from St. Petersburg and read to him in Russian and Tatar. He was to kiss the Quran and place it on his head. Then he would be awarded a sable coat, fox hat, saber, and khan's diploma, which he was to kiss and place on his head. At this point, cannon and rifles were fired, and the khan would return to Orenburg to resume the feast.[77]

The attempts by the Russian government to control its unruly nomadic neighbors by endowing the position of khan with more power and authority achieved limited success. Such government policies often backfired and instead contributed to the consolidation of opposition against the khan, who was seen as promoting Russian interests at the expense of the Kazakhs. On other occasions, when a khan chose to use his increased power against Russia, the government was compelled to seek help among influential Kazakh nobles and notables. This policy seesaw of first unite and then divide changed only in the 1820s, when the Kazakhs of the Lesser and Middle Hordes had become directly incorporated into the imperial administrative and political institutions, and the position of khan became superfluous.

RELIGION

Shortly after the fall of Byzantium to the Turks in 1453, the Muscovite tsar emerged as the only sovereign monarch of an Orthodox Christian state. Moscow subsequently spent much diplomatic energy before it succeeded in securing the consent of other Orthodox patriarchs to have the tsar appoint his own independent patriarch in 1589. A year later, the audacious Russian envoys to the Georgian king presented the issue differently. In the envoys' version, the Constantinople patriarch Jeremiah had traveled to Moscow to implore the tsar on behalf of himself and three other patriarchs of Alexandria, Jerusalem, and Antioch to appoint his own pope in Russia to replace the heretical pope in Latin Rome. They all would pray for God to help the tsar in liberating Christians and conquering the Muslims.[78]

Moscow's vanity, vision, and policies were splendidly displayed in the envoys' message. Like the native peoples, whose status could be described only in terms of a subject's service to the sovereign, the Orthodox patriarchs were expected to beseech the supreme ruler to act benevolently on their humble petitions. The Muscovite tsar and patriarch were non plus ultra, and it was only a matter of time before Moscow would liberate other Orthodox Christian brethren. Reality, different as it might be, was thus conveniently obscured by the official Muscovite rhetoric.

Even before the rise of Orthodox Christian Muscovy, with its own version of manifest destiny, the seemingly anonymous expanses of steppe, "the wild field," separated Christians from Muslims and peasants from nomads. It was not accidental that the Russian word *krestianin* implied both Christian and peasant. In time, the religious divide became further reinforced after "the wild steppe" became more "civilized and Christianized" by the late eighteenth century.

Naturally, appeals for religious solidarity driven by immediate political considerations were expected from both sides. In 1487 the khan of the Horde reproached Nur Devlet, the brother of the Crimean khan Mengli

Giray, for serving the grand prince. He invited him to join the Horde be-cause "you live among the infidels, and it is not befitting you [to reside] in the infidel land."[79] A century later, the Crimean khan Muhammed Giray used the same argument when he wrote to the Nogays inviting them to join him in a campaign against their Shi'a rivals in Safavid Persia because "it is appropriate for you to join us in the cause of Islam." And, as if understand-ing that an appeal based on religion alone would not suffice, he offered compensation for the campaign and promised that they would receive sup-plies from the Ottoman sultan.[80]

At various times the Ottomans and the Crimeans attempted to unite the Muslim Nogays, Kazakhs, Karakalpaks, and Bashkirs in a broad anti-Russian coalition. An unconfirmed report described the first such effort in a letter sent in 1551 by the Ottoman sultan, Süleyman the Magnificent, to Ismail, mirza of the Nogays. Purportedly the sultan accused Ivan IV of being haughty and arrogant toward the Muslims and complained of Ivan's war with Kazan and his control of the steppe and rivers, which Süleyman claimed for himself. The letter ended with an appeal for Islamic solidarity: "We are all Muslims and we should all unite against Moscow—the Crimea, Astrakhan, and you should help Kazan and Azov, which are too far away for me to aid; then I shall make you a khan in Azov."[81]

Yet religious differences did not preclude collaboration between Chris-tian Moscow and its Muslim neighbors, and the appeals of coreligionists remained largely subordinate to more immediate political and military goals. The letters of the Nogay chiefs to Ivan IV often began with the follow-ing words of respect: "God created us Muslims and you Christians," suggest-ing that the religious differences should not prevent their alliance.[82] When the exigencies of the situation demanded flattery, the Nogay rulers were unfettered by the apparent inaccuracies and incongruities in referring to the tsar as the "ruler of all Christians" and even a descendant of Chinggis khan.[83] In the end, however, the Muscovite ruler remained an infidel, as Belek-Bulat mirza made abundantly clear in his letter to the tsar. In a tone both courteous and condescending, his letter began: "Although he [Ivan IV] is an infidel, and we are Muslims, each has his own faith."[84]

Who was an infidel and whose faith was superior was not a matter open for discussion in Moscow, whose crusading spirit was on display for all to see in the summer of 1552, when the metropolitan Makarii blessed Ivan IV and his "soldiers of Christ" against the Kazan Tatars, who were "infidels and enemies of Christ, and who had always spilled Christian blood and destroyed holy churches."[85] The conquest of Kazan and Astrakhan by these soldiers of Christ further reinforced the religious divide between Christian Muscovy and its non-Christian neighbors.

Even so, notions of Christian solidarity remained largely at the service of Moscow's geopolitical interests. Just as the Russian princes had never hesitated to use the Mongols against their dynastic rivals, so Moscow employed various non-Christian peoples in its wars with the Christian monarchs of the West. Shortly before signing the Andrusovo Truce with Poland in 1667, the tsar wrote to the king with an appeal to conclude peace because they shared "the same Christian faith." Perhaps the tsar's appeal was so obviously disingenuous that the king's response was inevitably ironic: he first would have to consult the Crimean khan.[86]

Moscow's expansion into the North Caucasus, where other Orthodox Christians could be found beyond the line separating Christianity from Islam, provides a vivid illustration of the interplay between religion and politics. Since Russia's arrival in the region in the mid-sixteenth century, the Christian identity of the Russian state had been integral to its expansionist endeavor. The only Christians who possessed a state-organized political entity and found themselves on the other side of the frontier were the Georgians. Surrounded by the Muslim peoples of the Caucasus and compelled to pay tribute intermittently to the Persians or Ottomans, the Georgians often invoked the imagery of defiled Christianity to solicit Russian help. They appealed to Moscow to liberate them from the Turks, who had captured much of their land, and from the shamkhal and his people, described as "infidel dogs, who capture Christians at night and then convert them to Islam."[87]

Christians were not alone in appealing to their powerful coreligionists for help and intervention. While the Georgians were pleading for Russian help, the shamkhal of Daghestan, alarmed by rapid Russian expansion in the region, wrote to the Ottoman sultan in 1589. He described how the Russians had seized his river, built a fort, and were ready to send a large army against him. He warned that the Russians would take his land and convert his people to Christianity, and "then the cities that you took from Persia—Derbent, Shemakha, Shirvan, and Ghanja—will not be able to defend themselves; and the Russians will unite with the Persian shah and the Georgian king, and then they will march on Istanbul from here and the French and Spanish kings from the other side, and you, yourself, will not survive in Istanbul, and you will be captured and the Muslims will become Christians, and our faith will come to an end, if you do not intercede."[88]

At a time when religion and state sovereignty were not and could not be clearly separated, the major powers in the region often laid claims to lands and peoples on the basis of common religion. The Russian envoys were always prepared to argue for Russian sovereignty over western Georgia "because it was a Christian country." They also heard similar arguments from the Ottomans, who insisted that the Circassians and the Kumyks were Muslims, and therefore the subjects of the Ottoman Empire.[89] In 1645, one of the chiefs of southern Daghestan, the utsmii of Kaitag, rejecting Moscow's claim that two chiefs from northern Daghestan were Russian subjects, expressed his views unambiguously: "And you should know: Kazanalp and Burak are Muslims, and how can Muslims be the subjects [*kholopi*] of a Christian ruler? They are the subjects of our sovereign, the [Persian] shah."[90]

Such uncompromising rhetoric was, of course, both self-serving and untrue. By the middle of the seventeenth century, many Muslims in fact did find themselves within the borders of the Russian state, just as many Christians became the subjects of the Ottoman Empire. The numerous appeals of the Crimean khans to have Kazan and Astrakhan returned to them because the two khanates "were Muslim from days of old and belonged to the dynasty of the Crimean khans" held no validity in Moscow.[91]

The rhetorical power of religious appeals notwithstanding, such solidarity was often sacrificed to more pragmatic needs. Thus, the Georgians used their numerous laments about oppressed and suffering Christianity to seek Moscow's aid against the shamkhal, whose frequent raids devastated Georgian villages. But when military assistance was not forthcoming, the Georgians did not hesitate to collaborate with either the Persians or the Ottomans. Russia's best informants among the native peoples were often members of the local Islamic clergy, and both Christians and Muslims used pilgrims as spies and issues of faith as a cover for political purposes.[92]

Religious and political considerations caused constant clashes and often resisted reconciliation. During the Russian invasion of Daghestan in 1722, the Crimean khan wrote to the shamkhal, Adil Giray, "not to trust the words of the infidel Muscovites, but instead rally all Muslims against the infidels for the sake of Islam."[93] Fifteen years later, shortly after the Daghestani chief of Enderi was compelled to swear allegiance to Russia, he received instructions to dispatch his troops for a military campaign in Russia's war against the Ottoman Empire. He responded that it was not befitting him to help an infidel ruler (*giaurskii tsar*) against a Muslim one.[94]

All the regional powers—the Russian, Ottoman, and Persian governments—used religion for geopolitical purposes. Ottoman agents often were reported to have arrived in the Caucasus with letters from the sultan urging the local population to rebel against Russian oppression. St. Petersburg also sent its agents to the Christians residing under Ottoman or Persian rule to foment uprisings. In 1784, Russian agents were dispatched to the Armenians of Karabakh and Karadag "to convince them that they could use imperial protection to get rid of the Persian yoke."[95]

In fact, most of the time other Muslims were farther away than the Russians, and in their unceasing internal wars, various chiefs of the region conspired to obtain "infidel" Russian help against local Muslim rivals. The fact that Islamic identity alone was insufficient in uniting the peoples of the Caucasus became even more apparent in the 1780s, during the first major uprising against the Russians led by sheikh Mansur. During this uprising, one Muslim cleric wrote to the Russian authorities and volunteered to assassinate Mansur if they would pay him 2,000 rubles and keep his name secret. The Russian administration judged the offer credible enough to give the cleric 500 rubles as an advance for the promised assassination. Others also refused to join the uprising: the Avars confirmed their loyalty to Russia, and the Kabardinians resolved to remain neutral.[96]

Kabardinian nobles frequently needed Russian assistance against the devastating raids of their coreligionists from the Crimea and northwestern Caucasus. Reassuring the Russian administration that the Kabardinians had no choice but to be on good terms with Russia, Vasilii Bakunin, an insightful and knowledgeable Russian official in the region, reported in 1748 that even though the Kabardinians practiced the same religion as the Crimeans and the Kuban Nogays, they often suffered from their raids and would never leave Kabarda and cross the Kuban River to become Crimean subjects.[97]

One such story exemplified Crimean relations with Kabarda. Upon becoming the Crimean khan in 1708, Kaplan Giray demanded that 3,000 Kabardinian slaves (*esir*) be submitted to his court in order to mark his accession to the throne. In the region, which traditionally served as the largest supplier of slaves to the Crimeans and Ottomans, this was an old custom. Referring to the increasingly volatile Crimean political situation, the Kabardinians explained that in the past the khans had changed every fifteen or twenty years. Now the Crimeans changed them almost every year, and it was impossible for the Kabardinians to provide so many slaves so often. They added that most Kabardinians had now accepted Islam, that their children studied in village schools and mosques, so "how can we send these youth as slaves, as if they were some infidels?" But the appeal to Muslim sensibility did not help. Shortly thereafter, Kaplan Giray's army entered Kabarda. The Kabardinians promised to turn over slaves, but then tricked the Crimeans and utterly destroyed their entire force. Kaplan Giray narrowly escaped captivity, took refuge among the Nogays, and never returned to the Crimea.[98]

Differences among the non-Russian peoples notwithstanding, in the minds of the Russian officials the natives' religious identity or lack thereof continued to define their behavior and morals. In the early sixteenth century, Russian officials explained the natives' inability to keep an oath of allegiance by saying that they were Muslim and therefore could not be trusted.[99] Two centuries later, the governor-general P. S. Potemkin arrived at a very different conclusion, when he reported in 1784 that the Kabardinians' perfidious nature was due to their poor understanding of the tenets of Islam.[100]

Indeed, by the late eighteenth century, the Russian government began to see Islam as an antidote to pagan barbarism and the best way to tame and co-opt the empire's non-Christian subjects. In the 1780s, Catherine II advocated reliance on pro-Russian Muslim clergy to spread Islam among the Kazakhs in order to counteract the influence of the Islamic clergy from Bukhara and Khiva. Since the Kazakhs were "unaware of the most basic Islamic rites" and were thought so "savage and ignorant" as to be unsuited for conversion to Christianity, Catherine believed that they could be made more submissive and civilized if they became good Muslims first.[101] The empress's plans involved recruiting loyal mullahs from among the Kazan Tatars, providing them with cash payments, and sending them to the Kazakhs "in order to encourage the Kazakhs' loyalty and peaceful intentions." She envisioned the Kazakhs serving as irregular Russian military and the steppe transformed through the newly built towns, mosques, schools, and trading centers.[102]

While Catherine's grand vision of the Kazakh steppe had to wait, the government undertook an important step in its ongoing efforts to tighten its control and legitimize its jurisdiction over the increasing numbers of Muslims in the Russian Empire. In 1788 Catherine decreed the establishment of the Muslim Spiritual Assembly in Ufa. Later known as the Orenburg Muslim Spiritual Assembly, it was headed by a Muslim cleric with the title of *mufti* (the highest rank among the *ulema,* the official interpreters of the Islamic law) and appointed by the Russian government. The Assembly was charged with exercising authority over all the Muslims of the Russian Empire, with the exception of the Crimean Tatars.[103]

On more than one occasion, the Assembly and the mufti served to represent Russian interests. In one such instance, hoping to quell unrest among the Kazakhs in 1790, the government dispatched the mufti Muhammedjan Khusainov (Muhammed Jan al-Husayn) to the Kazakhs. After the negotiations, some notables conceded that while the local Muslim clergy had attempted to rally the Kazakhs in the struggle of liberating Muslims from the oppression of infidel Russia, the mufti had succeeded in convincing them according to his interpretation of Quran that "it was not against their law for the Muslims to be the subjects of the Russian Empire."[104]

But not everyone was convinced by such arguments, and, for Russia's Muslims, Islam more often served as a rallying cry against the infidel Russians. Despite the government's readiness to accept Muslims as subjects of the Russian Empire in the late eighteenth century, it was clearly understood that the empire was an Orthodox Christian one and that full privileges would be bestowed only on Christians and converts. Religion remained the most significant identity marker for all peoples within the Russian Empire.

IDEOLOGY THROUGH DIPLOMACY

Until the mid-eighteenth century, one would search in vain for any memoranda addressing Moscow's foreign policies or any attempt to reason and articulate its attitudes and policies toward the peoples along the southern frontier. It is hardly surprising that in highly centralized Muscovy, the opinions of local officials were not solicited, and any discussion of such issues was limited to a narrow and secretive circle of the tsar's advisors. Nonetheless, the evolution of Russia's perceptions of and attitudes toward its southern neighbors is clearly visible through the changes in the government's use of royal titulature and diplomatic procedures.[105]

Ivan III was the first ruler to appropriate the title of tsar, but it was not recognized outside Muscovy, and his son, Vasilii III, reverted to the less controversial title of grand prince. The elaborate coronation of Ivan IV in 1547 as tsar of all Russia was only one sign of Moscow's renewed confidence and assertiveness. In Roman Catholic Europe, only the pope could bestow the title of king, and in the steppe only those with claims to Chinggisid lineage could become khans. To assume the title of tsar was an act of tremendous diplomatic and political ambition, for it meant to declare the Muscovite ruler equal to the kings of Europe and the khans of the steppe.

But it was also more than that. In a direct challenge to the Holy Roman Emperor and the pope, Ivan IV confirmed the Muscovite rulers' claim to be heirs to Byzantium and his status as emperor and universal Christian ruler who "upheld the true Christian faith." Ivan's assumption of the title of tsar and his subsequent conquests of Kazan and Astrakhan were an equally unambiguous challenge to the status of the Crimean khan as the sole heir to the Golden Horde. Moscow was to be the center of the universe, as the Muscovites knew it, and its ruler was the tsar, the sovereign of all Christians, and the "white tsar." In other words, Moscow was the Third Rome, the New Jerusalem, and the New Saray, all at the same time.[106]

As a latecomer to the international scene, Moscow was acutely concerned with its status and prestige, sparing no effort to convince the neighboring monarchs of Moscow's legitimately equal, if not superior, status. One of the most revealing examples was the instructions given to the Muscovite envoy to the Polish king Sigismund II in 1553. If asked why Ivan called himself tsar, the envoy was to respond that it was because Grand Prince Vladimir had been named a tsar when he and the entire Russian land were baptized by the Greek tsar and patriarch, and because Grand Prince Vladimir Monomakh had been called so too, and finally because he, Ivan, had conquered the khanate of Kazan.[107] Even though Moscow's own credo was never formally stated, the government's instructions to the envoy made it abundantly clear that Moscow derived its sense of legitimacy from several sources simultaneously: the traditions of Christian Byzantium, Kievan Rus, and the Golden Horde.

At stake in the battle over the title of tsar was no less than the sovereignty of the Muscovite state, with its legitimate and recognized boundaries and the imperial ambitions of the Muscovite ruler. The Polish king and the

Christian West were not easily convinced by Ivan IV's arguments. In 1582, the pope's envoy and mediator between Poland and Muscovy, Antonio Possevino, declined to refer to Ivan as tsar without the pope's consent. In the end, a compromise was reached whereby Ivan was conceded the title only in the Russian version of the Polish-Muscovite treaty.[108]

Convincing its Muslim neighbors, the Crimeans and Ottomans, that Moscow was a sovereign state equal to its western counterparts was also an uphill battle. In 1474, Ivan III dispatched his envoy to the Crimea to negotiate and sign a peace treaty (*yarlyk dokonchatel'nyi*). The envoy was instructed to request that the Crimean khan show him his treaty with Poland-Lithuania and then to insist that the Russian monarch's name be referred to in the same fashion as that of the Polish king, that is, "I, Mengli Giray, am in peace and friendship with my brother, the king."[109]

The Muscovite sovereign's appropriate titulature was to be safeguarded at all costs. In 1515 the Muscovite envoy to the Ottoman Porte was to watch carefully that the title of the Muscovite sovereign not be belittled and that the sultan refer to the grand prince of Moscow as "brother," on the grounds that the grand prince was the brother of the Roman emperor, Maximilian, and other glorious rulers. To check whether the title was rendered correctly, the envoy had to request a Russian translation of the Ottoman text and take it to the Russian embassy's residence, where it could be checked against Moscow's version.[110]

Diplomatic protocol also had to reflect the new conquests of the Muscovite rulers—which was not easily accomplished. Thus, in 1655, the Crimeans refused to recognize the tsar's title, which described him as a grand sovereign of Lithuania, Little and White Rus, Volyn, and Podol'e. In response to the Muscovite envoy's protestations, the Crimean official stated that even if it were true in the past, the title was now obsolete and improper. In addition to demanding the appropriate titulature for the Russian ruler, Moscow instructed its envoys to communicate directly with the Crimean khan or sultan and to refuse to kneel in their presence. More than one Muscovite ambassador was thrown out of the courts of various Muslim rulers and Chinese emperors for arrogant and disrespectful behavior.[111]

The stubbornness of the Muscovite government's officials and its envoys abroad was, of course, more than bureaucratic rigidity. It concerned honor, prestige, and dignity, all of which Moscow was eager to acquire. Honor, however, was a product of the specific political culture, and it is not surprising that Moscow's expectations often differed from those of its neighbors. One symbolic and recurring issue was the Muscovite Christian custom of taking off one's hat as a sign of respect. Muslim custom demanded the opposite, to have the head covered. A number of confrontations over this issue testify to a remarkable and persistent Muscovite intransigence. Thus, in 1536 the Nogay chief, Sheidiak, bitterly complained that the grand prince had ordered the Nogay envoy in Moscow to remove his hat. To defuse the tension, Sheidiak suggested that his envoys be allowed to keep their hats on, and that the Russian envoys need not remove theirs.[112] In 1604 two Nogay rival chiefs were invited to Astrakhan to iron out their differences. During a dinner, when the cup was passed in honor of the Muscovite grand sovereign, one of the Nogay chiefs, Ishterek, who was favored by Moscow, took off his hat and knelt to drink the cup. The other, Jan Araslan, refused to remove his hat, explaining that it was a Muslim custom, and that even during prayers Muslims did not remove their hats. The Russians remained unconvinced, and he was forced to follow Ishterek's example.[113]

Taking off one's hat in honor of the Russian monarch became first and foremost a symbol of submission, and it was demanded from Muslims and non-Muslims alike. A comic compromise on the issue was reached between the Russian envoy to the Kalmyks, the diak I. S. Gorokhov, and the Kalmyk tayishi, Daichin, in 1661. During the reception, Gorokhov suggested that Daichin should stand up and take off his hat when the name of the tsar was mentioned. When Daichin replied that the Kalmyks did not have such a custom, Gorokhov reproached him, saying that monarchs of all states did so, and for Daichin to remain seated with his hat on was to show dishonor. An embarrassed Daichin explained that he meant no offense. As a compromise, he ordered his interpreter to stand up and continue to translate with his hat off. On this Daichin and Gorokhov agreed.[114]

The fact that removing one's hat had been seen in Moscow as an important sign of inferior political status was not lost on some native observers. One of them, the Kabardinian prince Sunchaley Cherkasskii, had spent several decades in Moscow's service at the Muscovite frontier fort of Tersk (Terk) and was familiar with Muscovite political vocabulary. In 1618, trying to dissuade Moscow from forcing the utsmii of Kaitag, Rüstem khan, to declare himself the tsar's subject, Sunchaley described the utsmii as an independent ruler who pays no yasak and submits no hostages. And to make sure that Russians would make no mistake about Rüstem khan's status vis-à-vis other local rulers, he added that Rüstem khan did not take off his hat in the presence of the shamkhal.[115]

Honor was commensurate with status and status with presents, which were of particular importance in steppe societies. Cycles of mutual dishonor sometimes appeared to be endless. Russian envoys at the courts of the Nogay chiefs were abused when they refused to submit the required presents and payments, and in return the Nogay envoys were thrown out of Moscow.[116] That these issues were of utmost sensitivity is clear from an exchange between Ivan IV and the Nogay beg Urus. In September 1580, Urus informed Ivan that the Nogays were at war with Moscow because Ivan had sent him an envoy at the rank of a service Tatar, whose low social status meant few presents and payments for Urus. Moscow's reply was that it had done so because the Nogays had detained the Russian envoys.[117] Again Urus tried to explain his frustration: "Is it not a dishonor when you are sending *deti boyarskie* [a rank of the Muscovite servitors] with payments to my brothers and nephews and [you send] to me a service Tatar? If an envoy is sent from a foreign land to your son and not to you, would you not be offended? And because of this I was angry and detained your envoy for a year, and also because your envoy came to me and addressed me without dismounting from his horse, saying that such was the sovereign's order." Ivan, confident of the Nogays' dependence on Moscow and resolute in insisting on the appropriate treatment of his envoys, remained unmoved by Urus' passionate appeal. He explained that the Russian envoy had not dismounted because Urus and his people were also on horses, and he reminded Urus of the humiliating treatment of the Russian envoy, who had been forcibly taken off his horse and then, like a prisoner, dragged to Urus on foot.[118]

Muscovite diplomacy was extremely prescriptive, rigid, and centralized. The embassy was expected to send regular messages back to Moscow as it proceeded toward its destination.[119] Discouraged from any personal initiative in negotiations, the envoy carried with him several versions (*spiski*) of the proposed treaty. He was to submit and insist on the acceptance of the first version. While appearing to negotiate, the envoy, after much bargaining, was merely to replace one fully drawn-up version of the treaty with another until one of the versions of the treaty was finally agreed to by the other side.[120]

The diplomatic terminology used by Moscow to signify a treaty with its neighbors in the south varied and often overlapped. Some terms were of Russian origin (e.g., *rota,* used at the time of Kievan Rus, was an oath and pledge of friendship; it was later replaced by *pravda*), some were inherited from the Golden Horde (e.g., *yarlyk*—a Mongol word for any written document), and others were of a distinctly Islamic origin and were borrowed from the Crimean khanate (e.g., *shert'*—derived from Arabic *shart* and originally used to designate a treaty between Moscow and the Crimea). The term *shert',* indicating an agreement between the Russian government and the Muslim and other non-Christian peoples in Russia's southern and eastern frontier regions, became prevalent in the early sixteenth century and remained in use until the mid-eighteenth century.

Traditionally, signing the shert' required the parties involved to take an oath in accordance with their religious rites. The animists were to call upon their spirits, the Muslims had to swear an oath on the Quran and the Buddhist Kalmyks on their book of prayers, while the grand prince was to kiss a cross laid over the agreement.[121] Throughout the sixteenth century, however, the meaning of shert' evolved from a symmetrical diplomatic relationship to a manifestation of subservience to the tsar. In the eyes of Moscow, shert' now signified an oath of allegiance of the new and faithful subjects of the tsar. Conscious of its spectacular rise, Moscow viewed the Golden Horde's numerous successors as repugnant in their religion, lacking the essential trappings of sovereign states and increasingly dependent on Moscow's economy and military might. By the mid-sixteenth century, Christian Muscovy was making increasingly clear its superior status through diplomatic language even before confirming it with military victories.

Both the Christian rulers in the West and the Crimean khans remained unconvinced by Ivan's ambitious pretension. Antonio Possevino advised Pope Gregory XIII to indulge the Russian prince and refer to him as tsar, despite Ivan's arrogation of the title, because "the hope of winning this Prince and the huge realm he controls to the better cause ever leads to further efforts and does not wear out all our pens."[122] The Crimean khans continued to regard themselves as the sole and supreme successors to the Golden Horde and always referred to themselves as "the great khan of the Great Horde" (*velikoi ordy velikii tsar*) in their correspondence with the grand prince. The latter neither objected nor attempted to insist on the status of tsar in his communications to the Crimea. When not at war with each other, Muscovite grand princes and Crimean khans referred to each other as brothers and friends, while not forgetting the religious divide—"to the sovereign of many Christians, to my brother," wrote the Crimean khan to Ivan IV in 1580.[123]

As long as the Crimea represented a serious military threat, the Muscovite rulers brought up the issue of their status occasionally and gingerly. The story was quite different when it concerned the Nogays, who by the middle of the sixteenth century had grown increasingly dependent on Moscow. The titulature and the tone of the Nogay letters had changed. The Nogay chiefs, instructed by the Muscovite envoys, exalted the grand prince in their letters to Moscow. In 1548, in addition to "the ruler of all Christians," the Nogays began to address Ivan IV as the "white tsar," a title that in the world of steppe diplomacy was reserved for the heirs of the Golden Horde.[124]

Of course, only those belonging to the Chinggisid dynasty were considered the Horde's legitimate rulers. Many pretenders, despite their military and political acumen, were foiled in their ambitions when they failed to prove Chinggisid origins. It was with the purpose of buttressing Ivan's claims and simultaneously aggrandizing his own status that the Muscovite loyalist among the Nogays, Belek-Bulat mirza, wrote to Ivan: "In your land you claim to be the legitimate heir to Chinggis [khan] and call yourself the legitimate Sovereign and Tsar, and here I am the son of Edige." He proceeded to lavish on Ivan other sonorous, if seemingly contradictory, titles: "the son of Chinggis, the white prince, and the Christian Orthodox Sovereign."[125] Twenty years later, the Nogay beg Urus, referred to Ivan as "the sovereign of all the Christians, the grand prince, and the white tsar" in the same breath.[126]

Because the great majority of Nogay letters survive only in copies of the Russian translations, reasonable doubt exists as to whether the tsar's titles were actually written by the Nogays or only rendered as such by subservient Muscovite translators and interpreters. Regardless, Moscow's continual efforts to appropriate various titles were intended to enhance its image and provide further legitimacy for its sovereign. The Russian tsar was to be the non plus ultra: a successor to Byzantine emperors and Chinggisid khans, a Christian ruler of the West and "white tsar" of the East. The importance attributed by Moscow to the Golden Horde's heritage was demonstrated resplendently when upon the conquest of Kazan in 1552, Astrakhan in 1554, and Siberia in 1580, the crowns of the respective khanates were transferred to the royal treasury in Moscow.[127] It was only in the early seventeenth century that the demise of the Nogays and consolidation of Moscow's supremacy in the Golden Horde's former realm rendered Moscow's claim to the Horde's legitimacy obsolete.

MAP 2.   The southern borderlands of Muscovy in the late sixteenth century.

[2]

FRONTIER CONCEPTS AND POLICIES IN MUSCOVY

Ne khvalis' v pole educhi, khvalis'—iz polia.

(Do not boast leaving for the steppe;
boast returning from the steppe.)

—RUSSIAN PROVERB

THE FRONTIER

There were no borders south of Muscovy, for borders required that neighboring peoples define and agree upon common lines of partition. Demarcating a conventional border in the steppe was simply impossible given the absence of the notion of territorial sovereignty among the nomads and the difficulty of maintaining such a border against nomadic predations. Instead, Moscow's southern frontier was an invisible divide in a seemingly endless steppe known as the *dikoe pole,* which implied both open, untamed expanses of land and a perilous frontier.

It is important to draw a distinction between the notions of a frontier and a border. A frontier is a *region* that forms the margin of a settled or developed territory, a politico-geographical *area* lying beyond the integrated region of the political unit. A border, by contrast, is a clearly demarcated boundary between sovereign states. To put it differently, to have a border requires at least two state-organized political entities. It is a state that, both physically and mentally, constructs, maintains, and enforces borders. In the west, where Russia confronted other sovereign states, the territorial limits of the states were demarcated by borders. In the south and east, where Russia's colonization efforts encountered disparate peoples not organized into states and with no clearly marked boundaries between them, the zone of separation between Russia and its neighbors was a frontier.[1]

Different terms were used to designate borders and frontiers until the late seventeenth century. The oldest term denoting a boundary in Kievan Rus was *mezha,* which referred to boundaries separating different land holdings.[2] *Rubezh* and *granitsa* were two other terms used synonymously with mezha, but in time they also acquired the meaning of a boundary separating different towns and principalities.[3] Both rubezh and granitsa were used to refer to the western borders of the Muscovite state and its borderlands (*mesta porubezhnye*). Beginning in the early seventeenth century, when Muscovy began to conceive of itself as a territorial nation-state, the terms rubezh and granitsa were used to designate Muscovy's national boundaries vis-à-vis those of another sovereign state.[4]

In the south and southeast, however, none of these terms was used in relation to the native inhabitants. Instead, several ambiguous terms were used to refer to the steppe frontier in the south. In the days of Kievan Rus, the term *dikoe pole* denoted a no-man's-land separating Rus from its nomadic neighbors. The terms *krai* and *ukraina* (edge, periphery)—hence the name Ukraine—were used in both Rus and Muscovy. The frontier was punctuated by *ukrainye gosudarevy ostrogi* (the sovereign's frontier forts) with residents in and around them known as *krainie liudi* (frontiersmen). Beyond the Muscovite southern outposts lay *pole,* steppe lands outside the control of the neighboring states.[5]

In Siberia, for example, from the point of view of the Russian government, the frontier separated those local peoples who paid yasak to the government from those who did not. Those natives who refused to submit themselves immediately to the Russian governors were classified as hostile, *nemirnye liudi*[6] (people who were not at peace with Russia), and were considered to reside on the other side of the frontier. It was only a matter of time before the Russian military would be sent into *novye nemirnye zemlitsy*[7] (new, unconquered territories) to build more forts and begin to collect yasak from the natives. Thus, the frontier would move farther away, the newly conquered territories would become known as *novoprivodnye zemli*[8] (new territories brought into submission), and their local residents would be termed *iasachnye inozemtsy*[9] (foreigners who pay tribute).

Such a concept of the frontier, as a zone separating a state-organized society from a people with a more primitive social organization, was also typical of Western Europe. The medieval empires of Europe had their numerous marches, defined as a frontier separating the Christian settlements from the pagan wilderness. However, in contrast to Russia, where government officials were appointed to administer the frontier provinces, the task of defending and expanding the European marches was left to the often powerful and independent nobles with the title of margrave (the Markgraf in German and the Marquess in most of the rest of Europe).[10]

The concept of frontier as the extremity, the outer boundary and the limit of civilization, is reflected in various geographical names throughout Europe: some survive as the names of countries (Denmark, the march of the Danes, or Ukraine, the edge or periphery), others as the names of provinces or states (the German state of Mark Brandenburg with the capital of Berlin, the Spanish province of Extremadura, and the former Habsburg Krajina, presently a part of Croatia). In all cases, from the times of the Roman Empire onward, the notion of the frontier as an outer limit implied boundaries destined to expand.[11]

The idea of *limites naturelles*, or natural frontiers, was one of the justifications for the expansionist policies of the states of Western Europe in the fifteenth and sixteenth centuries. France claimed that it was its "manifest destiny" to have a border along the Rhine River, and Spain made similar claims about the Pyrenees region.[12] The concept of natural frontiers suited the purposes of the Christian monarchs of Christian Europe, where territorial conflicts and disputes had been among Christian states. When theology was injected into politics and one Christian state was seen as infidel by another, some of the bloodiest wars in the history of pre-modern Europe took place.

In early modern Russia, the notions of natural law, natural frontier, and residence based on naturalization simply did not exist. Russia had been imbued with its own sense of manifest destiny since the late fifteenth century, and its ideology of expansion was fundamentally shaped by its encounter with the various pagan and Muslim peoples in the south and east. Moscow's military and political interests could no longer be separated from the ideological and theological rhetoric of expansion. It was only in the nineteenth century that the foremost historian of Russia, S. M. Solov'ev, used the concept of natural frontiers in a belated and anachronistic attempt to justify the expansion of the Russian state, claiming that "nature itself indicated at the outset [what] the broad borders of the state [were to be]."[13]

In the 1480s, Moscow's territory was largely bounded by the Oka River. In the early sixteenth century, Moscow considered Riazan and Putivl to be on the edge of its southern frontier, but by 1521 Vasilii III claimed the Muscovite frontier (*gosudarevy ukrainy*) to be farther south, along the Don tributaries of the Khoper and Medveditsa rivers.[14] Starting in the late sixteenth century, Moscow began building the *zaseka*, a series of fortifications forming a single defense line intended to prevent nomadic raids against Muscovite towns and villages. The frontier towns near the defense lines were known as *ponizovye* or *ukrainnye gorody*.[15] In time, such fortification lines were extended and moved farther south, marking the boundary of Muscovy and becoming the most effective tool of Russian colonization.

Moscow's claims of sovereignty over the steppe territory were not easily reconciled with its inability to control the area and its inhabitants. Sometimes the pleas of helplessness were only a diplomatic excuse, but most of the time it was indeed beyond Moscow's ability to stop brigandage in the steppe. Responding to complaints from the Nogays in 1538, a letter from Ivan IV stated: "As you are well aware, what place does not have bandits? There are many Cossacks in the steppe—the Kazan, Azov, Crimean, and other unruly Cossacks. And the Cossacks from our frontier also leave for the steppe, and you regard them as criminals just like we regard them as criminals and bandits; no one instructs them to commit banditry. And having committed banditry, they return home."[16]

Muscovy's frontier is best conceived as a multilayered concept in which political, military, fiscal, administrative, legal, and religious frontiers coexisted but did not overlap. For instance, some towns, even though recognized to be within the domain of either Muscovy or Lithuania, continued the old practice of paying tribute to the Horde (k Orde potiaglo) or the Crimea.[17] The "fiscal" frontier was not the only one that did not coincide with political boundaries. While the de facto frontier of the Russian state was its fortification lines in the south and the newly built forts in the east, Moscow's de jure territorial claims far surpassed its actual control. The numerous peoples whom Moscow claimed as its subjects remained for centuries beyond the reach of Moscow's military, administrative, legal, and missionary arms.

In contrast to the western borders, which were clearly demarcated, negotiated with the state-organized neighbors of Moscow, and agreed upon in written treaties, the southern frontier remained ambiguous and ever-changing. It was neither marked nor negotiated nor agreed upon with the steppe nomads. Moscow's boundaries in the south were not much more than an imaginary line between itself and those whom it deemed hostile. An oath of allegiance prepared by government officials for the Nogay beg Ishterek, in 1604 stipulated that he and the Nogays were not to communicate with or assist the Ottoman sultan, the Crimean khan, the Persian shah, the Bukhara khan, Tashkent, Urgench, the Kazakh Horde, the shamkhal, or the Circassians.[18] Moscow thus clearly delineated the other side of its southern frontier running through the steppe from the Crimea to the North Caucasus and Central Asia.

Unmarked and vague land boundaries in the south notwithstanding, Moscow's political vocabulary forcefully aspired to conceptualize and formalize its relationship with the steppe. In defining its rhetorical political boundaries, Moscow relied on several key concepts that were traditionally used in the Turko-Mongol world: shert', amanat, yasak, and pominki. All of the terms were used specifically along the southern and southeastern frontier. Only the last term was translated into Russian; the others remained in the original Turkic form, indicative of Moscow's assimilation of the political heritage of the steppe.

After the middle of the sixteenth century, while preserving the traditional terminology, Moscow began to infuse it with a meaning of its own, that is, a rationally understood concept of sovereignty. Henceforth these were to be policy concepts intended to emphasize the tsar's unquestionably superior political status. As usual, political rhetoric and reality did not match, and many of the steppe peoples continued to view Moscow in traditional terms.

SHERT': A PEACE TREATY OR AN OATH OF ALLEGIANCE?

> The expressions of [Indians'] subjection must have arisen from the ignorance of the Interpreter or from some other mistake; for I am well convinced that they never mean or intend, any thing like it and that they cannot be brought under our Laws, for some Centuries, neither have they any word which can convey the most distant idea of subjection, and should it be fully explained to them, and the nature of subordination punishment etc., defined, it might produce infinite harm.
>
> —Sir William Johnson to Lords of Trade in 1764, from Richard White, *The Middle Ground: Indians, Empires, and Republics in the Great Lakes Region, 1650–1815*

> They advised the khan to send the envoys only in order to have peace with Russia; they do not wish to be Russian subjects.
>
> —An explanation given by the Kazakh notables to the Russian envoy, Muhammed Tevkelev, in 1731

The rise of Muscovy in the late fifteenth century was particularly noticeable in its changing diplomatic practices and its increasing insistence on Moscow's superior political status vis-à-vis its many neighbors. Moscow was becoming a rather typical representative of the theocratic states and empires in which religious and political doctrines were fused in a single concept of "manifest destiny." The Chinese emperors ruled under the Mandate of Heaven and considered any other ruler a barbarian seeking their benevolent protection. The Ottoman sultans consistently belittled other rulers and considered them to be in the service of the Sublime Porte. Incidentally, this included the Holy Roman Emperor, who was referred to as the king of Vienna, and the Russian rulers, who could not compel the Porte to address them as emperors until 1774, when Article 13 of the Treaty of Küchük Kaynarja specifically stipulated it.[19]

The final recognition of the Russian emperor as an equal to the Ottoman sultan was the result of three centuries of struggle over Russia's political status and prestige. The first sign of change in Moscow's self-perception was evident far from its southern frontier. In 1487, the Hansa merchants who arrived to sign another trade treaty with Novgorod were presented with a document startlingly different from those they had negotiated with Moscow in the past. The new treaty raised a number of political issues, including Moscow's concern over the safety of the Orthodox churches in the Livonian cities. Most striking was the contrast to the previous treaties, which were signed by the Hansa and Novgorod as equal partners. The new document was presented as a petition of the Hansa merchants to the grand prince, who benevolently conferred it upon them. In the end, Ivan III had to submit to the merchants' protestations and compromised on the language of the new treaty, but his political message had been heard: Novgorod was now a part of Muscovy, and the grand prince was its supreme ruler.[20]

The Hansa merchants were not the only ones to rebuff the grand princes' growing ambitions. The Crimean khans continued to regard the princes as their subjects and demanded to be addressed as khans, that is, superior rulers. When in 1516 Vasilii III instructed the Crimean khan to send troops against Lithuania, Muhammed Giray reminded the grand prince of his improper commanding tone and inquired rhetorically: "Who is greater, the grand prince or the khan?" The Muscovites continued to oblige, even though some within the Crimea understood that the grand princes had, in fact, become sovereign and did not need to obey the khans.[21]

The Muscovite princes were nothing if not tenacious, and whenever possible they insisted on being addressed in accordance with their own self-image. In 1558 several pro-Russian Nogays advised the Nogay beg Ismail: "Save yourself an embarrassment, Ismail beg, address [Ivan IV] as your suzerain. The Livonians are more powerful than you, yet the Sovereign seized all their cities." To leave no ambiguity and to ensure Ivan's favor, Ismail was advised to state: "I, Ismail beg, am a servant to you, the Sovereign, with all the Nogays."[22]

Securing a pledge of loyalty from its perceived subjects became the cornerstone of Moscow's policies toward the peoples it confronted on its southern and eastern frontiers. From the first encounters, Russian officials routinely demanded that the local chiefs swear allegiance and declare themselves the tsar's faithful subjects. In 1589, on orders from Moscow, the commander of Tersk, a remote military outpost in the North Caucasus, instructed the Kumyk shamkhal to dispatch his envoys and petition to become the tsar's subject. When such envoys did not arrive, the commander was ordered to warn the shamkhal that a large army was ready to be sent against him "because he did not seek our favor and payment."[23]

Increasingly the autocratic Russian sovereign and the centralized state he represented could codify their relationship with the disparate tribal confederations only in terms of a suzerain bestowing favors on his subjects. The status of the various peoples, non-Christian and non-state-organized, was no longer negotiable, and Muscovite diplomatic language was becoming less diplomatic. In 1616 the Nogay beg Ishterek wrote to Moscow and, continuing the practice of his many predecessors, addressed Tsar Mikhail as a friend. What might have been seen as flattery a little over a hundred years before was now viewed in Moscow as an unpardonable familiarity and insolence. The response of the Muscovite officials was a sharp rebuke: "A servant [*kholop*] can never be the tsar's friend."[24]

While in the seventeenth century Moscow constructed an image of the tsar as a benevolent sovereign ready to reward his subjects in exchange for their service and loyalty, a hundred years later it was simply unthinkable for a Russian emperor, regarded as the embodiment of civilized European values, to be anything but a patron and protector of Russia's barbaric neighbors. The latter attitude was most forthrightly expressed by Muhammed Tevkelev, a Tatar translator in the Foreign Office charged with negotiating and executing the Kazakhs' oath of allegiance to the Russian crown. In response to some Kazakh notables who explained that they had sent an envoy to Russia solely to make peace, not to become Russia's subjects, Tevkelev declaimed that "it was not befitting for such an illustrious monarch to have a peace treaty with you, steppe beasts."[25]

Yet it seemed that the "beasts" did not appreciate the privilege of becoming Russian subjects. In 1762, succumbing to the demands of the Russian envoys, the Kazakh khan Nuraly swore an oath of allegiance to the newly enthroned Russian empress, Catherine II, only to explain later that he could not be responsible for his people, who were hostile to the Russian authorities because of their unaddressed grievances. Furthermore, his people disparagingly referred to him as "the Russian."[26] Despite a manifestly adverse reaction by the Kazakhs and the obvious fact that Moscow's rush to confer the status of subjects on the newly encountered peoples was little more than wishful thinking, the Russian government continued to insist on an oath of allegiance.

Easily extracted, albeit not easily enforced, such oaths were understood differently by both sides. From the late fifteenth century onward, the basis for Muscovy's relationship with the Crimea was the shert', a written document stipulating conditions of peace and military alliance. In time, Moscow extended the use of the term to its relations with other steppe peoples and, instead of a peace treaty, began to regard the shert' as an allegiance sworn by a non-Christian people to their Muscovite sovereign. The usual procedure involved one or more local chiefs pledging allegiance on behalf of their people in the presence of a Muscovite official. Moscow always tried to make sure that such a pledge of "eternal submission to the grand tsar" was made according to the native customs of its newly sworn subjects.[27]

Throughout the period, the Muscovite chroniclers, interpreters of the Foreign Office, and scribes were busily and deliberately constructing the image of the tsar's subservient subjects. One early example of Muscovite political incongruities was an account of a military expedition across the

Urals in 1483. The Muscovite officials described their encounter with the Khanty and Mansi peoples and the ceremony involved in formalizing a peace treaty between the local chiefs and the Muscovites:

> And their custom of making peace is as follows: they put a bear skin under a thick trunk of a cut pine tree, then they put two sabers with their sharp ends upwards and bread and fish on the bear skin. And we put a cross atop the pine tree and they put a wooden idol and tie it below the cross; and they began to walk beneath their idol in the direction of the sun. And one of them standing nearby said: "He who will break this peace, let him be punished by the god of his faith." And they walked about the tree three times, and we bowed to the cross, and they bowed to the sun. After all of this they drank water from the cup containing a golden nugget and they kept saying: "You, gold, seek the one who betrays."[28]

The same event was registered in the Russian chronicle, but described quite differently: "and the local princes swore not to bear any ill will, not to exhibit any violence, and to be loyal to the grand prince of Muscovy."[29] Obviously things did not look quite the same from the banks of a Siberian river as they did in Moscow. An uncensored eyewitness account lay bare the stark contrast between an unadorned contemporaneous description of the event and its later interpretation by the Muscovite "ideological department." What the local chiefs considered a peace treaty reached with the newly arrived strangers, Moscow maintained to be the chiefs' oath of allegiance to the grand prince and an act of their submission to Moscow.

Examples of this sort of official manufacturing of the indigenous peoples' subject status are abundant. When, in 1673, the envoys of the well-known and fiercely independent Oirat khan Galdan Boshoktu arrived in Moscow—the first such embassy to Russia—they were undoubtedly surprised to be told by Russian officials that their khan was a subject of the tsar. The Russian officials never tired of rebuking the steppe rulers whose letters to Moscow were written inappropriately. Where the remonstrations failed, the Russian translators and scribes preferred to edit away the differences. Thus, the letters of the Mongol ruler Lubsan, in which he had addressed the tsar as an inferior local ruler, became in Russian translation "petitions of the Mongol prince." While Lubsan offered peace and asked for military assistance, the Russian officials praised him for "seeking the sovereign's favor" and admonished him "not to violate his oath of allegiance."[30]

Vasilii Bakunin, a competent translator and knowledgeable Russian official stationed on the southern frontier in the first half of the eighteenth century, explained what the Kalmyk tayishis thought of their previous allegiances: "The Kalmyk tayishis never recognized their former allegiances as oaths of allegiance. Its very name, that is, 'shert',' is alien not only to the Russian, but to the Kalmyk language as well. They [the tayishis] referred only to the agreement concluded with Prince B. A. Golitsyn [in 1697]. It is obvious that they were not aware of [the contents of] those [previous] 'shert's.' It is clear from the copies found that the original allegiance records were written in Russian, and were only signed in Kalmyk."[31]

Even though unaware of the contents of the documents they were expected to sign, the local chiefs had at least one strong incentive to comply with Russian demands. It was not coincidental that such a procedure was often accompanied by the disbursement of an annuity or other payments and presents. When the Russian treasury was empty, the government recognized the difficulty of making the native chiefs affix their signatures without the expected distribution of gifts.[32]

During the eighteenth century, several prominent natives of the Caucasus, who had long been in Russian imperial service, advised the government to adopt a more realistic view of the indigenous peoples. In 1714 Prince Alexander Bekovich-Cherkasskii wrote to Peter I and stated unambiguously that "these peoples [the Kabardinians] were independent and submitted to no one." Bekovich-Cherkasskii explained that the nature of relations between the Kabardinians and Russia was no different than that of the Kumyks with Persia, whose rulers traditionally provided large payments for the Kumyks to ensure their amity.[33] Addressing the same issue in his report to the Senate in 1762, the Georgian prince and lieutenant-colonel in the Russian army Otar Tumanov stated emphatically that the peoples of the North Caucasus were Russian subjects more in name than in fact.[34]

Competent advice notwithstanding, any adjustment to the real situation on the ground was resisted in the Russian capital, and the authorities continued to demand relentlessly the oaths of allegiance to the Russian suzerain. One notable exception was the Ossetians. In the 1740s, carefully exploiting the loopholes in Russo-Ottoman and Russo-Persian peace treaties that recognized the Ossetians' political independence, the Russian government organized a Christian mission among them. But contrary to the wishes of the zealous missionaries, the Senate ordered that the Ossetians were not to be sworn as Russia's subjects, so that hasty efforts to secure their allegiance did not alarm them and jeopardize their conversion. The priorities of the government were clear: it was prepared to delay their formal allegiance in order to see them become Orthodox Christians.[35]

By the mid-eighteenth century, a new political vocabulary and more competent translations into native languages left no ambiguity about Russia's perception of the political status of its neighbors. The increasingly antiquated political terminology was being replaced by a modern imperial vocabulary. The native chiefs were no longer signing sherts. Instead, they and their people were now declared to be protectorates of Russia (*v Rossiiskoi protektsii*). Their allegiance as loyal subjects was referred to as *prisiaga na vernoe poddanstvo*, and its violation was now regarded as a crime (*kliatvoprestuplenie*).

Yet the political terms and notions of both old and new Russia continued to collide with the traditional notions of the native societies. One particular encounter illustrates the stark differences between the Russian notion of a political protectorate and the native peoples' notion of kinship-based patronage. When in 1779 the nobles of Greater Kabarda refused to swear allegiance to Russia and declared that they had traditionally been under Russian protectorship as guests or allies (*kunaks*) but not subjects, Russian troops marched into Kabarda, forcing the Kabardinians to sue for peace and to pledge unconditional allegiance.[36]

Where force could not be applied, the lure of presents and rewards worked to the same effect. Presented with a Russian demand to take an oath of allegiance to the empress in 1786, the Kazakh commoners agreed to do so under the instructions of their religious leader, the mufti, who told them that it was not against their law to lie to Christians, and therefore they could agree to the Russian demands in order to receive presents.[37]

Whether deliberately misled, induced by offers of gifts and payments, or intimidated by the force of the Russian military, the disparate peoples along the Russian frontier were expected to be reduced into submission and made loyal. The political identity of the natives as subjects of the Russian crown had to be constructed and reaffirmed through an oath of allegiance. This was the beginning of the long and arduous process of their political integration into the Russian Orthodox Christian empire.

AMANAT: HOSTAGES OF SORTS

I have reached an old age, and hitherto people believed my word in everything, and I have never given hostages or taken an oath to anyone.

—The Kabardinian chief, Alkas, to the Russian envoy in 1589

By teaching the hostages the Russian language, civilizing them, and discouraging their barbaric customs, in a short time there would no longer be any need for hostages, and they would convert to Christianity.

—1775 report of the Astrakhan governor
Petr Krechetnikov to Empress Catherine II,
in *Kabardino-russkie*, vol. 2

Oaths of allegiance notwithstanding, Moscow had few illusions that such oaths, oral or written, were of great importance to the natives. Moscow's view was succinctly expressed by two of its envoys to the court of the Georgian king Alexander in 1598. In instructing the king not to trust the Muslims, they described two Kabardinian princes who had sworn allegiance to the tsar and then violated it because "they were Muslim, did not keep their oath, and could not be trusted."[38] Apparently the oath alone did not suffice, and

Moscow demanded hostages in order to ensure the presumed loyalty of the newly sworn people to the Muscovite sovereign.

While hostages were supposed to be one of the guarantees against the natives' violations of a peace treaty, they were also a tangible symbol of Moscow's supremacy. That submitting hostages was tantamount to surrendering sovereignty was clear, and both were always mentioned together when referring to a local chief who "became a subject in the service of a sovereign and submitted his legitimate son as a hostage" or "was made to pledge allegiance and to give a hostage."[39] Such hostages, known as *amanat* (a Turkic term derived from Arabic *amanat*—something entrusted for safekeeping), or less often in its Russian variant as *zaklad* (a security deposit), were selected from among the natives and handed over to the Russian authorities.

The Russian officials insisted that the hostages be chosen from the best families, and they sometimes refused to accept hostages whom they deemed to be from lesser native families. Most commonly hostages were members of the chiefs' extended family: sons, brothers, and nephews.[40] The issue of who could be sent to the Russian towns as a hostage was a source of numerous quarrels between the Russian authorities and the natives. The most valuable hostages were the sons of the local ruler, and particularly the ruler's potential successor. Even if a native chief submitted his eldest son from the first wife, the Georgian king Alexander had warned the Russian envoys in 1589, he could not be trusted, because "the shamkhal has as many sons as dogs."[41]

Not only did hostages prove to be an unreliable guarantor of their people's loyalty to the Muscovite sovereign, but many natives were not prepared to submit immediately to their neighbor's arrogant demands. In 1606, upon their first encounter with the Kalmyk chief Kho-Urlük, envoys from the Siberian frontier town of Tara presented him with an ultimatum: he was to swear allegiance to the Muscovite suzerain and surrender hostages or else vacate the land. Kho-Urlük, insulted by such demands, ordered the Muscovite envoys put to death. Three decades later, the Kalmyks continued to refuse to submit hostages, and on one occasion they emphatically, albeit falsely, replied that they would never do so because their chiefs were the descendants of Chinggis khan. It was not until 1657 that the chiefs Puntsuk and Manjik consented to sending four hostages to Astrakhan. In a letter to Moscow, they remarked that although the case was unprecedented for the Kalmyks, they had decided to comply with the stubborn demands of the Astrakhan governor.[42]

The evolution of the Kalmyks' attitude from their initial refusal to eventual compliance with Moscow's demand for hostages was typical of the indigenous peoples' relations with Russia. To be sure, submitting or exchanging hostages was a widely known and frequent practice in the Eurasian steppe and elsewhere. Thus, a party defeated in war would surrender hostages to a victor as a sign of submission. Likewise, two equal parties could exchange hostages as a guarantee of their peaceful intentions. Yet Moscow demanded hostages neither because of its military victory nor because it sought to ensure peace between the equals. Not surprisingly, the initial reaction of the native chiefs alternated between insult and puzzlement. In the end, however, Moscow could always rely on one convincing argument that rarely failed to assuage the concerns of the local chiefs—a promise of presents.

This indeed was the best incentive in forcing compliance with Russian demands for hostages. In return for their oath of allegiance and hostages, the local chiefs were given cash, woolens, furs, and various luxury items, "so that other peoples would follow the example and come into submission at the sovereign's fort of Tersk."[43] Moscow's offers were hard to resist even for the proudest of chiefs. In 1589, in response to demands for pledging loyalty and submitting hostages, the Kabardinian chief, Alkas, replied: "I have reached an old age, and hitherto people believed my word in everything, and I have never given hostages or taken an oath to anyone." But for the Russians one's word was not enough, and they continued to insist on a written oath of allegiance. Finally Alkas consulted with his *uzdens* and agreed to comply on the condition that Moscow pay him an annuity, let his people hunt and fish along the rivers freely, transport them across the rivers, and help against their adversaries.[44]

No less proud, the Kalmyk chief, Daichin, sought to explain that the Kalmyks had never given hostages, and if he did so he would be disgraced in the eyes of the Crimea, Persia, and his own people. Eventually he too succumbed to the government's demands, as the lure of Russian presents, payments, and trade privileges proved to be stronger than his fear of disgrace. Realizing the importance of this concession for the Kalmyks, the government, in a conciliatory gesture, ordered the Kalmyk hostages boarded not in regular hostage quarters but in a special house and had them remunerated with an unusually high compensation.[45]

Hostages resided in a hostage residence (*amanatnyi dvor*) in the frontier towns. Such a dwelling was usually a cheaply constructed single hut. Most of the time hostages were under guard and were confined to their place of residence. Although they were to be provided with food and clothing, abuses by local officials were widespread, and hostages were routinely cheated, beaten, and fed carrion.[46]

While such abuses were common, it was clearly understood that hostages were not prisoners. They could become prisoners, however, in order to exert more pressure on recalcitrant native chiefs. In 1641, "to make the Kabardinian prince, Aleguk, petition the tsar and ask forgiveness for his violation of the oath," Moscow ordered its voevoda in Tersk to transfer Aleguk's son, who resided there as amanat, to a prison, to reduce his allowance from five to two rubles a month, and, perhaps more significantly, to eliminate his weekly supply of twenty-five cups of beer.[47]

Treatment of hostages varied: some were subjected to strict confinement and sometimes found themselves shackled, while others were allowed frequent leaves to visit home. Yet for most hostages the abrupt changes in diet and lifestyle from the unfettered freedom of the steppe to the confined quarters of a Russian town were often unbearable. Some tried to escape, while others died in captivity from illness and mistreatment.[48]

After a period of time, which could range from ten days to a year, hostages were supposed to be released, rewarded with small amounts of cash and presents, and replaced by new ones. However, if hostages happened to be valuable, the authorities detained them as long as possible until "their people become dependent and loyal." When numerous requests to have such captives released or replaced by others failed to convince the authorities, the natives often resorted to freeing their kin through daring raids into Russian towns or by siding with Moscow's adversaries in the region.[49]

In the eighteenth century, the practice of taking hostages assumed a new rhetorical disguise. In 1742, instructions from St. Petersburg directed the Orenburg governor, Ivan Nepliuev, to keep the children of the Kazakh khan and nobles as hostages under the pretext of their military service in the Russian army. Faithfully following his orders, Nepliuev rejected the new Kazakh hostage sent by Abulkhayir khan to replace the old one because "the new hostage was not Abulkhayir's legitimate son, but was born of a Kalmyk concubine," and therefore was of much less value. Abulkhayir's numerous protestations that his son had been held hostage in Orenburg for ten years, that his children were envoys, not hostages, and that "he became the subject of Her Imperial Majesty of his own will and gave his children into the military service, not as captives," were of no avail.[50]

Holding hostages not only was a measure of the natives' loyalty to Russia, but also served as a convenient argument in Russia's diplomatic squabbles with competing powers in cases of disputed suzerainty. Thus, Russian officials tried tirelessly to impress upon their counterparts in Qing China that the Kazakhs were Russian subjects because they submitted hostages.[51] Even so, the tangled loyalties in frontier regions were less clear-cut than the Russian authorities desired, and it was not uncommon for the various indigenous peoples to submit hostages and pay tribute to several alleged suzerains simultaneously.

Typically the Russian government and the native chiefs held different assumptions and expectations of hostage taking. Moscow continued to see in hostages a confirmation of the native peoples' oath of allegiance and their unconditional and exclusive submission to the Russian tsar and emperor. The natives, on the other hand, regarded submission of hostages as a reluctant but necessary act which accompanied a mutual nonaggression treaty and military alliance in return for payments and presents from Moscow. Such a peace treaty with Russia did not have to exclude a similar peace treaty with another party. To the Russians, however, such divided "loyalties" were unacceptable, and the repeated assurances from the chiefs that submitting hostages to others did not interfere with their allegiance to the Russian emperor failed to calm Moscow's suspicions.[52]

The Muscovite practice of keeping hostages continued throughout the eighteenth century, despite several proposals to abolish such practices and replace them with more effective means of exercising control over the natives. In the early 1760s, Russian officials in Orenburg proposed to replace hostages with a native court of law based in Orenburg, consisting of ten members: two or three Russians and others representing Kazakhs of all estates, so that "the Kazakhs would not consider this a hostage but a juridical institution."[53] At the same time, the Orenburg governor D. V. Volkov, in a passionate appeal to the empress to establish schools and educate the children of the native elites, asked: "Why should we not, for instance, treat their adolescent hostages better than cattle? Why should we not educate them in civility and morality instead of military skills?"[54]

Such proposals fell on deaf ears for several decades, until a new generation of Russian officials began to elaborate the same ideas in a broader colonial context. In the 1770s and 1780s, the Astrakhan governor, Petr Krechetnikov, envisioned the Caucasus transformed by the civilizing hand of the Russian administration. In his Caucasus, local languages and customs would give way to Russian ones, and Christianity would replace Islam. Since ignorance was one of the major handicaps on the way to civilization, Krechetnikov proposed to establish schools in Astrakhan for the sons of the local nobles. There they could be slowly introduced to Russian ways and inducted into the military, "so that there would be no longer need to take hostages, and they would convert to Christianity."[55]

Similar views of Russia's civilizing role in the Kazakh steppe, which was to be transformed by Russian justice, law, language, agricultural settlements, civilization, and Christianity, were held in Orenburg, where Russian officials did establish the Frontier Courts and schools for the children of the native nobles in the 1780s and 1790s. The sons of the khans, however, were sent to St. Petersburg. There they resided at the imperial court, were educated, awarded a military rank and honors, and often joined the distinguished ranks of the Russian nobility.[56] By the late eighteenth century, the former frontier hostages were becoming the empire's privileged subjects.

YASAK: TRIBUTE OR TRADE?

What was called the fur trade remained in reality a precarious amalgam of exchanges that ranged from gifts to credit transactions, to direct commodity exchanges, to extortion, to theft.

—RICHARD WHITE, *The Middle Ground:*
Indians, Empires, and Republics in the
Great Lakes Region, 1650–1815

If peace treaties and hostages were intended to formalize non-Christians' political subservience to Moscow, the imposition of tribute or tax in kind (*yasak*) was meant to be another and more tangible manifestation of the natives' subject status vis-à-vis the Russian suzerain. In the minds of Muscovite officials, the notion of peace and payment of yasak were often inseparable. Moscow considered the native territories that had not yet submitted yasak as hostile, and its voevodas were instructed "to call upon [the local population] to submit to the exalted protection of the grand sovereign to become his subjects and to pay yasak" and to demand that the natives pay yasak, not cash, because "it is more profitable to Moscow."[57]

Similar to the submission of hostages, yasak served to justify the tsar's territorial and political claims to the subject status of the indigenous peoples. In 1559 the Nogay beg Ismail wrote to Ivan IV disputing Muscovite boundaries and complaining that the Astrakhan voevoda had unlawfully demanded yasak "in grain from those who farm, and in fish from those who fish" from people who resided in the Volga estuary and whom Ismail considered to be his subjects. After numerous complaints, Ivan agreed that the Buzan, one of the smaller tributaries in the Volga delta, would be a border beyond which Moscow would not demand yasak.[58]

The concept of yasak (from the Mongol *yasa*—a law), like those of shert' and amanat, arrived in Moscow from the Turko-Mongol world. Originally one of many taxes collected by the Golden Horde, yasak, in Russian usage, became a generic levy imposed by the state specifically on the non-Christian peoples. What constituted yasak varied, however, and while the natives of Siberia submitted it in furs, the peoples of the Kazan region paid it in kind and cash.[59]

Yet, contrary to the government's wishes and its political definitions, yasak could not be immediately equated with the subject status of the indigenous peoples. By the early eighteenth century, some government officials realized that turning unruly native peoples into yasak-paying subjects of the empire required time and patience. This was particularly obvious in the Kazakh steppe, where in 1730 local Russian officials exacted a promise from the Kazakhs to make an annual delivery of yasak similar to that of the Bashkirs. The government cautioned its zealous agents not to insist on yasak, but to accept only if the Kazakhs offered it voluntarily. In return for "Her Majesty's high favor to grant the Kazakhs' petition and to permit the Kazakhs to become Russian subjects," the Russian officials dropped demands for yasak and hostages and emphasized to the Kazakhs the benefits of Russia's suzerainty: trade with Orenburg, freedom to graze their herds where they wished, and, in contrast to demands of the Oirats, no yasak payments.[60]

The government's case was undermined by peoples who were previously assuaged by similar assurances and later found themselves under the increasing burden of new demands. A powerful indictment of Russian policies came from fugitive Bashkirs, who told the Kazakhs that in the past they had become Russia's subjects of their own volition, performed various services, and paid yasak: "In time, however, the Russian government stripped them of their privileges and freedoms, increased taxes, demanded military recruits, imposed onerous services, converted them to Christianity, and brought them into such misery that they resolved to flee. The Bashkirs warned that the Kazakhs might soon find themselves in a similarly desperate circumstances."[61]

If Russia's strategic and political interests prevailed in the steppe, its economic interests were of far greater importance in Siberia. Here the government's insistence on the natives' payment of yasak in furs was less compromising, though not without ambiguities. Each time the natives brought their furs to the Russian officials, they were presented with the sovereign's compensation.[62] The Russians distinguished carefully between yasak paid by the natives and the sovereign's benevolent compensation or presents. Still, there is no indication that the native peoples separated the two notions, and they instead regarded such an exchange as a quid pro quo transaction.

Such transactions were accompanied by the distribution of government compensation, which ordinarily included axes, knives, tin and copper pots, woolens, flints, and tobacco. The most popular item, however, was beads, particularly crystal beads of different colors (odekui).[63] In addition, Moscow provided the natives with supplies of rye, butter, and fish oil. Upon the delivery of yasak, the authorities were expected to give a feast for the native representatives.[64]

In the seventeenth century, when Moscow often could not and did not deliver compensation or supplies regularly because of its own financial problems, the natives did not fail to voice complaints. On other occasions, the natives considered their compensation unsatisfactory and complained to the authorities that they were imposing items of poor quality upon them. According to some reports, the natives registered their displeasure by beating Russian officials, "and they throw the sovereign's presents, and tie them onto dogs' necks, and throw them into the fire, and they pay yasak with no courtesy, they kick it with their feet and throw it to the ground and they call us, your servants, bad people."[65]

The government was well aware of the quid pro quo nature of its relationship with the natives. The reports from Russian agents in charge of collecting yasak stated clearly that the natives submitted yasak only in exchange for the sovereign's compensation, and whenever they found their compensation to be inadequate, they did not deliver yasak in full. The agents added that they were running out of compensation and supplies, and, without them, the collection of yasak would cease completely. In response, Moscow instructed its officials in Siberia to give small amounts of compensation in accordance with yasak and to tell the natives that they should not regard this as a trade, but as the sovereign's compensation, and that they should be content with the amount they received.[66] That such explanations failed to convince the native peoples was clear from subsequent government actions. As late as 1766, seeking to improve the supply of furs in Siberia, the Yasak Distribution Commission suggested standardizing long-standing practices and recommended that, in exchange for yasak, the native nobles should be given presents in the amount of 2 percent of the furs' value.[67]

The evolution of yasak from an exchange of items between the indigenous peoples and Russian representatives into a fixed levy regularly submitted to the government was a long and slow process. The unruly natives continued to defy the Russian government's expectations that its imperial subjects pay tax or perform military service. Russia was yet to impose its effective control over the nomadic inhabitants of the steppe and migrating Siberian hunters. By the end of the eighteenth century, the imperial political language was slowly coming to terms with an illusive political reality.

PRESENTS AND PAYMENTS: BESTOWED OR EXTORTED?

> There everyone is afraid of this people, and particularly Persians,
> who in order to protect themselves give the Kumyk princes
> and the shamkhal what they call an allowance, but if one
> thinks about it, they pay them tribute, and the shah's
> annual expenditures on the Kumyk chiefs are great.
>
> —FROM THE REPORT OF PRINCE BEKOVICH-CHERKASSKII
> TO PETER I IN 1714

Neither an oath of allegiance nor any number of hostages could ensure the loyalty of Russia's purported subjects as efficiently as payments from Moscow. The regular supply of such payments and presents to the local ruler and his nobles was, in fact, the only way to secure the natives' cooperation. Similar to other frontier concepts, the system of payments and presents was a continuation of the Golden Horde's practices, and it too was based on ambiguous and different interpretations by both sides.[68]

By the time of the Golden Horde's collapse, payments and presents had evolved into a complex system, in which the two could not have been easily separated from each other or distinguished from tribute and taxes. From the mid-fourteenth century, when the Mongol khans entrusted the princes of Moscow with collecting tribute and taxes from other Russian princes, the Muscovites were regularly delivering the tribute (*dan'*, *vykhod* in Russian; *haraj* in Turko-Mongol) to the khan's residence along with an assortment of other levies (yasak).

FIGURE 6. Miniature from the *Litsevoi letopisnyi svod* showing the Grand Prince Mikhail of Tver bringing presents to Uzbek khan of the Golden Horde in 1319. The gifts did not prevent Uzbek khan from ordering Mikhail's execution. From O. I. Podobedova, *Miniatiury russkikh istoricheskikh letopisei: K istorii russkogo litsevogo letopisaniia* (Moscow: Nauka, 1966), p. 273.

The Russian princes specifically agreed to deliver to Moscow their part of the tribute and yasak, as long as the Horde continued to demand them. There was always a hope that "God willing, [if] there is a change in the Horde, then my children should not pay tribute to the Horde."[69] But after the Horde's disintegration, such payments did not cease. As late as 1531, Grand Prince Vasilii III was still given the sole right to collect tribute and other Tatar taxes (*tatarskie protory*) to be paid to the Horde, the Crimea, Astrakhan, Kazan, Kasimov (*tsarevichev gorodok*), and all the Chinggisids (*tsari i tsarevichi*) serving the grand prince.[70]

In time, the traditional terminology that expressed Moscow's relationship with the nomadic heirs to the Golden Horde became subsumed under different names. In Moscow's parlance, tribute was replaced by an allowance or annuity (*zhalovan'e*), and levies by presents (*pominki*). Such semantic changes were important for Moscow, where the zhalovan'e was considered a payment bestowed upon Muscovite friends and subjects by the tsar's divine mercy, and pominki were the presents brought to the ruler and his nobles as a measure of the recipients' honor and their good disposition toward Muscovy.[71]

While Moscow preferred to see zhalovan'e and pominki as rewards for loyalty and specific services to the tsar, Moscow's nomadic neighbors expected a zhalovan'e to be an annuity disbursed independently of any conditions and pominki a continuation of the traditional tribute and taxes paid by Moscow. Ivan III recognized as much when in 1473 he instructed his envoy to the Crimean khan to negotiate the issue and at first to refuse the Crimean demand to continue supplying the presents in undiminished quantities; only if his protestations proved fruitless was the envoy to sign a document obliging Moscow to make deliveries of presents.[72]

More than a hundred years later, the nature of the Muscovite-Crimean relations remained unchanged. In 1598, in the aftermath of devastating Crimean raids against Muscovy, the government dispatched to the Crimea its envoy, Semen Bezobrazov. He was given 1,000 gold pieces with instructions to discover the Crimea's intentions toward Muscovy. The envoy was to keep the money a secret, even from his interpreters, and to distribute it only if the Crimeans intended to launch a campaign against Muscovy: 700 gold pieces to a khan, 200 to a kalgay, and 100 to a nureddin.[73]

As late as 1665, Moscow's acceptance of the Crimea's demand for continued and ever-increasing tribute was one of the conditions leading to a peace treaty between a khan and the tsar.[74] Notwithstanding Moscow's rhetorical exercises, the Russian government was acutely aware that as long as Russia's military force remained ineffective against the Crimea, peace there could only be purchased. From the time of the initial protestations in the 1470s, Moscow's tributary relationship with the Crimea lasted for two more centuries. It was only the Peace Treaty of Carlowitz in 1699 which finally stipulated that Moscow no longer had to pay such tribute.

Throughout the centuries, the appetite of Russia's southern neighbors for payments and rewards remained undiminished. The annuity could be paid in cash, grain, clothing, or various valuable items. At critical moments the government was even prepared to pay in persons and herds to maintain the loyalty or neutrality of local rulers. Thus, in 1723, to counterbalance the entreaties of the Ottoman commander of Erzrum, Ibrahim pasha, Peter I ordered that the three Nogay uluses formerly belonging to Ishterek beg be given to the shamkhal, Adil Giray, to ensure the latter's peaceful intentions.[75]

The notion of presents included almost any possible payment: homage was manifested through tribute, taxes, financial aid, or loans. Various types of pominki were carefully distinguished. The first set of presents was submitted upon the arrival of a Russian envoy to the ruler's court (*pominki zdoroval'nye*), and then the customary presents, consisting of nine commodities (*deviatnye*), were disbursed to designated nobles (for instance, a good collection consisted of forty sable furs, one marten coat, and several other fur coats of lesser value). Some pominki contained items that had been specifically requested (*zaprosnye*), and others were direct cash payments (*kaznoiu pomoshch*). The most valued presents in the Crimea were furs (especially sables), falcons, walrus tusks, gold ducats, and armor. On several occasions the Crimean khan asked for cannon and silver goblets, which "our people cannot make so well." In the 1530s the Nogays requested and received from Moscow armor and helmets, gilded saddles and sabers, furs and fur hats, oils for dyeing and dyes, more than 300,000 nails, and Flemish woolens.[76]

In an endless chorus of growing demands, various local chiefs and nobles insisted on additional payments and presents for specific occasions: upon the marriages of their daughters and the births of their sons, to repay loans to merchants, to subsidize the construction of new forts, or for specific services they claimed to have provided.[77] More presents were needed because "what Mengli Giray khan had, he had already distributed [to his people] this summer," because Muhammed Giray khan wanted to be compensated for paying off the Nogays in order to avert their raids against Muscovy, because the Muscovite envoys did not bring sufficient presents, and because the greater the number of Nogays fleeing to the Crimea, the more a Crimean khan needed to pay them.[78]

The supply of payments and presents was critical to the local ruler's ability to maintain an elaborate network of patronage and loyalty by receiving and distributing valuable items among the ranks of the influential native nobles. This meant that Moscow had to provide an uninterrupted flow of payments to the nomadic rulers in hopes of enlisting their military support, or at least ensuring their neutrality. The mercenary character of the nomadic armies was an open secret. Some local nobles declared readily that "whether it is a grand prince or a [Polish] king, I will render better service to whoever pays more"; others were on Moscow's secret payroll and the recipients of secret gifts (*pominki sekretnye*).[79] That the services of the nomadic armies could be easily bought and sold meant that Moscow almost always found itself in a bidding war with other competing powers: Poland-Lithuania over the Crimeans and Nogays, and the Ottoman and Persian empires over the peoples of the Caucasus.[80]

Yet continuing the old practice of paying tribute and taxes to the nomads was increasingly at odds with Moscow's own self-image of a sovereign Christian state. At least since the 1470s, when Moscow's envoys were instructed to negotiate a reduction of the traditional tribute to the Crimean khan, Muscovite rulers engaged in a persistent effort to curtail and redefine the nature of these payments. The Russian envoys to the Crimea and the Nogays were under instructions to offer fewer presents, to refuse endless demands for numerous and seemingly arbitrary customary taxes, and to pay only those nobles who showed their loyalty to Moscow.

Moscow's attempts to change the nature of the traditional relationship with the nomads unleashed a flurry of protests on the other side. Writing to Ivan IV, who admitted that he had sent whatever he happened to have at hand, the Nogay beg Ismail lamented the measly number of presents and asked rhetorically: "How can we possibly divide what you are sending us?" In the early seventeenth century, the Nogays continued to complain that the Russian envoys were bringing "dry" letters, that is, missives unaccompanied by payments.[81]

But when the items arriving from Moscow were few, the responses of the native nobles grew less courteous. The Russian envoys were returning to Moscow with reports that their refusal to accede to the demands that they pay customary taxes was inciting fury among the local nobles, who assaulted and robbed them. In one such case, a Russian embassy to the Nogays in 1557 chose to defend itself against a group of Nogays and opened fire with muskets, killing one and wounding five others. Insulted and furious, Yunus mirza demanded that the embassy compensate him for the loss of his man with 500 live sheep or Russian goods worth 1,000 sheep. When the Russians refused, he seized goods worth 700 sheep. Such cases abounded, and the abuse of the Russian envoys was a matter of frequent discussion between the two sides. In the end, the complaints from Moscow were always met by the same argument in the steppe: they tried to take from the envoys only what was due to them.[82]

While demands for payments did not cease, the arguments for them varied greatly. Some nobles chose to exhibit humility and ask for an annuity because "my people are starving and poor." Others demanded respect for precedent and threatened their wrath if they were not honored as their predecessors had been. The eldest brothers indignantly claimed a larger payment than was brought to their younger brothers; some felt slighted and dishonored when their brothers received payments and they did not; and some claimed their high rank and accordingly a higher amount of payments.[83]

Honor and shame, two central concepts in any premodern society, were intrinsically connected to the distribution of payments and presents in nomadic society. Traditionally the tribute and taxes were brought to the court of the ruler, while smaller gifts were given to important nobles. As the central authority among the various nomadic peoples dissipated, the tribute diminished or disappeared with it. Instead, other payments and presents began to play a more important role and were in increasing demand by the independent and powerful nobles.

Realizing the growing dependence of the native nobles on the supplies from Moscow, the government boldly engaged in an effort to change the traditionally understood relationship with the nomads by taking the distribution of presents away from the local ruler and into its own hands, and by rewarding only those nobles who proved their loyalty. Such a policy was steadily undermining the traditional structures of the native societies, subverting the indigenous social hierarchy, and unleashing fierce internal rivalry for prestige and honor measured in size of payments. One Nogay, Urazly mirza, upon becoming a keikuvat, the third in the line of succession, wrote to Ivan IV in 1549 explaining his frustrations: "Among all the peoples there are important and less important men. And you know this but do not inquire who is who. And it so happens that the big men are honored like little ones, and the little ones like the big ones. And there is a custom that everyone needs his own levy [*poshlina*]. If our levy does not arrive, then we will be angry. Send us presents [*pominki*]: a suit of good armor, a gilded saber, and a good helmet."[84]

In the seventeenth and eighteenth centuries, the Russian government came into contact with other principal characters in the frontier drama: the Kabardinians and Kumyks in the North Caucasus, and the Kalmyks and Kazakhs in the Caspian steppe. But the dynamics of the government's interaction with its new neighbors remained unchanged. The relationships continued to rest upon the payments provided by Moscow, whether they were called taxes and mandatory presents by the nomads or payments and rewards by the Russian government.[85]

The most unembellished description of the natives' relationship with the neighboring empire came from the Caucasus' native son in the service of the Russian emperor. In his report to Peter I in 1714, Prince Bekovich-Cherkasskii argued that the only way to attract the peoples of the North Caucasus to Russia was to provide them with annuities and gifts. He gave an example of such a relationship between the Kumyks and the Persian shah:

> There everyone is afraid of this people, and particularly the Persians, who in order to protect themselves give the Kumyk princes and the shamkhal what they call an allowance [*zhalovan'e*], but if one thinks about it, they pay

them tribute [*dan*], and the shah's annual expenditures on the Kumyk chiefs are great. I will give you an example of the extent to which the Persians are afraid of them: if some Kumyk chief would wish to have a higher allowance from the shah, he receives it not through a request, but through a threat and destruction of Persian towns and villages, because when the shah learns of this, he writes to him, asking why he committed such robbery, and he responds that his allowance is smaller than that of others, and that is why he cannot restrain his people; and then, according to his wish, the shah adds to his allowance, so that he does not continue his destruction.[86]

That the nature of Russia's relationship with its southern neighbors was no different was well understood, yet never spelled out.

Pragmatism was only slowly winning out over the blunt denial or the politically correct rhetoric of official Russia. Thirty-four years after Bekovich-Cherkasskii's report, another native son from a different corner of the Eurasian steppe, the former Muhammed and now General Aleksei Tevkelev, had to argue again to his superiors in the capital that the khans of the Lesser and Middle Kazakh Hordes should be given annuities, because this was the only way to prevent their raids and to promote khans friendly to Russian interests—and "because the Kazakhs would do anything to receive presents."[87] The government offered annuities consisting of cash and grain, specific payments, rewards, and presents to the Kabardinian chiefs, the Kalmyk tayishis, the Kazakh khans, and other local rulers. That the loyalty of the nomads could be secured only by continuous payments, in whatever form, was no longer disputed.

TRANSLATING OR COLONIZING?

Friend and Brother! When those words were spoke to our chiefs by the governor they were much pleased with what he said, the Governor then wrote two papers which he told our chiefs contained the words he had just spoken to them and he wished them to sign them both that he would send one to the President of the United States and one they could keep themselves in order that the good words he had spoke might be kept in remembrance by the white and red people. Our chiefs cheerfully signed these papers.

Friend and Brother! You may judge how our chiefs felt when they returned home and found that the Governor had been shutting up their eyes and stopping their Ears with his good words and got them to sign a Deed for their lands without their knowledge.

—THE DELAWARE CHIEFS TO PRESIDENT JEFFERSON IN 1805,
FROM ANTHONY F. C. WALLACE, *Jefferson and the Indians:
The Tragic Fate of the First Americans*

Moscow's communication with its neighbors depended squarely on a few selected people: translators and interpreters. They were more than mere interlocutors rendering words from one language into another. Translating meant to relate Moscow's interests and policies, to transform Muscovite concepts into native terms, and to render native concerns in the appropriate imperial language. They were, in other words, a critical tool of Moscow's policies and principal actors in the long process of colonization of the natives' consciousness.[88]

Disparate peoples and tongues along the southern and eastern frontiers of Russia were connected not only by the political legacy of the Golden Horde but also by the Tatar language, which remained the lingua franca from the North Caucasus to the steppes of Central Asia. To maintain communications, Moscow employed a staff of translators (*perevodchiki*) and interpreters (*tolmachi*) at the Foreign Office. The two groups occupied different positions in the official hierarchy. The translators were literate, translated written documents, and were paid far better than the interpreters, who were usually illiterate and could only interpret orally.[89]

Despite an obvious need for translators and interpreters into Tatar and other local languages, Moscow was invariably and desperately short of both. Complaints about the matter from the local authorities were common. In 1589 the Tersk voevoda Andrei Khvorostinin wrote to Moscow: "There is a great damage to your sovereign's cause here because of the [lack of] interpreters, and there are no interpreters to be sent to the shamkhal, Georgia, Tiumen, the Circassians, and other lands. They sent to us interpreters from Astrakhan, and they were former captives, and some of them were freed a year ago, and others less than a year. And we, your servants, do not dare to dispatch such interpreters."[90]

Indeed, most of the interpreters were former captives who learned the local vernacular in captivity. One such story is of the interpreter Ivan Naumov, hired by the Foreign Office in 1682. Born in Ukraine and was a Cossack in the Zaporozhian Host when he fell prisoner to the Crimeans and was later sold into slavery in Istanbul. He spent twenty-two years as a rower aboard an Ottoman military ship before it was captured by the navy of Florence. The Florentines set him free, and after a long journey through the territories of the Holy Roman Empire and Poland, Naumov found his way to Moscow. There he petitioned to become an interpreter, claiming to speak Greek, Arabic, Turkish, and Italian. After being tested by the translators of the Foreign Office, he was deemed competent.[91] While the story of Naumov's captivity was rather typical, the attestation of his competence was less so. For most interpreters the subtleties of the local language and culture remained elusive, and even their basic competence was in grave doubt.

In 1580, one foreign observer asserted that "the only language the Muscovites knew was their own," and that the only Greek interpreter in the service of the grand prince was trained by Greeks who "taught their student the corrupt jargon the Greeks speak nowadays instead of ancient Greek or the language in which the early Fathers wrote their books."[92] A century later, however, the Foreign Office burgeoned to include a staff of twenty-three translators and twenty interpreters. The languages of their expertise—some claimed knowledge of two or three languages—clearly reflected the priorities of Moscow's foreign policy. Translators knowledgeable in various languages numbered as follows: Latin (8), Tatar (8), German (6), Polish (5), Dutch (2), Swedish (2), Greek (2), English (1), Turkish (1), and Mongol (1). Additionally, several translators into Tatar and Kalmyk were assigned to the Kazanskii dvorets, an office in charge of administering the Kazan region.[93]

While translators of Tatar and Turkish were slightly outnumbered by "Europeanists" in the Foreign Office, interpreters of the Asian languages held an undisputed majority: twelve interpreted into Tatar, three into Turkish, three into Persian, and one into Kalmyk. The remaining staff were two interpreters into Greek, one into Latin, one into Italian, and one into English. On the whole, Moscow employed more translators and interpreters of the Asiatic languages.

At the same time that Moscow employed translators to conduct its relations with the West, it continued to rely predominantly on interpreters in the southern and eastern regions. Most of these interpreters bore Russian names, a clear indication that they were freed Russian captives. By contrast, the translators into Tatar and Turkish had Turkic last names and Russian first names, betraying the fact that this more literate contingent of the Foreign Office consisted of converts who came from the indigenous population.

Moscow valued its translators. In the late seventeenth century, an average translator employed at the Foreign Office received a handsome payment by Muscovite standards: 300 chets of land (one chet equals about 1.2 acres), an annuity of 80 rubles, and 32 rubles for other annual expenses; interpreters were paid about half as much. Often employed outside their traditional role, the translators were also sent on sensitive missions to the natives and were sometimes generously rewarded if they were successful. In one such notable case, Muhammed Tevkelev, who had been sent to the Kazakhs in the 1730s, rose from the rank of translator to assume new titles of major-general of the Russian army and vice governor of Orenburg, and not incidentally a new name, Aleksei Tevkelev. Yet, most of the time the translators' incessant petitions for overdue payments suggest that their salaries, like those of many other Muscovites, were delayed or remained unpaid.[94]

Translations into local languages usually involved a two-step process: the original was first translated into Tatar, and then into the local language. At times the complexity of translating and interpreting was not helped by the rigid attitudes of the Russian officials. One example may illustrate how the task of translation was further handicapped by political and religious considerations. During the visit of the Muscovite embassy to the Georgian tsar Alexander in 1596–99, it turned out that the Georgians could no longer translate letters from Moscow because the Georgian translator had died. The Georgians suggested to the Muscovite envoys that they have their missives interpreted into Turkish, and the Georgians would then transcribe them in the Georgian alphabet. The envoys replied that although their interpreters knew Turkish, they were illiterate and could not read Russian or Turkish, and therefore they could not translate. Moreover, the envoys declared that "the letters contain many wise words from the divine scriptures, but the interpreters cannot translate them because these words are not used in the Turkish language." The Georgians continued to insist; the Russians continued to refuse, saying that it had never been done before, and one could not translate properly through three languages. In the end, the impatient Georgians suggested, "Then do not read the divine words, read to us only what concerns the substance of the matter and the interpreters will interpret that into Turkish." On this they finally agreed.[95] Contrary to what the Muscovite envoys claimed, translations "through three languages" were the only way to communicate with the natives and were used routinely until the mid-eighteenth century, when the Russian authorities learned to rely on natives with a knowledge of Russian.

Apart from sheer incompetence or concerns for sensitive theological propriety, translations were further compromised by the deliberate efforts at misrepresentation and selective editing, so that, for instance, letters from the natives, often written to the tsar as an equal, had to be rendered in the form of a supplication to the Russian sovereign. Translators and their censors took great pains in trying to avoid precise translations whenever the original phrasing could possibly harm the dignity of the Russian monarch; they rendered them instead into acceptable political and diplomatic terminology. Available copies of translations often show numerous signs of editing. The corrections spelled out fully the title of the tsar and introduced such polite expressions as "your royal majesty," "the grand sovereign," and others that were not mentioned in the original. Often the arrogant tone of a letter was changed, making it more humble and subdued.[96]

The political importance of translations and Moscow's ability to manipulate them were evident early on. The Muscovite embassy to the Crimea in 1500 was told that under no circumstances was it to give the Crimeans a Russian version of the proposed treaty. If the Crimeans insisted, then the text should be translated from Russian into Tatar at the Russian embassy, and if the Crimean khan wanted to have it translated in his presence, then a Russian scribe was to read the text and an interpreter was to translate it.[97] Obviously the Russian version and the Tatar translation contained some differences that Moscow did not wish to reveal.

Indeed, translations often deliberately misrepresented the issues. Most of the time the natives were not provided with a written copy of the documents they were expected to sign. Instead they had to rely on the Russian interpreters, who related the contents of the document to them. A contemporary Russian translator, Vasilii Bakunin, asserted that prior to 1724 the Kalmyks were not familiar with the contents of the treaties they had signed and that were regarded by Moscow as the Kalmyks' oaths of allegiance. In contrast to earlier documents, which had been written in Russian with the tayishis' signatures affixed to them, the document the Kalmyks signed in 1724 was written in Kalmyk and discussed among the Kalmyks in numerous meetings before they agreed to sign it.[98]

Translating was a serious matter fraught with serious consequences. Translators and interpreters walked a tightrope between the two sides, often in fear for their lives if what they translated was found to be offensive or provocative. The pope's emissary to Moscow in 1581, Antonio Possevino, recalled how the Muscovite interpreter hesitated to translate one of Possevino's questions to Ivan IV, because he thought it would provoke the tsar's ire. The steppe was no less dangerous than Moscow, and Russian interpreters accompanying embassies to the nomadic peoples were often held responsible for shortages of presents and were routinely threatened, beaten, and otherwise abused.[99]

Violence against Russian interpreters and the natives' complaints about them were not necessarily unfounded. The Russian authorities knew about and often agreed with many charges against their interpreters: stealing presents or taking bribes, distorting the contents of letters sent from Moscow, colluding with some local nobles at the expense of others, or simply lying and deceiving the locals in trade transactions.[100] Of course, the temptation to profit from the natives' ignorance of Russian was all the harder to resist inasmuch as the interpreters' salaries were haphazardly paid by Moscow. Additionally, and perhaps unintentionally, Moscow created personal incentives for its interpreters to distort the record. The interpreters who could claim success in securing the natives' allegiance to the Russian tsar were generously rewarded.[101]

While most interpreters were regarded by the natives with suspicion, some were able to win their trust. In 1560 the Nogay beg Ismail asked Ivan IV to have a specific interpreter included in the Muscovite embassy to the Nogays, because "he does good service to you and me." Moscow also had its preferences. When it came to relating certain secret matters to Moscow's loyalists among the Crimeans or Nogays, Muscovite envoys were under strict instructions to use the services of one Muscovite interpreter but not another. Curiously enough, the Muscovite interpreter who was distrusted by Moscow in this case bore the name of Petr Novokreshchennyi, his last name meaning "new convert" and one commonly given to converts. The interpreter requested by the Nogays was named Touzar, a Turkic name misspelled by the Muscovite scribes. If these cases are any indication, the old linguistic and racial affinities continued to matter more than the interpreters' new religion or place of residence.[102]

In the early eighteenth century, new imperial concerns demanded ever-larger numbers of translators and interpreters. In 1726 the Astrakhan and Stavropol metropolitan, Lavrentii, wrote to the Synod that there were no competent translators into Kalmyk and Tatar in Astrakhan, except for illiterate interpreters.[103] It was significant that this time the issue was raised by the ecclesiastical authorities, as it reflected the government's growing interest in religious conversion of the natives. The new spirit of proselytizing spurred the first concerted efforts to rectify the shortage of translators and interpreters and to improve their competence. It also marked a new realization of the importance of translations in converting new subjects of the empire to Christianity.[104]

In time, the social origins of both interpreters and translators changed. The former Russian captives who had acquired their knowledge of the native language and society while living there as slaves had been replaced by interpreters who came from the indigenous societies. They were new converts, who lived freely among the Russians and became equally competent in Russian and their native language. At the same time, pragmatic needs for more efficient imperial rule required more accurate translations and competent translators to express the new imperial language. The government learned to rely more heavily on the children of native nobles, who were often educated in the schools for translators set up for them in the cities of Kazan, Astrakhan, and Orenburg, and some were even sent to study in St. Petersburg.[105] In the eighteenth century, a new generation of better-trained and -educated translators into oriental languages emerged in the Foreign Office.

[   ]

This chapter has demonstrated that Russia's relations with its southern and eastern neighbors were based on a series of misnomers, misunderstandings, and deliberate misrepresentations. Altogether they comprised a set of mutual misconceptions that only reflected larger structural incompatibilities between the Russian and indigenous societies. Each side perceived the other through its own sociopolitical system and projected its own image upon the other. Thus, the Russian government's policies in the region should be understood not simply as a set of instructions emanating from the capital, but also as a function of the contested vocabularies and identities that the government labored to impose on the peoples and the landscape of the region.

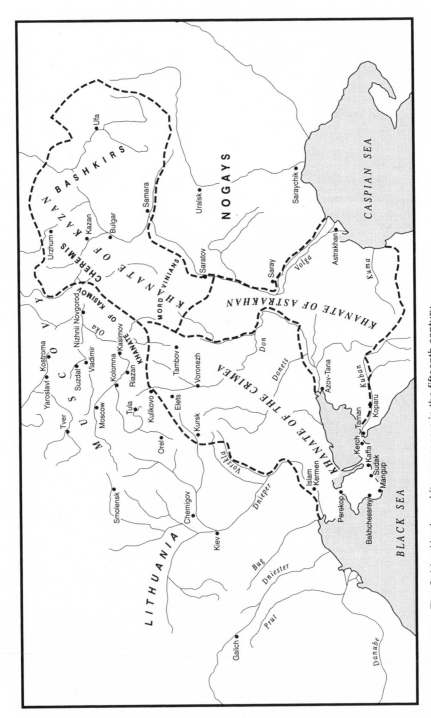

MAP 3. The Golden Horde and its successors in the fifteenth century.

[3]

TAMING THE "WILD STEPPE," 1480–1600s

MOSCOW AND THE GREAT HORDE: THE "UGRA STANDOFF" RECONSIDERED

Throughout more than two hundred years of its history, the Golden Horde, a powerful confederation of nomadic and seminomadic tribes dominating the vast territory from western Siberia to Moscow, withstood numerous challenges from constituents of its enormous empire as well as outsiders. But by the late 1470s the Golden Horde was in irreversible decline. It had become irreparably split between warring members of the Chingissid ruling families. The rivals were based in the peripheral regions of the Golden Horde's territory: in the khanates of Kazan and Astrakhan on the Volga, the Crimea, and Tiumen in western Siberia. The core of the Golden Horde remained a nomadic confederation known as the Great Horde (*Bol'shaia Orda*), which roamed the steppe between the Don and Yaik rivers. The khans of the Great Horde considered themselves successors to the khans of the Golden Horde and attempted continually to reassert their authority over other entities of the former Golden Horde.

It was at this time, in 1474, that a departing envoy of the grand prince of Moscow, Ivan III, was given detailed instructions about how to respond to various issues that the Crimean khan, Mengli Giray, might raise. In anticipation of Mengli Giray's insistence on Moscow's help against the khan of the Great Horde, Ahmad, the envoy was directed to reply that Moscow could not break relations with Ahmad because "the patrimonial lands [*votchina*] of the grand prince and Ahmad khan have a common steppe frontier, and every year Ahmad khan comes to his pastures near my sovereign's lands."[1] When in the following year Mengli Giray suggested similar terms of alliance, an exasperated Russian envoy explained that if the grand prince were to declare war against Ahmad, then Moscow would have to face two enemies on two fronts—Kazimierz IV, the king of Poland and Lithuania, and Ahmad khan of the Great Horde.[2] The grand prince had yet to overcome his fear of a direct challenge to Ahmad khan and was interested only in Mengli Giray's help against Poland and Lithuania.

The Crimea and Moscow had much in common. Both were locked in a struggle against traditional foes to recover their previous losses. In the case of Moscow, the issue was the loss of territory, "the old Russian lands," which were now under Lithuanian rule. For the Crimea, it was a fight over supremacy in the former Golden Horde and regaining from Ahmad those people and herds (*tsarev ulus*) that, Mengli insisted, belonged to his father. It was to be an alliance of two marginal rulers rapidly assuming major roles in regional politics.

In April 1480, Ivan wrote to Mengli Giray proposing an alliance against both Poland and the Great Horde. Ivan was finally compelled to seek closer ties with the Crimea not only by his increased confidence after the momentous victory over Novgorod or the threat of the alliance between Poland and the Great Horde against him, but also by the shifting winds of steppe politics. Mengli Giray, having survived several coups, had now been put firmly back on the throne by the Ottoman army, and his brother and former rival, Nur Devlet, had left his exile in Poland and offered his services to Ivan. The advantages of a Moscow-Crimea alliance were obvious to both sides: Nur Devlet, the potential pretender to the Crimean throne, was neutralized as long as Moscow and the Crimea remained allies and friends; the mutually profitable trade could continue and expand; the Crimean raids were channeled away from the Muscovite frontier towns and villages toward the Polish and Lithuanian frontiers; and their traditional foes, Poland and the Great Horde, would face a powerful military alliance of Moscow and the Crimea.[3]

At the same time that Ivan hesitantly took the risk of forming an alliance with Mengli Giray, the Polish king Kazimierz IV bought Ahmad khan's participation in a common military campaign against Moscow. Ahmad, unhappy with irregular payments of tribute from Moscow and hoping to take advantage of discord between Ivan and his younger brothers, could not refuse an opportunity for more spoils. In the summer of 1480, when Ahmad's army approached the Muscovite frontier along the Ugra River, the alliances were clearly drawn: Moscow and the Crimea faced Poland and the Great Horde. The rival alliances might have been locked in struggle for a

И помнюти дни при неупахоукыющеся,
и не оз могоша, не тон хиижждщи е гда
река станеть. Быша м разно единичто
гда река жемауастаоннтнеа, выишжеентра
на боон единидругн
бояхоуеа

FIGURE 7. Miniature from the *Litsevoi letopisnyi svod* depicting "the stand on the Ugra" in 1480. The Muscovite and Mongol troops appear virtually indistinguishable, with one notable exception. The headdress of Ahmad khan (*right*) is a royal crown worn by tsars, kings, or khans, whereas the headdress of the Grand Prince Ivan III (*left*) is a traditional and decidedly nonroyal cap of the Russian princes. The image testifies to contemporaries' clear understanding of the royal hierarchies. The sixteenth-century Russian illuminator correctly portrayed the khan of the Great Horde as superior to the grand prince of Muscovy. By contrast, in figure 8 (p. 108) Tsar Ivan IV is depicted wearing a crown as he enters Kazan in 1552. From Nikolai Borisov, *Ivan III* (Moscow: Molodaia Gvardiia, 2000).

long time had it not been for one other crucial player who, for the time being, remained behind the scenes. The khan of Tiumen, Abak (Ibak, Ivak), and the Nogays were observing developments from behind the Volga.

Ahmad arrived at the banks of the Ugra River only to be confronted by Muscovite troops waiting on the other side. Neither army was ready to engage the other, and, unable to invade Muscovy, Ahmad khan had to retreat. This event became known in Russian historiography as "the stand on the Ugra" and provided early Russian chroniclers and later historians with one of the more enduring myths in Russian history, namely, that "the stand on the Ugra" ended the "Tatar yoke" and that the might of the grand prince's armies was responsible for the ultimate demise of the Golden Horde.[4]

This image of victorious Moscow was carefully constructed by Muscovite chroniclers keenly aware of the necessity to provide the growing Muscovite state with a Russian Orthodox ideology of supremacy. Some chroniclers rebuked the grand prince for less than valorous behavior during the confrontation with Ahmad, and although they blamed it on Ivan's evil advisors, the unmistakable implication was that such behavior was unworthy of the Russian prince in the standoff with the infidels. Other chroniclers emphasized the disgraceful flight of Ahmad's army, attributing it variously to fear of the Muscovite troops, plague among the Tatars, or cold weather. In all cases, Russian historiography considers the "Ugra standoff" to have ended two centuries of "the Mongol yoke."[5]

In contrast to the Russian chroniclers, Ivan, in a letter to his ally Mengli Giray in 1481, described the event in much humbler terms: "Ahmad khan came against me, but all-merciful God wanted to save us from him and did so."[6] It is also purported that shortly after his retreat Ahmad wrote to Ivan III, demanded submission of tribute, and threatened to return, explaining that he had left only because "his people had no clothes and his horses no horsecloth." Even though this epistle has been convincingly shown to be a forgery, it is significant that its alleged seventeenth-century forger attributed Ahmad's retreat to a shortage of food and clothes rather than to victorious Muscovite arms.[7]

What precisely happened on the banks of the Ugra in 1480 may never be known, since the officials of the Great Horde were far more interested in keeping track of collected tribute than records of military battles, while the Muscovite chroniclers chose to present their information selectively. Yet circumstantial evidence and an understanding of traditional nomadic warfare and contemporary steppe politics may help to reconstruct the events of 1480 along the Muscovite southern frontier.

When Ahmad khan arrived at the banks of the Ugra, he had already lost the most crucial advantage traditionally enjoyed by the nomadic armies, the element of surprise. Most likely Ahmad was not seeking to surprise Ivan and ravage Muscovy. Instead, he might have counted on a commonly exercised strategy of intimidation, when the very sight of a large army led by the khan was sufficient to compel the Moscow prince into suing for peace and resuming the payments of tribute. This time, however, Ahmad's army was met by Muscovite troops gathered on the opposite bank. Crossing rivers had always presented a serious logistical challenge to nomadic cavalry even when the foe was not in sight. With the Muscovite troops already positioned at the known fords, such a crossing would have been extremely hazardous.[8] Ahmad chose to wait for the arrival of his ally, King Kazimierz of Poland. But the king's troops never arrived, because they were tied up by the campaign of Mengli Giray in the southern regions of Poland-Lithuania. The alliance between Moscow and the Crimea was paying off.

Ahmad waited for more than three months, expecting the grand prince finally to sue for peace and offer tribute. But this time, encouraged by church leaders and his alliance with the Crimea, Ivan did not concede. In mid-November 1480, as the weather turned cold and the surrounding pastures were depleted, Ahmad abandoned the campaign and turned back. The retreat of his army to winter pastures farther south was consistent with the typically seasonal campaigns of the nomadic cavalry. Winter campaigns did take place occasionally, of course, but they were usually narrowly targeted, brief, and feasible only if the horses were rested and had been well fed the preceding fall.

There could be another explanation for Ahmad's sudden retreat, however. It was not the first time that Ahmad had approached the Muscovite frontier only to retreat suddenly after plundering a few towns.[9] What the Muscovite chroniclers more than once attributed to divine intervention or the might of Muscovite troops was usually provoked by news of a raid against the Horde's uluses, where women, children, and herds were left defenseless. This was the most common tactic in nomadic warfare. Indeed, some chroniclers reported that Ivan dispatched Russian troops and Tatar cavalry down the Volga River to attack the uluses of the Great Horde. It is also possible that news that the Nogays were about to attack his uluses prompted Ahmad's speedy return.[10]

In early January 1481, Ahmad khan perished in an engagement with the Nogays led by Abak khan.[11] Abak's first act was to send an envoy to Moscow to inform the grand prince that Ahmad was dead. The envoy was generously rewarded by Ivan and sent back.[12] The fact that Abak knew very well who would benefit from Ahmad's death and where he could be properly rewarded indicates that some previous agreement might have been reached between Moscow and the Nogays. Indeed, in 1549 the Nogay beg Yusuf would trace the roots of the Moscow-Nogay friendship to the Nogay beg Temir, who had been on the side of Ahmad khan on the Ugra and who later assassinated Ahmad khan "because of friendship with the White Prince" (i.e., Ivan III).[13]

With the death of Ahmad khan ended the last attempt by the Great Horde to reestablish its authority over the entire territory of the former Golden Horde. For another twenty years the Great Horde, weakened and divided between Ahmad's sons, continued to be a nuisance, occasionally raiding frontier towns and pillaging trade caravans but no longer capable of major campaigns. Ivan permanently stopped paying tribute to the Horde, and Mengli Giray proclaimed that the Horde was no longer a threat to him.[14]

The slow demise of the Great Horde resulted from several factors. Moscow's rise as a significant commercial and military power was one of them. No doubt, Ahmad's indecisiveness on the Ugra also reflected the growing military power of Moscow. Given the factional struggle within the Muscovite government on matters of foreign policy, the grand prince could be credited with making clever and pragmatic choices in allying himself with the Crimea and the Nogays against the Horde.

Moreover, events of greater significance took place outside of Moscow, across its steppe frontier. When in 1475 the Ottomans occupied the strategic Crimean port of Kaffa, they believed that their control of the Crimea was secured. But in the following years a Crimean faction representing interests of the Great Horde was able to overthrow the Ottoman protégé, Mengli Giray. The Ottomans had to intervene again to finally install him on the Crimean throne in 1480.[15] The Ottomans' interest in Crimean affairs and their support of Mengli Giray meant that the winter pastures of the Great Horde were no longer safe from the Crimean raids.

Even greater danger to the Horde came from the east. In the middle of the fifteenth century, the struggle for pastures and control of the trading centers among the newly emerged nomadic confederations in the steppe of Central Asia produced a traditional pattern of nomadic migrations. Under the pressure of the Uzbek and Kazakh nomads, the Nogays had to move farther west and seized the pastures of the Great Horde.[16] In the 1470s the uluses of the Great Horde could no longer cross the Volga River to the east without fear of severe Nogay raids. By 1480, despite the threatening moves of Ahmad khan, the Great Horde was in a desperate situation. It faced a strengthened Muscovite military in the west, and it had lost its traditional pastures along the Don to the Crimeans in the south and pastures between the Volga and Yaik to the Nogays in the east. It was only a matter of time before the nomadic remnants of the Golden Horde would be replaced by new and more aggressive rivals.

THE END OF THE GOLDEN HORDE, 1481–1502: ON TO KAZAN

From the middle of the fifteenth century, the intensified internal wars within the Golden Horde produced ever larger numbers of rebels and outcasts who sought to escape their rivals. Some of them departed to the open steppe to become *kazaks,* better known as Cossacks among their Slavic counterparts, freebooters living off raids and enjoying their independence.[17] Increasingly, however, many Tatar nobles preferred the service of the Muscovite princes to the vagaries of life in the steppe. Content at first to join the Moscow princes on occasional military campaigns in return for rewards, the Tatar princes and nobles were soon ready to settle in Muscovy and perform military service in exchange for a stable income: grants of land, supplies of grain, cash, and generous gifts. One such well-known case was the arrival in Moscow of Kasim, the son of the khan of the Golden Horde, Ulu Muhammed. In 1452 the grand prince Vasilii II granted Kasim a frontier town in the Meshchera lands (*Meshcherskii gorodok*). Later known as Kasimov, it became the residence of numerous members of the Chinggisid dynasty for more than two centuries.[18]

By the late fifteenth century, the Tatars in the service of Moscow represented a sizable and significant contingent. Mengli Giray often specifically requested that all the Tatar princes, mirzas, and kazaks take part in campaigns against the Great Horde. Moscow also became a convenient exile destination for Mengli Giray's rivals. Thus, with Mengli Giray's encouragement Ivan harbored Mengli Giray's brothers, Aidar and Nur Devlet, and granted the latter the town of Kasimov. While far away from the Crimean throne and kept under the watchful eye of the Moscow prince, the khan's rival kin were also gainfully employed against the Crimea's foes. Ivan III was quite aware of the situation and, when necessary, did not hesitate to remind Mengli Giray of the burden of providing for the renegade Crimean princes.[19]

Ivan was not merely soliciting Mengli Giray's recognition of him as a loyal ally. Supporting Chinggisids in Moscow was indeed a costly matter. While Kasimov as a frontier town was simply a place of residence, provisions and revenue for Nur Devlet and his retinue came from the town of Kashira and many surrounding villages.[20] These expenses were worth the trouble, as Nur Devlet provided Ivan with crucial political leverage against both the Horde and the Crimea and played a pivotal role in securing Moscow's victory over Kazan.

Since its emergence in the 1440s, the Kazan khanate had paid close attention to its wealthy neighbor to the west, the prince of Moscow. Trade, profitable for both sides, was occasionally disrupted by Kazan's large-scale campaigns against Moscow, demanding Moscow's tribute. Far more frequent, however, were small-scale raids against Muscovite frontier towns. By the 1470s, Moscow was prepared to take advantage of endless internal strife within the Golden Horde and deep political divisions in Kazan. The political faction in power in Kazan relied on an alliance with the Great Horde, while the opposition increasingly turned to Moscow for help. Several times during the 1470s, Moscow had sent expeditionary forces to assist the opposition in deposing the ruling khan, but each time Kazan and the Great Horde successfully repulsed the Muscovite troops.[21]

In 1487 Mengli Giray's marriage to Nur Sultan, the widow of Ibrahim khan of Kazan, provided Ivan III with another reason to intervene in Kazan politics, and this time more successfully than before. When Nur Sultan wrote to Ivan and urged him to support her son, Muhammed Amin, who had fled from Kazan to Moscow, Ivan seized the moment to launch another campaign against Kazan. He sent Tatar cavalry led by Nur Devlet against the Great Horde and Muscovite troops against Kazan. In August 1487, Ivan triumphantly reported to his ally Mengli Giray that his troops had taken Kazan, deposed and taken to Moscow Alikhan (Alegam) and his family, and put Muhammed Amin on the throne.[22]

Kazan could not have been captured without help from Mengli Giray and Nur Devlet. While Mengli Giray harassed the Horde from the Crimea, Nur Devlet launched raids from Moscow; both prevented the Horde from aiding the besieged city of Kazan. The remaining sons of the deceased Ahmad khan, Murtoza and Seyyid Ahmad (Sedekhmat), turned their efforts toward playing off Nur Devlet against his old rival and brother, Mengli Giray. In the fall of 1487 Murtoza wrote to Nur Devlet inviting him to leave Moscow and join forces against Mengli Giray.

In his letter Murtoza addressed Nur Devlet as brother and khan (*tsar*) and called him "the pillar of our faith and the support of all Muslims and Islam." Murtoza reminded Nur Devlet that his father, Ahmad khan, and Nur Devlet had been friends until Mengli Giray sowed war between them, and now Murtoza again desired peace. He ended the letter with a reproach for Nur Devlet's service in Moscow: "It is not befitting your status, our brother, to live among the infidels. And if you want to leave the land of the infidels, I sent a letter concerning this to Ivan." Obviously an appeal to the common bonds of Islam intended to reinforce Murtoza's more pragmatic goals of waging war against Mengli Giray.[23]

It was Ivan who benefited the most from this ongoing rivalry between the Crimea and the Horde. Both Murtoza and Seyyid Ahmad of the Great Horde sent envoys to Moscow attempting to win Ivan's neutrality in the conflict.[24] Ivan dutifully dispatched their missives to his ally, Mengli Giray, causing great alarm in the Crimea. Concerned that Nur Devlet was quickly becoming a liability, Mengli Giray asked that Nur Devlet be sent back to the Crimea. But Ivan, assuring Mengli Giray that he had only the Crimean khan's interests in mind, declined. For several years Ivan continued to explain the issue away, suggesting that Nur Devlet's presence in the Crimea might endanger Mengli because "the same people that now serve you used to serve Nur Devlet," until finally, in 1489, he promised to let Nur Devlet go, if such was Mengli Giray's wish.[25]

In fact, Nur Devlet did not leave for the Crimea; nor was he ever mentioned again in Moscow's service. His name simply vanished from the written records. In 1490 the Tatar contingent of Moscow was led by Nur Devlet's son Satylkhan, and, a year later, when Mengli Giray requested that Ivan send Nur Devlet against the Horde, it was again Satylkhan who was dispatched. It is assumed that Nur Devlet died in Moscow around 1491.[26]

The tension surrounding the issue of Nur Devlet's return was only symptomatic of future conflicts in the Crimea-Moscow alliance. It was clear that the alliance had been based on common interests, not necessarily on trust. Mengli Giray worried that his brother could be used against him, and he did not quite trust Ivan's safekeeping. Ivan perhaps feared that to return Nur Devlet meant to provide the Crimea with a leader who was familiar with the roads to Moscow and its defenses. He was not willing to take such a risk, even if it meant a confrontation with Mengli Giray. Two decades later, in further testimony to the new confidence of the Muscovite princes, similar circumstances in a similar issue surrounded the case of Abdullatif, the son of Nur Sultan and Ibrahim khan of Kazan.

Ivan's stature among the steppe peoples rose dramatically after his victory over Kazan. For the conquest of Kazan in 1487 put Ivan in control of a city vital to the trade interests of the Nogays. Shortly after the fall of Kazan, envoys from Abak khan and the Nogay mirzas, Musa and Yamgurchi, arrived in Moscow to declare friendship, to ask for trade free of customs duties, and to insist that the deposed Ali khan and his family be released. Despite the stern tone of Abak's letter, Ivan responded that he would consider them friends only if they became allies of the new khan of Kazan. As for returning Alikhan, he had no intention of doing so.[27]

While the Horde and the Crimea were at war, Ivan established complete control over Kazan. Muhammed Amin, to whom Ivan referred as "brother and son," thus leaving no doubt of Ivan's superior position, was completely dependent on the grand prince of Moscow. And when Muhammed Amin sought to form an alliance with the Nogays by marrying a daughter of Yamgurchi mirza, both he and Yamgurchi had to ask Ivan's permission.[28]

Like the Nogays, Mengli Giray too was becoming visibly dependent on Moscow. He requested increased payments and presents and expected to receive sable furs, falcons, and walrus tusks for trade with Tabriz and Mamluk Egypt. Even more important, Mengli Giray needed Moscow's military help while the war between the Crimea and Horde continued unabated. In the spring of 1491, Mengli called upon Ivan to send the Kasimov and Kazan Tatars to finish off the Horde because the successful Crimean raids in the winter "undercut the enemy's feet, by seizing all of the Horde's horses."[29]

At the same time, Mengli was also seeking help against the Horde in Istanbul. The sultan's effort to reconcile the two rivals did not last long. The mutual raids intensified when the khans of the Horde (the *Naiman* [*Namagan*] *ulus*) broke a truce with Mengli by raiding the uluses belonging to the Baryn clan of the Crimea. While the Astrakhan khan chose to side with the Horde, the Nogays offered their alliance to Mengli Giray and were ready to attack Astrakhan. More aid to Mengli arrived from two other places: the Ottoman sultan sent 2,000 janisssaries, and Ivan dispatched his Tatar and Russian cavalry. Shortly thereafter the Muscovite envoy reported from the Crimea that there was a great upheaval in the Horde, and its Mangit clan had left Sheikh Ahmad khan and moved up the Dnieper River. In November 1491, the joyful Mengli Giray was able to inform Ivan that the Horde had moved away from the Crimea and that it had been routed by the Nogays of Musa and Yamgurchi mirzas. He added: "I do not think they will ever be able to recover after this."[30]

Mengli Giray's joy was short-lived. Weakened but not destroyed, the Horde continued to remain his deadly rival and encouraged the opposition to Mengli Giray within the Crimea. Having being deposed several times, he understood the danger of the situation, as did his wife, Nur Sultan, who wrote to her son in Kazan, Muhammed Amin, and explained that she was preparing to send her other son, Abdullatif, into safety to Kazan or Moscow.[31]

At the time the entire steppe was crisscrossed by an intricate pattern of rival nomadic alliances waging wars against each other and ready to claim spoils from the split and weakened Horde, whose deposed khan, Sheikh Ahmad, had been replaced by Murtoza. The political stability in the Crimea did not last long, as the Shirin clan remained hostile toward Mengli Giray; the latter was kept in power by the direct support of the Ottoman sultan and his alliances with Moscow and the Nogays. But the Nogays were also divided and destitute. Musa and Yamgurchi mirzas were at war, and while Musa chose an alliance with the Crimea and Kazan, Yamgurchi sent to Tiumen to invite Abak khan to join him against Musa mirza and Kazan. Shortly thereafter, Abak arrived from Tiumen at the pastures near the Volga, allegedly to claim his father's ulus, that is, the Great Horde.[32]

Divisions among the nomadic peoples inevitably reflected the decentralized nature of the nomadic confederations, whose constituent parts were pulled into different orbits of influence by the neighboring sedentary societies. Naturally Musa mirza, whose pastures were closer to Kazan, was more interested in trade with Kazan, and therefore an alliance with Moscow and the Crimea. Yamgurchi, whose pastures in 1491 were along the Emba River, forged closer ties to Tiumen in Siberia. On the other hand, the Shirins, one of the powerful Crimean clans, whose pastures were around Perekop and less exposed to the raids from the Horde, were inclined to ally with the Horde to promote their interests within the Crimea.[33]

In this atmosphere, the Muscovite-Crimean alliance withstood yet another test when, in 1492, the Polish king sent generous presents to Mengli Giray and, in exchange for peace, offered to grant him Kiev, which traditionally had paid tribute to the Horde, and revenue from the population along the frontier. Mengli reported this to Ivan. Despite Mengli's assurances of loyalty, Ivan instructed his envoys to the Crimea to watch carefully whether Mengli would send his envoys to Poland, and if so, whether they were of a senior rank. Ivan's suspicions proved to be unjustified. "Believe my word fully," insisted Mengli, and to dispel any doubts he launched devastating raids into Lithuania, seizing and selling into captivity many prisoners.[34]

In another reassuring sign, Mengli Giray dispatched his stepson, Abdullatif, to Moscow in 1493 and asked Ivan "to keep an eye on him and give him good people." While Mengli's concerns were political, his wife, Nur Sultan, had simply expressed her maternal gratitude to Ivan. Before her departure on pilgrimage to Mecca, she wrote to thank him for taking good care of her two sons, Abdullatif, who was granted the town of Zvenigorod, and Muhammed Amin, the khan in Kazan.[35] In 1496, when Muhammed Amin was deposed, her sons' fortunes changed. Having sheltered the fugitive Muhammed Amin, Ivan wrote to the worried Nur Sultan and assured her that he was safe and had been granted Muscovite towns and villages (Kashira, Serpukhov, and Khotun); Abdullatif was now declared the khan of Kazan. Once again, the rejoicing mother thanked Ivan for protecting her sons and praised him as "the ruler of those lands."[36]

The alliance between the Crimea and Muscovy continued to be based on their mutual interests against their respective foes, the Horde and Poland. In 1498, Mengli wrote to Ivan inviting him to march against the Horde, which was reported to be starving, badly beaten by the Kabardinians (Circassians), and in a desperate flight for safety. Seyyid Ahmad came to seek protection in Astrakhan but was not allowed in and remained outside the city, "exhausted, starving, and without horses." Sheikh Ahmad fled farther south and found refuge in Shemakha. In 1500 he sent to the Ottoman pasha of Kaffa a request to move to the pastures near the Dnieper in order to escape constant harassment by the Nogays and Kabardinians. The pasha declined Sheikh Ahmad's request and admonished him to reconcile with Mengli Giray, explaining "that these lands and waters belong not to me but to the free man, Mengli-Giray." When one of the Horde's Chinggisid princes (*oglans*) defected to the Crimea with 3,000 of his people, he informed Mengli Giray that the Horde was in the Kabardinian borderlands, near Piatigorsk (Beshtau), and its people had no clothes, food, or horses.[37]

Realizing that the Horde was mortally wounded, Mengli Giray repeatedly requested help from Moscow to finish it off. Yet, while the Crimeans actively assisted Moscow in its war with Poland-Lithuania, there is no evidence that Ivan reciprocated by sending his troops against the Horde. In 1501, Ivan promised his Crimean ally to send Muhammed Amin against the Horde with a large army of princes, mirzas, and kazaks and Russian and Kazan troops, but only after Mengli Giray promised to deliver Kiev and Cherkassk to Ivan. In the summer of that year, the Crimea and Moscow launched devastating attacks against Poland-Lithuania. The attempts by the king of Poland-Lithuania, Alexander, to pacify the Crimeans with new promises of numerous gifts were of no avail, and Mengli Giray proceeded to raid and burn the

Lithuanian towns and seize 50,000 captives. When the news came that the Horde was near the Don and might raid the Crimea, Mengli Giray wrote to Ivan to send boats with troops "to instill fear in the Horde."[38]

The North Caucasus steppe proved to be no more hospitable than elsewhere, and the raids from the Kabardinians forced Sheikh Ahmad with 20,000 of his people to move westward and cross the Don: "That is why we left and did not farm there" (*pashni ne pakhali*), he explained later. Hounded and despondent, Sheikh Ahmad sent his envoy directly to the Ottoman sultan Bayazit to ask for permission to come to pastures west of the Dnieper near the town of Belgorod (the Ottoman Akkerman, today Belgorod-Dnestrovskii) in the Ottoman territory, but he was once again rebuffed. Attempting to trap Sheikh Ahmad, Mengli Giray placed his cavalry on the eastern bank of the Don in order to block the Horde's possible escape to Astrakhan. In the meantime, fearful that the Nogays could assist Sheikh Ahmad, Mengli Giray again asked Ivan to dispatch his cavalry via the steppe and his fleet with arquebusiers and gunners along the Don. When Russian contingents failed to arrive, Mengli turned back.[39]

By the summer of 1502, the Horde could no longer find a safe haven. Its people were reported to have fled, some to Moscow, others to Lithuania, but most to offer their service to Mengli Giray. When the news reached the Crimea that the impoverished Horde was grazing its herds on the Sula River near the Dnieper, Mengli Giray resolved to act without help from Moscow and marched with a large force armed with arquebuses and cannon. On July 3, 1502, he triumphantly reported to Ivan that he had seized the Horde and its uluses and was moving them to the Crimea. A mere congratulation from Ivan for "acquiring the khan's Horde which belonged to your father" was not enough, and Mengli Giray asked Ivan to send him "good presents," so that he could send the envoys with the good news to all his friends, including the Ottoman and Egyptian sultans.[40]

This time Mengli Giray's claim that the Horde had suffered a final blow was neither an exaggeration nor wishful thinking. Sheikh Ahmad was able to escape, however, and continued to elude Mengli Giray for some time. He was sighted in the Kazan region near the lower Kama River with 4,000 horsemen and a few uluses. In search of new allies, Sheikh Ahmad dispatched his envoy to Ivan and promised to break with Lithuania if Ivan helped him become a khan in Astrakhan. Ivan promised, but under the same condition as was previously suggested by the Ottomans: not until Sheikh Ahmad reconciled with Mengli Giray.[41]

Instead of seeking peace with his archfoe in the Crimea, Sheikh Ahmad left for Astrakhan, entered an alliance with his uncle, the Astrakhan khan Abdulkerim (Abdyl Kerim), and invited the Nogays to join him against Mengli Giray. Ivan hastened to write to Mengli, allaying his fears about an imminent attack and assuring him that the Nogays were at peace with Moscow. The envoys from the Nogay mirza Yamgurchi soon arrived in the Crimea to inform Mengli Giray that they considered him their ally and "true sovereign" and promised to expel Sheikh Ahmad from their pastures.[42]

Forced to leave once again in 1504, Sheikh Ahmad's travails took him to various destinations. He was sighted near Astrakhan trying to dislodge his uncle Abdulkerim, in Kiev seeking help from the Lithuanian Grand Prince and king of Poland, Alexander, and in Belgorod appealing again to the Ottoman sultan. When Sheikh Ahmad finally returned to Kiev, his political capital was entirely spent. Like his brother Seyyid Ahmad, who ended his life in Lithuanian captivity, Sheikh Ahmad found himself a prisoner in Vilna, only to be used as a bargaining chip in Alexander's negotiations with Mengli Giray. Upon learning that Alexander had sued for peace with the Crimea, Ivan quickly and forcefully intervened and convinced Mengli to continue raiding Lithuanian territory. Once again Mengli Giray preferred his alliance with Moscow. In an enthusiastic letter to Ivan, Mengli envisioned that the new towns built along the lower Dnieper with the help of "his brother" in Moscow would become a base for the Crimea's further expansion, and that both Moscow and the Crimea would soon rule the Lithuanian lands.[43]

By 1506, while the Crimea, Moscow, the Nogays, and Lithuania remained the major players in the region, the cast of protagonists had largely changed. Moscow was now ruled by Ivan's son, Vasilii III. Sigismund I came to the throne in Poland-Lithuania, and the Nogay mirzas Musa and Yamgurchi were replaced by their sons, Alchagir and Alach, respectively. Unable to recover after the assassination of Ahmad khan in 1481 and the decisive rout and capture of its people by the Crimeans in 1502, the Great Horde finally dissipated. Only Mengli Giray lived to see his friends and foes pass away. With the Horde vanquished and Kazan ruled by his son Muhammed Amin, under the watchful eye of Moscow, Mengli turned his attention to another prized part of the former Golden Horde, Astrakhan. In 1508 Mengli wrote to Vasilii and secured his promise to dispatch troops down the Volga against Astrakhan.[44]

Mengli Giray's plan for a campaign against Astrakhan was forestalled by the Nogays, who had relocated from their traditional pastures between the Yaik and Emba rivers to the Volga steppe vacated by the Great Horde. The appearance of the Nogays in the immediate proximity of Muscovy and the Crimea compelled Vasilii to secure peace with them. Instead of raiding Muscovy, in the spring of 1509 a large force of Nogays joined the Astrakhan khan Abdulkerim and marched against the Crimea. Several months later, Mengli reported to Vasilii that he had sent a large army against these Nogays, routed them, and captured their uluses and numerous herds. The Russian spy in the Crimea, the mullah Baba Sheikh, confirmed the news of Mengli's victory and added that it was so decisive that it took more than twenty days to bring all the captured booty through Perekop into the Crimea.[45]

Until now the Muscovite-Crimean alliance had been maintained by generous payments from Moscow and military campaigns against their archfoes, Poland and the Great Horde, respectively. But by 1509 the Great Horde no longer existed, and Vasilii reached a peace agreement with Poland without any consultations with Mengli Giray. With diminished payments from Moscow and numerous Crimean appeals to send troops against Astrakhan all but ignored, Mengli Giray could no longer continue to overlook his growing discord with Moscow.[46]

One thorny issue was the fate of Mengli Giray's stepson, Abdullatif. For fifteen years, letters from the Crimea alternately beseeched and threatened the grand princes to let Abdullatif return to the Crimea—all to no effect. When, a few years earlier, Ivan had warned Mengli that the Lithuanians never released their prisoners, he might have mentioned that Moscow abided by the same principle. In the following eight years, the story of Abdullatif, who was detained in Muscovy until his mysterious death in 1517, was symptomatic of Moscow's growing confidence.

It began in 1502, when Ivan informed Mengli Giray that Abdullatif had not lived up to his expectations after being granted his father's *yurt* (an appanage, territory, land), Kazan. The Muscovite prince explained that the entire Kazan region had suffered under Abdullatif because he breached his oath when he took the throne of Kazan and committed violence against both the Russians and Muslims. Ivan was thus compelled to remove Abdullatif and give the throne of Kazan back to Muhammed Amin.[47]

Ivan III's stubborn rejection of appeals from Mengli Giray and pleas from Nur Sultan to allow Abdullatif's return to the Crimea was not necessarily a sign of partiality toward the Crimean prince. He was equally uncompromising toward his grandson Dmitrii for the latter's impertinence or toward those residents of Riazan who against his orders left to join the Cossacks on the Don; their families were executed or sold into slavery. Ivan's recalcitrant attitude and the severity of his punishment intended to send a clear message that disloyalty to the grand prince could not be tolerated "because only those who serve and obey us are bestowed with favors."[48]

In 1509, showing greater mercy than his father, the Grand Prince Vasilii brought Abdullatif back from exile. The Crimean request to grant him the town of Kashira was politely declined. Instead, after having Abdullatif take an oath in the presence of the Crimean envoys, Vasilii declared: "We grant you a place in our own lands."[49] The place was the town of Iur'ev (Pol'skii), "with all its villages, tribute, and customs duties." The significance of granting Abdullatif Iur'ev instead of Kashira was inescapable. Even though his father, Ivan III, had previously granted Kashira to Muhammed Amin, Vasilii implicitly asserted his right to grant Kashira to whomever he wished and not to turn it into the appanage of the Chinggisid princes. Of course, the desire to keep Abdullatif farther away from the Crimea and Lithuania must have been another consideration in tucking him into a safe and distant corner northeast of Moscow.[50]

Vasilii's concerns with Abdullatif's loyalty were quite apparent from the shert' that obliged Abdullatif not to have contact with Poland-Lithuania and to live in peace with other Tatar princes in the service of the grand prince: Yanay in Kasimov and Sheikh Avliyar in Surozhik (a town north of Zvenigorod). Nor was he supposed to leave "the lands of the grand prince" without Vasilii's permission, to send his troops against Kazan, or to attack the Moscow Cossacks who left for the steppe. Abdullatif was expected "to show goodwill to all the Christians," not to commit violence against Christians and their churches, and to help those Russians who escaped captivity to return to Moscow. Vasilii and Abdullatif agreed not to accept fugitives from each other, with the exception of the four Karachi tribes of the Crimea. Both sides swore to stand by this agreement, which the Crimean envoys confirmed on behalf of Abdullatif.[51]

This shert', like many others thereafter, reflected the perfect ambiguity of Crimean-Muscovite relations. While Moscow referred to the shert' as an oath sworn by Abdullatif to the grand prince, it was, in fact, executed as a written agreement between two sides with mutual pledges by Vasilii and Abdullatif, who was represented by the Crimean envoys. At the same time as the shert' left no doubt that Abdullatif was subordinate to the grand prince, was to reside in Christian lands, and was to have relations with no one outside of Moscow, Vasilii also referred to Abdullatif as a brother and granted him full autonomy within the Iur'ev province.

Such incongruities were a result of the complex intertwining of the new and the old in the steppe body politic. De facto, Moscow grew apart from its steppe neighbors, but de jure it remained within the Golden Horde's political system. Accordingly the Crimeans continued to consider Moscow to be a subservient tributary state. Moscow's struggle to eliminate the growing disparity between the old political forms and the new reality would continue in the following two centuries.

THE END OF THE CRIMEAN-MUSCOVITE ALLIANCE

By the early sixteenth century, it had become obvious that the rapidly changing status of Moscow from a backwater principality to a major economic and military power in the region required its affirmation through political and diplomatic means. Vasilii no longer wished to spend large sums of money on payments and presents to satisfy endless demands from the Crimea. Yet every attempt to curtail the delivery of the gifts or to bestow them only on those who showed sufficient loyalty resulted in abuse toward Moscow's envoys and raids across the Muscovite frontier.

In 1509 Mengli Giray submitted to Vasilii a list of increasingly typical complaints: the armor sent to him was of poor workmanship; his merchants had to pay customs duties (*tamga*) in Moscow; the Russian envoy had no inventory of the presents and was beaten because many Crimean nobles received none.[52] At a time when Moscow was reducing its payments to the Crimea, the Polish king Sigismund once again approached Mengli Giray and offered him an annuity of 15,000 ducats. This time, unable to resist such a handsome payment and frustrated in his futile attempts to secure Moscow's help against Astrakhan and freedom for Abdullatif, Mengli Giray accepted the offer and directed Crimean raiding activity against Muscovy.

In response to the hostilities from the Crimea, Vasilii decided to strengthen his relationship with the Ottoman sultan, whom the grand prince considered his "new" equal. A not too subtle indication of Vasilii's self-image was evident from his instructions to the envoys en route to the Porte in 1514. They were supposed to insist that the sultan refer in writing to the grand prince as a brother "because the grand prince was the brother of the Roman emperor, Maximilian, of the 'Roman king,' and of other rulers." Several versions of the treaty with the Ottoman Empire were prepared in advance; one of them provided for a Moscow-Istanbul alliance against Mengli Giray and Poland, but it failed to impress the sultan.[53]

With the death of Mengli Giray in 1515, his son and successor, Muhammed Giray, undertook a new initiative toward Moscow. In his first missive to Vasilii, Muhammed Giray expressed readiness to resume the alliance with Moscow, but only if Vasilii was prepared to meet several Crimean demands. The new Crimean khan laid the blame on Vasilii for deceiving his father, Mengli Giray. After all, it was Vasilii who three years before had attacked Smolensk without notifying Mengli, and it was Mengli who, upon signing a truce with Poland, had granted Smolensk to the Polish king. Muhammed reminded the grand prince that it was also his father, Mengli Giray, who had granted the towns of Briansk, Starodub, Pochap, Novyi Gorodok, Ryl'sk, Putivl, Karachev, and Radogoshch to Vasilii's father, Ivan III. Furthermore, he instructed Vasilii to look in the old *defters* (registers) to see that Ivan III had received from the Crimea thirty-five towns, all of which had formerly belonged to the Crimean khans. Ivan delivered tribute from them regularly, "and now not to cause you any hardship, he [the khan] wanted back only eight of the above mentioned towns" and the traditional yasak from the towns of Odoev and Riazan.[54]

The nature of the regional conflicts and politics was baldly set forth. Three powers—Poland-Lithuania, Muscovy, and the Crimea—were competing for control of the same lands: the first two with the intention to conquer, occupy, and annex, the last merely claiming the right to collect tribute. Muhammed Giray intended to continue the traditions of the Golden Horde and to reclaim the title of Great Khan and with it the Horde's former tributary possessions along the southern frontiers of Muscovy and Lithuania. It was not accidental that in the letter to Vasilii, Muhammed Giray referred to himself as "the Great Khan of the Great Horde."[55]

From the Crimean point of view, the cessation of raids against Poland-Lithuania was secured by lavish annuities and presents from the Polish king. If Moscow wanted stability along its frontier, it had to do the same. No one expressed this sentiment more clearly than Moscow's loyalist in the Crimea, Appak mirza: "How can one *not* be in friendship with the Polish king? His treasury, like the river, is flowing in both the winter and summer, and he pleases everyone, the nobles and commoners." He warned the Russian envoy that the king had promised to double his annuity if the Crimeans helped him to capture Moscow, and that the only way for Russia to counter the king's influence was to send more money and presents than he did.[56]

But the Kremlin saw things differently. From its vantage point, Moscow had paid the Crimeans for their alliance in the war against Poland. Once the Crimean raids against Poland stopped, so did the delivery of large sums of money and luxury items. What was even more important, Moscow no longer accepted the Crimean challenge to the grand prince's claim of sovereignty over the Russian towns and lands. The days of the Golden Horde were over.

In response to Muhammed Giray's initiative, Vasilii dispatched his own embassy to the Crimea. While flattering Muhammed Giray and referring to him as the Great Khan of the Great Horde, Vasilii found little room for compromise on any of the substantive issues. The embassy delivered payments and presents but made it clear that the annuities could not be guaranteed in the future and that they depended on Muhammed Giray's ability to maintain peace with Moscow. The Muscovite envoy was also instructed to pay no fees and customs (*daragi i poshliny*) to the individual Crimean officials or nobles, and if forced to do so, he was to remind Muhammed Giray that their agreements stipulated that envoys should pay none of the above.

The embassy was to allay Muhammed Giray's concerns and explain that Vasilii's relations with the Nogays and Astrakhan were based solely on trade and not directed against the Crimea. As for the towns and tribute from them, Muhammed Giray was ill-advised; the towns were Vasilii's patrimony and had been given to his father by God's will. Extending Moscow's territorial claims beyond the disputed towns in the west, Vasilii complained about the Crimean raids into the Meshchera region, unambiguously referring to the region as "our borderlands, the Mordovian lands." The embassy was also charged with a very sensitive mission. In strict secrecy, the envoy had to deliver a message to Muhammed Giray's brother, Ahmed. He was to reassure Ahmed Giray that if he chose to come to Moscow as he had requested, he would be welcome and free to leave at any time. However, if Ahmed Giray insisted on a specific town to be granted to him upon his arrival, the envoy was to give no specific promises.

While Ahmed Giray was secretly exploring the possibility of leaving for Moscow, the issue of Abdullatif's return from Moscow continued to plague the relationship between the Crimea and Moscow. In 1512, accused of assisting a Crimean war party, Abdullatif was once again arrested and exiled. The pleas for his release and return were routinely turned down, and even his mother Nur Sultan's visit to Moscow and Kazan in the previous year and the intercession of the Ottoman sultan failed to win Abdullatif's freedom. In 1515 Muhammed Giray appealed for a gesture of goodwill—to have Abdullatif released so that he could accompany his mother on her pilgrimage to Mecca. But neither the appeal to religious sensibility nor the promise of sending Abdullatif far away from Moscow was enough to convince Vasilii. In a compromise, Vasilii brought Abdullatif back from yet another exile and did what he had refused to do six years before—he granted him the town of Kashira.[57]

To a certain extent, the Russian strategy of dealing with the Ottoman sultan over the head of the Crimean khan paid off. Muhammed Giray was aware that the Ottoman Porte was interested in continuing its lucrative trade with Moscow via the Ottoman towns of Kaffa and Azak (Azov). Waging a full-scale war against Moscow would have brought such trade to a halt. Unwilling to jeopardize his relationship with Istanbul and not ready to give up hope for winning concessions from Moscow, Muhammed Giray chose to wait.[58]

Muhammed Giray's patience wore thin, however, when another Muscovite envoy, Ivan Mamonov, arrived in the Crimea in 1516 with no tangible signs of change in Moscow's attitude. The familiar diplomatic explanations no longer sufficed. He demanded that the envoy submit a payment (*kazna*) and three different types of presents. Muhammed Giray's demands that the presents be offered to his son, Alp, were met with stubborn resistance from the envoy, who insisted that Alp and others were not mentioned in his list. Obviously Moscow refused to reward those who raided its frontier. Moscow's loyalist Appak mirza interceded again to plead with Mamonov to offer generous gifts similar to those of the Polish king. Revealing unmistakably the Crimean interpretation of the political hierarchy within the former Golden Horde territory and Muscovy's place in it, he warned the envoy that the Crimean nobles would not approve of Moscow's behavior and would think that "the grand prince calls Muhammed Giray a khan [*tsar*], but he does not obey him and acts independently" (*tsaria kniaz' velikii ne poslushav sam, a tsarem nariazhaet*).[59] When the Muscovite envoy refused to budge, the Crimeans arrested, chained, and beat the Russian interpreter and the clerk, and Muhammed Giray informed Mamonov that Alp had left to raid the Muscovite frontier because "I had nothing to give to my son."[60]

Professing either poverty or loyalty amounted to the same expectation—more gifts from Moscow. Muhammed Giray's other son, Bogatur, illustrated the meager quantity of presents from Moscow in a graphic metaphor: "Even if I start chewing what the grand prince sent me and spit it on my people, even then there would be nothing left for my people." When this failed to convince the envoy, he explained that when one of his brothers had wanted to launch raids against Moscow, Bogatur had paid him 40,000 altyns (1,200 rubles; one altyn equals three kopecks) to stop him from doing it, and now he wanted to be compensated for serving Moscow's interests. When this argument failed as well, Bogatur seized presents by force.[61]

Continuing to hope that Moscow could still be convinced to join him against Astrakhan, Muhammed Giray announced to Ivan Mamonov that he was prepared to have peace with Moscow and would have a chance to convince all the Crimean nobles to do the same when they assembled to commemorate the first anniversary of Mengli Giray's death. But Vasilii had to meet two conditions: to return Abdullatif and to send a fleet with fully supplied arquebusiers against Astrakhan. To reassure Vasilii that his victory over Astrakhan was at hand, Muhammed Giray noted that all the major Nogay mirzas came to offer their service to him. Once Astrakhan fell, Muhammed Giray would send his troops against Poland. Chastising Vasilii for demanding that the Crimean troops be dispatched against Poland first, Muhammed Giray asked rhetorically: "Who is greater, the grand prince or the khan?"[62]

Without directly challenging Muhammed Giray's claim to his superior status, Vasilii responded self-assuredly, requesting an exchange of prisoners and ignoring the issues raised by the Crimean khan. In part, Vasilii's assertiveness was based on intelligence reports from the Crimea. Moscow's confidants there reported that Muhammed Giray's authority was weak, that the Crimean nobility was split between the pro-Muscovite and pro-Polish factions, that the Nogays were a burden to the khan and were disparaged by all the Crimeans, and that famine was forcing many Crimeans to abandon the Crimean peninsula and leave for the steppe with their herds. Finally, Muhammed Giray's brother, Ahmed Giray, informed Vasilii that the khan had feared a possible attack from Astakhan; assuring the grand prince of his loyalty, he explained that the khan could not launch any large campaign against Moscow without his, Ahmed's, help. In return, Vasilli wrote to his loyalists in the Crimea, encouraging them to continue to work on his behalf.[63]

Moscow's goals and policies were clear: to permit no challenges either to its sovereignty or to the legitimacy of its expansion. The grand prince had no intention of helping the Crimea to consolidate its grip over the former territories of the Golden Horde. Nor did he intend to continue the old practice of supplying tribute in its various forms. To keep the Crimean ambitions in check, Moscow relied on Astrakhan and the Nogays as the natural counterbalance to the Crimea. But the Nogays were engaged in bitter internal wars, and Astrakhan remained the only major impediment to the Crimea's ability to launch a larger campaign against Moscow.

Similar considerations accounted for Moscow's decision to install the traditional rivals of the Giray dynasty, the descendants of the late Ahmad khan of the Great Horde, in Kasimov and Kazan. In his letter to Moscow, the Crimean khan reproached Vasilii for not heeding a warning from the Shirin nobles, the most powerful clan in the Crimea, to remove their enemy Sheikh Avliyar, the nephew of Ahmad khan, from Kasimov. Muhammed Giray explained that his son Bogatur had raided the Kasimov region (*Meshcherskii yurt*) in 1517 to make it clear to Moscow that Kasimov had always been under Crimean control. He warned that such raids would take place again unless Vasilii placed Kasimov in the hands of Muhammed Giray's son.[64]

In this and other letters, Muhammed Giray portrayed himself as a friend of Moscow who had found himself under increasing pressure from his nobles. Indeed, the Crimean nobles chastised Muhammed Giray for considering Vasilii a friend, while the grand prince granted Kasimov to the Crimea's foe and refused to replace the dying Muhammed Amin with Abdullatif on the throne of Kazan. The latter issue was becoming a matter of some urgency. The Kazan nobles warned that, because Muhammed Amin had no offspring, they might send deputies to the Astrakhan khan with a request to dispatch his son to rule Kazan. Not only Kasimov, but Kazan, too, could end up in the hands of the Crimea's rivals.[65]

Neither warnings nor requests seemed to have an effect on Moscow's determination to advance its own interests by playing off the rivalry between the various descendants of Chinggis khan. Under conditions of strict secrecy, Vasilii's envoy to the Crimea was to offer the Kasimov throne to Moscow's loyalist, Ahmed Giray. Furthermore, to underscore Moscow's resolve to assert its independence and signal a change in its relationship with the Crimea, Vasilii sent an envoy to the Ottoman sultan in 1517 with the specific instruction to travel to Istanbul via Kaffa, not the Crimea. If the khan invited him to go through the Crimea, the envoy was to reply that he had been sent to the sultan, not the khan. At the same time, Vasilii reduced the status of his embassy to the Crimea by sending an envoy of middle rank with instructions to procrastinate and find various excuses when the Crimeans raised the issues of the campaign against Astrakhan, deposing Sheikh Avliyar, Abdullatif's freedom, or insufficient presents. In another unmistakable indication of dramatic changes in Moscow's attitude toward its former overlords, the envoy was instructed to refuse Crimean demands for ransom for Russian captives, but to offer instead an exchange of captives on both sides.[66]

Enmity or friendship with Moscow was defined largely by the deliveries of presents and payments. The Crimean aristocracy continued to be split between those who represented Moscow's interests and were well rewarded and those on the payroll of the Polish king. The most prominent representatives of the pro-Muscovite faction, Appak mirza and Ahmed Giray, tirelessly reminded Vasilii that he needed to send larger payments if he wished to keep the Crimeans at bay or enlist them into his service. Implying that payments spoke louder than words, Appak mirza wrote to Vasilii: "The red gold and the white silver are pouring from the king, and how can we make it wet with a dry tongue?" Only recently, he added, the king's envoys had brought twelve carts loaded with woolens, cottons, and fur coats.[67]

The generous payments from Poland proved to be effective in buying off the Crimeans for a short while, but in the long run Poland-Lithuania was unable to replace Moscow's strategic importance in the region; the former was simply too far away to be an active player in the rapidly changing steppe politics. Moscow, on the other hand, controlled the khan's seats in Kasimov and Kazan, exercised increasing influence over the Nogays, and could either make or break the power of the Astrakhan khan, the Crimea's ultimate foe. After a series of Muscovite military victories over Poland in 1517, Muhammed Giray again approached the grand prince. Even the news of Abdullatif's death under murky circumstances (Vasilii claimed that Abdullatif had died of an unspecified disease just before departing for Kazan) did not prevent Muhammed from seeking a rapprochement. In 1518 Muhammed Giray informed Vasilii that he had returned the king's annuity of 15,000 gold ducats, sent a large army into the Lithuanian borderlands, and was ready to renew their alliance against Poland and Astrakhan.[68]

In 1518 Vasilii sent his embassy to the Crimea with a prepared text of the agreement in both the Tatar and Russian languages. Resurrecting the old treaty between Ivan III and Mengli Giray, the agreement stipulated a Muscovite-Crimean alliance against the offspring of the Great Horde's dynasty ("Ahmad's children") and Poland-Lithuania. The Crimean side was obliged not to raid the frontier towns of Muscovy and those in the service of the grand prince. The disputed towns, which the Crimeans had previously claimed, were to be recognized as belonging to Vasilii. The Muscovite envoys in the Crimea were to pay no customs and to be protected from abuses. In return, the Muscovite envoy was instructed to promise Moscow's assistance against Astrakhan and Kiev, to bring presents in no smaller quantities than those from the king, and to allow Muhammed Giray's brother, Sahip Giray, to become the khan of Kazan. Yet if the Crimeans insisted that the Russian envoys swear an oath and sign a document listing such obligations, the envoys were to decline it.[69] It appeared that Vasilii had no intention of following up on his promises.

Moscow's concessions and promises were deemed inadequate in the Crimea, and in 1519 the scales of Crimean politics resolutely tipped in favor of the pro-Polish faction. Ahmed Giray, the most powerful of Moscow's allies in the Crimea, was reported to have been killed by the khan, and his sons fled to seek protection in Kaffa. Instead, Bogatur Giray, who consistently remained on the Polish king's payroll, was appointed kalgay. In his letter to

Vasilii, Bogatur Giray raised the old issues, demanding that the grand prince provide help against Astrakhan, recognize Crimean authority over the disputed frontier towns, which had belonged to the Crimea from the times of Tokhtamysh, and send the payments traditionally due to the kalgay.[70]

The khan also sent a missive to Vasilii, which was delivered personally by Appak mirza. The pleading tone of the previous letters had changed to dire warnings: if Vasilii did not send his troops against Astrakhan in the spring, their agreement would be null and void. Moreover, Muhammed Giray demanded 30,000 rubles to help him pay his debts and the restoration of the tribute from Riazan and three other frontier towns (*Odoevskii yasak*).[71]

Vasilii kissed the cross, swore to uphold the peace agreement, and promised to send troops against Astrakhan. At the same time, he sent Shah Ali, the son of Sheikh Avliyar, to assume the throne in Kazan. Acting against the advice of his loyalist Appak mirza, Vasilii again snubbed Muhammed Giray by ignoring the khan's wishes and his own promise to place Sahip Giray on the throne in Kazan. Now both Kasimov and Kazan were in the hands of the Crimean khans' traditional rivals and under Moscow's control. Even Appak mirza refused to represent Vasilii's interests in the Crimea any longer and offered his service to the Polish king. Compromise with Moscow was no longer possible.[72]

Muhammed Giray had to wait two more years before launching a large punitive campaign against Moscow. Astrakhan remained the main obstacle to his dominance in the steppe. In 1521, in a radical departure from his usual policies, he sent an envoy to Astrakhan to offer a truce to his rival, Janibek khan. Muhammed explained that his friendship with Moscow was over because Vasilii had betrayed him by installing Shah Ali in Kazan against the will of its population. Now, in response to the petition from the people of Kazan, he had sent his brother, Sahip Giray, to become a khan there. Muhammed Giray was prepared to march against Muscovy and invited Janibek khan to join him. But the old rivalry proved hard to overcome, and the Astrakhan khan refused the offer of truce.[73]

In the meantime Vasilii continued to pursue his strategy of establishing direct connections to the Ottoman Porte, thus excluding the Crimean khan. Indeed, the Ottoman sultan, Selim, was prepared to recognize Moscow's rising status, as he addressed Vasilii as the grand prince and tsar. Peace and trade were issues of serious concern to Istanbul, where furs, sables, black foxes, walrus tasks, and falcons were in great demand. Vasilii offered to secure the trade route along the Don via Azov and Kaffa, thus bypassing the Crimea, "because the Crimean khan is against our friendship."[74]

Both the Crimean khan and the grand prince were vying for the ear of the Ottoman sultan. After all, no matter how interested the sultan was in trade opportunities, he was also a protector of all Muslims, and Vasilii had to answer serious charges leveled against him by Muhammed Giray. In a letter to the newly enthroned sultan, Süleyman I, Vasilii disputed the legitimacy of the Crimean claims to Kazan. He argued that Kazan had never been a part of the Crimean yurt and that the khans of Kazan had always been independent (*oprishnye*). He built up his case by showing that none of the previous Kazan khans had belonged to the Giray dynasty and that his father, Ivan III, was de facto ruler there. Vasilii maintained that he had merely acted on the wishes of the Kazan people when he sent Shah Ali to be their khan. As for Muhammed Giray's other claim, that Vasilii destroyed mosques and built churches in their stead, they were lies and nonsense.[75] It is likely that trading interests proved to be more convincing than Vasilii's arguments as the Porte continued its good relations with Moscow at the expense of the Crimea.[76]

The Crimean khan seemed to have been entirely outmaneuvered by Moscow when unexpected and unsought help arrived in 1521. As in the past, the movements of the nomadic peoples in Inner Asia unleashed a chain reaction with a direct impact on regional steppe geopolitics. This time the Nogays, unable to resist the predations of the Kazakhs, abandoned their pastures east of the Yaik River and moved west, crossing the Volga into the pastures of the Astrakhan khan. The Muscovite envoys reported that the Nogay mirza Sheidiak (Shiidiak, Seyyid-Ahmad) had thoroughly routed the Astrakhan troops and captured the entire Astrakhan ulus. Only the city of Astrakhan survived the debacle, but, the envoys predicted, the Astrakhan khans would never be able to recover after this event.[77]

The Crimea's lot suddenly and dramatically improved. The danger from Astrakhan was diminished, and Kazan was recaptured when, in a successful coup against Moscow's excessive interference, the local aristocracy put Sahip Giray on the throne in Kazan. The Crimean alliance with the Polish king endured. The time was ripe for Muhammed Giray to wage war against Moscow. In the summer of 1521, a large army of about 50,000 to 60,000 horsemen set out from the Crimea under the khan's personal command. The khan's far-reaching plans became apparent when he took with him guides with knowledge of the Oka River crossings.[78]

Moscow was caught unprepared to confront such a large and rapidly moving army. Muhammed Giray crushed the Muscovite troops sent to block his advance and swiftly reached the walls of Moscow. The new khan of Kazan, Sahip Giray, ravaged the provinces of Nizhnii Novgorod and Vladimir and approached Moscow from the southeast to join his brother there. Compelled to follow the example of his many predecessors, the grand prince fled northwest of Moscow to gather troops and left his brother-in-law, Peter, a converted Chinggisid from Kazan, in charge of the city.[79]

The Crimean and Kazan armies limited their plunder to small towns and villages, and when the Moscow boyars sent generous gifts with an offer to resume paying tribute, Muhammed Giray lifted the siege. The Crimeans' failure to capture Moscow was due to both the improved city fortifications and the Crimeans' inability to sustain a long siege with the looming danger of attacks on their defenseless uluses back in the Crimea. Indeed, Muhammed Giray departed for home shortly after receiving the news that Astrakhan had launched raids against the Crimea. Nonetheless, the 1521 campaign by the combined Crimean and Kazan forces inflicted incalculable damage and left a deep imprint on the minds of the Muscovites. Rumor, even though greatly exaggerated, put the number of Muscovite captives at 800,000.[80] The dark days of the Golden Horde were not quite over.

Once again, Astrakhan proved to be a nuisance and a stumbling block to Crimean dominance in the region. In 1523 Muhammed Giray resolved to annihilate Astrakhan's challenge and successfully attacked and captured the city. The long-sought goal was finally achieved but quickly turned into a Pyrrhic victory. Muhammed Giray and his son, kalgay Bogatur Giray, were treacherously murdered by the Nogays of Mamay beg and Shigim and Temesh mirzas, and the Crimean army near Astrakhan was utterly destroyed. Those who escaped were pursued, and many were reported to have drowned crossing the Don.[81]

Within a short period, the Nogays proved to be an instrumental force in bringing about the collapse of the Great Horde and substantially undermining the Crimean and Astrakhan khanates. They became a critical, if often unpredictable, factor in the geopolitics of the steppe. By the 1530s their presence on both sides of the Volga was indisputable, and their relations with Moscow had acquired an ever-growing significance.

THE NOGAYS AND KAZAN, 1530s–1550s: KAZAN ANNEXED

The assassination of Muhammed Giray and the ensuing turmoil in the Crimea allowed Vasilii to turn his attention to Kazan. Two military campaigns in 1523–24 failed to subdue Kazan, and Moscow had to contend with establishing another advanced military outpost on the way to Kazan, Fort Vasil'sursk. The name of the new outpost (as it bore Vasilii's name) was suggestive of the grand prince's ambitious and earnest plans. In the meantime, the khan of Kazan, Sahip Giray, brought from the Crimea his thirteen-year-old nephew, Safa Giray, and put him on the throne of Kazan. Events in the Crimea, which had been weakened and torn by the civil war, convinced Sahip Giray that the Crimean throne could be his, were he to succeed in ingratiating himself with the Ottoman sultan Süleyman. In 1524 Sahip Giray left for Istanbul, where he waited patiently until 1532, when he indeed assumed the throne in the Crimea and became one of its most powerful and best-known rulers.[82]

Moscow was determined to regain its control of Kazan by any means necessary. Vasilii resorted to economic pressure by forbidding Moscow merchants to trade at the Kazan fair and establishing one in Nizhnii Novgorod.

In 1530 the Muscovite troops again marched on Kazan, reaching the city walls and bombarding the town. Moscow's diplomatic efforts to bring to power a pro-Moscow group among the Kazan leaders never ceased. In the following year, a combination of military, economic, and diplomatic pressure bore the desired fruit. The Kazan khan, Safa Giray, was overthrown in a coup and fled to his father-in-law, the Nogay beg, Mamay.

Despite the opposition to Safa Giray, there was no immediate agreement on who could replace him. One possible candidate, Shah Ali, the former pro-Moscow khan of Kazan, was discredited. A compromise was reached when Shah Ali's brother, Jan Ali (Ianalei), who resided in Kasimov, was installed on the throne. For the next three years Jan Ali represented the pro-Russian party in Kazan, until his assassination in 1534 in yet another coup brought Safa Giray back to Kazan.[83]

In a continuous reshuffling of rulers in Kazan, the Crimea, and Astrakhan, the Nogays continued to play a crucial role. Ruled by the numerous sons of the late Musa beg, Shigim, Sheidiak, Mamay (Sheikh-Mamay), Kuchum (Koshum), Yusuf, and Ismail, the Nogays also were split into pro-Russian and pro-Crimean factions. In September 1532, the envoys and horse traders of Kuchum mirza arrived in Moscow to sell their horses. A year later Yusuf put his support behind the pro-Russian party in Kazan by marrying his daughter, Süünbike, to the khan of Kazan, Jan Ali. In 1534, realizing the increased strategic importance of the Nogay partnership with Moscow, Sheidiak beg, together with other mirzas, sent a large embassy to Moscow to look for appropriate rewards.[84]

Moscow's response consisted of the kind of vague promises and procrastination that had served it so well in the past. But this time Moscow's tactics backfired, and the infuriated Sheidiak charged that the Kasimov kazaks had looted several trade caravans sent by the Nogays to Kazan, that during one such robbery alone sixty merchants and 200,000 altyns' worth of merchandise had been seized, and that Moscow had failed to return captured people and goods. In addition, Moscow had failed to please the principal Nogay chiefs, Sheidiak, Mamay, and Yusuf, who had asked for additional presents to supplement their regular delivery.

Sheidiak was prepared to take advantage of the fact that, after Vasilii's death in 1533, the Muscovite throne had become occupied by a minor, Ivan IV. So that no mistake was made about Sheidiak's superior status vis-à-vis the new grand prince of Moscow, he forbade Ivan to refer to himself as Sheidiak's father and brother. Instead, Sheidiak referred to Ivan as his son. And lest Moscow misunderstand his political ambition, Sheidiak demanded treatment equal to the status given the late Crimean khan, Muhammed Giray, with a corresponding tribute of 60,000 altyns and a tribute for his brother, Mamay, equal to that of the Crimean kalgay. Sheidiak backed his claims with an unambiguous warning: "If you engage in arguing and delays, we shall be at the gates of Moscow."[85]

101

Moscow could afford to disregard the Nogays' bombastic rhetoric as long as intelligence sources reported that the Nogays themselves were under siege from the advancing Kazakhs in the east and the Crimeans in the southwest. But in 1535 the situation began to change. Sheidiak beg wrote to Ivan IV boasting that he had routed the Kazakhs and seized the Kazakh yurt of the Ahmed khan (Hoja Mehmed) and his fifteen sons, and now had as many as 300,000 horsemen under his command. In undisguised contempt, Sheidiak referred to Ivan as one of the infidel faith.[86]

Threats and obscenities did not move Moscow, but pragmatic considerations did. The consolidation of power in the Crimea by Sahip Giray and Safa Giray's pro-Crimean coup in Kazan created a powerful and dangerous anti-Muscovite axis. When in 1535 intelligence reports informed Moscow of impending Crimean raids, the government urgently dispatched envoys to Ismail mirza, whose Nogays occupied pastures along the Volga. In return for presents to numerous mirzas and a gunner, an arquebusier, and a full suit of armor, which Ismail requested for himself, Ismail promised to prevent the Crimeans or his Nogays from launching raids against Moscow. Defense against Kazan and Poland was to be Moscow's responsibility.[87]

In the meantime the Nogays found themselves in increasingly desperate circumstances. Pressure from the Kazakhs, which did not stop after Sheidiak's short-lived victory, and the continuing enmity with the Crimea left the Nogays warring among themselves over limited pastures. Harassed by the Kazakhs, Mamay was compelled to abandon his pastures along the Yaik and to join Yusuf near Kazan. The renewed migration of the Kazakhs and Nogays disrupted the trade route between Kazan and Bukhara and severely undercut Sheidiak's source of income. Despondent and impoverished, many of his mirzas left for Astrakhan.[88]

In 1536 Sheidiak sent his envoys to threaten Astrakhan with a raid unless the fugitive mirzas were returned. At the same time, he dispatched an embassy consisting of 60 people and 500 horses to Moscow with specific demands: return the loot and provide woolens, armor, a golden saddle and bridle, a fur hat, 300,000 nails, dyes, and oil for dyes as a sign of friendship. Sheidiak explained that his people raided the Muscovite frontier because Moscow's Cossacks captured 10,000 horses from him every year. Moscow was unyielding; its answer was only a stern rebuke for raising the issue.[89]

Stubbornly Sheidiak again sent his envoys to Moscow to inform Ivan IV that the Nogays were united and he had become their khan (*tsar*), Mamay the kalgay, and Kuchum the beg. Far more than sheer vanity, the choice of terms was the clearest indication yet of Sheidiak's political ambitions, and a desperate attempt to impress the grand prince with the fact that he, Sheidiak, was an equal of the Crimean khan and entitled to the traditional tribute from Moscow. Ivan, of course, was aware that Sheidiak was a mere pretender and that only Chinggisids were permitted to assume the title of khan and privileged to receive tribute. New warnings to Ivan to avoid excuses and delays and submit tribute commensurate with that of the Crimean khan were to no avail.

Moscow was determined to reward only those who chose to forgo raiding and proved their loyalty. One such Nogay mirza was Sheidiak's nephew, Urak, whose pastures were along the Volga. Writing to Ivan in 1537, he explained that he had been charged by the Nogay mirzas with guarding the Volga from Crimean raids, and that his service to Moscow was no different from Ivan's Cossacks: "I shall never leave the Volga. It is as if I do not live among the Nogays but at your court." He promised to remain on Ivan's side, even if his uncle Sheidiak launched war against Moscow.[90]

It was Urak's efforts that kept the Nogays at peace with Moscow. After all, Moscow and the Nogays had overlapping strategic interests in the area. For Moscow, the Nogays were a critical force capable of checking the Crimean raids and aiding Moscow in its conquest of Kazan. Indeed, throughout the 1540s, the Nogays thwarted several Crimean campaigns against Moscow and launched raids against the Crimea proper. The Crimean khan, Sahip Giray, began to doubt even the loyalty of the Nogays in the Crimean service and specifically blamed the Nogay Baki Bey for the Crimean failure in 1541 to cross the Oka River expediently and plunder Moscow.[91]

To most Nogay mirzas, Moscow was a natural counterforce to their rivals in the Crimea and Astrakhan, and when the Crimeans supplied Astrakhan with cannon and light firearms, the Nogays likewise requested from Moscow several gunners and a cannon, "one that could be used by the nomadic people." Even more significantly, cut off by the Kazakhs from the markets in Central Asia, the Nogays were growing increasingly dependent on Moscow as an attractive horse market. In 1548 alone, Mamay sent to Moscow his merchants with 16,000 horses, and Yusuf dispatched 400 merchants with 2,000 horses.[92]

The balance of power in the region was irreversibly changing in Moscow's favor. In 1547, to reflect the newly crystallized sense of Moscow's political theology, its growing geopolitical ambitions, and its rise to become a major military and economic power in Eastern Europe, Ivan IV was crowned tsar of all Russia. In the world of steppe politics, the coronation and the title of the tsar implied a status equal to the descendants of the Chinggisid family and thus a direct challenge to the rulers of the Crimea, Kazan, and Astrakhan. Even if such an act of unilateral declaration of sovereignty, as illegitimate and self-aggrandizing as it might have been viewed in the steppe, were accepted, one unbridgeable difference between the Russian tsar and all other Chinggisids remained: Ivan was not a Muslim.

From this time on, the ideological divide between Moscow and the Muslim world would become more pronounced, and the issues would be articulated more frequently in terms of the religious differences. While some

Nogay mirzas began to refer to Ivan as the "white tsar" and "the Christian sovereign," the new Nogay beg, Mamay, continued to call Ivan a "white grand prince" and clearly drew a distinction between himself as a Muslim ruler and Ivan as a Christian one. Mamay insisted that Ivan release all his Muslim captives, in particular Mamay's nephew Dervish (Derbysh Ali), the heir to the khan of Astrakhan.[93]

It had been a strict tenet of Moscow's policies not to allow the return of the Chinggisid princes who at different times sought refuge in Muscovy. They were to be kept as potential pro-Muscovite marionettes, serving to legitimize Moscow's various claims in the world of the former Golden Horde. This time, however, despite Dervish's preference for staying in Moscow, Mamay beg's request was granted. Having pledged to serve Moscow's interests among the Nogays, Dervish was allowed to leave. The reason for such an unusual concession was the new realization that the Nogays' cooperation was crucial in Moscow's large and decisive military campaign against Kazan. The Nogay mirzas understood this and did not hesitate to restate the case in soliciting more presents and rewards: "We are at war with the Crimea and Kazan because of the Christian tsar [Ivan]."[94]

Moscow was well aware that releasing Dervish into the Nogays' hands would strengthen the latter's claims on Astrakhan. But for the time being, Astrakhan was too far away, the Nogays appeared to be allies, and the conquest of Kazan was an immediate priority. In 1549 the khan of Kazan, Safa Giray, died, and the Kazan government sent to the Crimea to request a new khan. The time had come to act decisively.

In the summer of 1549, the Muscovite troops, led by Shah Ali and guided by their Nogay allies, once again appeared near Kazan. The Nogay beg, Yusuf (1549–55), who had succeeded his deceased brother, Mamay, sent to Ivan his envoys and 200 merchants with 3,000 horses. Making clear that it was his help that had secured the throne of Kazan for Safa Giray, Yusuf now offered to assist Shah Ali in capturing Kazan. Inflating his status, Yusuf mentioned his recent reception of the envoy from the Ottoman sultan and then proposed friendship to Ivan. Yusuf requested specific presents (paper, saffron, fur coats, dyes, woolens, and armor) and raised the already familiar issue of the Muscovite Cossacks, who had built several fortifications on the Don and pillaged his caravan near Voronezh.[95]

This time, in addition to the traditional concerns of security, trade, and presents, Yusuf's offer was also motivated by a deep yearning for revenge against the Crimeans and Kazan. Only two years earlier the Nogays had endured a crushing defeat by Sahip Giray khan. Those who were captured suffered a brutal reprisal: some were impaled; others were hanged upside down; yet others were beheaded, their severed heads piled up in towers (*bashta*). The humiliation was almost as great when the Nogays led by Yusuf's son, Yunus, laid siege to Kazan, but after seven days, unable to take a city well-defended with cannon and muskets, they were compelled to retreat with great losses. By 1550 the Russian tsar and the Nogay beg had formed an alliance against Kazan.[96]

In a rare insight into the tributary relations among the various parts of the former Golden Horde, Yunus mirza explained to Ivan why he was so eager to avenge himself in the war against Kazan. He and his father, Yusuf, had been deceived by Safa Giray, who had promised to give them control of the highland and Arsk sides of the Volga (i.e., part of the east bank of the Volga near the Kazanka River) and to grant Yunus the rank of the Kazan beg, with the right to receive tribute traditionally paid to the Nogays. Yunus suggested that Ivan install Shah Ali as khan, and he himself would be the beg there. He then gave Ivan precise advice on how to approach Kazan, which roads to cut off first, and offered more help if Ivan dispatched fifty to sixty boats to transport the Nogays across the river.[97]

While Yusuf and his son Yunus were forging closer ties with Ivan in order to seize Kazan, Yusuf's brother Ismail mirza tried to secure Ivan's aid against Astrakhan. He informed Ivan that the Astrakhan khan Akkubek had fled to the Kabardinians, who had then captured Astrakhan and restored the fugitive khan to the throne. He encouraged Ivan to take advantage of the turmoil in Astrakhan to capture the city and install Dervish khan there. Ismail made it clear that the Nogays could not seize Astrakhan without Moscow's help because "we have no cannon, no muskets, and no boats."

To reassure Moscow of his loyalty, Ismail added that he had rejected a proposal from the Ottoman sultan, Süleyman I, who had extended to the Nogays an offer to join an anti-Muscovite alliance of the Crimea, Kazan, and Astrakhan. The Russian envoy to the Nogays reported in detail the sultan's offer, which showed the extent of the Ottomans' concern over the Muscovite expansion. In his letter to Ismail, Süleyman accused Ivan of being haughty and arrogant toward the Muslims. He charged that Ivan controlled the steppe and rivers, which belonged to the Porte, and that his Cossacks had blockaded and exacted payments from Azov, routed the Crimeans near Perekop, taken over Astrakhan, raided the Nogay uluses, and captured Dervish khan. And now Ivan was at war with Kazan. "But we are all Muslims and we should all stand united against Moscow," continued the sultan. Finally, realizing that an appeal to Islamic solidarity might not suffice, Süleyman promised to make Ismail a khan in Azov if he helped Kazan and Azov, which, the sultan admitted, were too far away for him to aid.[98]

Whatever the hopes for an Islamic axis might have been, they were dashed when, in the summer of 1551, Moscow set up its own candidate in Kazan, Shah Ali. The Muscovite government skillfully took advantage of the turmoil in the Crimea caused by the assassination of the Crimean khan, Sahip Giray. His victories against Astrakhan in 1546 and the Nogays and Kabardinians in the following years reignited the old enmity of the Crimean karachis, who were fearful of the strong central authority of the khan. Persuaded by the intrigues of the karachis that Sahip Giray had grown dangerously independent, the Ottoman sultan supported the coup that eliminated him.[99]

On the eve of the final campaign against Kazan, the Nogay pastures were distributed as follows: Yusuf beg and Dervish khan occupied the pastures along the Yaik River near Saraychik; Ismail and the sons of Kuchum were on the Volga near Astrakhan; Mamay's son Kazy (Kasai) and others could be found on the Syr-Darya River near the Kazakh Horde; and Sheidiak and his sons were near Urgench.[100] By the summer of 1551, in its plan to conquer Kazan, Moscow could count on cooperation from the Nogays on the Volga under Ismail and Belek-Bulat and those between the Volga and the Yaik under Yunus mirza.[101]

At the same time, Ivan and the Nogay beg Yusuf were again sharply at odds over the usual issues of presents and raids. Aware that Yusuf's forces were distracted by the anticipated raids of Sheidiak and Mamay's sons against Saraychik, Ivan rejected Yusuf's demands in a most severe and uncompromising tone. In 1551 he wrote to Yusuf concerning the Nogays who had been captured while raiding the Muscovite frontier: "There is a custom now in our land, whoever comes to wage war in our borderlands shall not live." Refusing to accept Yusuf's letter, Ivan reiterated that the captives would not be returned, and those who attacked Muscovy would be dealt with severely. To give Yusuf a taste of his own medicine, he ordered the Nogay envoys robbed in return for the abuses suffered by their Russian counterparts.[102]

Open threats no longer seemed to have an effect on Moscow, so Yusuf tried another approach. Writing to Ivan in September 1551, he informed him that the new Crimean khan, Devlet Giray, had asked Yusuf to join a Crimean campaign against Moscow. Yusuf did not forget to mention that he had an army of 300,000 horsemen under his command, and his eight sons had 10,000 each of their own troops, and that he was still deciding whether to take up the offer of the new Crimean khan.[103] In other words, Yusuf was open to bargaining.

Neither Yusuf nor other Nogay mirzas yet realized the full extent of recent changes in Moscow's self-perception and in its consequent attitude toward the steppe. With Moscow as a perceived center of the Christian universe, its divinely ordained tsar was determined to discontinue the traditional payments and to stop the demands from the steppe once and for all. It no longer befit Moscow's image to surrender to the old extortionary practices.

In January 1552, Ivan sent another letter to Yusuf. In the same uncompromising tone, Ivan asserted his right over Kazan as the yurt conquered by his grandfather and now inherited by him. It was his both by right of conquest and by dynastic inheritance.[104] Additional and curious support for Ivan's claims came from the Moscow loyalist Belek-Bulat mirza, who referred to Ivan as a direct descendant of Chinggis khan. It is not clear whether such a claim was initiated in Moscow or whether Belek-Bulat resorted to deliberate flattery to win Ivan's favors. At any rate, the significance of belonging to the Chinggisid dynasty was apparent to anyone in the world of steppe politics.[105]

In the meantime, infuriated by Ivan's annexation of the Volga's west bank near Sviiazhsk and the city's virtual loss of sovereignty, Kazan was poised to rebel. In the ultimate act of its attempted peaceful annexation of Kazan, Moscow dispatched a viceroy (*namestnik*) to replace the unpopular Shah Ali khan, but it was too late.[106] Kazan refused to accept the Russian viceroy, massacred the Russian garrison stationed there, and invited Yadyger Muhammed of the Astrakhan dynasty to become khan. Of course, such a coup would not have been possible without the tacit consent of the Nogays. Writing to Ivan in April 1552, Yusuf poignantly blamed him for breaking their written agreement, in which Ivan had promised to share power with the Nogays, whereby Ivan would have his khan and the Nogays their beg in Kazan. He reminded Ivan that he, Yusuf, had kept his word and had not aided Kazan against Moscow, but Ivan had violated their agreement and lied to him.[107]

The disappointment among the Nogay mirzas over Moscow's intransigence was unanimous. Kazy mirza informed Ivan that the Nogays had all agreed that there would be no peace with Moscow until Ivan returned the widow of Safa Giray khan, Yusuf beg's daughter, Süünbike, her son, Utemish Giray, and other prominent Kazan captives. Even Moscow loyalists, Ismail and Yunus mirzas, confirmed that Kazan was the yurt of the Crimean khans, and in the past they had shared it equally. But Ivan was adamant, and his only promise to the Nogay mirzas was to grant a Muscovite town to Utemish Giray when he grew up.[108]

Ivan was not to be distracted or intimidated on the eve of his crusade against the rebellious Kazan. After a brief siege, the Muscovite troops, under Ivan's personal command and armed with artillery and modern siege equipment, stormed the city in October 1552. Added to the Muscovite crown and mentioned among many other royal possessions in the title of the tsar, Kazan was now one of the Muscovite cities governed by a Russian viceroy. The annexation of Kazan was complete, and its conquest was seen as no less than the God-sent victory of the Orthodox Christian monarch.

Three months later, in his letters to the Nogay leaders, Ivan reiterated the fact that Kazan was a yurt of Moscow dating from the old days and that he had punished the residents of Kazan for their sedition. He then proceeded to describe with undisguised pride how the male population of the city had been slaughtered, women and children taken captive, and Yadyger khan shown mercy—not hanged, but taken to Moscow and bestowed with an estate. In a friendly overture to the Nogays, Ivan assured them that they could come and trade safely in Kazan and that for the Nogays' sake he had ordered the Cossacks to vacate the Volga.[109] The Nogays were thus presented with an even starker choice between accommodating Moscow or waging war against it.

FIGURE 8. Unfinished miniature from the *Litsevoi letopisnyi svod* depicting Ivan IV in a royal crown triumphantly entering Kazan in 1552. From *Rasskazy russkikh letopisei 15–17 vv.* (Moscow: Detskaia literatura, 1978).

THE NOGAYS AND ASTRAKHAN, 1550s

The fact that Moscow's ambitions did not end with the annexation of Kazan was made clear in Ivan's letters to Ismail in early 1553. Ivan asked Ismail to let him know of an opportune moment to begin their campaign against Astrakhan and to advise him how best to conquer the Crimea.[110] These plans, however, had to be shelved temporarily when news reached the Kremlin that Yusuf was preparing for a large campaign against Muscovy. Intelligence reports claimed that the Astrakhan khan had promised to assist Yusuf in transporting his troops across the Volga. Then, since the steppe along the Khoper River had been burned, an estimated 120,000 troops of Yusuf's army were expected to use the Crimean route to Voronezh and Riazan, where they would wait for the Oka River to freeze so they could cross it easily. To provision themselves, his troops were to take with them camels, sheep, and grain.[111]

It is hard to know what devastation Yusuf would have inflicted on Moscow had such a campaign taken place. In the end, Ismail refused to participate in the campaign, under the pretext that the Crimeans might launch raids against him while he was gone, and he dissuaded Yusuf from waging war against Moscow. Ismail used a colorful and revealing metaphor to explain his reasoning to Yusuf: "Your people trade in Bukhara and mine are in Moscow. And if I get into war with Moscow, I myself shall go around the world naked, and there will not be even enough for a cover for the dead."[112] Ismail understood what subsequent generations of other nomadic leaders would also come to realize: the Nogays' proximity to the Muscovite frontier and their growing destitution were making them increasingly dependent on Moscow.

Trying to convince Ivan that Moscow would stand to benefit from some concessions, Ismail suggested that Ivan release the captured khan of Kazan, Yadyger, and install Dervish khan in Astrakhan. Appreciative of Ismail's services and advice, Ivan explained firmly that Yadyger could not be returned because he had converted to Christianity of his own volition, had taken the name Semen, and was now married and granted an estate. Ivan added that it was because of Ismail that he bestowed so many favors upon the captive.[113]

Ivan's answer was the same to friend and foe, and when Yusuf requested to have his daughter, Süünbike, freed, he received a predictable response. In his letter to Yusuf, Ivan explained that Yusuf's daughter was married to Shah Ali and lived in Kasimov, and that he treated Yusuf's grandson as his own. And so that Yusuf would not make the mistake of resorting to new threats and intimidation, Ivan flatly stated that Moscow's enemies were now at his will because "our cause is right, and putting trust in God, we fear no foe."[114]

Putting trust in Ivan's god did not preclude relying on some of his ungodly allies, Ismail and Dervish. In the spring of 1554, following Ismail's advice, Ivan sent Dervish khan and an army of 30,000 men down the Volga to rendezvous with Ismail's Nogays and lay siege to Astrakhan. Unlike Kazan, the conquest of Astrakhan took place without much struggle or drama. The Astrakhan khan, Yamgurchi, fled to Azov with no attempt to resist the Muscovite siege of the city, and Moscow declared Dervish to be the new khan of Astrakhan. Ismail was given thirty Muscovite musketeers and was expected to guard the land approaches to Astrakhan, while Ivan was to secure the water routes.[115]

Ismail's delivery of Astrakhan into Muscovite hands revived the dormant hostilities between Yusuf and Ismail. As in the past, the internal wars among the Nogays were waged along the factional lines of pro-Russian versus anti-Russian coalitions. Kazy mirza confirmed to Ivan that his and Ismail's alliance with Moscow was indeed the reason for their conflict with Yusuf. A series of clashes throughout 1554 were indecisive, until Araslan mirza, a son of Kuchum, unexpectedly switched sides and murdered Yusuf. Asking for rewards and professing his loyalty, Araslan assured Ivan that he had now chosen an alliance with Muscovy, and his people and herds had come to use the Volga pastures: "The Volga became our mother, and the forest our father."[116]

In early 1555, the members of the victorious pro-Russian coalition assumed the leadership positions among the Nogays: Ismail became beg (1555–64), Kazy nureddin, and Araslan keikuvat. The size of the enormous booty captured from Yusuf was apparent when in November 1555 Ismail dispatched to Moscow a thousand envoys and merchants with 20,000 horses and 4,000 sheep. Intoxicated by his victory, the new ruler of the Nogays, Ismail, changed the tone of his letters to Moscow, referring to Ivan as "my son, the white tsar." In an unusual personal letter to the head of Moscow's Foreign Office, I. M. Viskovatyi, Ismail placed Viskovatyi in the category of those who "live there, but serve us." He explained that in the past Kazan had paid him an annuity of ten barrels of honey and sixty rubles in cash. He demanded the restoration of this payment in addition to numerous presents.[117]

Ismail's good fortune changed quickly, and with it the superior tone of his letters to Moscow. Avenging their father, the sons of Yusuf seized Ismail's uluses and Saraychik. Desperate, Ismail tried to convince Ivan that he remained the beg of the Nogays and loyal to Moscow. He informed Ivan that Dervish khan had betrayed them and sided with the Crimeans, whom he had ferried across the Volga. Ismail urged Ivan to retake Astrakhan by force and asked that Muscovite forts be constructed near Astrakhan, in the estuary of the Samara River, on the Irgiz River, and at Perevoloka (the shortest distance between the Don and Volga). Such forts would have prevented his enemies from crossing the rivers and protected Ismail's pastures stretching from the Volga in the west to the Emba in the east and to the Samara in the north.[118]

In July 1556, the ever-confident Ivan rebuked Ismail for the inappropriate tone of his letters and informed him that troops had been dispatched against Astrakhan. Ivan reassured Ismail of Moscow's protection and offered him and his family a residence in Astrakhan, if it were taken, or in Kazan, if the campaign failed. The campaign proved to be a success. Dervish khan fled in advance of the approaching Muscovite troops, and Astrakhan fell to the Cossacks without resistance. Shortly thereafter, expecting the defection of many Crimean nobles, Ismail suggested an immediate combined attack against the Crimea. This time he addressed Ivan as "the ruler of all Christians, the white tsar."[119]

By the end of 1556, it was clear that only Moscow's support allowed Ismail to retain the title of beg. But it was equally clear that the simmering discontent among other mirzas against both Ismail and his Moscow supporters was not going to disappear. The new keikuvat, Yunus (the eldest son of Yusuf), and the nureddin, Belek-Bulat, wrote to Ivan from their pastures in the lower Volga and demanded that he remove his voevodas from Astrakhan, allow them to use pastures in the Volga estuary, and send payments and presents in accordance with their new titles. In return they offered friendship and alliance against the Crimea. Ivan's answer was merely to order the voevodas to allow the Nogays to trade in Astrakhan.[120]

The tsar responded more positively to the complaints from Ismail, who confirmed that the Volga estuary had traditionally been the Nogay yurt and that the Astrakhan khan had formerly paid an annuity of 40,000 altyns. Bitterly, he reminded Ivan that now he received no annuity from Astrakhan and that the Astrakhan voevoda, Ivan Cheremisinov, did not share customs duties with him and refused to return Nogay fugitives. Ismail's grievances were followed by his promise to start a war with the Crimea after the issues were settled. Ivan sent him food, promised to replace the Astrakhan voevoda, and assured Ismail that he could rely on his musketeers for protection.[121]

In the summer of 1557, squabbles over dividing the uluses led to a new and devastating round of hostilities among the Nogays. Most of the mirzas sided with Yunus and against Ismail. The Muscovite envoys reported great turmoil among the Nogays. Ismail fled, and his uluses were divided between Yunus and his allies. Realizing that they could not prevail over Ismail completely unless Moscow stopped supporting him, Yunus and other mirzas assured Ivan of their good intentions. They explained that they had expelled Ismail because he had killed their father, not because of his alliance with Moscow. If Ivan wanted to accept Ismail into his service, they had no objections, but he should not support Ismail by providing him with musketeers.[122]

In the meantime, numerous reports sent to Moscow indicated that the Nogays were starving, had lost most of their horses, and were ruining themselves by raiding and looting each other. In addition to the destructive civil war, flood and severe winter storms had caused widespread famine among the Nogays. Ismail lamented that in the last four years of fighting with his rivals, he had lost all his herds and property. Now that his farmland near Saraychik was flooded, a despondent Ismail pleaded with Ivan to send him boats with seeds, grain, honey, gifts, and cash.[123]

By the summer of 1558, the situation among the Nogays had reached a new level of desperation. Some of the Nogays moved away, crossing the Yaik to join the Kazakhs. Ismail's two sons crossed the Don and left for the Crimea. Belek-Bulat moved south to the Kuma River. Abandoned and starving, Ismail was compelled to send his people across the Volga and Kuma to buy fish and grain in the Caucasus. Even then, nature refused to cooperate: on their way back, his people became stranded on the Volga's west bank when the ice broke. Completely dependent on aid from Moscow and driven to despair by war and famine, Ismail wrote to Ivan: "We can no longer subsist."[124]

Unable to move anywhere else and plagued by continuous defections, Ismail decided to have a fortified residence built for himself on the Buzan River, east of Astrakhan. In another appeal to Ivan, to whom he now referred as "our sovereign," Ismail submitted his most detailed list of grievances and unfulfilled expectations. He reminded Ivan that he remained loyal to Moscow even though his people had abandoned him and accused him of becoming a Russian ("ty dei budesh' rusin"). And what was the reward for his loyalty? Ivan's promises to place Ismail in Astrakhan and allot him two-thirds of the customs duties collected there had not been carried through. His annuity from Kazan had ceased. The presents from Moscow were so meager that it was impossible to divide them among the mirzas. The new Astrakhan governor, Ivan Vyrodkov, imposed yasak on the grain and fish, shared nothing with Ismail, and was even less cooperative than the previous governor had been. Ismail was concerned that because of the governor's disrespectful behavior, "others would say that we were not allowed to be in possession of our own people." The Astrakhan people committed raids against him. In particular, he blamed the four Nogay mirzas who had found refuge in Astrakhan and who had incited the governor, attacked Ismail, and then divided the spoils with the governor and the interpreters. In short, he and his people were abused and starving. Once again, Ismail urged Ivan to dispatch without delay five boats of grain and two hundred musketeers to protect him during the winter against the Crimea.[125]

It was apparent that, contrary to the Nogays' expectations, the Muscovite conquests of Kazan and Astrakhan had severe negative consequences for them. The newly acquired territories were to be subject to the Muscovite government's policies: yasak was imposed on the vanquished population, and the traditional tributary payments to the Nogays ceased, leaving them solely dependent on their service to the Muscovite sovereign. When the Nogays' demands to return to the status quo failed, Ismail offered an arrangement to share territory between the Nogays and Moscow. The Volga and Yaik, he reminded Ivan, had always been the Nogay yurt in possession of the nureddin and beg, respectively: "And now the Volga is yours, but it is the same as ours because we are brothers. And there are your people in the Volga estuary and there are our people there too, whom we left there poor and hungry."

But even this toned-down proposal was rejected by Moscow. Faced with the divided and impoverished Nogays, Moscow was not interested in negotiating with these nomads, who were to be treated like other subjects of Moscow and rewarded if they provided service to "the ruler of all Christians, the white tsar." Ivan IV left no doubt that he would provide for Ismail only if the latter attacked the Crimea. According to Moscow's plan, the Muscovite troops were to sail down the Don and Dnieper rivers and join forces with the Nogays and Kabardinians. As an incentive to Ismail, Ivan granted the Nogays a three-year exemption from customs duties on their trade with Moscow.[126]

The campaign against the Crimea never took place. Instead, Ivan turned his attention toward Muscovy's weakened rival in the west and invaded Livonia. Yet the developments on the Livonian front were closely linked to the events on the southern frontier. Because of the traditional nomadic tactics of launching raids into Muscovy while its troops were engaged elsewhere, fear of Crimean raids was ever present. It was Ismail and his Nogays whom Moscow entrusted with harassing the Crimeans and forestalling their raids. In the summer of 1560, Ismail sent his horsemen against the Crimea, but they were intercepted by the Nogays of Kazy mirza. Frustrated in his political ambitions, Kazy, who had been the nureddin and next in line of succession, fled to the pastures along the Kuma River after Ismail declared his son, Tin Ahmed, heir apparent. Until his death in 1577, Kazy and his followers preferred the steppe of the North Caucasus to the pastures of the Volga, and alliance with the Crimea to the service of the Muscovite tsar.

Ismail assured Ivan that he would have attacked and destroyed the Crimea had it not been for the threat of Kazy's raids. To annihilate his rival, Ismail requested 2,000 to 3,000 Muscovite troops, including 600 musketeers, because Kazy's residence was well fortified and it would be impossible to capture him without the musketeers and guns. There was another reason, Ismail contended, which had prevented him from launching successful raids against the Crimea—the Astrakhan governor, Ivan Vyrodkov, who supported Ismail's enemies and helped them to capture Saraychik, seize herds, capture many Kalmyk and other prisoners there, and sell them into slavery in foreign lands.

It is possible that Moscow finally realized the extent of the misrule and corruption in Astrakhan when the governor was charged with profiting from the sale of the captives instead of bringing them to Muscovy to be converted to Christianity. Or perhaps the worrisome news that Ismail had moved away from Astrakhan and was about to enter negotiations with the Crimea finally convinced Moscow of the need to appease Ismail. In 1561, Ivan informed Ismail that the Astrakhan governor Vyrodkov had been arrested and put in chains until the next spring, when he would be sent to Moscow.[127]

Sensing that Moscow was in a compromising mood, Ismail decided to push for further concessions. He reminded Ivan that Moscow had been able to take over Kazan and Astrakhan because of Ismail's complicity, and that Ivan had reneged on his promise of tributes from Kazan and Astrakhan. Now all that Ismail was asking was to be allowed to graze his herds near Astrakhan and to have the Tumaks (a farming community of captives, presumably of Turkic origin) from Astrakhan settled on the Buzan River nearby. Denying that he made any past promises to the Nogays, Ivan agreed that Ismail could have the Tumaks, but that they should be settled on the Yaik, not on the Buzan, "because Astrakhan could not survive without farming on the Buzan." To make his case more convincing, Ivan drew an analogy with

Saraychik and inquired rhetorically whether the residents of Saraychik would have given up their farmland had the Russians come to settle there.

The final exchange of arguments over the Buzan River indelibly captured the new and old images of power relations in the region. The embattled Ismail tried to relate his predicament to Ivan when he insisted that his authority among the Nogays was further undermined because this was the Nogays' old yurt and his people had reprimanded him thus: "There are one hundred thousand rivers flowing into the Volga, and you cannot even get [from Ivan] one Buzan." Ivan countered with his own reference to tradition, stating unequivocally that Buzan was farmland, which from the days of the Golden Horde ("under the tsars") had belonged to Astrakhan, and Buzan should remain the border (*rubezh*) between Astrakhan and the Nogays.[128] Ivan's appeal to the legitimacy of the Golden Horde clearly intended to put the issue to rest.

Moscow's success in securing control over the newly conquered region was as much a function of its economic and military superiority as of considerable diplomatic skills. To justify the conquest of Kazan and Astrakhan to other Christian rulers, Moscow did not hesitate to declare the khanates to be former Russian patrimonies. At the same time, Moscow equally confidently used the legitimacy of the Golden Horde in arguing its case among its Turkic neighbors.

When necessary, Ivan IV showed an understanding for religious sensibilities in the region inhabited by Muslims and ruled by the Christian monarch. With one eye on the Ottoman sultan and another on the rapidly growing number of Muslims in his own domain, Ivan explained to Ismail how Moscow's policies in the region were necessarily constrained by the delicate issue of religion. In 1563, responding to Ismail's charge against seven nobles in Astrakhan who had secretly collaborated with the Crimea and Kazy mirza, Ivan, in a conspicuously rhetorical display, wrote:

> We cannot remove them because [when] we took Astrakhan and appointed our governors there, we gave our word to the Astrakhan nobles that they would be protected. And we are the Christian sovereign, and they are Muslims. If we remove them and keep them away from Astrakhan, the Astrakhan people might run away, and in the foreign lands some would say that we did not keep our word, that the two faiths could not live in peace, and that the Christian sovereign was destroying the Muslims. And it is written in our Christian books that it is not allowed to convert to our faith by force; people should have whichever faith they wish. And then God will decide in the future whose faith is right and whose is not; a man cannot judge this. And in our lands there are many people of the Muslim faith who are in our service, and they live in accordance with their law.[129]

Ivan's letter did not reach the intended addressee. In January 1564, the Nogay envoys brought news that Ismail had died and had been succeeded by his son, Tin Ahmed (Tinekhmat) (1564–79). Upon the pledge of the new Nogay beg to follow his father's policies, Ivan granted him an annuity of 400 rubles. Tin Ahmed and his father-in-law, the Kabardinian Prince Temriuk, whose other daughter had recently become Ivan's second wife, were ready to attack the Nogays of Kazy, their sworn enemy and Crimean ally.[130]

THE ASTRAKHAN CAMPAIGN OF 1569

Moscow's policies in the region were first and foremost concerned with the possible reaction of the Ottoman sultan, the ruler of the most powerful empire and protector of all Muslims. In Istanbul, despite initial concern over Moscow's conquests of Kazan and Astrakhan, the issue of containing Muscovite ambitions did not become a priority while the Porte was engaged in a protracted struggle with the Habsburgs in the west and Safavid Persia in the east. By the early 1560s, however, it became apparent that Moscow's rapid expansion southward along the Volga and Don rivers was threatening Ottoman strategic interests in the area and could no longer be ignored. The Don Cossacks' raids disrupted overland communications with the Ottoman fort Azov, and the Russian military governors in Astrakhan did not allow safe passage for Muslim pilgrims from the Central Asian khanates to Mecca.

The first attempt to organize an Ottoman-Crimean campaign against Astrakhan and to dig a canal connecting the Don and Volga rivers was conceived in Istanbul in 1563. But the Crimean khan dissuaded the sultan, Süleyman, citing difficulties in supplying troops for such a campaign. The plan was shelved. Four years later, the sultan and khan discovered that the Muscovites were constructing a fort on the Terek River in the eastern corner of the North Caucasus. Moscow's relentless expansion farther south suddenly endangered the Porte's vital communications with its newly acquired possessions on the western shore of the Caspian Sea and threatened the Crimea's control of parts of the North Caucasus and its Circassian subjects. The Porte revived its plan to send an expeditionary force in order to construct a canal connecting the Don and the Volga. Ottoman success in building such a canal would have allowed Istanbul to conquer Astrakhan and to dominate the entire North Caucasus region—a crucial area of contest between the Porte and Persia—and to control one of the most profitable trade routes connecting Bukhara, Khiva, Urgench, and Tashkent with the Ottoman markets.

In 1567, news reached Moscow that the new Ottoman sultan, Selim II, was preparing an armada of 7,000 ships to sail to Azov under his personal command, and then he and the Crimean khan would set out against Astrakhan. The Crimean khan, Devlet Giray, expressed his concern over Moscow's expansion to the Russian envoy in the Crimea: "Before Ivan used to send tribute to Kazan, and then he seized Kazan and Astrakhan, and now he has founded Tersk." With the support of an Ottoman army behind him, Devlet Giray wrote to Ivan, raising the price of peace with Moscow. He demanded that Ivan return Kazan and Astrakhan to the Crimea, "because from the old days Astrakhan and Kazan were part of the Muslim world and the yurt of the khans of our dynasty," and that he send valuable and numerous presents and give up building the fort on the Terek. Otherwise, the khan warned, there would be no peace.

The Crimean claim to common Islamic identity with Kazan and Astrakhan left Ivan unimpressed. Instead, he countered that both cities were the yurt of his ancestors and had become an indivisible part of Muscovy. As far as a Muslim yurt was concerned, Ivan had one, Kasimov, and if Devlet Giray desired friendship, he could send his son, and Ivan would make him a khan in Kasimov. Ivan's answer dispelled any doubt about Devlet Giray's participation in the Ottoman campaign against Astrakhan. Plied with promises of handsome payments from Poland and fearful that Moscow's victory over Poland would mean more Muscovite forts on the Dnieper River, the Crimean nobles also advised the khan against peace with Moscow. Even the Nogay beg Tin Ahmed, whose various requests were rebuffed by Moscow, promised to help Devlet Giray. In the spring of 1569, a large Ottoman-Crimean force set out on the campaign.[131]

Digging a canal between the Don and the Volga at their nearest point proved to be too formidable an undertaking, and the work was soon abandoned. The Ottoman-Crimean expeditionary force approached Astrakhan in September 1569. Instead of continuing the campaign so late in the season, the decision was made not to storm the city but to build a fort nearby and winter there in anticipation of reinforcements the following year. Less than enthusiastic about the campaign, which, if successful, could only expand Ottoman control of the region at the Crimea's expense, the Crimean khan tried to convince the Ottoman commander to give up and return to Azov. In the end, rumors of a large Russian army sailing down the Volga and a Persian army dispatched to assist Astrakhan forced an Ottoman retreat.

Supplying troops for such a distant campaign proved to be an impossible task, and the Ottoman retreat through the arid and inhospitable steppe of the North Caucasus took a heavy toll; only one-third of the original force was reported to have returned to Azov. More than a century later, in 1689, a similar fate befell a Russian expeditionary force into the Crimea, and for similar reasons. Regular armies dependent on massive supplies were not yet capable of launching a successful large-scale campaign in the hostile environment of the steppe.[132]

Although a military fiasco, the Astrakhan campaign of 1569 convinced Moscow that the Porte's concerns had to be taken seriously. Ivan IV's assurances that he meant no harm to Muslims and the Islamic faith, and that he had conquered the Volga khanates merely to ensure their loyalty, did not satisfy Selim II. The sultan insisted that the regions of Astrakhan and Kabarda in the Caucasus were traditional Ottoman domains with Muslim residents. He demanded that the pilgrims and merchants from Bukhara and elsewhere be allowed to proceed through Astrakhan on their way to Mecca. In 1571, eager to prevent another campaign against Astrakhan, which Moscow could ill-afford to defend at the time, Ivan IV informed the sultan that Fort Tersk was being demolished and the Astrakhan route reopened.[133]

While war with the Ottoman Empire was avoided, raids from the Crimea were not. Throughout the 1570s, taking advantage of the social turmoil within Muscovy and with the knowledge that its troops were tied up on the western front in Livonia, the Crimeans launched both large- and small-scale raids. The most damaging campaign occurred in 1571, when a large Crimean army of more than 100,000 horsemen led by the khan himself was able to cross the Oka River and reach Moscow unimpeded. Unwilling to take the risk of storming the city, the Crimeans looted and burned the suburbs of Moscow and seized large numbers of Muscovite captives.

In the aftermath of the successful campaign, Devlet Giray threatened more raids unless Ivan gave him Kazan and Astrakhan. Desperate and besieged on both fronts in the west and in the south, Ivan IV sent his envoys with payments and presents to the khan and promised to return Astrakhan. Devlet Giray adamantly insisted that Kazan should also belong to him. To show that he meant business, the khan again led a large army against Moscow in the spring of 1572. This time, however, Russian troops were ready for the encounter and routed the Crimeans in several battles. Ready for a compromise, Devlet wrote to Ivan suggesting that Astrakhan alone would suffice. Ivan, however, was no longer interested in concessions and instructed his envoys to curtail the presents to the khan and assert firmly that Kazan and Astrakhan would remain a part of Muscovy.[134]

CONTAINING THE NOGAYS, 1577–1582

Tin Ahmed's promise to follow in the footsteps of his father also meant that Moscow continued to be besieged with similar complaints and requests over the Buzan River, construction of a fort in the Volga estuary, the return of the captured Nogays, and of course, more payments and presents. If the requests were familiar, so too were Moscow's responses. In one curious attempt to influence the outcome of decisions in Moscow, Tin Ahmed wrote to the diak Andrei Vasil'evich [sic] in 1564 and promised to treat him like one of his own karachis in exchange for representing his cause to the tsar. This none too subtle attempt to recruit a Muscovite official, in a manner similar to Moscow's paying its loyalists among the Nogays, betrayed a thorough misunderstanding of the nature of Muscovite autocracy.[135]

117

БЕССЕБѦКНѕьоеᴌнісіі ноєноᴌаграсіси.
оустронстіногрᴌᴅепоушісіі іітіиці
ᴌіпрнісᴌзᴌᴌіь . ігрᴌсісіі
ᴌюᴅеѪнноітьіно
Знтіиᴌогрᴌ
попеᴅь

FIGURE 9. Miniature from the *Litsevoi letopisnyi svod* depicting a town preparing for a siege. From O. I. Podobedova, *Miniatiury russkikh istoricheskikh letopisei: K istorii russkogo litsevogo letopisaniia* (Moscow: Nauka, 1966), p. 245.

As long as raids against the Muscovite southern borderlands offered rewards greater than those sent by Moscow, both the Crimeans and the Nogays continued to engage in them. Moscow's attempt to push the Nogays away from the Volga did not bring about the desired result. Informers among the Nogays reported that both Tin Ahmed beg and Urus mirza had sent their horsemen to participate in the Crimean raids against Muscovy.

If the Nogay complaints were not heeded in Moscow, neither did Moscow's grievances find a receptive audience among the Nogay chiefs. In 1577,

Tin Ahmed dismissed the charges of the Muscovite envoy against him, insisting that it was Urus' people who took part in the raids, not his. Even then, he bitterly pointed out, Moscow sent Urus larger payments. When the issue was raised with Urus, he asserted that without sufficient payments from Moscow he could not control his people and was considering leaving for the Crimea. With his own undeniable logic, Urus referred to precedent from the days of the Golden Horde and put a precise price tag on his alliance with Moscow: his ancestor Nureddin had once received payments from the khan of the Golden Horde, Timur Kutlug, and his father, Ismail beg, had received 40,000 altyns' worth of fur coats, honey, and cloth from Kazan and the same amount from Astrakhan. Now, since all of these yurts belonged to Moscow, it was Ivan's turn to send him the same payments. Then he would be able not only to induce his people to stop the raids, but also to attract back those who had deserted him and fled to the Crimea.[136] His argument could not have been more transparent: Moscow's control of the region formerly belonging to the khans of the Golden Horde was no longer disputed, but neither was its obligation to continue the payments of its glorious predecessors.

While the Nogays tried to restore and maintain the old system of tribute, Moscow struggled to turn the traditional payments into rewards bestowed only on those who showed their loyalty. But sending the appropriate payments and presents was not an easy matter. Rewards sent to one mirza immediately provoked demands from others for a similar or larger payment. Fathers demanded payments at least equal to those of their sons and those of uncles to their nephews, and political rivals claimed higher status vis-à-vis each other and commensurate higher payments. Such a spiral of extortionary demands was endless because it reflected the scale of honor and kinship relations among the Nogay mirzas.

Moscow's policy to reward selectively the loyal mirzas regardless of their status amounted, in effect, to taking the distribution of payments out of the hands of a Nogay beg. On the one hand, such a policy allowed Moscow greater leverage among the individual Nogay mirzas by circumventing a Nogay beg and providing a manifest link between the loyalty of the mirzas and their rewards. On the other hand, Moscow's attempts to turn a tributary system into a service further undercut the power of a Nogay ruler, encouraged internal rivalries, and had a disruptive effect on the entire traditional hierarchy of the Nogay society. Such policies had at least one undesirable and significant consequence for Moscow. Substituting itself for a Nogay beg meant that it was now held directly accountable for a failure to deliver payments, and Moscow bore the brunt of the mirzas' discontent.

These contradictions could not be easily resolved. There were always those mirzas who found their payments inadequate. They often vented their anger by beating and humiliating the Muscovite envoys and interpreters and seizing the payments and presents by force.[137] It seemed that Moscow's policy had only accelerated demands for more payments. To cut short the unceasing claims on his treasury, Ivan offered a compromise. He had no intention of continuing the old practice of paying large tribute, but he would provide payments of 8,000 and 5,000 altyns to Tin Ahmed and Urus, respectively. Other mirzas were reproached for their inappropriate demands.[138] Apparently Moscow found it more expedient to extract itself from a direct distribution of payments and let the Nogay rulers themselves satisfy the insatiable appetite of their noble brethren with the greatly diminished tribute.

Upon Tin Ahmed's death in the summer of 1579, Urus (1579–90) sent his envoy to Moscow to inform "the sovereign of all the Christians and the grand prince, the white tsar" that he was now in charge of all the Nogay uluses along the Yaik and the Volga. In return for payments, exemption from customs duties, and the return of the captive Nogays, he offered assurances of his loyalty. Congratulating Urus on becoming a Nogay beg, Ivan confirmed that the desire for friendship was mutual and agreed to grant most of his requests.[139]

Assurances and promises apart, the policies of the new Nogay beg were closely watched. A Muscovite envoy reported that the Nogays had exchanged embassies with Bukhara, Tashkent, Urgench, and Siberia, discussing the issues of trade, peace, and marriages. Moscow was particularly suspicious of the embassies from the Crimea. This time, however, the Crimeans were more interested in raids against Persia than against Muscovy. The letter from the Crimean khan to the Nogay nureddin on the Volga, Tinbay mirza, asked Tinbay to join the Crimean campaign against Persia "because it is fitting that we together should defend our Islamic faith." In return the khan promised that Tinbay would be rewarded by the Ottoman sultan. Believing that he had more to gain from his relationship with Ivan, Tinbay instead forwarded the letter to Moscow and was handsomely rewarded by the tsar.[140]

The cordial exchange between Urus beg and Ivan did not last long. Moscow's distrust of Nogay intentions and the unsatisfactory payments from Moscow again led to mutual recriminations. In September 1580, Urus informed Ivan that the Nogays were at war with Moscow because Ivan had sent an unacceptable envoy, a Tatar of military service rank. Urus charged that the envoy's low rank and correspondingly small payment were a personal insult to him. The Muscovites replied that they had done so in response to the Nogays' detainment of the Muscovite envoys. But the envoys had been detained because they did not bring any payments, was the Nogays' reply. Without adequate payments and presents, the cycle of mutual complaints and Nogay raids against the Muscovite frontier was destined to continue.

To avenge his honor, Urus resolved to attack the Kasimov and Riazan regions. All the Nogay nobles and elders arrived at Urus' ulus to discuss the issue. Opinions differed. Some supported the decision to attack Muscovy; others disapproved because "we live off the tsar's payments," and "if the tsar orders the Cossacks to take away from us the Volga, Samara, and Yaik rivers, then we and our uluses will perish, and the Cossacks will seize our wives and children." In the end, news of the impending raids leaked to Moscow, and the campaign had to be canceled.[141]

Abandoning a large-scale campaign did not mean that the smaller raids were also given up. In 1581, the Nogays joined the Crimean and Azov Tatars in a series of raids against the Muscovite provinces of Tula, Kashira, Shatsk, and Alatyr. Hoping to prevent the raids and enlist several thousand Nogay troops in his war against Lithuania, Ivan sent envoys with instructions to give fifty rubles to Urus and several others mirzas in secret and to assure them of Moscow's peaceful intentions.

But empty assurances from Moscow, accompanied by a paltry sum of fifty rubles, were unlikely to satisfy Urus. In April 1581, Urus' envoy arrived in Moscow and was personally received by Ivan. A message from Urus was bitter and unyielding. His ancestors had spared no effort to help Ivan, even if it meant turning against their own brothers and uncles, and in return Ivan offered not gratitude but dishonor. Urus demanded the return of the German and Lithuanian captives who had fled from his uluses to Astrakhan and an annuity of 500 rubles, as had been paid to his late father, Ismail.[142]

Ivan assured him that he meant no offense and promised that those captives who had run away to Astrakhan would be sent back to the Nogays. In exchange he asked Urus to contribute 2,000 horsemen for a campaign against Lithuania. If the Nogay raids continued, Ivan threatened to stop restraining his people from moving into the frontier regions of Kadoma, Temnikov, Shatsk, Alatyr, Arzamas, Kurmysh, Sviiazhsk, and Tetiushchi and to unleash the Kazan, Don, Volga, and Astrakhan Cossacks against the Nogays.[143]

The threats from Moscow did not seem to impress Urus. In the spring of 1581, bolstered by his alliance with the Crimea and with his major grievances unaddressed, 30,000 Nogays joined the Crimeans in raiding the entire Muscovite frontier from Belev to Alatyr. The severe damage from these raids and the large number of captives prompted bitter recriminations from Ivan, who accused Urus of violating the peace and reproached him in a helplessly moralistic tone: "Are you not *ashamed* of attacking our lands with so many people? We trusted you, and that is why we had no people [i.e., troops] along the frontier." Succeeding in neither threatening nor shaming Urus into compliance, Ivan finally yielded and promised to deliver annuities and payments in the amount demanded by the Nogays.[144]

As soon as the payments to the Nogay chiefs were remitted, Urus demanded more. Confidently addressing Ivan as his equal by sending "many bows from the ruler of the Mangits to the ruler of all Christians," Urus offered to dispatch a Nogay contingent to join the Muscovite troops against Lithuania, if Ivan promised to reward him appropriately. Moreover, Urus demanded that Ivan "honor him more than his father"—in other words, submit a larger annuity and presents, because only the khans of the Golden Horde (*velikie tsari*) had formerly possessed Kazan and Astrakhan, which were now in Ivan's hands, and because Urus too was now in higher esteem, receiving most recently a tribute of 100,000 tangas ("in the Bukhara currency") from Bukhara and Tashkent.[145] In Urus' view, the higher status of both the Muscovite tsar and the Nogay beg required higher tribute; the price of peace between the Nogays and Moscow had just gone up.

In order to secure its southern frontier from Nogay raids, Moscow was prepared to deliver annuities, payments, and presents and permitted the Nogays to trade in Moscow and Kazan. But when the Nogays continued to press their demands to have returned those German and Lithuanian captives who had fled to Astrakhan and to have compensation paid for fugitive Russian captives, Moscow refused. The government's argument sounded strangely familiar: the Russians had fled captivity, and many of them had joined the Cossack service and thus could not be returned. Such a line of reasoning should have been familiar to the Nogays, who, in response to the Russian demands to have the Russian captives freed, often maintained that they could not free them because the captives had already been sold to Bukhara.[146] Moscow only replicated the Nogay chiefs' traditional excuse in professing the limits to its authority; how could the Nogays object to that?

This time the arguments from Moscow were supported by the actions of the Volga Cossacks. Now it was Urus' turn to complain of the violence and brutality of the Cossacks, who "this summer burned Saraychik, and not only did they lash those who were alive, but they also dug the dead out of the ground and looted their graves, and we were deeply insulted by it." Furthermore, because of the fear of Cossack raids, he could not take advantage of the internal war among the Kazakhs. Once again, Moscow's response sounded suspiciously similar to those traditionally given by the Nogays—that these Cossacks were brigands and not under Moscow's control. While the Nogays' request to remove all the Cossacks from the Volga and Yaik went unanswered, both sides agreed to the conditions of peace stipulated in the shert'. Urus promised to control his people and prevent them from raiding the Muscovite frontier, while Moscow assured him that it would keep a close eye on Cossacks who committed banditry.[147] In the end, it appeared that the tsar and the Nogay beg were not as helpless against their insubordinates as both had previously professed.

DEBILITATING THE NOGAYS, 1582–1600

Humiliating defeats by Poland-Lithuania and Sweden compelled Ivan IV to seek peace with his neighbors in the west and north. In January 1582 he concluded a ten-year truce with Poland-Lithuania, and the following year one with Sweden. Now Moscow could shift its resources to the southern frontier, which had continued to suffer heavy damage from the destructive campaigns by the Crimeans and Nogays. It was at this time that Moscow resolved to strengthen its southern defenses by placing farther south advanced "frontier regiments" (*ukrainnyi razriad*) in addition to the regiments traditionally stationed at the key locations along the Oka River (*beregovoi razriad*). The Muscovite troops were also sent to quell the protracted unrest in the Kazan region, where the pagan Maris (Chesemis) and Chuvash and the Muslim Tatars rose against Moscow's increasingly intrusive presence in the area. Several large and brutal campaigns were required before the Kazan province was finally pacified three years later.

Throughout the mid-1580s, new forts mushroomed in the Kazan province, marking a further advance of Muscovite military colonization toward Siberia: Forts Urzhum and Malmyzh were founded on the Viatka River in 1584, and two years later and much farther east the Muscovites were already constructing Fort Ufa on the Belaia River. Following the natural flow of the rivers, Moscow also rapidly expanded south, along the Volga. Fort Samara was built in 1586, followed by Tsaritsyn and Saratov in the next four years.[148]

For the Nogays, construction of Muscovite forts along the Volga meant further dependence on Moscow, which now could more effectively control the river crossings and the Nogays' access to the nearby pastures. In a last attempt to secure help against Muscovite expansion, Urus beg pleaded with the Crimean khan to appeal to the Ottoman sultan on behalf of the Nogays. But help was not forthcoming—the Ottoman Porte had other priorities, and the Crimea was plunged into a dynastic struggle.

In 1586, taking advantage of instability in the Crimea, the Nogays agreed to help one of the fugitive Crimean pretenders, Saadat Giray, to avenge his father's death and to recover the Crimean throne. Only Ottoman intervention saved the ruling Crimean khan, Islam Giray. The Nogays' support of the rebel against the Ottoman interests distanced them even further from Istanbul. In 1587 Urus wrote to Istanbul, and, as if tantalizingly reminding the sultan of the missed opportunity to help the Nogays and to expand Ottoman influence, explained that "he, who controls Astrakhan, the Volga and the Yaik, also controls the Nogay Horde." Thus, he informed the sultan, he reluctantly submitted to the Muscovite tsar.[149]

Of course, such "submission" was short-lived, and more often than not the Nogays' statement of their reluctant submission was a useful bargaining chip in bidding themselves up to the other side. In 1588, finding the Astrakhan authorities to be hostile to Nogay interests, some Nogays chose to leave the Volga and moved to the pastures along the Don to seek Ottoman-Crimean protection. Triumphantly, the new Crimean khan, Gazi Giray, wrote to Moscow announcing that 100,000 Nogays had come to join him in the Crimea.

Not only was the number of Nogays greatly exaggerated, but their submission to the Crimea proved to be just as short-lived as it had been to Moscow. No sooner did the Nogays arrive on the banks of the Don than they found themselves under attack by their old rivals. Some Nogays had to flee back to Astrakhan, while others were captured by the Kazy Nogays. This clash unleashed a series of mutual raids between the Astrakhan and Kazy Nogays, raids so severe that by 1590 many Nogay chiefs on both sides had perished in the battles, including Urus beg.[150]

In the meantime, two forceful campaigns by the Crimeans in 1587–88 convinced Moscow to abandon any idea of manipulating the fugitive Crimean pretender, Murad Giray, who first fled to Moscow and was then sent to Astrakhan to be in charge of the non-Russian contingent there. Threatened with more devastating raids unless Murad Giray was returned to the Crimea, Moscow agreed to let him choose either to stay in Muscovy or to leave. In 1590, shortly after Murad Giray decided to leave, he and his son were found dead, apparently poisoned, in Astrakhan. Moscow blamed the Crimeans, but a previous pattern of similar incidents with Nur Devlet and Abdullatif strongly points to a plot originating in Moscow.[151]

The civil war among the Nogays continued unabated. After the death of Urus beg, the title of beg was assumed by his brothers, Ur Mamed (1590–97), and after his death by Tin Mamed (1597–1600). Their succession, and particularly that of their younger brother, Ishterek (1600–1618), was strongly opposed by a group of Nogay nobles led by Urus' son, Jan Araslan. It was a typical struggle for succession between uncle and son—Ishterek, representing the lineage of Tin Ahmed and his sons Ur Mamed and Tin Mamed, and Yan Araslan, representing the lineage of Urus. Moscow clearly chose sides when, in 1600, in the first open display of its direct involvement in Nogay affairs, a decree of Tsar Boris Godunov invested Ishterek with the title of beg. He was declared beg in a traditional Nogay ceremony, which took place in Astrakhan. Later Ishterek admitted that he could have neither survived nor become the beg without Moscow's help.[152] Moscow's continuous support of Tin Ahmed's faction led to a protracted civil war among the Nogays, and there are indications that debilitation of the Nogays was indeed a deliberate government policy.

For the time being, the Nogays could not present any sustained threat to the Muscovite southern frontier. But the Crimeans continued to do so, embarking on two successive large-scale campaigns in 1591 and 1592. Having successfully foiled the former, Moscow was caught completely unprepared by the Crimean invasion in the following year. The Crimeans devastated the regions of Riazan, Kashira, and Tula and brought back numerous captives. Forced to comply with some of the Crimean demands, Moscow gave up its attempt to influence the internal struggle within the Crimea and promised to resume payments. The Crimeans were now ready to join the Ottoman wars against the Habsburgs and turned their raiding activity toward Hungary.[153]

In 1598, Moscow abandoned its traditional defense line along the Oka River and the surrounding frontier towns. Instead, the government relied on the advanced frontier regiments stationed in several southern towns in the form of a triangle pointed toward the south and on a chain of newly built forts: Liven and Voronezh in 1586; Kursk, rebuilt in 1587; Elets, built in 1592; Krom in 1595; Belgorod and Oskol in 1598; Valuiki in 1599; and Tsarev-Borisov in 1600.[154]

By 1600, Muscovy's line of southern defense advanced far from the Oka River, the traditional natural barrier where Russian troops had faced various nomadic armies since the days of the Golden Horde. Moving Muscovite frontier defenses farther into the southern steppe was more than a measure of confidence and testimony to the fact that the city of Moscow was now relatively safe from raids emanating from the steppe. It also meant that the legacy of the Golden Horde was becoming less relevant. The heirs to the Golden Horde, the former city-states of Kazan and Astrakhan, were administratively integrated into the Muscovite state; the Nogays, weakened and subdued, were dependent on Moscow; and the Crimeans were at peace. Having absorbed various entities of the Golden Horde, Moscow also inherited the vast spaces that were to be transformed in Moscow's own image. The formerly uncontrolled frontiers had become the Muscovite borderlands.

[4]

FROM STEPPE FRONTIER TO IMPERIAL BORDERLANDS, 1600–1800

The beginning of the seventeenth century brought a temporary reversal in the traditional roles of Muscovy's relations with its steppe neighbors. Throughout the sixteenth century, as the Muscovite state was becoming increasingly autocratic, the steppe nomadic societies were torn by incessant civil wars. But from 1598 to 1613 it was Muscovy that found itself amid the most severe crisis: the extinction of the royal Riurik dynasty, a disastrous famine, a bloody civil war, and foreign intervention. Still, during this civil war, also known as the Time of Troubles, the importance of the southern frontier did not diminish, and the threat of raids and military campaigns from the south remained ever-present.

Negotiations between the envoys of Tsar Boris Godunov and the Nogay beg, Ishterek, in 1604 registered Moscow's broad concerns over the anti-Muscovite policies of its Islamic neighbors. An oath of allegiance prepared for Ishterek by government officials stipulated that he and his Nogays, known as the Greater Nogay Horde, were not in any way to communicate or assist the Turkish sultan, the Crimean khan, the Persian shah, the Bukhara khan, Tashkent, Urgench, the Kazakh Horde, the shamkhal, or the Circassians. According to the government's plans, the Nogays were to graze their herds near Astrakhan, between the Volga and Terek rivers, and were to be used specifically for campaigns against the hostile Kazy Nogays (the

Lesser Nogay Horde), the renegade bands of the Volga and Don Cossacks, and particularly the Crimea. Ishterek made his commitment conditional on Moscow's help. He explained that he could send a sizable force against the Crimea only if Astrakhan musketeers were sent to protect his uluses, which otherwise would become easy prey to the raids of the Kazy Nogays, Kazakhs, or Kalmyks.[1]

The shert' between Ishterek and Moscow soon became irrelevant, as the civil war in Russia worsened and Astrakhan rose in an open rebellion against Moscow. Both Moscow and the rebels attempted to win over Ishterek, who chose to support neither side and instead moved away to the traditional Nogay pastures between the Volga and the Yaik and launched numerous raids against the Muscovite provinces. Complaints from Moscow officials had no effect, and the Nogays continued to capture and sell large numbers of Russians on the Central Asian markets. The situation changed only in 1613, when an advanced Kalmyk detachment of 4,000 horsemen crossed the Yaik and forced the Nogays to flee southwest across the Volga. There, in the steppe of the North Caucasus, Ishterek found himself under attack from the Kabardinians; in search of safety, he moved farther west, into the vicinity of Azov.[2]

In 1613, the civil war in Russia was near its end, and the Russian tsar Mikhail Romanov ascended the throne. The new royal dynasty and new government did not mean that Moscow was about to change its policies in the south. In 1615 a Russian embassy arrived at Ishterek's camp to have him confirm his oath of allegiance to the new tsar. Upon receiving the presents, Ishterek pledged allegiance, which remained as meaningless as it had been in the past. Shortly thereafter, Ishterek entered into an anti-Muscovite alliance with the Polish king and swore allegiance to the Ottoman sultan. Convinced of the continuing weakness of the Russian government and its inability to defend him against the approaching Kalmyks, Ishterek was looking for protection and rewards elsewhere.

Moscow's informers corroborated reports that Ishterek had received embassies from the Polish king, the Ottoman sultan, and the Persian shah. Sigismund III, the king of Poland, urged the Nogays to continue their raids against Russia in return for his payments, and he even invited Ishterek to move to the pastures along the Dnieper and join the Zaporozhian Cossacks. The Ottomans, who had not quite abandoned their plan to capture Astrakhan, welcomed Ishterek's oath of allegiance to the sultan and offered him military assistance "to expel the Christians from Astrakhan." Finally, the Persian shah was interested in securing the Nogays' help in new confrontations with the Ottomans in the North Caucasus.[3]

With no shortage of allegiances to pledge and alliances to enter into, an old rivalry stood in the way of Ishterek's rising ambition. The Crimean khan, Janibek Giray, was furious that Ishterek had approached the Ottoman Porte, bypassing the Crimea. Portraying himself as the ruler of all the steppe north of the Crimea, Janibek Giray demanded that Ishterek pledge allegiance directly to him, not to the Ottoman sultan. In an open challenge to Janibek Giray, Ishterek responded that both he and the Crimean khan were Ottoman subjects and therefore equal in status.

In the following year, 1616, as part of the Ottoman campaign against Persia, the Crimean army marched through the North Caucasus and devastated the Kabardinian allies of Ishterek. In anticipation of Janibek Giray's campaign against him and in the wake of the resurgent rivalry among the Nogays, Ishterek fled to Astrakhan, pledged allegiance to the tsar yet again, and crossed the Volga looking for safety from the Crimeans and Kazy Nogays. Later that same year, during Muscovite-Ottoman negotiations, both sides agreed that Moscow would restrain its dependents, the Don Cossacks, from raiding the Ottoman borderlands, and the Ottomans would restrain theirs, the Azov Tatars, from raiding Russia. As for Ishterek's Nogays and the Kazy Nogays, the Ottoman government declared them to be independent and outside of the Porte's sphere of influence.[4]

If the Ottomans were prepared to give up their claim over the Nogays, Moscow was not. Fearful of Crimean raids, Ishterek chose to stay on the pastures along the Volga's east bank. From there he maintained lively relations with his neighbors, Shah Abbas of Persia and the Kalmyks, while also demanding and receiving generous payments from Moscow. On one occasion, Ishterek demanded that Moscow pay him the same amount that the Crimean khan and Ottoman sultan were receiving. Surely even increased payments were not about to buy Ishterek's loyalty or peace. In 1618, Ishterek beg and the nureddin Shayterek died in unknown circumstances. Given the Russian government's policy in the region and the grave doubts about Ishterek's loyalty, Moscow's involvement in their death cannot be ruled out. In elaborating their views, the Astrakhan voevodas reported to Moscow that it was in the government's interests to keep the Nogays fighting each other, "for if they reconciled their enmities, then there would be no peace in the sovereign's borderlands."[5]

Indeed, after Ishterek's death the Greater Nogay Horde was plunged into interminable civil war. Attempting to win over the Russian authorities, each Nogay faction denounced the other as disloyal to the Russian sovereign. The Astrakhan voevodas sent musketeers to assist various factions and to ensure that the disputes and rivalries continued, so that "their internal wars result in their complete destruction." In 1619 some 3,000 Nogays arrived in Astrakhan and requested to be settled near the city to join the Yurt and Yedisan Tatars there. Others fled farther east and crossed the Yaik, but they were attacked by the Kalmyks and forced to return to the Volga. The reports from Astrakhan informed Moscow that the Greater Nogay Horde was now split into two parts, and that the Nogay nobles had submitted hostages and pledged an oath of allegiance. The voevodas added that they no longer expected any trouble from the Nogays.[6]

Drained by the continuous internal strife, impoverished, and dependent on Moscow, the Nogays seemed to have been pacified. But peace along Moscow's southern frontier was always an illusive notion. The steppe was already disgorging other numerous invaders, the Kalmyks, who were more warlike and better prepared to control the steppe pastures than their Nogay predecessors. Long accustomed to the incursions of the vanguard Kalmyk detachments, the Russian voevodas and the Nogays now were faced with the ominous movement of this entire people toward the Caspian steppe. In 1632, while most of the Kalmyks were reported to occupy the pastures along the Tobol, Ishim, and Turgay rivers (today north-central Kazakhstan), some uluses were already grazing their herds along the banks of the Emba and the Yaik. A year later the Kalmyks were at the gates of Astrakhan.[7]

The arrival of the Kalmyks in the Caspian steppe was about to reverse the government's short-lived success in stabilizing its southern frontier. The Nogays proved incapable of defending themselves against the more numerous and militant Kalmyks. In 1622, news that the Kalmyks were crossing the Yaik sent the Nogays fleeing to Azov. There, in an alliance that only recently had seemed inconceivable, they joined the Kazy Nogays and launched raids into the Muscovite borderlands. Shortly thereafter, Moscow's renewed promises of protection against the Kalmyks and the Nogays' distrust of the Crimea convinced them to return to the Volga. But the realization of the potential danger of the new developments in the steppe was not lost on the Russian government. The Astrakhan voevodas were sternly instructed to be more accommodating to the Nogays and to discourage enmities between the Nogays and Kalmyks. Otherwise, the government warned, the Nogays would again flee from their more powerful foe, the Kalmyks, and join the Crimea in combined raids against Russia.[8]

But the Kalmyks were already too close. In 1628, in a final and desperate move, the Nogay mirzas appealed to the Russian government for protection. They explained that their people were scattered, destitute, and unable to defend themselves against the Kalmyks, who were taking advantage of the Nogays' discords and weakness. In a highly unusual supplication betraying their utter helplessness, the despondent Nogay nobles asked for protection and pleaded that "they could no longer resolve their disputes in accordance with the Muslim laws" and therefore were ready to submit to the tsar's court and Russian laws to help them reconcile their rivalries. Despite warnings from the Astrakhan governors that a rejection of the Nogays' appeal might lead to their complete destruction, Moscow was not prepared to assume such a responsibility. The government responded that even though the tsar wanted to see them reconciled, he could not grant their present request, for this would mean "oppressing the Nogays and taking away their traditional freedoms."[9] This sudden concern over the Nogays' freedom and independence was only a thinly veiled excuse for Moscow's present inability to assert its own interests in the region. Unwilling to jeopardize its recent peace agreement with the Ottomans, Moscow was not ready to declare the Nogays its subjects, let alone to replace their Muslim laws with Christian ones.

When, in the early 1630s, the Kalmyks moved in force toward the Volga, neither the Nogays nor a small contingent of Astrakhan musketeers sent to aid them could do anything to stop the Kalmyks' advance. Nor could the small Russian garrisons stationed in the forts along the Volga prevent the Nogays from crossing the Volga and moving toward Azov. Before their departure, the Nogay mirzas listed their seemingly endless grievances against the abuses of the Russian authorities. They recalled how Astrakhan officials had forcefully seized and appropriated their horses and sheep, how they had captured and brought to Astrakhan Nogay women and seized Nogay hostages. They reminded the authorities with particular bitterness how the Astrakhan governor, A. N. Trubetskoi, had threatened to turn all the Nogays into peasants, so that they would settle down and farm like the Kazan Tatars.[10]

In 1634, the Nogays of the Greater Horde joined the Nogays of the Lesser Horde near Azov. Together they unleashed a new wave of devastating raids against Russia. Two years later, news of the imminent Kalmyk campaign against the Nogays near Azov forced the Nogays to flee farther across the Don and to seek refuge in the Crimea. But this refuge was only temporary, as the Nogays and their Crimean coreligionists could not overcome their deep-seated and mutual distrust. In the following years, the Nogays, displaced from their traditional pastures by the Kalmyks and in search of safety, periodically would flee back and forth between the Crimea and Russia. In the end, surrounded by hostile powers on all sides—the Crimeans and the Don Cossacks in the west and north, and the Kalmyks and the Kabardinians in the east and south—the Nogays found themselves scattered among neighboring peoples. Some would stay in the Crimea, some near Astrakhan, and some would join the Kalmyks and the peoples of the North Caucasus. The Greater Nogay Horde ceased to exist as a single political or military power. It was now replaced by a new and formidable nomadic confederation, the Kalmyks.[11]

NEW STRATEGIES

The arrival of the Kalmyks in the 1630s had a dramatic impact on the entire southern region. The decades of Moscow's careful strategies of weakening, dividing, and impoverishing the Nogays and its significant expenditures to implement such policies seemed to have been wasted. Together with the Crimeans, the Nogays launched raids against Russia, and in the three years 1632, 1633, and 1637 alone, they captured and brought to the Crimea more than 10,000 Russians. The newly colonized southern region, with its towns and peasants, urgently needed protection. The danger that the Nogays and Crimeans would break through the southern defenses and approach Moscow was not exaggerated. The new situation demanded that Moscow rethink its frontier policies and restructure its southern defenses.

In a change from previous policies, Moscow decided to play the "Cossack card." Instead of restraining the Don Cossacks to avoid provoking the Ottoman Porte, Moscow was now prepared to arm the Cossacks further and encourage their raids. Such raids, however, were to be carefully calibrated, and the Cossacks were instructed to limit their attacks to the Nogays and Crimeans alone, and not to raid Ottoman possessions, Azov and Kaffa in particular.[12]

To be sure, controlling the Cossacks was no easy matter, as the interests of the government and the Cossacks did not always coincide. After all, it was not the impoverished Nogays that the Cossacks were after. Their eyes were set on the wealthy Ottoman and Crimean towns and villages along the Black Sea coast. The only obstacles between the Cossacks and the promise of rich booty and numerous captives were the fortifications of Azov, the Ottoman fortress in the estuary of the Don, which prevented the Cossacks from sailing down the river to the sea.

When in 1636, enticed by the Crimean khan and under constant pressure from the Kalmyks and Cossacks, the Nogays abandoned the area around Azov and crossed the Don on the way to the Crimea, the Don Cossacks quickly moved to lay siege to Azov. In June 1637, Azov was in the hands of the triumphant Cossacks. In the next five years, taken aback by this unexpected and undesired development, Moscow was presented with an unpalatable dilemma: to support the Cossacks and thus enter war with the Ottoman Empire, or to avoid war by having the Cossacks abandon the fortress. After much hesitation and deliberation, the government chose avoidance over confrontation.

The Cossacks continued to be an important element in the government's strategies along the Muscovite southern frontier, where the line between defensive and offensive measures was often blurred. Cossack raids penetrated deep across the frontier, pillaging caravans traversing the steppe, attacking hostile nomadic raiding parties, or preying upon the villages and towns in the North Caucasus and along the Crimean and Ottoman coasts. Moscow's direct support of the Cossacks and the effectiveness of their naval raids were all but acknowledged by the Crimean envoys in the 1660s, who stipulated that one of the conditions for peace was Moscow's willingness to deny Cossack boats access to the Black and Azov seas.[13]

But the Cossacks' degree of independence from Moscow and the history of their unruliness and participation in popular revolts made the government suspicious of their true intentions—and, as the Azov affair proved, not unreasonably so. Use of the Cossacks along the frontier had to be supplemented by a more reliable strategy. In 1635, the government undertook a new and bold initiative: it began the construction of fortification lines in the south. The length of time taken for the construction, the expenditures on these extensive fortification networks, and the utilization of human and natural resources made the project Russia's single most ambitious and important strategic undertaking in the seventeenth century. It was to become Moscow's own Great Wall to fend off the "infidels" from the southern steppe.

Constructing a fortification line in the southern region was not an entirely new idea. Such fortification lines were already known in tenth-century Kievan Rus, and more recently, in the middle of the sixteenth century, they had been constructed just south of the Oka River. By the 1630s, numerous forts and towns emerged far south of Moscow. Still, these proliferating vanguard military outposts had to be supplied from the central regions of Russia because agriculture remained a dangerous undertaking on the frontier. It was paramount to provide further security if peasant colonization of the region was to take place. The fortification lines were to serve exactly that purpose, becoming in time both the primary means of Moscow's defense against predations and an effective tool of Russia's territorial expansion.

Realizing that stability on the southern frontier was inseparable from successful colonization and settlement of the region, the government assumed complete control of the process. Despite complaints from the landlords of the central regions about their fugitive peasants who had found refuge in the frontier area, the government forbade its frontier commanders and governors to return the runaways. Instead, they were enlisted as soldiers and dragoons. In 1637 the government issued a decree concerning so-called forbidden towns. This decree banned any acquisition of land in and around twelve frontier towns by anyone outside the region. By effectively encouraging small landholdings, Moscow intended to turn the newly arrived population into a military frontier force capable of living off the land, granted by the government. Throughout the seventeenth century, defending and populating the southern frontier remained the principal interest of the government, and it continued to reject petitions from the landlords to have their runaways returned.[14]

In the decade between 1635 and 1646, Moscow moved its frontier defenses much farther south, connecting, in one uninterrupted defense line, natural obstacles, such as rivers and swamps, with manmade fortifications: several rows of moats, felled trees, and palisades studded with advance warning towers and forts armed with cannon. The first such fortification line (*zaseka* or *zasechnaia cherta*), stretching for more than 800 kilometers from the Akhtyrka River in the west to Tambov in the east, became known as the Belgorod line. The Greater Regiment, which was stationed in Mtsensk in 1600, was relocated farther south to Belgorod in 1640. It took the government another decade to extend the fortification line farther east, from Tambov to Simbirsk on the Volga. By the mid-seventeenth century, both the colonists arriving in the southern regions of Russia and the residents of the Kazan province found themselves in relative safety behind the Belgorod and Simbirsk fortification lines.[15]

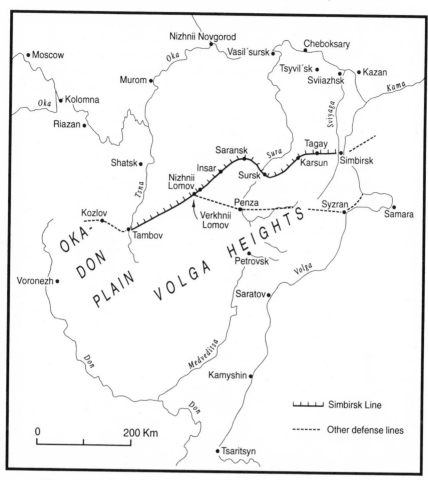

MAP 4. Muscovite defenses in the mid-seventeenth century. The
Simbirsk fortification line was built in the 1640s and 1650s and linked up
with the Belgorod fortification line constructed a decade earlier.

THE KALMYKS

The reshuffling of regional political alliances, the increasing raiding activity of the Crimeans and Nogays, and Moscow's new strategy of securing the unstable southern frontier were all, in no small measure, caused by the new wave of nomads arriving from the Inner Asian steppe, the Kalmyks. In contrast to the current residents of the region, the Kalmyks were a distinctly foreign group—Tibetan Buddhists—and neither Christians nor Muslims could find any immediate affinity with the newcomers.

Moscow was not alone in its concern about the Kalmyks' presence in the region. The arrival of the newcomers disrupted the traditional trade routes connecting Russia with the markets of Central Asia and Persia; in fact, the first appeals to form an alliance against the Kalmyks came to Moscow from the rulers of Bukhara, Khiva, and Balkh. No less concerned were the Crimean khan and the Kabardinian chiefs of the North Caucasus. For a short while, Moscow and the Crimea were united by the common threat. The entire region had to brace itself to face the dangerous outsiders.

On their arrival in the lower Volga area in the 1620s, the Kalmyks left behind a wide swath of destruction. They burned and looted towns and villages in southern Siberia and the Ufa and Saratov regions and seized many Nogay uluses. Moscow dispatched reinforcements to Astrakhan and other Volga towns and instructed its governor in Astrakhan, A. N. Trubetskoi, to inform the Kalmyks that if they did not cease pillaging and leave the area, the tsar would order his troops against them. The Kalmyk tayishis chose to bypass Astrakhan and instead pursued those Nogays who had fled to the pastures along the Kuban and Terek rivers.[16]

After having swept effortlessly across the steppe from Inner Asia to the Caspian Sea, the Kalmyks suffered their first major defeat in the mountains of the North Caucasus. In 1644 a large Kalmyk contingent was trapped in a mountain pass and decimated by a group of Kabardinians, Nogays, and Crimean Tatars armed with muskets. Their chief tayishi, Kho-Urlük, his two sons, and a grandson were killed in the battle. Other Kalmyks were run to the ground by the Kabardinians and Nogays with assistance from the Tersk and Astrakhan garrisons. Both the Crimea and Moscow achieved their goals for the time being, and the Kalmyks were pushed back east of the Yaik River.[17]

However, the reprieve was a temporary one. Under pressure from their rivals in Jungaria, the Kalmyks had little choice but to move farther west. In 1648 they resumed their campaigns against the Nogays and subjected the residents of the Kazan and Ufa districts to increasing raids. A Russian envoy, Ivan Onuchin, was sent from Ufa to convince the new chief tayishi, Daichin, to vacate the lands and to live in peace with the sovereign's subjects in accordance with the Kalmyks' oath of allegiance to the tsar. Daichin's response was blunt. He accused the Russian envoy of being a liar because the Kalmyks had never lived in submission to anyone and had always been independent. As far as the lands were concerned, Russians had nothing to do with it. The Kalmyks had seized these lands and rivers from the Nogays; why should they not use them for pastures?[18]

In 1651, after Ivan Onuchin's departure, Daichin sent his own envoy to Astrakhan. In a clear snub to the Russian monarch, Daichin referred to him briefly as "the grand sovereign, the white tsar," while assuming more sonorous titles for himself: "the grand sovereign, Daichin khan, the son of Urlük khan, the ruler of Kalmyks and Tatars, and the sovereign of many other peoples." In a confident and assertive tone, Daichin demanded that the Russians return the remains of his father and brothers and release his people from captivity in Astrakhan.[19]

Later that same year, Daichin's brother, Louzang tayishi, with a force of 10,000 Kalmyks, routed the Crimean army and captured 40,000 horses. To prevent further damage, the Crimean khan urgently evacuated the Nogay uluses to the interior of the Crimean peninsula behind the safety of the Perekop fortifications and canceled his campaign against Wallachia. Moscow officials were beginning to realize that the Kalmyks were not going to leave, and that rather than waging war against them it was more expedient to encourage their raiding activity against the Crimea and its Nogay allies. The new Russian envoys brought the remains of Kho-Urlük and other tayishis who had perished in Kabarda in 1644, and even though Daichin rebuffed repeated Russian demands, which included signing an oath of allegiance, submitting hostages, and leaving the Volga area, some understanding of a military alliance had been reached.[20]

The increased Kalmyk raids against the Nogays and the Crimea were frequently coordinated with the Don Cossacks. The Crimean khan accused Moscow of violating their peace treaty and threatened to attack the Russian lands unless the tsar stopped using the Kalmyks against the Crimea. In 1654, after the Russian government annexed parts of Ukraine, Moscow no longer needed to encourage Kalmyk raids against the Crimea in secret. Rival alliances were formed when Poland and the Crimea joined forces against Russia. The Kalmyks were to become Moscow's crucial ally against the Crimea.

The First Written Treaties

In February 1655, the Kalmyk tayishis swore allegiance to be the tsar's faithful subjects and confirmed it by affixing their signatures to a shert'. Even though the usual attributes of subject status—submission of hostages and payment of taxes or tribute—were not mentioned, the treaty, written in Russian, was unmistakably phrased as an oath of a subject to a suzerain. At least, such was Moscow's intention, for it was inconceivable for the Russian tsar to relate to the steppe chiefs in any other way.

Reality, however, was quite different. The clauses of this first written treaty between Moscow and the Kalmyks addressed the issues of the return of Russian prisoners, the Kalmyks' participation in Moscow's military campaigns, and cessation of their raids against other peoples, subjects of Russia. Even though the government's commitments to the Kalmyks seemed to be absent from the treaty, a series of separate decrees, which immediately followed, testified to the extent of the government's concessions. Moscow dropped its objections to the Kalmyks' use of the pastures along the Volga and Akhtuba rivers, ordered its local governors and the Bashkirs to cease hostilities, and allowed the Kalmyks to trade in nearby towns. Obviously, in whatever servile form the Russian officials had chosen to solicit certain commitments from the Kalmyks, in reality both sides, Moscow and Kalmyks, entered into an alliance with an implicit understanding of their mutual obligations to maintain peace, trade, and military cooperation. And this was exactly how the Kalmyks viewed it.

Such treaties were easier signed than implemented. Despite its promises, Moscow was not always capable of restraining its own subjects, who continued to raid the Kalmyks. The Kalmyks then complained that they could not keep their promises and participate in the military campaigns because they feared attacks from the Bashkirs or Don Cossacks. Sometimes such arguments were genuine; sometimes they were merely a convenient excuse. In either case, Moscow was expected to continue providing payments, and when they were delayed or withdrawn, others were ready to step in to lobby among the Kalmyks. Thus, in 1657, in response to the promise of handsome payments from the Crimea, the Kalmyks agreed to attack the Kazan and Ufa provinces, and the joyful Crimean khan, Muhammed Giray IV, announced to Moscow that, with God's help, the Kalmyks had become his subjects.

The Kalmyks, to be sure, were no more subjects of the Crimea than of Russia. They were simply maximizing their bargaining power by extracting increasingly advantageous terms of military cooperation from each side. This was clearly understood in Moscow, and the government made a higher bid for the Kalmyks' loyalty. In 1657, Moscow urgently dispatched its envoys to the Kalmyks to have them sign another shert'. This time, in addition to agreeing to the Kalmyks' demands for more extensive pastures and duty-free trade in Russian towns, the envoys brought presents and promised annuities to the tayishis. Daichin received a sable coat, a fur hat, and 200 rubles. Other tayishis received presents and annuities of smaller value.

But higher rewards were also accompanied by increasing demands from Moscow contained in several new clauses of the shert'. One specifically obliged the Kalmyks not to serve the interests of either the Ottoman sultan or the Crimean khan; another provided for several Kalmyk hostages to be placed in Astrakhan. Even though these hostages were to reside in special quarters and be given large allowances, agreeing to this demand certainly represented a change from Daichin's previous assertions of complete independence. It seemed that the temptation of presents and payments had proved irresistible, and a few minor concessions worth the trouble.

The cycle of growing expectations continued on both sides. In 1660, the government sent the diak I. S. Gorokhov to secure the Kalmyks' participation in the forthcoming military campaign. Shortly before the departure of the embassy, Moscow prudently sent the Kalmyks two years' worth of annuities, and the diak personally brought presents worth more than 1,000 rubles. Yet Daichin was unhappy, complaining that his annuity was smaller than the one

Moscow paid to the Crimean khan. In the end, some cajoling and promises of further payments secured his cooperation. Another treaty was signed. One of its new clauses abrogated the Kalmyks' right to maintain independent contacts with the Crimea. They were to arrest and turn over to Moscow anyone advocating the Crimean cause among the Kalmyks; and instead of the traditional practice of ransom, they were to sell captured Crimeans and their herds in Russian towns. Step by step, the Kalmyks were embarking on a slippery road that would inevitably lead to their growing dependence on Moscow.

Moscow's temporary success in harnessing the power of the Kalmyks and redirecting it away from its frontiers in the early 1660s had long-term consequences for the entire region. Just as the threat of nomadic invasions had compelled Moscow to embark upon the construction of the fortification lines in the south, the Crimeans began to fortify their northern frontiers against increasingly damaging predations from the Zaporozhian and Don Cossacks and Kalmyks. Between 1661 and 1665, the Crimeans undertook the construction of a rampart connecting their newly built forts along the Dnieper and Don rivers with the Azov Sea, thus protecting the Nogays' pastures north of the Crimean peninsula. At the same time, the khan ordered the mobilization of the entire population of the Crimea to build a stone wall along the old rampart of Perekop to safeguard the Crimea proper from the Kalmyks. The relative success of the Crimean defense efforts was evident from the Don Cossacks' inability to use their traditional raiding routes along the Don, instead switching the direction of their raids first toward Persia and then against Russia in 1669–71. Such, indeed, were the origins and circumstances of the Stepan Razin Uprising.[21]

In 1664, Moscow sent a new chief tayishi, Puntsuk, a gilded silver mace, a white banner, and valuable presents. The political meaning of this gesture was unmistakable. The Russian government sought to assert its prerogative of confirming and, in time, appointing the Kalmyk chief. By vesting Puntsuk with symbols of authority, Moscow was claiming, in ever more transparent terms, that the Kalmyks had become its subjects and were now considered a part of Russia's irregular military forces, similar to the Zaporozhian and Don Cossacks. Of course, Moscow still lacked any effective means of controlling either the Cossacks or the Kalmyks, and the loyalty of both peoples remained largely dependent on the short-term military interests of their leaders and their insatiable appetite for presents and payments. When the situation in the region changed and the flow of presents dried up, neither written treaties nor symbols of authority were sufficient to keep the Kalmyks on the Russian side.[22]

After Puntsuk's death in 1669, his eldest son, Ayuki, initially continued his father's policies of close cooperation with Moscow. He was able to consolidate his position as the chief tayishi, in no small degree thanks to Moscow's support. But such support also had a price, and the government's demands and expectations increased accordingly. The number of restrictions and obligations imposed on the Kalmyks grew to thirteen clauses in a new treaty that the government presented to Ayuki. The Kalmyks, of course, had to refrain from doing any damage to the sovereign's towns and his subjects. Trade was limited to two cities—Astrakhan and Moscow.

One new clause was indicative of a new and troublesome issue. In response to the growing number of Kalmyk fugitives to Russian towns, the authorities promised to return only those fugitives who did not convert to Christianity. Since most of the time such fugitives were either forcibly converted by the Russians or opted to convert in order to stay among the Russians, few such fugitives found their way back. In addition to the Crimea, contacts with which had already been prohibited in the previous treaty, the new treaty extended the list of banned diplomatic relations to the Ottoman sultan, the Persian shah, Azov, and various peoples of Daghestan. The Kalmyks were thus effectively barred from any relations with their neighbors.

The expectations on both sides continued to differ. Moscow's attempts to turn the Kalmyks into its subjects and an irregular military force were unsuccessful, and the Kalmyks' participation in Russia's military campaigns was insignificant. In response to Moscow's complaints, the tayishis responded that the government's annuities were insufficient and the presents irregular. Ayuki continued lively relations with the Crimea and peoples of the North Caucasus, sent envoys to the Ottoman and Persian courts, and traded actively with the Crimea and Azov. The promises made in the treaties remained committed to paper alone.

In Moscow the Kalmyks were seen as traitors who had violated their oath of allegiance signed and sealed by the written treaties. The Russian government decided to resort to different policies, encouraging the Don Cossacks' raids against the Kalmyks and urging the Nogays to leave the Kalmyks and return to the vicinity of Astrakhan. Ayuki's reaction was swift: he abandoned his neutrality in the Russo-Crimean conflict and launched an outright war against Russia. In the early 1680s, a large army of Kalmyks ravaged the Kazan and Ufa provinces, and small-scale raiding activity along the frontier surged.

With the Russian conquest of Azov in 1696 came a change in Ayuki's anti-Russian policies. While Ayuki realized that, for the time being, his fortunes lay with Russia, Moscow came to the conclusion that it would gain more by mollifying the Kalmyks than by confronting them. In July 1697, Ayuki and a high-ranking Russian envoy, the boyar Prince B. A. Golitsyn, signed a treaty that was strikingly different from the previous ones. This time it was the Russian side that undertook commitments to assist the Kalmyks, to put a stop to the Bashkir and Cossack raids, not to dictate the boundaries of the Kalmyks' pastures, and neither to give refuge to nor to convert runaway Kalmyks.[23]

138

In addressing the Kalmyks' grievances and putting in writing its own obligations, the government was ready to admit that ensuring the cooperation of the Kalmyks and achieving a modicum of peace along the frontier required more than emphasizing the Kalmyks' submissive status and their obligations. Rather, it required a clearly articulated recognition that such a relationship was a two-way street with mutual obligations and commitments. The Kalmyks needed Russian help to recover the Nogays, who had recently fled to the Kuban, and to deal with the increasing raids from the Kazakhs and Karakalpaks in the east. For Moscow, the cooperation of the Kalmyks was crucial in securing its control of recently conquered Azov and checking the Nogay and Crimean raids in the Volga and Don steppe. For the moment, the alliance between the two seemed like a perfect deal.

Control and Colonization

With the conquest of Azov and Russia's continuous expansion in the early eighteenth century, Russia's southern frontier was rapidly approaching the Ottoman northern frontier in the Caucasus and the Crimea. Both sides could claim only a tenuous control of the frontier region that separated the two empires and acknowledged as much in the peace treaty signed between St. Petersburg and Istanbul in 1711. One of the clauses stipulated that neither Kalmyk predations against the Crimeans, Nogays, and Circassians across the frontier nor the latter groups' retaliatory raids against the Kalmyks should be construed by either side as a violation of the treaty. While maintaining that these respective peoples were their subjects, both Moscow and Istanbul implicitly conceded their limited control and their inability to impose law and order in the frontier region.[24]

Throughout the first two decades of the eighteenth century, the Kalmyks evolved into a major military power in the area, widely courted by the neighboring competing powers, Russia and the Ottoman Porte, and even by more distant rulers in Qing China and Tibet. In 1718, the newly appointed governor of the newly designated Astrakhan province was determined to put an end to what he saw as the Kalmyks' "frivolous behavior." The governor, Artemii Volynskii, considered the Kalmyks to be "his children," and as such they had to be disciplined and their submission enforced through Russian laws and regulations.

From the beginning, Volynskii proved to be an overzealous and foolhardy Russian administrator. In the spring of 1719, after realizing that the aging Ayuki khan was losing authority among the Kalmyks to his more energetic and popular son, Chakdorjab, whose pro-Russian orientation could not be taken for granted, Volynskii made this recommendation to St. Petersburg: "In my opinion, it would have been very useful to have him [Chakdorjab] murdered or poisoned secretly by some of his people, but in the meantime to encourage through various factions a strife between him, his father, and other tayishis."[25] Whether Volynskii's enthusiasm for physically eliminating an unsuitable candidate was shared in the capital is not known, but three years later, in 1722, Chakdorjab was found dead, allegedly from alcoholic intoxication.

The extremes of his personality notwithstanding, Volynskii's arrival in Astrakhan marked a new course in the government's policies in the region. Russia's strategic, economic, political, and military dominance was indeed overwhelming, and St. Petersburg was prepared to use it in order to transform the previous and largely rhetorical claims to the Kalmyks' status as Russian subjects into political reality.

In 1718 the government completed construction of the Tsaritsyn fortification line, which stretched from the Volga to the Don and effectively locked the Kalmyks within distinctly delineated boundaries. To the east was the Volga, with the pastures on its eastern bank increasingly off limits to Kalmyks fearful of Kazakh raids. In the west there were expanding Cossack settlements along the Don, and in the south the Nogays dominated the steppe of the North Caucasus. Now the traditional summer pastures in the north were also cut off by the Russian troops stationed along the Tsaritsyn line, and the Kalmyks' access to these pastures was controlled entirely by the Russian authorities.[26]

The Russian government was fully aware of the Kalmyks' predicament and was intent on taking full advantage of the new circumstances. Upon the death of Ayuki khan in 1724, the government resolved to dispense with any niceties and to interfere directly in Kalmyk affairs. The title of khan was to be abolished. Instead, the ruler of the Kalmyks was to be appointed by St. Petersburg at the rank of a viceroy. Ignoring several legitimate successors to Ayuki and not bothering to consult the Kalmyks, the government chose to appoint its loyalist, Dorji-Nazar tayishi.

The unceremonious attempt by the Russian authorities to impose their will on the Kalmyks backfired when Dorji-Nazar refused to become the viceroy. He argued that he would not be accepted by other tayishis as a Kalmyk ruler, and his rivals would assassinate him. Even the promise of sending Russian troops for his protection failed to change his mind. Tensions were further exacerbated by various rumors. Some foretold impending Crimean raids against the Kalmyks, who, hemmed in by Russian forts and settlements, would be unable to escape. Others warned that the Russians were bent on converting all the Kalmyks to Christianity, and that troops and priests already had been dispatched for that purpose. In this explosive situation, some Kalmyk tayishis seriously considered departing for Jungaria, while others suggested seeking refuge in the Crimea. The crisis was only temporarily averted when the Russian government, worried lest the Kalmyks join the Crimeans, the Nogays, and the Kazakhs in an anti-Russian alliance, agreed on a compromise candidate. In September 1724, Cheren-Donduk was proclaimed the Kalmyk viceroy.[27]

Russia's heavy-handed management of the crisis in 1724 and subsequent events showed that as long as the region remained a porous frontier zone, direct rule over the Kalmyks would remain impossible. The prospect of the Kalmyks' abrupt departure, or even worse, their anti-Russian alliance with the Crimeans or Kazakhs, demanded more cautious and conciliatory approaches from St. Petersburg. But when in 1732 the government once again used a heavy hand and resorted to military means in eliminating the challenge to its protégé, Cheren-Donduk, by his more popular nephew, Donduk-Ombo, the latter moved away to the Kuban region with a large number of Kalmyks. The Russian troops sent to intercept them were rendered useless by poor intelligence, lack of mobility, and the harsh conditions of the steppe. Three years later, the Russian government was prepared to meet Donduk-Ombo's demands, and he triumphantly returned to the Volga steppe to become the next Kalmyk khan.[28]

Still, concessions by the Russian authorities were only temporary, and St. Petersburg's ability to impose direct rule over the Kalmyks was only a matter of time. Nothing could change the fundamental fact that the Russian presence in the region was irreversible. German agricultural settlements, Don Cossack villages, and Volga fishing hamlets continued to spill over into the Kalmyks' pasturelands. Control over trade was entirely in the hands of the Russian administration, which demanded that merchants register with the Russian military authorities on their way to and from the Kalmyk uluses.[29] Fortification lines, effectively marking the borders of the Russian Empire, advanced farther south. In 1762, a newly completed Mozdok fortification line undergirded the southern border of the Russian Empire along the Terek River and put a limit on Kalmyk migrations south. Once again, the Kalmyk tayishis considered plans for leaving the Caspian steppe.

In a half-century or so, since the first attempts by the Russian government to assert its direct control over the Kalmyks in the 1720s, Kalmyk society had changed dramatically. The position of khan was significantly weakened, and the Kalmyk elites were bitterly divided into warring factions of those advocating a pro-Russian course and those opposed to it. The Russian government's deliberate policy of supporting its Kalmyk loyalists and playing off factions against each other could result only in protracted and frequent conflicts among the Kalmyks.

The Final Rebellion: Exodus

Despite the civil wars and differences of opinion, the Kalmyk tayishis were united on two issues, which were of equal importance to all of them: the loss of people and the loss of herds. Russian control of shrinking pasturelands had led to a significant reduction in the Kalmyks' herds. As a result, impoverished Kalmyks were fleeing in ever larger numbers to look for employment in Russian towns and fisheries. Caught in this vicious cycle of impoverishment and fearing that the government intended to turn them into farmers and make them Christians, the Kalmyks resolved to take a desperate step and to leave for Jungaria.

Catherine II's policies of settling and civilizing the region provided the final straw for the Kalmyks' decision. Arrogant and dismissive of her subordinates, Catherine demanded that the local officials ignore the Kalmyks' complaints and continue to encourage colonization of the region. Against the advice of the governor of Astrakhan and the regional commanders, she insisted that the Kalmyks provide an army of 20,000 cavalry for a war with the Ottoman Empire. When regional officials warned of the Kalmyks' possible departure, Catherine II snubbed them, accusing them of ignorance and an inability to read maps or to think rationally.

In 1770, Count Nikita Panin carefully considered the protestations of the Kalmyk viceroy, Ubashi, over Russia's onerous demands on the Kalmyks but chose to reject them. Having exhausted their last appeal, the Kalmyks resolved to leave Russian territory. In January 1771 the majority of the Kalmyks, about 31,000 households, or more than 150,000 people, started their long trek to Jungaria. Even then, the Russian empress was convinced that the Kalmyks intended only to displace the Kazakhs and to stay on the pastures east of the Yaik River. In a lofty decree of January 21, 1771, she instructed Nuraly khan of the Kazakh Lesser Horde to exhibit his loyal service by attacking the Kalmyks and forcing them to return.

By early March, new reports made it clear that the Kalmyks had been approached earlier by the Chinese emperor, and that they indeed intended to leave the territory of the Russian Empire for Jungaria. Avoiding pursuit by the Russian military, the Kalmyks with their herds moved swiftly through the steppe, but predations from the Kazakhs and a march through the ice- and snow-covered Caspian steppe and later the waterless steppe of Lake Balkhash exacted a heavy toll. Their herds perished or were captured by the Kazakhs, and less than one-third of the people were able to reach the frontier of Qing China. Within the next few decades, those who had left the Russian Empire in hope of finding freedom in Jungaria found themselves incorporated into the Qing military system.[30]

But not all Kalmyks departed for Jungaria. Some remained on the Volga's west bank, unable or unwilling to join the departing majority, while others were apprehended during their flight and were forced to return. All in all, about 11,000 households remained on the Volga. In late November 1771, after receiving intelligence reports that the remaining Kalmyks also intended to depart from the Volga, the Astrakhan governor, N. A. Beketov, took measures to avoid any surprises. He forbade the Kalmyks to cross the

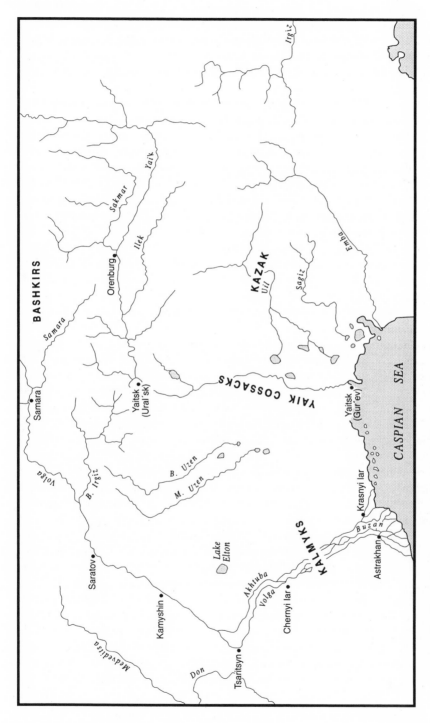

MAP 5.   The North Caspian steppe in the first half of the eighteenth century.

Volga and rewarded the tayishis by distributing among them about 5,000 Kalmyk households that had belonged to the departed Kalmyk viceroy, Ubashi. The largest share, 2,000 households, was awarded to a Kalmyk convert, Prince Aleksei Dondukov.[31]

The government saw in Prince Dondukov an ideal candidate to promote Russian interests. He represented that new breed of native colonial administrators which the government tried to cultivate in the frontier regions of the empire. The son of the late Kalmyk khan, Donduk-Ombo, he was taken as a child to St. Petersburg and converted to Christianity together with his mother and siblings in 1744. He grew up in Russia, but in the early 1760s he returned to the steppe to inherit his father's ulus and to reside under Russian protection at Fort Enotaevsk on the Volga.

In May 1771, Count Panin advised the Astrakhan governor to appoint Dondukov chief supervisor over the other tayishis "because by race [or by birth—*po prirode*] he is a Kalmyk tayishi, but in his loyalty and faith he is like us."[32] Of course, what was seen as an assurance of loyalty to the local Russian administration was a source of anxiety and suspicion to the Kalmyks. The fact that Dondukov was an Orthodox Christian brought back fears of forced conversion, and with them protests against his appointment.

In the meantime, the governor, Beketov, continued to tighten administrative control over the Kalmyks. He dismissed Colonel A. Kishenskii, who resided among the Kalmyks as a liaison officer between the government and the tayishis and whose early warnings about the Kalmyks' desperate situation had gone unheeded. In a more significant development, all matters regarding Kalmyks were to be under the jurisdiction of the newly formed Kalmyk Expedition attached to the Astrakhan administration.[33]

An imperial decree of October 19, 1771, abolished the titles of Kalmyk khan and viceroy, thus dismantling the last vestiges of Kalmyk independence and putting an end to the idea of a single Kalmyk political entity under a single ruler. In the wake of the Kalmyks' departure from the Russian borderlands, the government was finally determined to place the Kalmyks under the authority of the Russian administration and submit them to Russian laws.

Accordingly, each tayishi was to become independent from the others, but all of them were to be subordinate to the Astrakhan governor. Primogeniture was to replace the traditional division of the ulus between heirs. Those without a legitimate heir would forfeit their ulus to the state treasury. The authorities made clear their determination to enforce the law when ten years later Prince Aleksei Dondukov died without an heir. The government chose to compensate his brother, Iona, with 3,000 serfs in the Mogilev province and took both uluses of the Dondukovs into the state treasury. In the nineteenth century, this particular regulation opened the way for numerous and fierce disputes with the government over the tayishis' rights to their uluses.

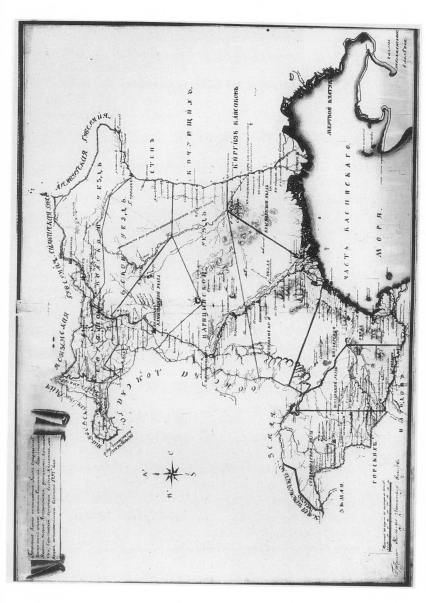

MAP 6.   The Astrakhan province in 1797, including the districts of the North Caucasus after the administrative restructuring of several provinces of the Russian empire in 1796. Courtesy of the Central State Archive of the Military History of Russia, Moscow.

In further curtailment of the Kalmyks' rights, the Kalmyk institution of *zargo*, a traditional court of law and advisory council to a khan, was to be attached to the Kalmyk Expedition in Astrakhan, with no authority other than to help the governor adjudicate disputes among the Kalmyks. In other matters the Kalmyks were to be judged by the laws of the Russian Empire. No longer shy about asserting its direct control over the Kalmyks, the government detained those who, it believed, opposed Russian interests. In 1772 three tayishis, including a sixteen-year-old, were deemed disloyal, arrested, and dispatched to St. Petersburg. Within two years, all of them had died.[34]

At the same time, a series of governmental decrees aimed at encouraging rapid settlement of the vast territories in the south of the empire. As early as 1765, one such decree made the state lands in the region available to the gentry, on the condition that they would bring their peasants to settle and farm there. The Kalmyks' departure in 1771 only accelerated colonization of the region, and gentry willing to relocate their peasants from central Russia received land grants along the Mozdok fortification line. By 1796, huge tracts of land along the Mozdok line and the Volga ended up in private hands. In addition, the government sent 11,000 state peasants to the region without designating any specific lands for them.[35]

In the following years, the Kalmyks found themselves administered by different government agencies. At various times, for reasons of political expediency, the government chose to empower the zargo and to restore the title of viceroy, but at all times the Kalmyks were to be closely watched by a specially appointed Russian chief supervisor (*glavnyi pristav*). Zargo and the offices of the Kalmyk Expedition, Kalmyk Chancellery (*kantseliariia*), and Kalmyk Administration (*pravlenie*), as well as the positions of viceroy and chief supervisor, were all intermittently created, abolished, and restored, only to be abolished again shortly thereafter.[36]

This seemingly endless litany of institutions and positions was clear testimony to the government's continuous search for an effective means to place the Kalmyks within the Russian administrative structure. In 1825, in an unmistakable sign of the evolution of the Kalmyks' status within the empire, supervision of Kalmyk matters was transferred from the Ministry of Foreign Affairs to that of the Interior. While integration of the Kalmyks into the political and economic structures of the empire was virtually complete by 1800, their incorporation into imperial administrative and legal institutions continued. By this time it was no longer avoidable.

THE KAZAKHS

If Russia's relations with the steppe were dominated by the Nogays in the sixteenth century and the Kalmyks in the seventeenth, the Kazakhs took center stage in the eighteenth century. Although the first news of the Kazakh

Horde and its victories over the Kalmyks and Tashkent reached Moscow in the 1520s and 1530s (see chapter 2), it was not until two hundred years later that the expanding Russian Empire came into direct and systematic contact with the Kazakhs. Previously the Kazakhs had simply been too far away from the Russian frontier, and only occasional embassies were exchanged.

The first diplomatic contacts between Moscow and the Kazakhs were recorded in the 1570s and 1580s. It was Moscow's spectacular conquests of Kazan and Astrakhan, and particularly its rapid expansion into Siberia, that attracted the Kazakhs' attention. As always, such contacts were prompted by the search for a military alliance, and the Kazakhs offered their help to Moscow if it stopped supporting their rivals, the Nogays, and instead aided them in conquering the Central Asian khanates. Moscow's initial interest in their offer was quickly dampened when the Nogays threatened to ally with the Crimea if the Muscovite government seriously considered the Kazakhs' proposal.[37]

Contacts resumed in 1594, when the Kazakh khan (*tsar*), Tevekkel (1586–98), dispatched his envoy to Moscow with an offer of a military alliance. In the usual bidding pitch, the envoy first described the greatness of Tevekkel khan, who ruled both the Kazakhs and the Kalmyks, and who, although presently at peace with the Nogays and the Bukhara khan, was prepared to turn against them if the Muscovite tsar rewarded him appropriately. The envoy suggested that the Kazakhs could conquer Bukhara with no outside help if Moscow supplied them with firearms.[38]

Moscow's plans, however, were somewhat different. Little concerned with the Nogays, who were embroiled in squabbles of their own, and even less concerned with Bukhara, Moscow promised "to place Tevekkel under the tsar's exalted arm, to bestow on him a generous stipend," and to provide him with military aid on one condition. The Kazakhs were "to capture and deliver Kuchum khan of Siberia to his majesty, the tsar's threshold, as a sign of their loyalty and sincere service." Kuchum, who for more than a decade continued to elude the Muscovites and resist their further expansion in southern Siberia, was finally hunted down in 1598. He was able to escape one last time to the Nogays, where he died under unknown circumstances.[39]

Throughout the seventeenth century, the Kazakhs' relations with Muscovy were limited to a few encounters with the provincial governors in Siberia. Only distant echoes of the Kazakhs' falling political fortunes occasionally reached Moscow. The Kazakhs' temporary decline was due, in part, to the establishment of the Ashtarkhanid dynasty in Bukhara (1599–1753) and its aggressive policies in the region in the early seventeenth century. In 1616, after a protracted war with the khan of Bukhara, Imam-Kuli (1611–45), the Kazakhs were forced to retreat and abandoned Tashkent.[40]

But even more significant was the rise of the Kalmyk and Oirat nomadic confederations to the north and northeast of the Kazakhs. As early as 1616, the Greater Kazakh and Kirgiz Hordes submitted to the authority of the Oirats, but the wars between the two continued unabated throughout the seventeenth century, almost invariably ending in resounding victories for the Oirats. The two Oirat envoys sent to the Irkutsk governor, L. K. Kislianskii, in 1691 offered a curious explanation for this continuous hostility between the two steppe peoples. They related that the Oirat khan, Galdan Boshoktu (1671–97), had invited the Kazakhs to join him and to accept the authority of the Lama rather than the Prophet Muhammad. When they refused, Galdan Boshoktu razed many of their towns and seized numerous Kazakh captives. It is entirely possible that among other, more traditional reasons for hostilities in the steppe, the Oirat ruler and Tibetan Lama had indeed contemplated turning the Muslim Kazakhs into Tibetan Buddhists.

Upon further inquiry by the Russian officials, the envoys provided detailed information about the Kazakhs. They controlled eleven towns: Turkistan (Yasy), Sayram, Menket, Kharasman, Chimyget, Tekek, Baban Elgan, Kharamurol, Tashkent, Chinak, and one more that the envoys could not recall by name. The Kazakh towns were built of wood and bricks, surrounded by a wall but not defended with cannon. The towns had grand mosques, courts, houses, and plentiful gardens, while crops and numerous herds were raised outside of the towns. The Oirats had destroyed most of the towns, and only Turkistan continued to be the residence of the Kazakh khan, Tauke (Tevke) (1680–1716), who was capable of assembling more than 10,000 Kazakh troops armed with bows and arrows and small firearms.[41]

The Russian government's interest in the Kazakhs increased as Russian forts and garrisons in Siberia moved farther south and came within reach of Kazakh raids. Amid reports of increasing clashes between Russians and Kazakhs in the 1690s, Russian officials were instructed to keep a close eye on both the Kazakhs and Oirats, so that neither could pose a threat to Russian expansion in Siberia. In fact, Moscow's most important concern was its lucrative trade with Bukhara. The arrival of the Kalmyks in the Caspian steppe cut off the traditional caravan routes connecting Bukhara with Astrakhan and Kazan. Increasingly, trade with Bukhara was maintained through the southern Siberian towns of Tobolsk and Tara, and the Kazakhs' cooperation was critical if the caravans were to pass through the steppe safely.[42]

The Russian Empire's growing appetite for Asian trade, its search for natural resources, and its geopolitical ambitions in Central Asia led to renewed contacts with the Kazakhs in the early eighteenth century. While Peter the Great is widely and correctly perceived as a Westernizer, his commitments to Russian expansion in Asia were as significant, even though less successful. In 1714 Peter sent out two well-armed expeditionary forces, one to Khiva in Central Asia, another to Yarkand (Erket) in Jungaria. Both expeditions ended disastrously, and long before they were able to achieve their goals—to verify rumors of vast natural resources, particularly gold deposits—the Russian troops were decimated by disease and hostile armies.

FIGURE 10. Kazakh horseman. From Aleksei Levshin, *Opisanie Kirgiz-Kazach'ikh ili Kirgiz-Kaisakskikh ord i stepei* (St. Petersburg: Tip. Karla Kraia, 1832), pt. 3, p. 42.

The failure of the two expeditions was only a temporary setback for Russia's ambitions in Asia. Upon his return from the unsuccessful military campaign in Persia in 1722, Peter realized once again that "even though the Kazakhs were nomadic and unreliable people, they were both the key and the gates to all of Asia," and he urged his lieutenants to spare no effort and cost in making the Kazakhs Russian subjects.[43] Peter appeared no less interested in the Oirats, and in the same year he dispatched an envoy, Captain Ivan Unkovskii, to the Oirats. Russia's overtures to the Kazakhs and Oirats were only a logical continuation of its imperial ambitions and the empire's renewed attempts to project its geopolitical interests farther into Inner Asia.

St. Petersburg's search for closer ties with both the Kazakhs and Oirats was frustrated by the simple fact that the two were implacable enemies. In desperate need of help against the Oirats, the Kazakhs sent numerous embassies to the Siberian governors, offering to field 20,000 to 30,000 Kazakhs, who could join the Russians in an assault on Yarkand, the principal city of the Oirat ruler. The Russian response was a cautious one, and the officials were instructed to find out more about the Kazakhs' intentions.[44]

In the meantime, the Kazakhs continued to suffer devastating defeats at the hands of the Oirats. A few attempts to unite the dispersed Kazakh clans and to launch a counteroffensive inevitably ended in the Kazakhs' defeat. The worst debacle occurred in the winter of 1723. One year after the death of the Chinese emperor K'ang Hsi, the Oirats sent a large force against the Kazakhs, forcing them to flee west across the Syr-Darya River. There, at what they considered a safe distance, they were taken completely by surprise when the Oirats overran them later that year. Having lost the towns of Tashkent, Turkistan, and Sayram and having found no safe haven from the Oirat raids, the Kazakhs fled in panic farther west, approaching Khiva, Bukhara, and Samarkand. Many people and herds died during the exodus; many more people were taken captive. The year 1723 and those that followed would become known in Kazakh history as the time of the "Great Calamity."[45]

The arrival of desperate and destitute Kazakhs spelled disaster for the Central Asian khanates. The inhabitants of Samarkand and Khiva deserted the cities, Bukhara was besieged, and farmland and gardens were trampled by the Kazakhs' herds. More Kazakhs were compelled to move to the pastures along the Emba and Yaik rivers, thus putting themselves in direct confrontation with the Kalmyks and, once again, in the orbit of Russian interests.[46]

While the mutual raids between the Kazakhs and Kalmyks were not a new development, the news of the internal turmoil among the Kalmyks prompted the Kazakhs to move closer to them and undertake even larger campaigns. In 1726, as many as 30,000 Kazakhs camped two days' journey from the Yaik. The Kalmyks' urgent pleas for help were at first cautiously rejected by the Russian authorities. Soon rumors surfaced that the Kalmyks were negotiating with the Kazakhs and were planning to combine their forces in raids against Russia. In the end, having considered the consequences of the Kazakhs' possible victory over the Kalmyks and their alliance with the Kuban Nogays and the Crimea, the Russian government decided to provide the Kalmyks with ammunition and cannon. When 10,000 Kazakhs of the Lesser and Middle Hordes crossed the Yaik to attack the Kalmyks, they quickly found themselves surrounded by the more numerous and better-armed Kalmyks. To avoid bloodshed, both sides agreed to a peace for the next several years.[47]

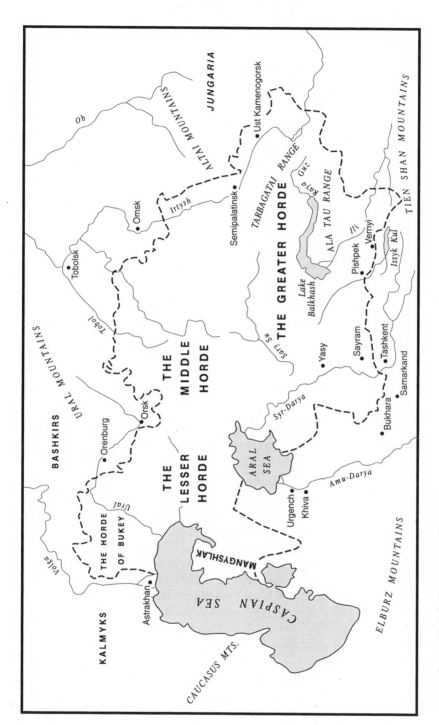

MAP 7.   Central Asia in the nineteenth century.

New and Unwilling Subjects

In the early 1730s, Russian officials began to pay closer attention to the state of affairs among the Kazakhs and dispatched more systematic and substantive reports to St. Petersburg. Officials reported that the Kazakhs were divided into three *juz,* or hordes: the Lesser, the Middle, and the Greater. A 1732 report put the combined number of the Lesser and Middle Kazakh Hordes at 80,000 households, or more than 300,000 people. Two years later the Russian officials gave a specific account of the Hordes' military capabilities and the location of their pastures. The Lesser Horde under Abulkhayir khan numbered about 30,000 horsemen and occupied pastures along the Emba and Yaik rivers and near the Aral Sea; the Middle Horde under Shemiaka khan could assemble 20,000 horsemen and grazed its herds along the Turgay River; the Greater Horde, whose pastures were farther southeast and bordered on the territories of the Oirats, Bukhara, Tashkent, and Turkistan, was the most numerous, capable of fielding 50,000 horsemen.[48]

The Lesser Horde's proximity to the Russian frontier and the example of the military and material benefits that other neighboring peoples, such as the Kalmyks and Bashkirs, derived from their ties with Russia prompted the khan of the Lesser Horde, Abulkhayir, to approach the Russian authorities. His first offer of a military alliance with Russia in 1718 was not immediately welcomed. Instead, Abulkhayir was told to show his loyalty to the tsar by preventing Kazakh raids and returning Russian captives.

When in 1730 Abulkhayir again sent his envoy to Moscow, he received a much more favorable response. This time his offer met and exceeded the government's expectations. He proposed to serve the tsar and pay yasak, in exchange for which he wanted Russia's protection from the Kazakhs' adversaries, in particular from the raids of the Bashkirs and other Russian subjects. Captives would be exchanged.

The Foreign Office found such conditions agreeable and even suggested that the payment of yasak was only voluntary. Abulkhayir could become a Russian subject if he pledged his loyalty to the tsar, lived in peace with Russia's subjects, the Bashkirs, Yaik Cossacks, and Kalmyks, and protected the caravans traveling to Astrakhan. Abulkhayir would then be vested with an imperial decree, a formal insignia, a caftan, a hat, a saber, and small presents. In 1731 Abulkhayir accepted these conditions and volunteered to pay yasak of 4,000 foxes annually. Shortly thereafter, following Abulkhayir's example, a group of Karakalpaks arrived to meet the Russian envoy to the Kazakhs, Muhammed Tevkelev, and offered their allegiance to Russia on behalf of the Karakalpak khan.[49]

Such is the testimony of official records, and the traditional historiography regards 1731 as the year when the Kazakhs became Russian subjects. But a rare look behind the scenes gained from the diary of Muhammed Tevkelev reveals quite a different picture. Tevkelev had been instructed to keep a detailed diary, and he did so diligently.

In October 1731, Tevkelev arrived for a meeting with Abulkhayir to execute the oath of allegiance. Unexpectedly Abulkhayir confessed that he was the only one interested in a Russian protectorate, that the Kazakh notables (*mukhtar* in Kazakh, translated into Russian as *starshiny*—elders, headmen) were against it, and that they could be convinced only if offered numerous presents. He explained that after losing his towns and his wife to the Oirats, he had found himself surrounded by enemies: the Oirats in the east, Bukhara and Khiva in the southwest, the Kalmyks and Bashkirs in the northwest. He now was at peace with Bukhara, Khiva, and the Kalmyks, although the latter were unreliable. If he could secure peace with the Bashkirs, he could then avenge himself against the Oirats. But because the Bashkirs refused to reconcile without the tsar's permission, he wished to become Russia's subject, so he could make peace with them.

Abulkhayir's motives in his search for Russian protectorship could hardly have been more prosaic. The following events exhibited the inner workings of Kazakh society and displayed both Abulkhayir's ability to appropriate the Russian political vocabulary by promising to become Russia's subject (*vstupit' v poddanstvo*) and the popular Kazakh opposition to his subservient relationship with Russia. A week later Tevkelev witnessed a sharp exchange between the notables and the khan. While the notables loudly protested that the khan had written to Russia and asked to become an imperial subject without the customary consultation with them, Abulkhayir complained that he had no power over the Kazakhs and was a khan only in name. When the notables emphasized that they had advised the khan to have his envoys sent to Russia only to conclude a peace treaty, and not to submit to the Russian sovereign, it was Tevkelev's turn to respond. His tirade was one of pride and indignation: "The Russian Empire is in high repute among many states in the world, and it is not befitting such an illustrious monarch to have a peace treaty with you, steppe beasts, because the Russian Empire has no fear of the Kazakhs and not the least need of them, while the Kazakhs are in great danger from Russian subjects, the Kalmyks, Bashkirs, Yaik Cossacks, and from the Siberian towns." He added that even sovereign tsars and khans were Russian subjects (Georgians, Kalmyks, Kabardinians, et al.), and signing a peace treaty with the Kazakhs would only defame the Russian Empire.[50]

Abulkhayir, together with a prominent Kazakh notable, Bukenbay batyr, and twenty-seven other notables, chose to pledge an oath of allegiance to the Russian emperor on the Quran. However, the majority of the notables refused. When Tevkelev distributed presents only among those who had taken an oath, other notables made an attempt to seize the goods from him by force, and only Bukenbay's intervention saved Tevkelev and his embassy from being looted.

The lure of the presents proved irresistible to some notables, and they were prepared to oblige Tevkelev in order to obtain the valuable goods. On November 21, 1731, about thirty of them approached Tevkelev and promised to pledge allegiance in return for presents. After receiving 100 rubles' worth of presents, they took an oath. On December 9, Tevkelev received the envoys of the Karakalpak khan, Gayib. The Karakalpaks also wanted to become Russian subjects. They were told that they could do so only upon meeting certain conditions, which they agreed to with the exception of the following: they refused to pay yasak, surrender hostages, or return Russian captives without a ransom. Tevkelev agreed, and the envoys took an oath and affixed their seals to the written statements.[51]

It was apparent that the two sides, Russians and Kazakhs, were interested in one another for different reasons. The main concern of the Kazakhs was to secure peace with the neighboring nomadic peoples and to ensure payments and presents from Russia. If the only way to achieve these goals was to swear allegiance to the Russian monarch, the khan and some notables were prepared to do so. The Russian government, on the other hand, insisted that the Kazakhs first had to become the subjects of the empire, and only then could they be protected and rewarded. The government was yet little concerned with the practical side of such allegiance by the Kazakhs, what their status as Russian subjects really meant, or whether the government could indeed deliver on its promises. Instead, the Russian government's priority was to formalize the status of the empire's new subjects.

St. Petersburg could hardly have found a better person to represent its interests among the Kazakhs. Tevkelev, a Muslim Tatar, had no difficulty in communicating with the Kazakhs and winning their trust. Upon his urging, Abulkhayir sent his envoys to the khan of the Middle Horde, Shemiaka, to convince him to submit to the Russian monarch. Realizing Abulkhayir's interest in playing a role in Russia's trade with Khiva, Tevkelev also encouraged the khan to send his envoy to St. Petersburg with a request to have a fort built where the Or River flowed into the Yaik, so that the trade with Khiva would be more secure and the khan could spend winters there in comfort. The location would become the future site of Orenburg.

Tevkelev's growing influence over Abulkhayir and Bukenbay caused considerable anxiety among other Kazakh notables. They threatened Bukenbay and refused Tevkelev's demand to return Russian captives without ransom. In a meeting of notables opposed to Russian suzerainty, some suggested that Tevkelev should be killed because he knew the location of their pastures, and they threatened to kill Abulkhayir, too, if he allowed Tevkelev to escape. Others within the opposition group were more cautious and voiced concern that they could be destroyed in revenge by Russian forces and would be forced to abandon their present pastures. Even then, some continued to insist on Tevkelev's assassination, arguing that the khan of Khiva had annihilated Prince

Bekovich-Cherkasskii and his entire force in 1717 with impunity. In the end, the more moderate voices prevailed, and the plan was abandoned. Abulkhayir could only helplessly explain to Tevkelev that the Kazakhs were "free and unfettered people" and that he could not restrain them.[52]

The opposition to the khan and his pro-Russian stance received additional encouragement when the Kalmyk tayishi Dorji-Nazar, whose pastures were along the Yaik River near the Kazakhs, proposed that they combine their forces and launch raids against the Russian towns. The Kalmyks became similarly divided when the Russian government placed its support behind the Kalmyk khan, Cheren-Donduk, and forced Dorji-Nazar and other tayishis into opposition.

The final confirmation of the doubts that many Kazakhs had about their khan's relationship with Russia came with the news of the Bashkirs' successful raids against the Kazakhs of the neighboring Middle Horde. It was additional proof that Russia's protection was worthless, if the Russian government, despite its promises, could not control the Bashkirs and prevent their raids. With renewed threats against him, Abulkhayir decided to send Tevkelev away promptly. Before Tevkelev's departure, Abulkhayir told the Russian envoy that he had no objection to having a Russian fort built on the Or River. Then he could lure his notables there with promises of presents and have them arrested, sent to Moscow, or executed. Reassured of Abulkhayir's loyalty, Tevkelev secretly departed for Ufa.[53]

Tevkelev's diplomatic mission to the Kazakhs of the Lesser Horde revealed a classical dilemma faced by the Russian government on its steppe frontier. It was not difficult to insist on the nomadic peoples' status as subjects of the empire. But by doing so, the government was taking upon itself a responsibility to protect them, in particular from those other peoples whom it also claimed to be its subjects. This was far easier said than done, since the open frontier and the mobility of the nomads hampered the government in exercising efficient control. Such inability to prevent mutual raids among its purported subjects had served to undermine the government's credibility and to force the nomadic peoples to look for other alliances which did not always coincide with Russia's interests.

Upon his return to Russia, Tevkelev presented his ideas to the Foreign Office on how best to assert Russian interests among the Kazakhs. Befriending the Kazakhs, he stressed, required a generous distribution of presents to the khan and notables. The government should build a fort on the Or River on the pretense that Abulkhayir had requested its construction. The new fort would have a number of advantages over Astrakhan and would be indispensable in securing trade with Central Asian cities, while the Kazakhs could be paid for protecting the passing caravans. Because the notables refused to surrender hostages, the government should establish a Kazakh judicial body in the new fort, in which each clan would be represented by one notable, who then could be treated as "political hostages." Moreover, the fort could be used to project Russian military power into the steppe and to deny the Kazakhs the use of their summer pastures if they conducted raids along the Russian frontier.

Exhibiting uncommon insight and pragmatism, Tevkelev explained that Abulkhayir's submission to Russia was involuntary and doubtful. Rather, the khan was forced into it because of his military losses to the Oirats and his desire to have absolute power over the Kazakhs. Finally, he warned that the Kazakhs, Kalmyks, and Bashkirs were all unbridled and untrustworthy peoples, but if one of them rebelled, the other two could be used to destroy the rebels without the intervention of Russian troops. Presented in 1733, Tevkelev's memorandum laid the foundations of Russian colonial policies in the region. It was a combination of economic incentives, commercial interests, and political and military pressure that was to help the government achieve its objectives: to pacify the Kazakhs and expand the imperial frontiers farther into Asia.[54]

Orenburg: Window to the East

One year later, acting on Tevkelev's recommendations, the government appointed an official, Ivan Kirilov, to head the Orenburg Expedition and charged him with the planning and construction of Fort Orenburg. This expedition, along with the Siberia and Kamchatka expeditions undertaken shortly before, was to be another grand project destined "not only for immortal glory, but also to expand an empire and to explore its boundless wealth." In March 1734, after studying the issues, Kirilov presented a memorandum far more detailed, comprehensive, and sophisticated than the one submitted by Tevkelev. It was appropriately titled "A Project of the Ober-Secretary Ivan Kirilov on How to Retain the Kazakhs as Russian Subjects and the Ways to Govern Them."[55]

Kirilov stressed the strategic importance of the planned fort, which would be "right in between the Bashkirs and Kazakhs, separate the Volga Kalmyks from the Bashkirs, put us in proximity to the Oirats," and prevent Kazakh raids into the Kazan region and against the Bashkirs. But Orenburg was to be much more than just the means of controlling the nomadic peoples and securing Russia's southern frontier. It was also to be the gate to the East, opening the road to a bountiful trade with Asia and its limitless natural resources.

Comparing Russian expansion into Asia with the Spanish discovery of America, Kirilov urged the government to spare no effort in annexing Central Asia. For if Russia hesitated, it could lose the region to the militant Oirats, or the Persians, who were aware of its wealth, or even the Dutch, who had already established themselves in East India. Like the Spanish and Por-

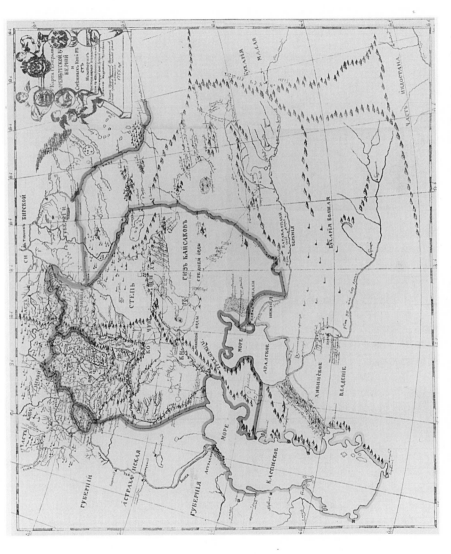

MAP 8. A map of the Orenburg region in 1755. From V. N. Vitevskii, *I. I. Nepliuev i Orenburgskii krai v prezhnem ego sostave do 1758g.*, 3 vols. (Kazan: Tip. V. M. Kliuchnikova, 1897).

tuguese, who shipped wealth from the Americas, Russia could avail itself of the region's riches: lead, salt, gold, silver, rubies, lapis lazuli, and many other metals and precious stones. Kirilov drew a grandiose picture of caravans from Khiva, Bukhara, and India bringing exotic goods, and Bukharan, Indian, Armenian, and even European merchants coming to trade in Orenburg. If St. Petersburg was known as a window to the West, Orenburg, in Kirilov's imagination, was to be Russia's window to the East.[56]

On May 1, 1734, the project ceased to be confined to paper when the Empress Anne approved the plan and decreed that Kirilov be given all the necessary means to implement his ideas. A flurry of decrees instructed the heads of factories in Ekaterinburg to have cannon, munitions, and construction tools ready, the governor of Ufa to dispatch the construction teams, and the Astrakhan governor to send troops. The empress personally sent secret instructions to Kirilov authorizing him to manipulate and play the Bashkirs, Kazakhs, Oirats, and Khiva off against each other.[57]

Colonization of the mid-Volga region and the southern foothills of the Ural Mountains had been an ongoing process since the middle of the sixteenth century. Construction of Orenburg was intended to continue an ever-growing Russian presence, but it also signified a dramatically new, accelerated, and far more intrusive colonization. In 1730–31, a series of new forts formed the Kama fortification line, which separated the Bashkirs from Kazan. Orenburg, like other new forts and industrial towns in the region, was also to be built on Bashkir land and with Bashkir labor. Twenty thousand Bashkir *tarkhans* (lesser nobles who provided military service instead of paying yasak) were to be drafted to provide protection for Orenburg, and 20,000 *tepters* and *bobyls* (registered and unregistered Tatar, Chuvash, and Mari migrants working on Bashkir lands) were to be mobilized for work because "it was cheaper and more efficient to use them instead of using Russian peasants." With the construction of Orenburg in 1736, another fortification line connecting the forts of Samara and Orenburg along the Samara River cut the Bashkirs off from the southern steppe. Separated from the Kazan region in the north and from the steppe in the south, and increasingly surrounded by Russian troops and colonists, the Bashkirs rose up in numerous revolts throughout the eighteenth century.[58]

While the Bashkirs correctly viewed the construction of Orenburg as another step in their slow encirclement within the Russian Empire, the Kazakh khans welcomed it. For them the Russian presence meant increased security from Oirat and Bashkir raids, an opportunity for expanded trade, and, most important, an enhancement of their own power among the Kazakhs. Writing to Tevkelev, who had been promoted to the rank of colonel and assigned to the Expedition, the khan of the Middle Horde, Küchük, offered his help against the rebellious Bashkirs in exchange for Russia's support, so that "the Bashkirs would be fearful of you, General [*sic*], and our Kazakhs would be in fear of their own khans."[59] In 1736, urged on by Kirilov, the Kazakhs of the Lesser and Middle Hordes launched raids into the Bashkir lands, killing or capturing many Bashkirs in the Siberian and Nogay districts.

If the construction of Orenburg helped the government to achieve some of its military objectives and use the Kazakhs to police the region, Russia's commercial objectives were lagging behind. On one occasion, merchants from Bukhara, Turkistan, Tashkent, and Khojand arrived in Orenburg only to find that their Russian counterparts were not yet there. In a classical case of state intervention, the government took measures to encourage Kazakh trade in Orenburg by forbidding the Kazakhs to trade with the Yaik Cossacks "because the Russian merchants in Orenburg would suffer losses." And if proscriptive means failed to convince the Kazakhs, the authorities also ordered that prices be raised on Russian goods and lowered on Kazakh goods in the town of Yaitsk, and that the Kazakhs be sold only a limited amount of grain at higher prices.[60]

The support of the Kazakh khans for the Russian presence in the region notwithstanding, the expectations on both sides remained unmatched by reality. The Russians demanded that the loot captured in Kazakhs raids against passing caravans or frontier settlements be returned, that fugitive Bashkir rebels hiding among the Kazakhs be seized and handed over, and that Russian, Tatar, and Kalmyk captives be set free. In response, Abulkhayir khan once again pled his helplessness, because "here it is not like in Russia, they [the Kazakhs] do not obey my orders."

Seeking to strengthen his authority over the Kazakhs, Abulkhayir asked the government to send troops to be placed under his command and to build a fort on the Syr-Darya River; only then would he be able to instill fear in the Kazakhs and address Russian grievances. Abulkhayir was telling the truth: hostility toward him and his Russian friends was widespread among the Kazakhs. In 1740, having robbed and beaten the Russian envoys en route to Khiva, the departing leader of the Kazakh raiding party starkly reminded the Russians that "only Abulkhayir himself is the subject of the empress, and he receives presents from Russia in exchange for his written oath; but we are not subjects."[61]

Just as Abulkhayir could not deliver on Russian demands, the Russians, too, failed to keep their promises. Thus, the khan continued to insist that a fort be built on the Syr-Darya. But the Russian officer sent to evaluate the situation in the region, Dmitrii Gladyshev, deemed the construction of the fort unnecessary because "Abulkhayir wanted it in order to rein in his Kazakhs, but such a fort would be of no use to Russia." Abulkhayir's hopes of becoming khan of Khiva with the help of the Russian troops were also dashed. His policies of ingratiating himself with Russia and counting on its military support, even though at the expense of the majority of the Kazakhs, yielded bitter fruit. Described by one government official as "adventurous,

FIGURE 11. I. I. Nepliuev, Orenburg governor. From V. N. Vitevskii, *I. I. Nepliuev i Orenburgskii krai v prezhnem ego sostave do 1758g.*, 3 vols. (Kazan: Tip. V. M. Kliuchnikova, 1897).

ambitious, and a man not without cunning," Abulkhayir warned the Russian authorities that if his requests were not granted, he would offer his services to the Oirats.[62]

Instead of realizing the limitation of Russian power in the area and the incongruity of the government's political rhetoric with the ever-shifting reality in the steppe, Gladyshev recommended stiffening Russian resolve and ordering that Abulkhayir and the notables confirm their allegiance. To prevent any wrongdoing, the Kazakhs should surrender four hostages from each clan, in the same way that the Greater Horde submitted them to the Oirats. Furthermore, suggested Gladyshev, because the Kazakhs were a barbaric people and could not understand Russian decrees, it was paramount to have an adviser appointed who knew their language and customs, who would have the power to make decisions, and who could be given 1,000 rubles in goods to be used for rewarding the Kazakhs and ransoming captives. Gladyshev recommended a Russian officer, Prince Urakov, who was born in Ufa, knew Kazakh customs, and spoke Tatar, to serve as such a plenipotentiary intermediary. Finally, read Gladyshev's memorandum, some Kazakhs had previously sought refuge in the vicinity of Orenburg, but they were forced to go back because Russian officials seized their Kalmyk wives and the Bashkirs raided their herds. If such abuses were prevented, then more Kazakhs would move closer to Orenburg and slowly become dependent on trade and abandon their nomadic lifestyle.[63]

In contrast to the previous centuries of dealing with its various nomadic neighbors, Russia's present approach to the Kazakhs was characterized by increasing and conscious reliance on trade and economic incentives, which were intended to turn the Kazakhs into civilized and loyal subjects of the empire. Spelled out by Orenburg's founder, Kirilov, these policies were followed and amplified by his successors: Vasilii Tatishchev (1737–39), Prince Vasilii Urusov (1739–42), and Ivan Nepliuev (1742–58). In 1742, a military commander of Orenburg pointed out the potential benefits to the treasury if he were allowed to barter grain for young, strong horses capable of dragoon service; two or three *chetvert* (a measure of grain equal to about eight poods, or 277 pounds, in the eighteenth century) of grain per horse. Even sheep could be profitably bartered, because they could be sold to merchants for 80 to 100 kopecks each, while the Kazakhs were given two *chetverik* (a measure equal to one-eighth of a chetvert, i.e., about one pood or thirty-five pounds) of grain worth 50 kopecks for one sheep. He expected the Kazakhs to grow slowly accustomed to relying on grain and to grazing their herds near Orenburg, as the Kalmyks did near Astrakhan and Tsaritsyn.[64]

Governed by a new, Westernized generation of the Russian elite pursuing active mercantilist policies, the region was undergoing a rapid change. In search of a better natural location, the town of Orenburg was moved in 1744 farther west along the Yaik and refounded at the confluence of the Sakmara and Yaik rivers. The original Orenburg Expedition was first renamed "the Commission," and then in 1744 the "Orenburg *guberniia*," marking its administrative transition from an exploratory project into a fully incorporated region of the empire. The new guberniia was one of the largest in the empire and consisted of four districts (*provintsii*): Stavropol on the Volga in the west, Cheliabinsk in the east, Ufa in the north, and Orenburg in the south.

Colonization of the region proceeded at a rapid pace, in part because of the arrival of non-Christians fleeing the Kazan region, where the government had confiscated their lands, imposed a burden of heavy taxation, and sought to convert them to Christianity by force. But the government did not intend to leave the region to the spontaneous colonization of non-Christians. In fact, the official policy of Russifying the region was believed to be the most reliable guarantee of securing Russian control. The Bashkir lands could be purchased to build a new factory or develop a mine or could be confiscated for military reasons, such as the construction of roads or forts.

The government brought in Russian state peasants to settle along strategic roads and to assign to the growing numbers of forts and industrial enterprises. The new fortification lines and Russian settlements continued to encircle the non-Christian population of the empire.[65]

Russia's increasing military and economic presence in the steppes of Central Asia and its claims of suzerainty over the Kazakhs of the Lesser and Middle Hordes inevitably drew it into the whirlwind of regional politics. In the south, there was the Persia of Nadir Shah, whose ambitions increasingly clashed with Russian interests in the area. It was reported that the shah treated his new subjects well, and Bukhara, Khiva, the Turkmens of the Aral Sea, and the Karakalpaks were tempted to accept Persian protection. In the east there were the Oirats, whose envoy came to Abulkhayir in June 1742 to inform him of the approaching Oirat army and to present demands from the Oirat khan, Galdan Tseren. The Kazakhs were to offer ten hostages along with their families from among the Kazakh notables and a tribute of one fox from each tent; if Abulkhayir refused to accept these conditions, the Oirats threatened to destroy him.[66]

The Oirat demands were deemed unacceptable by the Russian officials stationed among the Kazakhs. After all, the Oirat envoys were informed, Abulkhayir was already a Russian subject. It turned out that it was Abulkhayir who had approached the Oirats with an offer of peace, in exchange for the return to him of the towns of Turkistan and Tashkent. Explaining himself to the Russian officials, Abulkhayir asserted that his sole goal was to make the towns a part of the Russian Empire.[67] Certainly, the khan had learned how to make his interests palatable to the Russian authorities.

Caught between demands from the Russians, Oirats, and anti-Russian Kazakh notables, Abulkhayir once again chose to pin his fortunes on Russia and asked for protection. He explained that the Kazakh notables wanted him to move farther away from the Russian frontier, and if he refused, they would renounce him as their khan. Some of them planned to force their way through the Volga pastures of the Kalmyks and join the Nogays on the Kuban. Others suggested moving back to the Syr-Darya, giving hostages to the Oirats, and making peace with the Karakalpaks, thus confronting Russia together with the Oirats and Karakalpaks. Abulkhayir warned that if the Russians did not protect him, he would flee to the Kuban River, where he was always welcome.[68]

But the Russian government was more concerned with the possibility of an Oirat attack against the Kazakhs than the latter's internal disputes. The new governor of the Orenburg region, Ivan Nepliuev, recommended to his superiors that if the Oirats attacked, Russian troops should protect Russia's "new subjects, the Kazakh peoples." Nepliuev also warned of the risks of such a policy, describing one potentially troublesome scenario, whereby the Kazakhs might be expected to flee and ask for protection in the forts at

Orenburg and Yaitsk. If they were allowed to enter, the Oirats, who had a large army equipped with artillery, could try to attack the forts and break through the fortification lines. For this reason, Nepliuev asked that three regiments intended for a reinforcement of Astrakhan from possible attack by Nadir Shah remain where they were: in Kazan, Ufa, and Sheshminsk. The Senate approved these recommendations.[69]

At the same time, Russian envoys were sent to Abulkhayir to have him sign yet another pledge to remain faithful, and to the Oirats to inform them that the Lesser and Middle Kazakh Hordes and Karakalpaks of the lower Syr-Darya were Russian subjects. In a personal letter to the Oirat khan, Galdan-Tseren, Nepliuev presented his government's view: Abulkhayir had already been under Russian protection for many years when in 1738 he swore allegiance to Her Majesty, the empress, and two years later the khan of the Middle Horde, Abdul Muhammed (Abul Mamet), did the same.

During the negotiations that followed, the Oirats made clear the nature of their grievances against the Kazakhs: they pillaged the caravans sent by the Oirat khan to the Kalmyks, Russia, Bukhara, and Urgench and launched raids against the Oirats when they were at war with China. Now the Kazakhs sued for peace and promised to submit hostages. When Nepliuev again insisted that the Kazakhs were Russian subjects, the Oirats responded that without submitting their hostages, the Kazakhs could not be trusted, and that in the end this was a matter between the Oirats and Kazakhs.[70]

By asserting its suzerainty over the Kazakhs, the Russian government inevitably found itself on a collision course with the Kazakhs' rivals. While claiming the Kazakhs as its subjects and therefore assuming responsibility for their actions, the government had no means of controlling the Kazakhs and stopping their raids into the Russian borderlands, even less against other nomads. The Russian claims of sovereignty were of little help in resolving the traditional conflicts between two rival nomadic peoples.

Frontier Dilemmas: Force or Trade

Russian authorities in the region continued to face a familiar dilemma: how to strengthen Russian control over the Kazakhs without putting too much power in the hands of their khans. Abulkhayir's desire to become absolute ruler of the Kazakhs with Russian help was never in doubt. Trying harder than ever to convince the authorities that this would also serve Russian interests, he related to Nepliuev an old Nogay proverb: "If a snake has one head but many tails, the tails all easily follow the head into the hole; but if the snake has many heads and one tail, then it is difficult to do." Nepliuev was not impressed. He reported that Abulkhayir was interested only in receiving more presents from Russia and using Russia in his intrigues against other Kazakh rivals. Informers reported that on one occasion, when visiting

163

the Kazakhs of the Middle Horde, Abulkhayir had boasted that Russia was under his sway.[71]

Nepliuev, given by the empress full powers "to retain by all means the newly admitted Kazakh Hordes as Russian subjects," decided to tighten his control over the Kazakhs. The construction of the Orenburg fortification line was sped up. Abulkhayir's plea to cross the Yaik to better pastures was denied "because the pastures on the other side were necessary for the use of regular and irregular troops," and because this could lead to renewed squabbles with the Yaik Cossacks and Kalmyks. Instead, the khan was to graze his herds near the Russian forts in the upper Yaik, where he could be supplied with grain in the winter. Nor was he permitted to exchange his son kept in Russia with another one, on the grounds that the hostage he offered as a replacement was less worthy because he was the son of a Kalmyk concubine, not of a legitimate wife. In his secret report, Nepliuev made clear that he considered taking the eldest son of the khan as a hostage the best way to guarantee the Kazakhs' loyalty.[72]

That Russian policies were inevitably leading to the Kazakhs' loss of independence was now apparent even to those who were prepared to offer their limited loyalty, the Kazakh khans. The first to rebel against tougher Russian policies was Abdul Muhammed, the khan of the Middle Horde. When it became known that Abdul Muhammed had entered into negotiations with the Oirats, Nepliuev recommended to his superiors that he be immediately denounced as a traitor and rebel and deprived of the title of khan, which had been bestowed on him by the Russian authorities. Abulkhayir too was profoundly unhappy with Nepliuev's policies and submitted his detailed grievances. He objected to his son's hostage status because "he gave his children to serve Her Imperial Majesty, not to be kept as hostages." Later he compared his son to an envoy sent to Russia and detained there, even though he had never detained Russian envoys. He complained that his prestige among the Kazakhs had been undermined by the humiliating reception he had received in the Russian fort at Orsk, where some of his people had been fed rotten rye bread and died. Worst of all, his people were convinced that his reliance on Russia would ruin them all. They mocked him by pointing out that in contrast to his meager rewards from Russia, a certain Turkmen chief, who had offered his service to the Persian shah, had been rewarded with seven towns and so many presents that it required forty camels to transport them. In the end, a bitter Abulkhayir assured Nepliuev that, despite having suffered an injustice and lacking rewards for his service, he remained loyal and steadfastly refused offers from others to leave for Turkistan and Tashkent. He hoped to mend the relations in a personal meeting with Nepliuev, but to make sure his message got across, Abulkhayir also sent a letter of complaint to the empress.[73]

In contrast to the written petitions of their khan, ordinary Kazakhs and notables chose to express their dissatisfaction with Russian policies by launching raids against the Yaik Cossacks and Russian forts along the Orenburg line. In 1743, the Senate considered and rejected the idea of directing the Bashkirs against the Kazakhs because the former were unreliable. Instead, the Yaik Cossacks, the Volga Kalmyks, and the regular troops from Astrakhan were to be used. It was now Nepliuev's turn to appeal for a more cautious approach, as he explained to his superiors in St. Petersburg that the use of force should be the last resort, and that persuasion and realization of the advantages of peace with Russia would pacify the Kazakhs better than war. As for the bitterly contested issue of the khan's sons kept as hostages, Nepliuev suggested that there should be a special imperial decree allowing them to be educated and to reside at the imperial court, instead of remaining in a frontier town.[74] Frontier hostages were to become imperial captives.

In the following years, Nepliuev continued to advocate peaceful co-optation of the Kazakhs through trade. He disagreed with the suggestions of the Foreign Office to use non-Russian irregular troops against the Kazakhs, who, in the view of Foreign Office officials, were only causing damage and were of no use to the empire. The irregular troops would not be able to do much harm to the Kazakhs, Nepliuev argued. In fact, the Russian borderlands were safe from Kazakh raids when the Kazakhs grazed their herds in the vicinity of the frontier, for it was when they planned raids that they moved farther away. For this and other reasons, Nepliuev continued, it was best to keep the Kazakhs nearby and soften them up by encouraging their growing trade with Russian towns. He assured the officials that the success of such a policy was already visible, and that within the last four years, between 1743 and 1747, the Kazakhs had traded more than 14,000 horses, which were later sold at a profit by Russian merchants in Astrakhan. Now that the ordinary Kazakhs also had incentives to trade with Russia, he continued, they could serve to check Abulkhayir's ambitions and diminish Russia's reliance on him.[75] In contrast to St. Petersburg, which was prepared to resort to military actions, Nepliuev advocated a more gradual, evolutionary approach of first co-opting the elite, then the commoners, and in the end playing the two off against each other to further Russian interests.

Trade in the newly founded Russian towns was indeed growing rapidly. In 1747 alone, the Kazakhs bartered 7,000 horses and 28,000 sheep. The Kazakhs, like the Kalmyks, were exempt from customs duties, which were paid instead by Russian and foreign merchants. Relatively safe travel allowed numerous merchants from Kashgar, Bukhara, and Khiva to bring their goods to trade in the Russian towns of Orsk, Orenburg, Yamyshev, and Semipalatinsk.[76]

But increasing caravan trade and the lure of valuable goods on the Russian market further added to the existing hostilities between various Kazakhs groups contesting the control of the trade routes and vying for a bigger share of the trade in Russian towns. It was over this issue that Abulkhayir once again quarreled with his rival from the Middle Horde, Barak sultan. Their argument over safe passage for merchants ended in a fight, in which Abulkhayir was killed. Such was the story presented by Tevkelev, who arrived in the region in 1748, shortly before Abulkhayir's murder. Two other reports, one from Abulkhayir's widow, Bupay (Pupai), and another from a Russian interpreter among the Kazakhs, Emagul Guleev (also known as Yakov Guliaev), explained that the quarrel was, in fact, over spoils—2,000 Kazakh families captured on their way from the Karakalpaks to join their kin in the Greater Horde.[77]

Whatever the circumstances, Abulkhayir's death presented the Russian government with another policy dilemma: Who should become the new khan? Nepliuev and Tevkelev offered their advice to the government in St. Petersburg. Nepliuev explained that Kazakh khans had no real power and did not inherit the title, but were elected from among the sultans. Therefore, it was important to make sure that in choosing their nominee they sought the approval of the empress, so that in the future it would be possible to have a khan appointed by the government. Tevkelev submitted a detailed account with the names of the principal clans and subclans of all three Kazakh Hordes. There were two likely candidates: Nuraly, the son of Abulkhayir, and his heir apparent and Abulkhayir's murderer, Barak. Tevkelev and Nepliuev disagreed on the issue. Believing that one strong khan would better control the Kazakhs, Tevkelev supported the candidacy of Barak. Nepliuev argued that Russian interests would be better served by encouraging the existing divisions among the Kazakhs, thus allowing neither side to become too strong or too weak.[78]

As envisioned by Nepliuev, Russian support of Abulkhayir's son Nuraly set off a new round of hostilities between the Lesser and Middle Hordes. With the help of the Russian administration, Nuraly was elected khan by a few renowned notables but lacked general support. The majority of notables of the Middle Horde refused to accept him and instead declared Barak to be their khan. To convince more Kazakhs to offer their support to Nuraly, Tevkelev advised that the newly elected khan be given a cash and grain annuity, which would send a clear signal to other Kazakhs that Nuraly and his people had become Russia's true subjects.

In May 1749, an imperial decree invested Nuraly with the title of khan. Nuraly knelt on a carpet embroidered with gold, took an oath according to the form sent from St. Petersburg, and kissed the Quran. His notables stood or sat around him "according to their Asiatic custom." He was then given a saber, fur hat, and coat and a specially decorated decree, to which he attached his seal.[79] Nuraly's investiture with the title of khan by the Russian authorities was yet another step, both symbolic and real, in Russia's continuing efforts to transform the unruly Kazakhs into the empire's faithful subjects.

Nuraly Khan and the Limits of Loyalty

Despite the pomp and circumstance and the new khan's assurances of loyalty, the traditional disagreements between the Kazakhs and Russian authorities could not be easily resolved. The new khan, however, proved to be more pliable than his father. Initially, when asked to collect and return Russian captives among the Kazakhs, Nuraly gave a familiar answer: he did not have such power over the Kazakhs because "they were free people of the steppe." He added that in this case he could not use a *barimta,* a nomadic custom of ensuring justice by allowing the victimized side a forcible seizure of herds or property from the offenders. Then the Russian envoy suggested that the Russians could capture some Kazakh notables and exchange them for captives. Nuraly was delighted to oblige and submitted a list of about fifty Kazakh notables, who, he suggested, should be detained when they arrived to trade in Orenburg. For the time being, a new type of cooperation was forged between the Russian authorities and the Kazakh khan.[80]

Inevitably, the khan's collusion with the authorities led to further feuds. Some sided with Nuraly and tried to convince others that had it not been for Russian protection, they would have perished at the hands of the Oirats. But the majority were increasingly alarmed by the presence of Russian forts near their pastures and believed that Russia's intention was to surround and subjugate the Kazakhs, as they had done earlier with the Bashkirs. Upon the death of Barak sultan in 1750, the Kazakh opposition rallied around Batyr sultan of the Middle Horde and elected him khan.[81]

The analogy with the Bashkirs was not far-fetched. In 1755, a group of more than 1,500 Bashkir households, having fled their homes in the Russian Empire, came to seek refuge among the Kazakhs. The fugitive Bashkirs explained that they had become Russian subjects of their own volition, had agreed to pay yasak, and had provided numerous services and labor. In the beginning, they, too, like the Kazakhs, had been granted privileges, but then the government had begun to demand from them more than from their ancestors. Every year they were getting worse off, and now they were in such misery that they could not even feed themselves. Their petitions did not reach the empress, and their petitions to the governor went unheeded. The governor forbade them to petition the empress and seized, tortured, and killed many of their people; they were no longer free in their own lands and waters. How could they live without the land? Military regiments came and ruined them; they cut the trees with their beehives, built forts, and forced Bashkirs to fell trees, dig ditches, cut stones, provide transportation, join military patrols, and buy salt at a higher price. And the poorest Bashkirs were converted to Christianity. Finally, desperate and destitute, they resolved to flee, even though the Russian authorities tried to prevent them from doing so by ordering the execution of one remaining Bashkir resident for each fugitive: "And if the empress had no longer needed her faithful servants, then they too did not want to reside there." The Bashkirs warned that the same fate would soon befall the Kazakhs.[82]

Nuraly remained unmoved by the grim tale of the Bashkirs and their stark warnings. Trying to impress the Russian authorities with his faithful service and enriching himself in the process, Nuraly informed Nepliuev that he had ordered fugitive Bashkirs and those who harbored them plundered without mercy. In the ensuing melee, many Bashkirs were killed. Those who were captured were appraised at ten mares per man, fifteen mares per woman or girl, five mares per child, and "fathers were separated from children and mothers from daughters" and dispersed among the Kazakhs.[83]

Yet even Nuraly could not close his eyes to the steady encirclement of the Russian forts. Writing to Nepliuev about the new Russian fort built near the salt mine on the Ilek River, he asked that the fort be razed. He explained that the Kazakhs badly needed land for grazing their herds, and that because of the Russian forts the pastures not only along the Yaik River but also along the Ilek would soon become inaccessible. He cautioned that if the authorities ignored his plea, the Kazakhs would move away, and he would be a khan over no one. Nepliuev remained adamant, and the imperial decrees continued to forbid the Kazakhs to cross the Yaik.[84]

"Enlightened" Governors

For many years the Russian government was intimately involved in supporting the Oirats in order to check Chinese expansion into Central Asia. In 1758, however, the Oirats ceased to exist as an independent political entity, finally destroyed by Chinese armies and decimated by a smallpox epidemic. Now, more than ever, it became imperative to secure the loyalty of the Kazakhs, who remained the only buffer between the two expanding and competing empires, Qing China and Russia.[85]

Aleksei Tevkelev, a few years earlier promoted to the rank of major-general, and Petr Rychkov, appointed to replace the retired Nepliuev, urged their superiors at the Foreign Office to act immediately and win over the Lesser and Middle Hordes to the Russian side. They had no doubt that the Kazakh chiefs could be easily enticed with gifts, because "the Kazakhs are fickle and greedy people eager to lay their hands on anything."[86]

Readdressing Russia's policies in the region, in 1759 Tevkelev and Rychkov submitted a detailed memorandum advocating Russia's continuous engagement with the Kazakhs. First they described the location of the Kazakhs' pastures, which, according to the Orenburg map, occupied a circumference of more than 7,000 versts across the steppe: from the Caspian Sea near Gur'ev, to the upper Yaik, along the Ui and Tobol rivers to Fort Zverinogolovskaia, and then in the Siberian province past the Ishim and Irtysh rivers and the upper Irtysh to Fort Yamyshev. In the north they faced the forts and redoubts of the Orenburg and Siberian fortification lines. In the south their neighbors were the Turkmens, Khivans, Arals (Turkmens of the Aral Sea), Lower Karakalpaks, Bukharans, Turkistan, Tashkent, and Oirats. Tevkelev and Rychkov emphasized that together the Lesser and Middle Hordes were the most formidable force in the region, and had both Hordes been united under one strong leader, they could have mustered an army of 50,000 to 60,000 horsemen, primarily armed with firearms. It was only because of their traditional independence and dislike of the strong authority of a khan that their army more typically numbered from 10,000 to 20,000 horsemen.[87]

Several local military commanders held a different view. Claiming that the Kazakhs had caused damage only along the Russian frontier, they were eager to pacify them once and for all by a punishing military campaign which would either destroy the Kazakhs or force them to leave. Tevkelev and Rychkov accused such commanders of sheer ignorance in matters concerning the steppe and pointed out that there were not enough Russian troops to rout the Kazakhs. Nor, they insisted, would a military campaign be able to accomplish these goals, because the Kazakhs would flee and later launch retaliatory raids.

Instead Tevkelev and Rychkov submitted an "Enlightenment Manifesto" of their own: "Even though to change the national mores and old customs of the entire people is the most difficult undertaking, yet in the matters of governing the new subject peoples [*novopoddanye narody*], as they are, it is most essential from the very beginning to be aware of their mores and customs, and to guide them through fairness and moderation in the direction required by the interests of the state." They stressed that the Kazakhs were more amenable to Russian influence than the Bashkirs, who, having been Russian subjects for two hundred years, only now were reaching a human and civilized state (*liudskost'*). In contrast, the Kazakhs were already getting used to trading, eating a diet of bread, and making and storing hay for the winter. In time, trade would pacify them, and they could be expected to settle down, just as the nomadic Bashkirs had before them.[88]

They elaborated some of the specific policies that had been suggested by Tevkelev two decades earlier. For instance, they proposed stopping the practice of demanding hostages, instead creating a council of several local notables who would reside in a Russian town. Then the Kazakhs would believe this to be an institution for dispensing justice rather than thinking of the Kazakh notables as Russian hostages. The authority of a khan should be somewhat strengthened to allow for better control of his people, but not too much. A khan should be appointed by the Russian government, thus insulating the candidate from the influence and pressure of the Kazakh notables. It was important to favor one of the sultans in preparing him to assume the position of khan. A khan and the sultans should be given annuities, and the notables granted the status of tarkhan.

FIGURE 12.   Karavansaray in Orenburg. Built in the early 1840s, it was
originally placed outside the city walls to house Bashkirs in Russia's
military service when they were traveling through the region. The
architect was Alexander Briullov. From V. V. Dorofeev, *Nad Uralom-rekoi*
(Cheliabinsk: Iuzhno-Ural'skoe knizh. izd., 1988), p. 122.

The memorandum proceeded to explain that it was not advisable to use
regular military against the Kazakhs because of their large numbers and
mobility. Instead, it was best to control them by encouraging feuds among
the Kazakhs and by playing off the Bashkirs, Kalmyks, and Kazakhs against
each other. Finally, all efforts should be made to prevent the Kazakhs from
being enticed by a Chinese invitation to move farther east into the vacant
parts of the steppe previously occupied by the Oirats.[89]

This detailed exposition offered by Tevkelev and Rychkov clearly defined
the means and objectives of the Russian policies toward the Kazakhs. In the
long run they were expected to settle down, partake of the fruits of civiliza-

tion, and become faithful subjects. In the meantime, however, they were to be kept divided and weakened enough to prevent any threat to the Russian borderlands, but strong enough to be used against their neighbors and against the encroaching Qing China.

In 1761, similar policies, but with a slightly different twist, were detailed by Major General von Veimarn, a Russian commander of the Siberian fortification lines. The general also wanted to "soften up" (*iznezhit'*) the Kazakhs by building houses for them and pens for their animals. At the same time, he recommended secretly working toward impoverishing the Kazakhs' sheep and horse herds. One way to do this was to get the Kazakh herds accustomed to hay, so that they would no longer be able to survive in the open steppe. The special secret commission considered and in principle agreed with the recommendations. It found that the only undesirable consequence of such policies would be a growing number of impoverished Kazakhs who would have no other choice but to resort to raids. For this reason, the project of encouraging Kazakh settlements near the Russian frontier was found to be unfeasible.[90]

It was the Orenburg governor D. V. Volkov who expounded most eloquently Russian ideas and attitudes during Nuraly khan's visit in 1763. For years Nuraly's frequent requests went unheeded—whether they were about returning Kazakh runaways, allowing Kazakhs to cross the Yaik toward their traditional winter pastures, releasing Kazakh hostages, or permitting duty-free trade. Accused of a pro-Russian stand and derided by his own people, who derogatorily referred to him as "the Russian khan," Nuraly arrived in Orenburg to plead his case in a personal meeting with the governor.

He and the four sultans who accompanied him were received in the governor's house by the governor and several generals. Except for permission to make duty-free purchases of grain for three years, the negotiations did not bring the two sides any closer to a resolution of the traditionally thorny issues. But the governor took the opportunity to explain to the Kazakh khan how fortunate the latter was to be able to become more civilized and to enjoy Russia's benevolent protection and help. Were the khan to choose to settle down, he would see that "the almighty force of civilization at the hands of the emperor was such that it could transform nature, and through the wisdom of the grand sovereigns and the obedience of their subjects . . . the winters are turned into summers, and summers into winters." The development of peoples, he continued, was similar to the development of a human being: at first there is a child, then a young man, and then an adult. The Russian people, too, had gone through these stages and had now reached their adulthood.

The implications of the governor's exhortation were quite obvious: the nomadic Kazakhs were similar to children. In time they would change and grow, if they settled down under the guidance of their benevolent Russian patrons. Nuraly agreed that the Kazakhs indeed were like small children and added that he could improve them more quickly if he had more control over them; without towns and troops, he was powerless to enforce their obedience.[91]

At the time, however, Russia's military presence was far more visible than the civilizing one. The growing number of forts and towns continued to squeeze the Kazakh pastures, and the Lesser and Middle Hordes were now forbidden to cross the Irtysh River. Ablay khan of the Middle Horde sent embassies to the Chinese emperor and the Ottoman sultan and considered leaving the region altogether. Even Nuraly khan dispatched his embassies to China and Persia with the same purpose, and the Kazakhs were reported to have forced their way across the Yaik more frequently.

Yet the Russian government remained undisturbed by these warnings. In a detailed memorandum submitted to Catherine II by the Foreign Office in 1764, the officials assured her that there were no reasons to worry about the situation in Asia, because "were even all of Asia to come into turmoil, there are plenty of ways to check the trouble there." As for the Kazakhs, they could be tamed by the Yaik Cossacks, Kalmyks, or Bashkirs, although the latter, being Muslim, were less reliable. The memorandum advised that the policies toward the Kazakhs remain unchanged: the practice of keeping hostages should continue, crossing the Yaik should be banned, and the return of baptized Kazakh fugitives was against the Christian laws. In the end, even though it would have been beneficial to have the Kazakhs close to the imperial borders, the memorandum continued, the Kazakhs were still in such a state that they could not be relied upon, and keeping them at a distance was the only way to prevent clashes with other subjects of the empire.[92] It seemed that many of the previous recommendations made by Tevkelev and Rychkov had fallen on deaf ears in the capital.

The Pugachev Uprising

The Russian government's confidence in its ability to manage the situation in the southern borderlands was shattered when the entire southern rim of the empire erupted at a most inopportune time, during Russia's war with the Ottoman Empire (1768–74). The departure of the Kalmyks in January 1771 set in motion a chain of rebellions and uprisings, the violence and enormity of which would send shock waves across Russia and Europe.

The expansion of the Russian Empire and the government's policies of further integration of the borderlands and peoples into the imperial military, economic, and administrative structure had an adverse effect on various peoples along the southern frontier. By 1771 the Kalmyks found themselves hemmed in by the Russian fortification lines, the Cossacks, and farming and fishing settlements. After repeated warnings, which were not taken seriously by the government in St. Petersburg, the Kalmyks chose to leave the banks of the Volga and return to the Jungar steppe, which had been left vacant by the Qings' destruction of the Oirats. Even though the vagaries of the journey and raids by the Kazakhs took a high toll on the fugitive Kalmyks and their herds, their flight proceeded unimpeded by the Russian authorities.[93]

The Kalmyks' departure revealed the vulnerability of the Russian frontier garrisons, which, undermanned and underarmed, could do little to stop their flight. During the summers of 1771 and 1772, a series of small disturbances broke out among the Yaik Cossacks. The reasons for the disturbances were similar to the often-heard complaints from the Kalmyks and Kazakhs. The Yaik Cossacks complained that they were exhausted by increasing government demands to perform military service, and most recently by the pursuit and confrontations with the fleeing Kalmyks. At the same time, the government owed the Cossacks six years' worth of cash and grain allowances. The arrival of Russian military commanders who tried to impose rigid military discipline among the Cossacks proved to be the last straw.

A Russian officer sent in 1772 to investigate the disturbances among the Cossacks reported that there were no serious reasons for concern, that the Cossacks had everything in abundance and enjoyed their privileges of free trade in salt and spirits. As for riots, he continued, they were caused by the abuses of the local commanders, and this could be easily rectified.[94] Less than a year after this reassuring report, the Yaik Cossacks, led by Emel'ian Pugachev and joined by the Bashkirs and numerous other non-Christian peoples of the empire, rose against the authorities in what became the largest Jacquerie of the eighteenth century. Reversing its previous plans to use the Kalmyks, Bashkirs, and Cossacks against the Kazakhs, the Russian authorities in the region now appealed to the Kazakhs for help against Pugachev.

The Kazakhs, of course, had their own interests in mind. While assuring the Orenburg officials of their loyalty, Nuraly and his brother Dosaly at the same time wrote to Pugachev and, addressing him as Emperor of All Russia, promised their services to him. As always in such circumstances, the nomads positioned themselves to take advantage of the situation by not aligning themselves with either contender for power until one had gained a clear upper hand.[95]

Pugachev was well aware of the issues that were important to the Kazakhs. In his appeals, written in Tatar, he promised to reward the Kazakhs generously with "land, water, pastures, arms and munitions, salt, grain, and lead." Some Kazakhs chose to join Pugachev's army; others, seeing an opportunity for booty, launched raids against Russian settlements. Nuraly defended himself against Russian charges by citing his inability to control the Kazakhs and accusing his rival brother, Dosaly sultan, of being an active supporter of Pugachev. There were rumors that Nuraly sided with Pugachev and the

Kuban Nogays, and that they were ready to launch an attack along the entire Russian frontier. In fact, Nuraly remained neutral and was simply awaiting the outcome. Nuraly did nothing to help the Russian administration, but neither did he help Pugachev, who, rebuffed in his demand for assistance, threatened to hang Nuraly by the rib.[96]

The most visible sign of the struggle between the government and the rebels was the strategically important regional citadel, Orenburg. The rebels, "unable to capture Orenburg with arrows and spears," besieged the city. "If only we could capture Orenburg, then all other places would fall to us," some Kazakhs were heard to say. Instead the siege was lifted in the spring of 1774 with the arrival of a sizable contingent of the regular Russian army, against whom the rebels were no match. A Russian officer, Major M. Vaganov, sent to Nuraly to assure him of Russia's inevitable victory over the rebels, demanded that the khan find and return 256 Russians captured in recent Kazakh raids. Once again, Nuraly pleaded lack of authority and control over his people.[97]

Nuraly was not exaggerating. While he and most of the Kazakh sultans refrained from anti-Russian activity, many Kazakh notables and commoners did take part in the raids along the Russian frontier. In the summer of 1774, when the Russian troops stationed along the Orenburg fortification line were ordered to the Kazan region to suppress Pugachev's last attempt to reignite the uprising, the Kazakhs launched more than 240 raids along the frontier and captured many people and herds.[98] The most prominent leader in these raids was Syrym (Srym) batyr.

The Syrym Affair

Syrym batyr attracted the attention of the Russian authorities as one of the most active supporters of Pugachev. In June 1775, one of the Russian local commanders was ordered to pursue Syrym and his people at all costs and to either capture him or kill him on the spot. By the end of 1775, the Pugachev uprising was over, and Pugachev ended his life drawn and quartered in Moscow. But Syrym remained at large, emerging eight years later to lead the Kazakhs against Nuraly khan and his Russian supporters.[99]

The Pugachev uprising was brutally suppressed. But instead of reevaluating its policies in the region, the Russian government saw in the uprising a measure of its weakness, and its logical conclusion was to increase its military presence in the area and tighten its control over the local inhabitants. Long-standing Kazakh grievances remained unresolved, and with the encroaching Russian forts, the Kazakhs' ability to reach pastures became the most urgent issue.

The government repeatedly denied the Kazakhs' request to use the pasturelands between the Volga and Yaik, which remained unoccupied after the Kalmyks' exodus. In 1782 the Russian authorities finally conceded, allowing the Kazakhs limited access to the pastures on the Yaik's west bank. Significantly, the government now referred to this territory as the lands "inside the border" (*vnutrenniaia storona*) and stipulated that the Kazakhs could cross the Yaik only if they obtained permission from the border authorities and paid crossing fees. The Kazakhs' response to Russia's imposition of the imperial territorial boundaries on the steppe was similar to the Kalmyks': "The grass and water belong to Heaven." Why should they pay any fees?

The frustration among both Kazakh commoners and notables reached new heights by the summer of 1783. They accused Nuraly khan of being a Russian puppet and the only one to benefit from Russian rules and restrictions. Hoping to find redress in the Russian capital, they wrote to Catherine II and charged Nuraly with conspiring with the Yaik Cossacks against his own people. They explained that the khan had secretly informed the Yaik Cossacks about Kazakhs who crossed the Yaik, and after they were captured by the Cossacks he collected ransom from the captives' relatives, which he shared with the Cossacks.[100]

The situation was exacerbated by a natural disaster that struck the steppe in the winter of 1783. Freezing of the steppe caused massive losses among the Kazakhs' herds. The Kazakhs' attempts to cross the Yaik to save their remaining herds were again rebuffed by the Russian authorities. A despondent Syrym batyr and many other notables lashed out by launching a series of punishing raids against the Yaik Cossacks. Unable to stop them, Nuraly asked for Russian troops to help him in suppressing the rebels. But by 1785 the rebels represented the majority of the Kazakhs, and they moved away from Nuraly. Baron Osip Igelstrom, the newly appointed governor-general of the Simbirsk and Ufa provinces, which included Orenburg, became convinced that Nuraly was no longer capable of controlling the situation. Igelstrom wrote directly to the rebellious notables, promising to forgive their hostile acts against Russia if they returned the captives and pledged allegiance.[101]

In the summer of 1785, Kazakh notables met to discuss the Russian offer. Reluctantly they agreed to suspend the raids, but only if they were allowed to use the pastures between the Volga and the Yaik, the latter recently renamed the Ural River to erase memories of the Pugachev uprising and any association with the Cossacks' traditional freedoms. In addition, the Kazakhs insisted that the Ural Cossacks stop their raids against them and that Nuraly khan be deposed. Uncertain whether to accept these conditions, Igelstrom described the great hatred of the notables toward Nuraly khan and requested instructions from the capital.

Detailed directives concerning the abolition of the title of khan, division of the Lesser Horde into three parts each led by an elected chief notable, and establishment of a Frontier Court came personally from Catherine II. The empress also found it prudent to recruit loyal mullahs from among the Kazan Tatars, provide them with cash payments, and send them to the

Kazakhs in order to encourage the Kazakhs' loyalty and peaceful intentions. She believed the Kazakhs would soon be transformed into an irregular Russian military, settled in urban centers yet to be built, and adapted to civilization and commerce.[102]

Changes in Russian policies in shifting the government's support from the khan to the notables, dividing the Kazakhs, resolving the disputes through the Frontier Courts, and civilizing the Kazakhs through the influence of the Tatar-Bashkir Muslim clergy were all part of Catherine's consistent policies of applying the ideas of the Enlightenment to tame "the violent" and to civilize "the wild" subjects of the Russian Empire. Although encouraged, expanded, and approved by Catherine, these policies were attributed to Governor-General Igelstrom and later became known as the "Igelstrom reforms."

Throughout his long service in Russia's eastern and western borderlands, Igelstrom was instrumental in implementing his empress's enlightened ideas. His appointment in Orenburg meant to capitalize on his previous and relatively successful experience as the first governor of the Crimea. There, as in the Kazakh steppe, the core of his policies was the same: to integrate the respective Muslim populations into the empire through a slightly modified Russian administrative and legal system. To do so, Igelstrom identified and

FIGURE 13.   Edict of Catherine II to the notables of the Bayul clan of the Kazakh Lesser Horde in 1789 announcing the imperial favor for their loyalty and good behavior. From Kazanskii Universitet, Rukopisnyi otdel, Kazan, Tatarstan, no. 4875.

relied on cooperation with various local groups interested in assisting Russian policies. In particular, members of the Islamic clergy among the Crimeans and Kazakhs were his primary target, and many had indeed been successfully co-opted.[103]

Unaware that the governor-general's plans enjoyed the full support of St. Petersburg, Nuraly khan saw in Igelstrom the sole source of his misfortunes. In a last attempt to save his position, Nuraly appealed directly to the head of the War Office, Prince G. Potemkin. He complained that, while he remained a loyal subject of Russia, Igelstrom had chosen to ignore him and to rely on Syrym and other rebels who attacked the Russian frontier. But loyalty without power no longer sufficed, and the complaints went unanswered.

In 1786, with the open support of the Russian administration, Syrym attacked Nuraly, seized his wives, and forced the khan to flee to Uralsk (formerly Yaitsk). Later the same year, Nuraly was brought to Orenburg, stripped of the title of khan, and transferred to Ufa. When Nuraly's brother, Eraly, appealed for the khan's return, Igelstrom replied that Nuraly had come to him of his own will, and to return him now, amid the continuous Kazakh discords, would be unsafe. Polite hypocrisy apart, the baron laid out his case in a long letter to Eraly. He explained that when he had first arrived to govern the region, he found that the Kazakhs had abandoned their allegiance to the empress and were engaged in raiding, pillaging, and looting. His appeals to the khan to stop the violence on the frontier were in vain, as the latter pleaded his inability to control the Kazakhs. Igelstrom, then, had no choice but to appeal to the people (*narod*) directly. As a result, Syrym batyr, seven sultans, and 168 notables, altogether representing 21,900 households, took an oath of allegiance. His friendly advice to Eraly was to join the rest of the Kazakhs, participate in the Frontier Court, or else move away.[104]

The government continued to meet the Kazakhs' conditions for peace by ordering the Yaik Cossacks to cease their raids and opening up pastures between the Volga and Ural—all of which had an immediate and positive effect on the Kazakh economy. More than 45,000 Kazakh households crossed the Ural River to graze their herds. The cattle trade in Orenburg jumped from 204,164 sheep and horses in 1785 to more than 370,000 in each of the following two years.[105]

At the same time, Russian policies directed at instituting structural changes among the Kazakhs were producing an inevitable backlash. The Kazakh nobility of both the Lesser and Middle Hordes demanded the release of Nuraly khan. Even commoners made it clear that they wanted to replace Nuraly, but not to abolish the position of khan. Finally, the strategy of placing support behind Syrym and the commoners was questioned when it became known that Syrym was in contact with an Ottoman envoy and ready to join Bukhara and Khiva in the Ottoman-organized coalition against Russia.[106]

In the middle of another Russo-Ottoman war (1787–91), Colonel D. Grankin, stationed in Orenburg, was ordered to prepare a report on the situation in the steppe. His detailed and critical report, submitted to the War Office in 1788, bluntly pointed out the problems. Disabusing the government of any notion of loyalty on the Kazakhs' part, Grankin explained that when the Kazakhs of the Lesser Horde had accepted Russian suzerainty in 1786, they had done so purely out of greed in order to receive numerous gifts. Moreover, only commoners swore allegiance, while most nobles and notables (*znatnye bei i starshiny*) refused. But even the commoners had done so only after the mufti Muhammedjan Khusainov, newly appointed by the government to head the Muslim Spiritual Assembly, told them that it was fine to cheat the Christians and to agree to Christian demands in exchange for presents. The mufti then told the Russians that all the Kazakhs had sworn allegiance to the empress. In fact, no more than 2,000 households, or one-fifth of the Lesser Horde's population, had taken the oath, since at the time the Kazakhs were scattered about in different locations and did not know about the oath. The mufti later confessed that he had lied about the Kazakhs' allegiance because he wanted to please Her Majesty. The Kazakhs' connection to Islam was weak, continued Grankin's bleak report, and they had very few mullahs. The Frontier Court did not work because the elected Kazakhs were unfit for the position. The new policies had failed to stop the raids against the Russian settlements and passing caravans. The cost of patrolling the frontier with the Bashkirs and Ural Cossacks had increased, and that year alone the Kazakhs had caused more than 70,000 rubles' worth of damage.

In the colonel's military mind, the solution was to pressure the Kazakhs by further administrative and military means. He recommended convincing Nuraly, in return for the promise of a pension, to write to his people and explain the necessity of abolishing the title of khan, dividing the Lesser Horde into four parts, and reconstituting the Frontier Court with six notables from each part of the Horde, one Russian secretary with a knowledge of Tatar, and one mullah. Finally, peasants from the Kazan and Simbirsk districts should be invited to settle along the Samara, Uil, Ural, and Sakmara rivers, while the Stavropol Kalmyks and the Ural and Orenburg Cossacks were to live along the fortification lines. The policies of dividing and ruling the Kazakhs were to be made more effective by the forceful presence of Russian settlements and irregular military units along the entire frontier.[107]

By 1789, the government's policies in the Kazakh steppe had led to the emergence of two antagonistic factions: one consisted of notables and commoners led by Syrym, the other of nobles and notables who supported the ruling dynasty led by Eraly. It became increasingly clear that a policy of supporting the commoners in order to check the influence of the khan and his faction had succeeded neither in pacifying the Kazakhs nor in stabilizing the frontier. Part of the problem was that traditionally thorny issues between the administration and the Kazakhs continued to affect the interests of both the Kazakh nobles and commoners. Kazakhs in both factions protested that permits to use the pastures west of the Ural were granted selectively, their fugitives to Russia were not returned, and the abuses by the local authorities had not ceased. They also resented the Russian attempts to ban the traditional barimta between the Kazakhs and Ural Cossacks and replace it with the Frontier Courts. The government countercharged that the Kazakhs had continued their raids along the frontier, and Syrym, like the Kazakh khans before him, was also unable or unwilling to stop the raids.[108]

St. Petersburg instructed Igelstrom to revise his policies in such a way as to strengthen the khan's position, while at the same time dividing the Kazakhs. Unwilling to abandon his plans to impose the Russian political and legal system on the Kazakhs, Igelstrom submitted another proposal in October 1789. He suggested establishing one principal administration over the Horde, while dividing the Horde into six parts with a local court in each. Nuraly could be a chief administrator of the Horde with the title of khan. But the mood in St. Petersburg was rapidly changing. The news of active agitation by mullahs from Bukhara encouraging the Kazakhs to attack Russia and the increasing Kazakh raids along the frontier prompted the government to reverse its policy. Instead of supporting the commoners and dividing the Kazakhs, it was now once again inclined to exercise its control through strengthening the position of khan.

FIGURE 14. Reading the Quran in Bukhara. From *Aziatskaia Rossiia* (St. Petersburg: Izdanie Pereselencheskogo Upravleniia, 1914), vol. 1, p. 176.

A change in policies was clearly signaled in the spring of 1790 by the appointment of A. A. Peutling, who replaced Igelstrom as governor-general of Ufa. Unlike his predecessor, Peutling shared the belief of Colonel Grankin that the issues should be solved by military means. He forbade the Kazakhs from crossing the Ural River and at the same time permitted the Ural Cossacks to launch raids against them. To counteract the influence of Islamic clergy from Bukhara, he dispatched the mufti Muhammedjan Khusainov from Ufa to represent Russian interests in negotiations with Syrym. The mufti was instructed not to appease the Kazakhs by bestowing gifts upon them or promising the release of Kazakhs in Russian captivity. Instead, they were to be warned of severe retribution if they failed to accept the Russian conditions.

During the negotiations, it became apparent that, capitalizing on the Kazakhs' discontent, the Muslim clergy had attempted to rally the Kazakhs in a struggle to liberate Muslims from the oppression of infidel Russia. Even Syrym admitted that he had been accused of being an infidel for favoring relations with Russia. After the negotiations, some notables conceded that the mufti had succeeded in convincing them that according to his interpretation of the Quran, it was not against their law for Muslims to be subjects of the Russian Empire. A fragile compromise was reached when Syrym and his followers reluctantly agreed to Nuraly's return to the Kazakhs, but without the power or the authority of a khan.[109]

But the compromise came too late. The imperial government resolved to abandon Syrym and his faction in favor of the restored authority of a khan as a more effective way to project Russian interests. In the summer of 1790, Nuraly khan died in Ufa. His son Esim was elected khan by the majority of the notables but was deemed unacceptable by the Russian administration. Instead, the government pushed through its candidate, Eraly. The nobles of the ruling dynasty and some notables gathered near Orsk to agree on who should become khan. To dispel any doubt about the outcome of the election, the governor-general dispatched to the election site a sizable contingent of regular and irregular Russian troops armed with artillery. In January 1791, Eraly was declared khan.

Syrym, still hoping for a deal with the authorities, appealed to them in search of another compromise. He was ready to accept the restoration of the authority of a khan on the condition that the Kazakhs be allowed to choose their own khan. He insisted that Eraly had no popular support and would not be able to dispense justice. Syrym charged that the Russian government had violated his agreement with Baron Igelstrom. That agreement stipulated that no khan from the Abulkhayir dynasty was to be elected, and that payments were to be made directly to sixty-one notables. Instead, Eraly was appointed khan, and the notables had received no payments in the last three years.[110]

His pleas ignored, Syrym launched a war against Russia. A letter signed by Syrym and other notables and delivered to Governor-General Peutling charged that the governor and his administration had abused their authority and wanted to make the Kazakhs obedient slaves and soldiers by either oppressing them or buying them off with payments and gifts. The signatories noted that this was exactly what had happened to the Nogays, Bashkirs, and Kalmyks and assured him that they would not allow this to happen to the Kazakhs. Supported by the anti-Russian Muslim clergy, Bukhara, Khiva, and numerous Kazakh commoners and notables, Syrym and his followers attacked Russian fortifications and settlements along the frontier. Governor Peutling rejected any mediation. Instead he offered a 3,000 ruble bounty for Syrym's head, unleashed the Ural Cossacks against the rebels, and sent reinforcements.[111] His recalcitrant position, constant restrictions on the Kazakhs, the abuses of the local administration, and severe freezing of the steppe forced more Kazakhs to join Syrym in raiding the Russian borderlands.

Increasingly, reports from the local military commanders urged the government to rely more on notables and less on the khan. They recommended that the best way to pacify the Kazakhs was not by military means but "by encouraging them to settle down." These reports calling for dividing the Hordes, establishing the Frontier Courts, and building mosques, schools, and hospitals essentially revived recommendations made by Baron Igelstrom a decade earlier. Trying to make his case more convincing, General Ia. Bouver wrote to Catherine II and explained that the benefits of dividing and settling the Kazakhs were also advocated by the late Prince G. A. Potemkin-Tavricheskii, and that achieving security in the Kazakh steppe would open a direct land trade route to India.[112]

When Eraly died in the summer of 1794, the Russian government was no longer willing to impose its own candidate as khan. The realization that reliance on military solutions had backfired forced St. Petersburg to recall Governor Peutling and replace him with a far more moderate successor, S. K. Viazmitinov. Almost immediately the new governor issued orders restraining the Ural Cossacks and allowing the Kazakhs to cross the Yaik. In 1795 the administration confirmed Esim, who had been rejected by Peutling five years earlier, as the khan of the Lesser Horde.[113]

Syrym and his followers cautiously explored opportunities for working with the new khan, but Esim saw Syrym's popularity as a threat to his authority, and the two remained apart. The moderate approach of Governor Viazmitinov in supporting the authority of the khan and the nobles, while at the same time appeasing Syrym and his notables, failed to bring the two factions closer. In 1796, further adjusting its policies in the region, the government brought back mufti Muhammedjan Khusainov and appointed Baron Igelstrom governor of a now separate Orenburg district. Syrym interpreted the arrival of the two familiar and friendly faces as St. Petersburg's support of his antikhan attitude. Shortly thereafter, Esim khan was assassinated by a group of Kazakhs.[114]

The situation in the Kazakh steppe remained complicated. Exhausted by the long war between Syrym's and the nobles' factions, the Kazakhs were ready for a compromise. Igelstrom, urgently recalled from his retirement, had arrived in the region with instructions to restore calm along the frontier. Attempting to bring the two sides together with a new proposal, the baron suggested the establishment of a Khan's Council consisting of six notables representing major clans. Igelstrom chose Nuraly's son, Aichuvak, to be the Council Chair and mufti Khusainov to represent the Russian government. But the idea satisfied no one. Syrym was disappointed by such half-hearted support from Igelstrom and chose to wait. The nobles, however, took a more hostile position toward the Council, correctly realizing that such an institution favored the notables more than the ruling nobility.

Eventually Igelstrom decided that it was more important to move closer to the position of the Kazakh nobility than it was to please Syrym and his supporters. In a compromise reached with the Kazakh nobles, the baron agreed to abolish the Council but successfully insisted on his own candidate to become the khan of the Kazakhs. In 1797 he appointed Aichuvak the khan of the Lesser Horde. At the same time, the government continued to co-opt the notables and awarded those who proved their loyalty the Russian military ranks of lieutenant and captain. All of these measures by the government contributed to a further erosion of Syrym's power. Having lost many of his supporters and pursued by hostile Kazakhs, Syrym sought refuge in Khiva, where he died several years later.[115]

Syrym's flight was not necessarily a victory for the Kazakh nobles, as the rapprochement with the Russian authorities proved to be short-lived. Deprived of the ability to choose their own khan, some members of the ruling dynasty launched a war against the weak and ineffective khan appointed by the Russian administration. Others, such as one of Nuraly's sons, Bukey, chose to submit to the Russian authorities and sought permission to cross the Ural River in order to take up "permanent residence" as a Russian subject. In 1801 Bukey, together with 5,000 Kazakh households, crossed the river to lay the foundation for the new Kazakh entity, the Bukey Horde. Invested with the title of khan in 1812, Bukey and his people continued to reside within the imperial boundaries, separated from their relatives in the Lesser Horde.

It would take another decade before the successors to Baron Igelstrom would be able to implement the ideas he first put forth in the 1780s. In 1822 the governor-general of Siberia, Mikhail Speranskii, abolished the title of khan in the Middle Horde and imposed on it Russian imperial administrative, fiscal, and legal systems without the slightest consideration for the traditional structures of Kazakh society. Two years later, the Kazakhs of the

Lesser Horde found themselves divided into three parts and the title of their khan abolished. Their last khan, Shirghazi, was moved to Orenburg to take the honorary title of First Member of the Frontier Commission with an annual salary of 150 rubles. To underscore the Kazakhs' incorporation into the Russian Empire, the government began to refer to both the Lesser and Middle Hordes as "the Orenburg and Siberian Kazakhs" and considered moving its fortification lines deep into the Kazakh steppe.[116] Only the Greater Horde retained its independence, but not for long. Russia's relentless expansion into Central Asia continued, and by the 1860s the Greater Horde had also come under Russian rule.

CONCEPTS AND POLICIES IN THE
IMPERIAL BORDERLANDS, 1690s–1800

For a century and a half after Moscow's conquest of Kazan, Russia's rapid and forceful expansion pushed its frontiers farther south and east, taking Russian settlers far afield: to the foothills of the Caucasus as well as the shores of the Pacific Ocean. By the early eighteenth century, the initial stage of expansion was largely over. Undergirded by the new and continuing construction of fortification lines, which effectively contained nomadic raids, the government's security concerns of the past gave way to new priorities. Consolidation of the recently acquired territories and colonization of the new frontiers required a new ideology of expansion: Russia was now destined to bring Civilization and Christianity to the numerous non-Christian peoples who would become part of the "glorious and rising" empire.

The old practices did not immediately vanish, and the government persisted in demanding that the natives comply with its demands through the familiar rituals of taking an oath of allegiance, surrendering hostages, and paying yasak. Yet by the middle of the eighteenth century, the same frontier concepts were increasingly expressed through a new political vocabulary. The oath of allegiance was frequently referred to as a "protectorate" (*protektsiia*), hostages were assuming the ranks of Russian military officers and members of the Frontier Courts, and yasak was becoming a regular tax. The frontier was conceptualized in more precise terms, and the government was eager to appoint the Frontier Commission and to set up the Frontier Courts to deal with "frontier affairs." The natives' proximity to imperial borderlands and the government's new goals required an additional set of policies and strategies, which proved in the end to be far more destructive to the indigenous societies.

Several such policies became particularly visible throughout the eighteenth century. Previously sporadic efforts to convert the non-Christians to Orthodox Christianity now became a cornerstone of Russian policies in the southern borderlands. The natives were encouraged to convert and settle within the boundaries of the Russian Empire. Many of the new converts were resettled deep inside the Russian territories, while settlers from Russia were brought in to populate the frontier. The newly appropriated lands had to be transformed from the former grazing grounds of the indigenous peoples to farmlands of the Christians. By the late eighteenth century, Russia's expanding frontiers reached those of the Ottoman and Persian empires in the south and Qing China in the southeast. The frontiers of the Russian Empire were rapidly becoming imperial borders.

REPRESENTATIONS

It was the "wild steppe" that separated Kievan Rus from its nomadic neighbors. "Wild" implied not only lawless and dangerous space, but also the untamed nature of its nomadic inhabitants. Accordingly, the residents of Kievan Rus regarded their towns as centers of civilization, culture, and religion, while the nomads were wild, barbaric, and godless people at the edge of civilization. Such a view, which was common in many societies, changed when "civilization" was conquered by the Mongols. The steppe inhabitants, who exerted their power over fragmented and debilitated Russian principalities, could no longer be dismissed as "wild." From that time on, Russian merchants and officials were departing for "the steppe," and the epithet "wild" in this context was effectively dropped.[1]

The nearly simultaneous rise of Christian Moscow and the conversion of the Golden Horde to Islam in the fourteenth century added a new dimension to the conflict between the nomadic rulers and their sedentary subjects. Religion became the primary marker identifying and dividing the two sides and could not be easily separated from other collective identities. In 1390, the Muscovites described a certain new convert as "a newly enlightened who prior to this was a Tatar," while one Nogay mirza thought it was perfectly normal to address Ivan IV in the following way: "You are the Christian, and I am the Mangit." Even language was now seen as an attribute of religion, and Moscow referred to the letters from its steppe neighbors as written in a Muslim script, while the Muslims considered the correspondence from Moscow to be written in "Christian letters."[2]

As late as the nineteenth century, the pagan peoples of the middle Volga area failed to distinguish between ethnic and religious identities. Christianity was considered to be a Russian faith and Islam a Tatar one, and pagans who converted to Islam were regarded as Tatars (*ushli v Tatary*). Religion also implied certain moral and political qualities, and on various occasions the Russian officials made it clear that the natives were not good at keeping their oath and could not be trusted because they were Muslim.[3]

In the eighteenth century, while remaining a predominant identity marker, religion was increasingly fused with the notion of civilization, as reformed and Westernized Russia also began to conceive itself as a part of a European civilization. As such, Russia, not unlike its European counterparts, began to see itself as ordained by destiny to bring both Christianity and Civilization to the "wild and uncivilized" peoples along its frontiers. It was at this time that the notion of the "wild" steppe nomads was resurrected, and the Russian officials in charge of the southern and eastern frontier districts described the neighboring Kazakhs, Kalmyks, and Bashkirs as "wild, untamed horses," "wild animals," and "wild, unruly, and disloyal peoples" whose khans practiced "savage customs." On other occasions, the government officials described the nomadic peoples as the "wind," while the Russian Empire was proudly portrayed as a "pillar of stability and a glorious state under the sun." Obviously, in the political universe of Russian officials the non-Christian nomads represented the savage, the brute, the unreliable and unruly, while Russia stood for civilization, morality, and a state order, like a "pillar of stability" untouched by the "steppe winds."[4]

It was not until the 1830s that the image of the steppe nomads, engulfed by the Russian Empire and no longer presenting a military threat, began to evolve into "noble savages." Alexander Pushkin's famous musing about the "peaceful Kalmyks who were protecting the southern frontier of the Russian Empire" and who were "a good-natured, innocent, and docile people" driven into a desperate exodus by the abuses of the Russian administration was but only one example of a new romanticized image of the steppe and its inhabitants.[5] First feared, then despised, and finally pitied, Russia now acquired its own version of "a noble savage."

The description of the steppe inhabitants in the eighteenth century revealed as much about Russia's self-image as about its neighbors and reflected the government's newly developed realization of its civilizing mission among the non-Christians. In 1761, the Secret Commission charged with the task of developing a strategy of subduing the Kazakhs reported that the best way to deal with them was to eradicate their "useless customs and habits" through "softening them up" and introducing them to a sedentary lifestyle. It was explicitly and implicitly clear that in order to transform the "savage nomads" into civilized Russian subjects, the former had to settle down, farm, and eventually convert to Christianity.[6]

This vision of the Russian government was antithetical to the values of nomadic society, where settling down and farming were equated with loss of cherished freedom and scorned as incompatible with the warrior lifestyle. Russia's view of the natives as savages or children in need of civilization caused different reactions across the frontier. One Kalmyk tayishi, Dorji Nazar, whose pastures were closer to the Kazakhs and the Central Asian khanates than to the Russian frontier, reportedly wrote to the Kazakhs in 1732, dismissing the Russians as "not warriors and military men, rather they were farmers and townsmen," whom he regarded as "mice, and he could take them by their ears and give them to the Kazakhs."[7]

But the increasing and overwhelming presence of Russian forts, soldiers, merchants, and settlers could not be easily ignored; nor could Russian rhetoric. The Kazakh khans, for instance, often chose to ingratiate themselves with government officials and repeatedly referred to their own people as "wild and savage." Others, such as the Kabardinian nobles, resorted to verbal resistance when in 1768 the Russian commander of Mozdok, General N. A. Potapov, refused to negotiate with them because "it was below his dignity to speak to such people." Determined to seek justice within the confines of the empire, they warned the general that they would complain to the empress, because "we are only the servants of our empress, but not yours, and you cannot intimidate us with such letters of yours."[8]

The natives' appropriation of the dominant discourse was not surprising. Yet their ability to manipulate the same colonial system that sought to subjugate them was limited. While the general might have overstepped the boundaries of haughtiness, in the end his views were only a reflection of the official attitude formed and articulated in the capital. The natives were simply wild animals to be tamed and pacified by the benevolent imperial government, and Catherine II's own instructions to the frontier commanders sounded like exhortations to the trainer of the circus animals: first "restrain the local unbridled peoples from raids and predations," and later "cajole the savage peoples to be under our rule."[9]

It was only natural that such "wild beasts" and their societies were not deemed worthy of being either studied or described. Until the middle of the eighteenth century, the Russian government showed little interest in the different mores, customs, languages, and laws of the various indigenous peoples. As late as 1784, the report submitted by the Russian governor-general of the Caucasus, P. S. Potemkin, ended on such a note: "And because the differences between the peoples of the Caucasus are insignificant, by submitting the description of the Kabardinian people, I am describing all other peoples of the North Caucasus."[10]

Undoubtedly, Muscovite merchants, officials, and colonists who initially encountered non-Christians in the frontier areas observed different markers: haircuts, clothing, smells, food, marriage customs, lifestyle, language, and race.[11] Yet the government remained remarkably unconcerned with various outward signs of difference, which it considered malleable upon conversion to Christianity. This lack of curiosity was abundantly compensated for by the official interest in the political, economic, and religious classification of Russia's new subjects. As the number and the significance of non-Christians within the Russian Empire grew, it became even more important to describe and classify them. The first attempt at a comprehensive classification of Russia's subjects was made by the late-eighteenth-century Russian writer and historian Prince Mikhail Shcherbatov. In a 1776 treatise, Prince Shcherbatov suggested that the peoples of the empire should be divided into six categories in accordance with their lifestyle, taxation, military service, and religious affiliation:

1. Russians and all non-Christians who pay the soul tax and provide recruits
2. Russians and non-Christians who pay taxes but do not provide recruits
3. Christians other than Russian Orthodox
4. All kinds of Cossacks and other military settlers
5. Bashkirs and other savage peoples who practice Islam and
6. Kalmyks and other nomadic idol-worshippers.[12]

Unable to draw a clear distinction between religious, ethnic, and social identities, Shcherbatov presented an array of overlapping categories typical of premodern mentalities. But in contrast to the previous concerns with taxation, military service, and religion alone, his classification now offered as additional criteria lifestyle ("nomadic") and civilization or the lack of it ("savage"). It laid the groundwork for Mikhail Speranskii's landmark classification of the non-Christian subjects of the Russian Empire in the 1820s.

By the late eighteenth and the early nineteenth centuries, Russia's diverse empire included Orthodox, Catholic, and Protestant Christians along with Jews in the west and Muslims, Buddhists, and pagans in the south and east. Throughout the three hundred years since Moscow's initial expansion, the perception of the newly vanquished peoples had undergone several transformations. At first they were assigned an extra-territorial identity (*inozemets*, literally a person of a different land) and considered foreigners (etymologically similar to the German *Ausländer* and the English "foreigner"). Shortly thereafter, they were considered to be Russia's subjects and were referred to by their specific ethnic names.

It was not until the mid-eighteenth century that the collective terms for Russia's non-Christian subjects emerged in the official Russian language. The non-Christians were now more systematically referred to as *inovertsy* (of a different faith), and by the early nineteenth century as *inorodtsy* (of a different origin, descent, and later race). The two terms conflated notions of people and faith, emphasizing unmistakably that the non-Christians were different from the Russians in both religion and race. Religion also marked the boundaries in the usage of the term "nation" (*natsiia*), which by the late eighteenth century was largely reserved for the Christian peoples (e.g., Georgians and Armenians) within the Russian Empire, while the non-Christians were referred to as a people (*narod* or *liudi*).[13]

Redefining the status of the non-Christians clearly reflected a change in the self-perception of the Russian state and its evolution into a nation and empire, which despite its diverse populations was conceived of as a Christian one. It was all the more ironic that with a further integration of the non-Christians into the Russian Empire, their foreignness was emphasized in starker terms. Even then, the boundaries of the ostensibly hardened categories could be crossed, and the difference erased, if the empire's non-Christian subjects became Christian.

NON-CHRISTIANS INTO RUSSIAN ORTHODOX

> Nothing can tame their barbarity better and make them more docile than
> their conversion to Christianity. Then, through contact with our people, it
> will not be difficult to eradicate their language and customs.
>
> —MEMORANDUM OF THE ASTRAKHAN GOVERNOR PETR KRECHETNIKOV IN
> 1775 CONCERNING RUSSIA'S POLICIES IN THE NORTH CAUCASUS

At the heart of the Russian policies in the eighteenth century was an overwhelming sense of the imperial mission to bring Civilization and Christianity—two concepts inseparable in the minds of the Russian officials—to the indigenous peoples. Curiously, such a mission was to be achieved without a mission or missionaries in a traditional sense, that is, a group of priests trained for missionary activity and residing among the non-Christians in a mission compound. Instead, the natives were to be transplanted to the Russian towns and villages to be converted and resettled among the Russian population.

The word "mission" was not to be found, and even the first missionary institution established by the government in the middle of the eighteenth century and charged with missionary activity in the middle Volga area was named the Agency of Convert Affairs (Kontora novokreshchenskikh del). Significantly, its name indicated that it was meant to be a part of the civil, not the church, bureaucracy. On a rare occasion when the government sent a mission to the North Caucasus in 1744 to preach among the Ossetians, this short mission was referred to as the "Ossetian Commission." It was only in the nineteenth century that the term and concept of a mission appeared in Russia, suggestive of both the evolution of a missionary consciousness and the government's recognition of the fact that missionary matters fell more within the purview of the church than of government agencies.[14]

189

FIGURE 15.   Bishop Antonii with converted animists from the Khevsur region in northeastern Georgia. From *Pribavleniia k Tserkovnym Vedomostiam,* vol. 27 (1914), pt. 1, no. 1.

Yet the concept of traditional missionary activity was not unknown in Moscow prior to the nineteenth century. The story of St. Stefan's life is the best-known case of Moscow's earliest attempts to proselytize among the non-Christians. The story is significant, not only because it is one of the few available accounts of early missionary activity by the Russian Orthodox church, but also because St. Stefan's approach stands in sharp contrast to the missionary work of the church after the 1550s.

His vita, recounted shortly after his death, begins in the 1380s, when St. Stefan arrived in the Perm region in the foothills of the Ural Mountains determined to spread Christianity among the indigenous pagan population. Impressed by his success, the metropolitan of Moscow and the grand prince appointed St. Stefan the first bishop of Perm. Until his death, St. Stefan continued his efforts to convert the natives of the region, where he created a native alphabet, translated the Scriptures from the Russian language, and conducted services in the vernacular.[15] Such an approach to winning converts was quite common. After all, Rus had likewise received an alphabet from Greek monks in the tenth century and adopted Christianity shortly thereafter.

However, before Moscow's dramatic expansion in the 1550s, such efforts at proselytizing among the pagans occurred only sporadically. It was not until Moscow acquired the Kazan and Astrakhan regions, with their numerous non-Christian population, that the idea of religious conversion began to enjoy the all-embracing support of a government imbued with an overpowering sense of manifest religious destiny. After the mid-sixteenth century, the missionaries took a back seat to the interests of the government, as they were to preach in lands that had already been conquered and governed by Moscow.

The new missionary spirit of the increasingly self-conscious Orthodox Muscovy was forcefully expressed by the triumphant Russian tsar. In his 1556 letter to Archbishop Gurii of the newly founded Kazan diocese, Ivan IV suggested that converting pagans was a divine duty, adding that missionaries "should teach the pagans [*mladentsy*, lit. children] not only to read and write, but to make them truly understand what they read, and [they], then, will be able to teach others, including the Muslims."[16]

But immediate political considerations continually dampened Moscow's missionary zeal. Ivan IV had to answer charges from the Ottomans and Crimeans of harm caused to Muslims and the Islamic faith, and more than once he had to abandon his projects to appease the concerns of the Ottoman sultan.[17] An additional constraint was Moscow's dependence on a local Muslim elite in the initial postconquest stage. Writing to the Nogay Ismail beg in 1563, Ivan IV explained that he could not remove the Astrakhan princes because "we are the Christian sovereign, and they are the Muslim people. If we removed them and keep them away from Astrakhan, the Astrakhan people might flee to other lands and they would tell that we did not keep our word, that two faiths could not live in peace, and that the Christian sovereign destroyed the Muslims. . . . And in our lands there are many people of Muslim faith who are in our service, and they live in accordance with their law."[18]

Whether Ivan's words indeed expressed his idea of tolerance, were dictated by the immediate necessity of political accommodation, or were simply a convenient excuse, the issue of converting non-Christians did not come to the fore until the early 1590s. In his letter to the tsar, the Kazan metropolitan Germogen complained that because of the neglect of the local voevodas, the Tatars flouted earlier prohibitions and built new mosques, and converts did not observe Christian laws and continued to live among their non-Christian kin. In response, the tsar's decree of 1593 stipulated that converts should be resettled in a separate compound near Kazan and given farmland, and that they should reside among the Russians. Russian officials were to ensure that converts practiced Christianity and did not intermarry with Tatars or foreign prisoners of war. Furthermore, children of mixed marriages and the slaves of the converts were to be baptized. Those converts who did not follow Christian ways were to be put in chains and thrown in jail to

191

make them forget the Tatar faith and become firm believers in Christ. All mosques were to be destroyed.[19]

Moscow's increasingly militant stance against the Crimea and the Ottoman Empire in the seventeenth century was accompanied by more aggressive policies toward Muslims inside Russia. In 1654 these Russian policies compelled the Crimean khan, Muhammed Giray IV, to denounce Moscow's treatment of its Muslim subjects. He noted that many Christians lived under the protection of the Ottoman sultan and were free to worship, whereas the Muscovite tsar burned the Quran, destroyed mosques, tortured Muslims, and forced them to convert.[20]

Russia had long defined itself as a crusading state and the depository of the only true religion. By the late seventeenth century, the idea of Russia's destiny as a Christian state at the forefront of the struggle with the Islamic world had further crystallized as the government prepared to confront the Ottoman Empire. In 1696, Peter I conquered the Ottoman fortress of Azov and was nurturing plans for a broad anti-Ottoman coalition of European states. Such plans had to be shelved, however, because European powers had other priorities. In 1699, at Carlowitz, Russia became a reluctant signatory to a peace treaty with the Ottoman Porte.

The importance and duty of converting non-Russians was reiterated by Ivan Pososhkov, a contemporary of Peter the Great and often referred to as "the Russian Adam Smith." In a treatise written in 1719, Pososhkov contrasted the feeble missionary efforts of the Russians with those of the Roman Catholic church and chastised the Russian government and the Orthodox church for their inability to attract non-Russians to Christianity:

> And these peoples have been the subjects of the Russian Empire for two hundred years, but they did not become Christians and their souls perish because of our negligence. The Catholics are sending their missionaries to China, India, and America. [Despite] the fact that our faith is the right one—and what could be easier than converting the Mordva, the Maris, and the Chuvash—yet we cannot do this. And our non-Christians are like children, without a written language, without a law, and they do not live far away, but within the Russian Empire, along the Volga and the Kama rivers; and they are not sovereign, but the subjects of Russia.[21]

Inspired by the missionary work of the Catholic church and particularly the Jesuit order, Ivan Pososhkov was primarily concerned with saving the souls of non-Christians and making them good Christians. His views were shared by the government, albeit for different reasons. Defined by Russia's crusading spirit in its struggle with Islam, government policies of religious conversion acquired additional importance in securing the political loyalty of Moscow's non-Christian subjects.

New efforts to convert non-Christians were also prompted in part by Russia's strategic concerns, in particular the government's constant fear of

192

an emergence of a hostile Islamic axis—a united front of various Muslim peoples under the Ottoman umbrella. No less important, however, were disturbing reports of a growing number of non-Christian converts to Islam. The news that some non-Christians were lured by the "disgusting faith of Muhammad" prompted Peter I to order that missionaries be taught native languages and sent to preach among non-Christians.[22]

Not relying on preaching alone, the Russian government also resorted to discriminatory legislation and the confiscation of lands to induce the conversion of its Muslim subjects. In contrast, converts not only were allowed to retain their lands but also were promised the lands confiscated from their more stubborn brethren. Upon conversion, converts were rewarded with cash: 10 rubles per Tatar noble, 5 rubles for his wife, and 1.25 rubles for each child.[23] Finally, converts were offered three-to-six-year tax breaks and other exemptions, while other Muslim and pagan subjects of the Russian Empire found themselves carrying rapidly increasing burdens of corvée, military service, and taxation.[24]

Although the numbers of converts had continued to grow on paper, reports from the field lamented the fact that the conversions were only nominal and converts remained ignorant of Christianity and did not observe any of its precepts. It was becoming more apparent that reliance on sheer force or material incentives to effect conversions was insufficient.[25] The government and the church responded by focusing missionary activity less on reporting large numbers of converts and more on spreading the Gospel among them and ensuring their attachment to Christianity. The idea of civilizing the savage ("wild," "ignorant," "unenlightened") became a major driving force behind proselytizing efforts throughout the eighteenth century. The language of the church officials reflected a change of attitude, as the converts were now more frequently referred to as the "newly enlightened" (*novoprosveshchennye*).

Despite the new emphasis on proselytizing among the non-Christians, some major impediments to conversion could not be easily overcome. Many non-Christians were deterred from converting, fearful of either retaliation from their kin or abuses from Russian local authorities. Indeed, widespread corruption in the Russian frontier towns and forts subverted efforts to convert the natives. Local officials abused the rights of the converts, often withholding their due rewards or continuing to collect taxes instead of making a promised exemption. Corruption, however, could work both ways: non-Christians were also known to bribe officials and priests so that the pagans could continue their traditional practices and Muslims could build new mosques and religious schools. Aware of the corruption and unsatisfied with the progress of its proselytizing efforts, the government once again decided to resort to more coercive measures and to centralize missionary policies under a newly created umbrella organization, the Agency of Convert Affairs.

Established in September 1740, the Agency of Convert Affairs was supposed to operate in four provinces: Kazan, Astrakhan, Nizhnii Novgorod, and Voronezh. The agency consisted of three priests, five translators, several staff members, and couriers, with a budget of 10,000 rubles and a 5,000 chetvert grain allowance. About one-fourth of their budget was to be used to pay the salaries of agency employees, while the rest was allocated toward founding four schools for non-Christians in addition to the rewards bestowed upon conversion. Instructions to the agency consisted of twenty-three articles explaining in great detail how to proceed with converting the non-Christians.[26]

The Elizabethan reign (1741–62) marked one of the most violent assaults on non-Christians' religious beliefs. The government put new emphasis on using force and legislative decrees, rather than teaching Christian doctrine. Missionary activity focused on the Kazan province, which was, in the words of Father Dmitrii Sechenov, the first head of the Agency of Convert Affairs, "a center of all the non-Christians residing in southeastern Russia."[27]

Orders to destroy mosques and resettle non-Christians by force indicated the beginning of renewed efforts to expedite the conversion process. These policies were implemented with particular enthusiasm by the Kazan bishop, Luka Konashevich. In 1743 the government ordered that 418 out of 536 mosques in the Kazan region be demolished. The remaining 118 mosques were left alone because they had been built prior to the Kazan conquest, and the government feared that their destruction would cause a popular uprising. In other Volga provinces, only one mosque was allowed in each village, and only if the village had an exclusively Muslim population with no fewer than 200 to 300 males.[28]

Preventing the spread of Islam and discouraging its practice remained one of the government's highest priorities. In 1756, the government added its own bleak statistics to the agency's reports. In addition to the mosques destroyed in the Kazan province, the authorities destroyed 98 of 133 mosques in the Siberian provinces of Tobolsk and Tara and 29 of 40 mosques in the Astrakhan province.[29]

In addition to a series of decrees once again intended to encourage the conversion of non-Christians, the government also used Russian criminal and military systems for this purpose. Thus, those convicted of petty crimes and, between 1741 and 1760, even of capital offenses continued to receive pardons upon conversion, while non-Christians who converted to Islam as well as the Muslims who converted them were severely punished. Non-Christian recruits who converted to Christianity received an exemption from military service, while the non-Christians drafted in their stead faced additional pressure to convert from priests in the Russian army.[30]

The desire to avoid diplomatic confrontation with the Ottoman Porte was probably behind the government's decision to formalize the conversion procedures aimed at its Muslim population.[31] The 1750 decree stipulated that non-Christians should not be baptized without first submitting a voluntary petition in writing. The petition was prepared in advance, and a petitioner needed only to add his or her name to it. The prescribed form required that a Muslim petitioner first denounce and reject "the most false Prophet [Muhammad] and his most false and ungodly laws [the Quran]," and then state his or her "sincere desire to be baptized into the Christian faith of salvation." Apparently it was decided that pagans did not have to denounce their idols or to praise the virtues of Christianity at any great length, as their petitions were much shorter than those required of Muslims.[32]

Reports of the Agency of Convert Affairs boasted of the large numbers of converts: more than 100,000 in the Kazan province in 1747. Yet there was a striking contrast between the Muslim and pagan populations of the region. In 1763, converted Tatars represented about one-third of the Tatar population of the province (13,615 converts and 35,079 Muslims), while almost 95 percent of the pagan Maris, Mordva, Chuvash, and Votiaks were registered as converts.[33] The government's draconian laws favoring neophytes at the expense of their Muslim kin could lead only to a growing resistance to missionary activity. The Muslim Tatars and Bashkirs revolted numerous times throughout the seventeenth and eighteenth centuries. Together with other non-Christians, they were a crucial force in Russia's two largest popular uprisings, those of Stepan Razin in the early 1670s and of Emelian Pugachev a century later.[34]

It is not surprising that conversions induced either by force or through promises of rewards were less than sincere. Government officials reported that the converts did not choose to receive baptism voluntarily but did so in order to avoid punishment for their crimes.[35] Local priests complained that since the agency did not keep a register of converts by name, it was difficult to keep track of non-Christians, who often came to convert several times in order to receive rewards. In 1757 the government responded by ordering that those who had converted more than once be dispatched to monasteries to perform hard labor. The missionaries further complained that the converts did not allow preachers into their villages and houses, claiming that they had been granted exemptions by the government. The converts even threatened to beat the priests if they failed to provide the rewards that the converts considered to be their right.[36] The excessive force used by the Agency of Convert Affairs, the complaints of church officials and converts against each other, and the large-scale but nominal character of conversion made it clear that missionary work in Russia in the middle of the eighteenth century was badly flawed.

In April 1764, Empress Catherine II instructed the government to issue a decree that inaugurated the most tolerant period in Russia's relations with non-Christians since the middle of the sixteenth century. The decree also ended the twenty-four-year existence of the Agency of Convert Affairs. It put converts under the governance of the same civil and religious administration that oversaw all other Russian state peasants. Missionary activity was to be continued by educating non-Christians. For this purpose, the decree stipulated that preachers with annual salaries of 150 rubles should be sent to spread the Gospel without any coercion, and that schools for the converts should continue to teach their children. The government recognized that the number of converts had grown to such an extent that those who remained unbaptized could no longer carry the burden of paying taxes or supplying military recruits in the converts' stead. The neophytes would continue to receive a three-year tax exemption, but other rewards had to be scaled down. They were to be given an icon and a cross, and a voucher that would be credited against their future taxes when their tax exemption expired.[37]

Religious tolerance in the reign of Catherine II was a product not only of her enlightened ideas but also of sheer pragmatism. The introduction of reforms, the incorporation of the new territories of the Crimea and Poland, and the importation of German colonists required a manifestation of toleration toward the non-Christian subjects of the expanding empire. With Russia's military superiority over the neighboring Islamic states and peoples no longer in doubt, St. Petersburg tried a new approach: to ensure the loyalty of its Muslim subjects through toleration and collaboration with the Islamic clergy rather than through coercion and discriminatory laws. Missionary work did continue, although less by force and more by the teaching of the Gospel.[38]

The cumulative effects of the government's policies of religious conversion became fully apparent in 1766, when delegates from different corners of the Russian Empire arrived in the capital to participate in the Legislative Commission in charge of compiling the new legal code. The delegates from the Penza province, representing local Tatars in Russian military service, complained that Muslims who had committed crimes were choosing to convert to Christianity in order to escape punishment. The delegates suggested that such criminals should be punished.[39] The Tatars from Orenburg explained that although they were experiencing a severe labor shortage, they were forbidden from hiring converted Mordva, Maris, or Votiaks. The delegates requested that they be allowed to hire converts and promised to let them practice Christianity. The yasak-paying Chuvash of the Kazan province objected to the converts' being granted a tax exemption while they had to pay additional taxes and provide recruits and means of transportation in the converts' stead.[40]

The most detailed grievances were submitted by the Tatars of the Kazan province. They complained that they suffered greatly as a result of the privileges granted to converts, such as exemptions from taxes, military service,

FIGURE 16. A missionary school for Mari women converts in the middle Volga region. From *Pribavleniia k Tserkovnym Vedomostiam,* vol. 13 (1900), pt. 2, no. 43.

and current debts, and because of land speculation by converts, who were selling land to Russian gentry. The Tatars objected to the discrimination in taxation that required them to pay 1.10 rubles for each serf, while Russian landowners paid only seventy kopecks. They asked for permission to cut timber and to bear sabers and arms at home and on the road. Their most urgent plea was for greater religious freedom: they asked the government for permission to construct mosques, send their elders on pilgrimage to Mecca, and punish those who mocked their religion.[41]

Remonstrances were not limited to non-Christians; converts, too, submitted numerous grievances. Those from Siberia lamented that their ignorance of the Russian language and laws made them vulnerable to abuse by Russian peasants and landlords. In one instance, converts were lured by a one-year contract to work at ironworks and then were not allowed to return home. Other converts complained that they had lost their lands to Russian landlords, that their farms and forests had been taken away from them for the use of factories, that merchants did not allow them to trade, that officers stationed to protect them took food and fodder by force, that judges kept them in jail for months, and that their well-to-do brethren were ruined by jealous Russians.[42]

197

The number of converts continued to grow relentlessly. In 1781, government statistics for the Kazan region presented the following numbers:

Tatars—10,631 converts and 66,072 not converted
Chuvash—89,995 converts and 926 not converted
Maris—25,630 converts and 739 not converted
Mordva—3,296 converts and none not converted
Votiaks—1,863 converts and 305 not converted.[43]

Unimpressed by the numbers of converts, some contemporary observers judged the government's efforts in converting the natives to be a failure. The results of Russia's proselytizing of its non-Christian subjects were summarized by Prince Mikhail Shcherbatov. He was not surprised that non-Christians remained attached to their native beliefs, observing that it could not have been otherwise because they had been converted by force. He lambasted the Russian Orthodox Church, which

> neither attempted to teach converts first, nor sent preachers who knew their language, but instead brought them to baptism in the same way they would have been brought to a bath; gave them a cross, which, in their ignorance, they considered some kind of a talisman, and an image of Christ, which they regarded as an idol; and forbade them from eating meat on fast days, a prohibition that they did not follow, while priests took bribes from them for overlooking this. Likewise, no attempt was made to translate the Holy Scriptures into their languages, nor to teach these to the priests, so that their preaching could be understood.[44]

At the same time that Prince Shcherbatov was pointing out the reasons why the church had failed to achieve a genuine conversion of non-Christians, Amvrosii Podobedov, the newly appointed archbishop of Kazan, simply observed the facts when he reported to the Synod on the situation in his archdiocese: "I find that the ignorant [*neprosveshchennye*] non-Christian peoples, the Chuvash and Maris who reside here, have not only insufficient, but not even the slightest notion about the precepts of the faith into which they were converted by holy baptism."[45]

Such was the state of affairs in the middle Volga area, which in the course of two and a half centuries had been transformed from the frontier into the core region of the Russian Empire. Intimidation, force, revocation of privileges, confiscation of land, legal and economic discrimination—all of these coercive measures could have been used only in the territories already under the firm control of the Russian military and bureaucracy. In the frontier areas, however, where the government's hold over the new territory remained tenuous and the need for the natives' cooperation was acute, Russia's conversion policies had to rely more on carrots than on sticks. Accordingly, the church officials were instructed to win converts not by force, but by "love." The converts were rewarded with presents and cash; some were enlisted and assigned to the frontier garrisons, but most were resettled farther away from the borderlands.[46]

Geopolitical considerations of the frontier compelled the government to exercise more caution than in the areas already under Russia's firm administrative control. When the issue of sending a mission to the Ossetian people in the North Caucasus came up in 1744, the Senate instructed the Synod to send only Georgian, not Russian, priests, and to give them no written instructions, so as to avoid any suspicion on the part of the Ottoman or Persian governments.[47]

In a few cases when missionaries were sent to reside among the Ossetians and Kalmyks, they proved short-lived and ineffective. After several years among the natives, the missionaries complained of the hardships and burdens of everyday life and the difficulty of learning the natives' languages; they often pleaded for transfers back to their monasteries in St. Petersburg, Moscow, or Kazan. The support of the government also fell short of the missionaries' expectations; they reported that they had insufficient funds to build new churches and reward converts.[48]

The idea of converting the natives received additional impetus in the late eighteenth century, when Russia's continuous triumphant expansion allowed government officials to equate anew Russian imperial ambitions with the propagation of Christianity. In 1784 the governor-general of the Caucasus, P. S. Potemkin, concluded that it was quite possible that the Kabardinians had become duplicitous after they converted to Islam, but that their perfidious nature might be explained by their poor understanding of Islam's tenets. Before this conversion to Islam, the governor continued, they were Christians, and if suitable priests were sent to preach among them, "undoubtedly, they would soon shed the light of divine bliss among all the peoples scattered in the mountains."[49]

P. S. Potemkin was not the first to introduce the idea of the "re-Christianization of the Caucasus." A visible testimony of Peter I's intentions was a newly founded fort in northern Daghestan, which he chose to name the Holy Cross. In 1748 an unsigned report about Kabarda was prepared by the Foreign Office. Referring to the testimony of one of the Kabardinian nobles, it maintained that the Kabardinians had always been Christians, and that their origins could be found among the fifteenth-century Ukrainian Cossacks who had come to settle at Fort Tersk and in its environs. At that time they were known as Circassians or Kabardinians and became Russian subjects, but they were later seized by the Crimeans and forced to convert to Islam. When they returned to the Terek River, they had forgotten their language and their Christian faith. A similar memorandum, originating from the same office in the 1770s, went one step further in concluding that this was why the Ottomans had claimed them as their subjects.[50] Despite the absurd nature of such reports, their implications for policymakers in the Russian capital were obvious: the Russian government had grounds to dispute the Ottoman suzerainty over the Kabardinians and to legitimize its efforts to "re-Christianize" them.

While some argued that conversion was justified because these peoples had been Christians in the past, others suggested that Islam prevailed among them because they had been Christians in name only and, essentially, remained pagan. Both arguments, however, led to the same conclusion: a more active evangelization would bring them back to Christianity.[51] Yet, despite the various plans for missionary work among the natives, these proposals remained mostly committed to paper and were left unrealized.

Instead of being "re-Christianized," the region was continuously "re-Islamicized." A new wave of Islamic influence was brought to the region in the middle of the eighteenth century by the Nakshbandi dervishes of the mystical Sufi order. These mendicant Muslim preachers needed no missions, resources, or government support. Expelled from Persia, they brought their austere and uncompromising version of popular Islam to the mountainous villages, where they found a receptive audience. An anti-Russian, anti-Christian uprising led by sheikh Mansur in the 1780s was a direct result of the increasing influence of the Sufi order in the Caucasus.[52] Even though unsuccessful in pushing back the Russian "infidels," the uprising left an indelible mark on the memory of the peoples of the North Caucasus and was only the first in a series of uprisings declared by the Muslim clerics as *ghazawat* (holy war) against the Russians. Inevitably the continuous Russian expansion in the region drove the natives closer into the arms of the local Muslim clergy and to resistance under the green banners of Islam.

Whether in the mountains of the North Caucasus, the forests of the middle Volga, or the steppe of Central Asia, the non-Christian peoples inevitably perceived Russian colonization as inseparable from the government's attempt to convert them to Christianity. The indigenous peoples responded with frequent and violent uprisings against the Russian officials and their policies. Sometimes the rumor of an impending forcible conversion was sufficient to stir anxiety among the native population. It was such a rumor that finally pushed the Kalmyks toward their tragic exodus from Russia in 1771 and forced many Kazakhs of the Bukey Horde to flee to their old pastures east of the Ural River in 1820.[53]

Yet to some the attraction of opportunities and rewards in Russia proved to be irresistible, and they chose to cross the boundaries—geographical, social, and religious—and convert to Christianity. In the frontier regions, as elsewhere, the government policies of religious conversion achieved the same results: creating and exacerbating social and economic divisions and rivalries within the indigenous population. The continuous and increasing exodus of natives to Russia, their conversion, and the government's refusal to have them returned emerged as one of the most important concerns to both the natives and the imperial government.

MIGRATION OF THE NATIVE ELITE AND COMMONERS

> The Russian people are permitted to purchase the Kalmyks, Kumyks, Chechens, Kazakhs, Karakalpaks, Turkmens, Tomuts, Tatars, Bashkirs, Baraba Tatars and other Muslims and idol worshippers. . . . Priests, merchants, Cossacks and others are allowed to buy, convert, and teach the non-Christians, who are to remain their serfs until the owners' death.
>
> —SENATE DECREE OF 1755

> I regard the separation of the commoners from the nobles as the surest way to secure our frontier.
>
> —PRINCE G. A. POTEMKIN-TAVRICHESKII INSTRUCTING THE COMMANDER OF THE RUSSIAN TROOPS IN THE CAUCASUS, GENERAL P. S. POTEMKIN, NOT TO RETURN THE FUGITIVE KABARDINIAN COMMONERS TO THEIR NOBLES

By the early eighteenth century, the Russian government achieved a remarkable reversal of a long-established frontier pattern. The protracted hemorrhaging of the Russian population, which had been captured and sold into slavery outside of Russia, for the most part had been stopped. Increasingly, the former non-Christian raiders were transformed into converts and settled within the borders of the Russian Empire. Some of them were captured and sold into Russian households, but most came to seek refuge of their own volition. Now it was the turn of the native nobles across the frontier to complain and demand the return of their people.

The migration of Russian settlers into the new territories in the second half of the eighteenth century is well known and is rightly considered to be a major element of Russian colonization policies.[54] Less well known is a mass migration of the vanquished indigenous population toward the frontiers, such as the case of the thousands of Tatars, Maris, Chuvash, and Bashkirs who, deprived of their lands and escaping the military draft, high taxation, and forced conversion to Christianity, abandoned their residences in the middle Volga area and fled toward the southeastern frontiers in the early eighteenth century.[55]

Several official reports give a clear indication of the extent and impact of such mass dislocation of the native population. In 1734, Ivan Kirilov suggested that as many as 20,000 fugitives from the Kazan region could be used in the construction of Orenburg. Thirty-two years later, the governor of Orenburg, Prince Putiatin, informed the Senate that the region was overwhelmed with non-Christian Chuvash and Tatars who had fled their villages near the Volga to avoid converting to Christianity. The dubious loyalty of the non-Christians to the Russian state and of the new converts who, the governor admitted, had converted involuntarily had compelled him to recommend that Russian peasants (*velikorusskie liudi*) be brought in to make them a predominant majority in the region. He urged specifically, and the Senate agreed, that the lands around the newly constructed and strategically important New Moscow Highway be confiscated or purchased from the Bashkirs and distributed among the Russian settlers.[56]

While many from among the native peoples tried to escape the Russian military and administrative arms by fleeing into the more distant imperial borderlands, others preferred to abandon their native society and seek opportunities across the frontier in Russia. The Russian authorities directly and indirectly encouraged the escape and migration of the indigenous population into Russia in what became one of the cornerstones of the government's colonization policies in the frontier regions.

Russia's growing impact on the neighboring native societies was simply inescapable. Attracted by the Russian government's offers of generous rewards and payments, some of the native elite continued to leave for Russia. But even those who stayed behind found the benefits of trade with Russia irresistible. To maximize the profits from such trade, they increased the taxation of their own population, inadvertently adding to the numbers of refugees to Russia. Now émigrés were also commoners fleeing to avoid oppression by their own nobles.[57] This migration of the indigenous population, both elite and commoners, and its larger implications remained virtually unnoticed and unexamined in the historiography.

Throughout the fifteenth and sixteenth centuries, the simultaneous demise of the Golden Horde and the rise of Moscow attracted a number of non-Christian nobles who left their uluses for the Muscovite court in search of protection, service, and privileges. We have already seen in chapter 3 many examples of such "aristocratic diasporas" and Moscow's policy of seeking out and attracting them into Muscovite service.[58] One contingent of such possible emigrants was fugitives in the steppe, who found temporary refuge there from their rivals. Upon learning of the desperate situation of a certain fugitive Tatar noble ("v chuzhom iurte stoish, i sam vsi istomen, i kon' tvoi poten"), the grand prince would dispatch his representative and offer to harbor the noble and his retinue. Such offers were often accepted, as the fugitives hoped to recover their lost uluses with Moscow's help.[59]

Another contingent of would-be defectors was disgruntled Crimean and Nogay nobles, who were secretly approached by Muscovite envoys during their official diplomatic mission to the Crimean khan or Nogay beg. The envoys promised generous rewards in exchange for the nobles' service and the unconditional freedom to depart from Muscovy. Tempted by handsome rewards or protection from their rivals in the steppe, many non-Christian nobles elected to join the service of the grand prince.[60]

One of the earliest and most spectacular examples of Moscow's ability to attract such fugitives into its service was the arrival in Moscow of two royal princes from Kazan, Yakub and Kasim. In 1452 the latter was rewarded for his loyalty and granted the town of Gorodets (also known as Meshchera), which bordered on the Kazan region.[61] In one daring move, Moscow acquired political leverage over Kazan by having within its borders a legitimate challenger to the Kazan throne. Moscow's confidence and ability to manipulate the royal rivalries of the Chinggisid descendants were on display for other disgruntled princes to see. Kasim and his descendants lived up to Moscow's expectations, and the town, renamed Kasimov, remained in the possession of the Kasimov dynasty of khans for over two centuries.

The rivalry among factions of the native societies was a critical source of noble émigrés to Moscow, which was rapidly becoming a dumping ground for the recalcitrant native nobles. The Crimean and Kazan khans, the Nogay begs, and the Kalmyk tayishis often disposed of their rivals by sending them to Moscow to keep the pretenders at a safe distance. Moscow was ready to oblige and granted the exiles towns and villages to live off. Although the grand princes often reminded the local rulers of the high cost to the treasury of providing for such exiles, Moscow never refused to accept them. The exiled nobles usually arrived together with their retinues, which could number several hundred horsemen, a small army by the standards of the time and a valuable addition to the Muscovite military.[62]

As legitimate successors to their khans, begs, and tayishis, such exiles were extremely valuable as unofficial hostages and could be used to blackmail and potentially unseat the local rulers. In a few conspicuous cases when the Crimeans or the Nogays wished to have their exiles returned, Moscow stubbornly refused their entreaties. One particularly poignant correspondence ensued between Moscow and the Crimea regarding the fate of Abdullatif, the son of the Crimean khan. Despite continuous pleas to have him sent back to the Crimea, Moscow alternately refused and procrastinated until finally Abdullatif died in Moscow under suspicious circumstances. Later, in the seventeenth and eighteenth centuries, the Kalmyk and Kazakh khans continued the practice of disposing of their rivals by surrendering them to the Russian authorities. This time a more confident Russian government no longer needed to use such exiles in frontier politics, and after being granted an annuity and land estates, they were forced to convert and enlist in the regular Russian military.[63]

The political power of Moscow was particularly visible in the increasing number of requests from the Crimean ("give me a Riazan yurt and make me a khan in Meshchera [Kasimov]") and Nogay nobles ("give me Kazan or Kasimov") to be granted lucrative positions to rule Kazan, Kasimov, Riazan,

Kashira, and other towns.[64] After Moscow's conquests of Kazan and Astra-khan in the 1550s, conversion to Christianity was the best way to secure generous grants and privileges from Moscow, and various members of the Chinggisid dynasty from Astrakhan, Crimea, Kazan, Siberia, and Kasimov were compelled to convert.[65]

Chinggisid princes from Siberia to the Crimea, non-Chinggisid Tatar nobles of the Kazan region, Kabardinian nobles from the Caucasus, Nogay and Kalmyk chiefs from the Volga steppe—all at different times and for different reasons chose to convert to Christianity. Upon their baptism, non-Christian nobles were granted a title of Russian nobility, and, in exchange for military service, they were given generous annual compensation in land and cash.[66] The converted nobles intermarried with the Russian nobility, held high military positions, and often served in the frontier regions as Russia's trusted intermediaries.[67] Within two generations, their names often no longer betrayed their non-Russian and non-Christian origins.[68] Assimila-tion was complete when a dynasty entered the Genealogical Book of the Russian nobility.[69]

While the offspring of the Chinggisid dynasty were assured of a virtually seamless transition into the ranks of the highest nobility in Muscovy, the lesser non-Christian nobles also enjoyed opportunities for social mobility in Muscovy and imperial Russia. One of the best examples was the impressive rise of Muhammed Tevkelev through the echelons of the government bu-reaucracy. A Muslim Tatar mirza named Muhammed Qutlu Tawakkul, he was employed as a translator in the Foreign Office in the 1720s. In 1733 the government entrusted Tevkelev with a mission to the Kazakhs of the Lesser Horde to convince them to become Russian subjects. In 1734 Tevkelev re-turned to St. Petersburg, bringing with him an oath of allegiance signed by the Kazakh khan, Abulkhayir, and his plans for the development of the Kazakh steppe. Apparently the government judged his mission a success, and Tevkelev was rewarded with the rank of colonel and holy baptism. By the late 1740s, the colonel Aleksei Ivanovich Tevkelev was promoted to the rank of major general, and throughout the 1750s he was cogovernor of Oren-burg. His son, Osip Tevkelev, was a captain in the Russian army in the 1750s. Of course, the price for Tevkelev's spectacular rise along the military-bu-reaucratic ladder was his conversion to Christianity. It is significant that the Kazakhs seemed to be unaware of his religious conversion, and they contin-ued to refer to Tevkelev as "mirza and general" or "the most esteemed mirza."[70]

No doubt the government intended Tevkelev to be an example of the favors and benefits that other non-Christians could expect in exchange for their loyal service to the emperor. Tevkelev's remarkable career notwithstanding, there were limits on what a first-generation convert could achieve in the Russian Empire. Despite the fact that it was Tevkelev who initiated most of the

Russian policies in the region and was a de facto governor of Orenburg throughout the 1740 and 1750s, he had never been officially appointed governor. Instead, the names of his contemporaries Ivan Nepliuev and Petr Rychkov, the Orenburg governors who mostly followed his advice and policies, became far better known to the Russian public than the name of the obscure but indispensable convert Aleksei Tevkelev.

Migration and assimilation were not the only terms of cooperation with Moscow. Some nobles preferred to rely on Moscow's protection and help in order to project their ambition and power locally. At different times, the Kabardinian chiefs, the Nogay begs, the Kalmyk tayishis, and the Kazakh khans had petitioned (or more often were encouraged to petition) Moscow to build a fort nearby with a Russian garrison for their protection. Tersk in the North Caucasus, Orenburg in the Kazakh steppe, and a number of other Russian forts and towns emerged in precisely this way.[71]

Some nobles chose to relocate to the newly built forts or elsewhere within Russian borders. The government continued to express interest in such defectors and provided them with strong incentives to resettle and convert. In one such typical instance, in 1762, a Kabardinian noble convert, formerly Korgoka Kanchokin and now known as Andrei Ivanov, petitioned to be resettled within Russian borders. To encourage him, the Senate granted him the rank of lieutenant colonel and a new title and name, Prince Cherkasskii-Kanchokin. The Senate also listed several options available to him. He would receive an annuity of 500 rubles if he relocated within the Russian borders with his people. If he could not convince his people to convert and join him, he could move to the Russian frontier town of Kizliar and receive 300 rubles. Finally, if he chose to stay in Kabarda, he would receive 150 rubles, but he had to come to Kizliar three times a year to receive his annuity and have his Christianity confirmed. The Senate expressed hope that he and his people would thus convert and resettle.[72] It is revealing of Russia's attitude toward its new noble subjects that, despite inflation and other factors, the Russian government maintained the annuities to the local chiefs and nobles at the same level of 500 rubles, more or less, for at least the three centuries discussed here.[73]

If the continuous departure of the nobles further contributed to the divisiveness among the native elite, the flight of native commoners proved to be even more detrimental to the indigenous society. By the seventeenth century, the fleeing nobles were joined by a host of others: lesser nobles and notables fleeing justice or looking for better terms of military employment; impoverished Nogay, Kalmyk, and Kazakh nomads looking for jobs near the Russian towns; Nogays fleeing captivity among the Kalmyks; captive Persians and Jungars fleeing bondage among the Kazakhs; North Caucasian peasants escaping onerous labor; and enslaved Georgians and Armenians seeking freedom among fellow Christians.

The first signs of this troublesome issue appeared early on. In the 1550s, the Nogay nobles complained to Moscow about the Astrakhan voevodas, who refused to return fugitive Nogays. The nobles tried to convince the Russian authorities that it would be in Moscow's interests if they, the Nogay nobles, had more people. Still, the escape of the Nogays into Russian towns continued unabated.[74] Others preferred to stay in Moscow, enticed by presents and payments. Such was the case of a certain Kabardinian servitor, who accompanied his noble on a visit to Moscow in 1603, and then petitioned the tsar to stay and convert. In an indication that this was not an isolated occurrence, his noble reacted swiftly by withdrawing the prospective convert's payment, explaining that "others will follow you and convert, and then I will have no one in my service."[75]

The issue was rapidly becoming of great significance to the local rulers. Many similar complaints of the Kalmyks tayishis, who came to replace the Nogays in the mid-seventeenth century, found their way into the Russo-Kalmyk treaties. Since the 1670s, such treaties with the Kalmyks, known in Moscow as oaths of allegiance, had included a clause regarding those Kalmyks who fled to the Russian towns and converted to Christianity. The Kalmyk tayishis, concerned with the loss of their people, demanded that these fugitives be returned unbaptized. The government initially rejected such demands but often, in exchange for the Kalmyks' cooperation, placated the chiefs and instructed the governors in the Volga towns to return Kalmyk fugitives or pay the Kalmyk chiefs a thirty ruble fine for each Kalmyk converted by force.[76]

By the 1720s, the construction of the new fortification lines and debilitating wars among the nomads brought a dramatically improved sense of security along Russia's southern frontier, and with it a more recalcitrant attitude on the part of the government. Repeated requests and demands to return the fugitive commoners, and threats of retribution if they were not returned, failed to move the authorities, who insisted that those fugitives who converted to Christianity could not be sent back. The Russian administration encouraged such conversions, and instead of returning the fugitives offered compensation to the nobles who claimed them. Like the Kalmyks, the Kazakh nobles were given cash or presents valued at twenty to twenty-five rubles for each fugitive.[77]

The baptized fugitives were listed as new converts, even though they had little idea of their new religion and continued to practice their old one. To secure converts as Christians and to protect them from their kin's revenge, the government moved them away from the frontier area and settled them in towns founded especially for this purpose. On government orders, Fort Nagaibak in the Ufa province was built for Bashkir converts in 1736. Three years later, the town of Stavropol was founded to settle Kalmyk converts near the Volga River north of the city of Samara.[78] None of the settlements proved to be far enough away to prevent the escape of many converts seeking to reunite with their coreligionists and kin. When the issue of the settlement of Kazakh converts came up in 1763, the Senate decreed that they should be sent farther away from the Orenburg, Astrakhan, and Kazan provinces and settled on state lands deep in the Russian interior.[79]

At different times, when the chorus of complaints from the native chiefs was about to turn into an open rebellion and threaten Russia's geopolitical interests in the region, the government forbade the seizure and sale of the natives and ordered the fugitives returned. Even then, however, several considerations militated against the new policy. Harboring fugitives or purchasing natives became one of the major sources of enrichment for Russian officials in the frontier towns. The government's orders failed to prevent the growing enserfment of non-Christians by local officials, and in 1737 the Senate conceded and ruled that converts could be purchased and enserfed.[80]

In 1756 the Kazakhs requested to have their Persian, Karakalpak, and Jungar captives who had fled to the Russian forts along the Yaik returned unbaptized because "they converted to your majesty's faith not by their own will, but only because they wanted to escape slavery." The Senate rejected the petition and permitted Russians to purchase or barter and retain these prisoners of the Kazakhs because of the labor shortage in Siberia. No less important was the Senate's concern that these prisoners not be purchased by Muslim merchants and converted to Islam. Instead, they were to become Christians and be enserfed by Russians.[81]

The government's principal concern with transforming non-Christians into Russian Orthodox underpinned Russian policies in the frontier area throughout this time. In 1755, responding to the undeniable reality of the massive exodus, purchase, and conversion of the natives, the government acquiesced to those who wished to purchase and convert the natives in the frontier regions of Astrakhan, Orenburg, and Siberia. In a remarkable violation of the exclusive privilege of the Russian nobility to purchase and own serfs, the government permitted priests, merchants, Cossacks, and others to buy, convert, and teach non-Christians, who were to remain their serfs until the owner's death. The Senate sanctioned the purchase of Kalmyks, Kumyks, Chechens, Kazakhs, Karakalpaks, Turkmens, Tomuts, Tatars, Bashkirs, Baraba Tatars, and other Muslims and idol-worshippers. Thus, the non-Christians would be acquired without force, "so that they could be converted to Christianity." Such transactions were to take place only with the written permission of the native chiefs or parents of those offered for sale, and with reasonable assurances that those to be sold had not been kidnapped.[82] Of course, given the desperate situation of many natives and the corruption of both the Russian officials and the native chiefs, these conditions were unlikely to prevent any illegal sales. The government's direct involvement in and encouragement of a wide-ranging enserfment and Christianization of the non-Christians in the frontier regions was unmistakable.

The situation in the North Caucasus in the second half of the eighteenth century illustrates with particular clarity the nature of Russian frontier policies and their intended and unintended impact on the indigenous societies. As elsewhere, the numerous pleas from the Kabardinian and other local chiefs to have their fugitives returned continued to fall on deaf ears. But in the mid-eighteenth century, with the construction of Mozdok, a new fort a short distance away from some Kabardinian villages, the issue of the fugitives' return took on a different dimension. Despairing Kabardinian nobles asserted that they could no longer exercise control over their people, who were threatening to flee and convert to Christianity in Mozdok, Kizliar, or Astrakhan. Others complained that many had already left, and few people remained to perform any work. That such complaints were not exaggerated was confirmed by the Kabardinians who spied for the Russians and by the Russian officers stationed in the region.[83]

One particularly detailed and knowledgeable report prepared by Captain M. Gastotti for the Foreign Office in 1770 stated that the Kabardinians had indeed suffered greatly from the loss of their people. The report explained that Kabardinians usually paid about 100 rubles per captive, and the loss of 1,000 such captives would amount to a significant sum of money. The report suggested that Muslim fugitives should be handed back and that the Kabardinian nobles could be appeased if the government offered them a compensation of 60 to 70 rubles for each Muslim who wished to convert and 50 to 60 rubles for each Christian fugitive.[84]

Another, more urgent argument in favor of returning the fugitives from the Caucasus was presented in a secret report by a commander of Kizliar, N. A. Potapov. He reported that on the eve of the war with the Ottoman Empire in 1768, the forts of Kizliar and Mozdok, as well as the Cossack towns along the frontier, were poorly fortified and had few troops. If the various local peoples were aided by the Crimeans, their raids could cause significant damage. His recommendation was not to accept fugitive Muslim peasants, thus winning the loyalty of the Kabardinian nobles, who could then help the Russians defend the frontier.[85]

A temporary reprieve for the local nobles was achieved in 1771, when Catherine II personally wrote to the Kabardinian people, trying, as always, to reconcile her ideas learned from the books of the Western *philosophes* with the incongruous realities of the Russian Empire. While she nobly declared that "there is no such law in the entire world to reject those who seek Christian faith," she then conceded to the demands that the Kabardinian peasants should be returned "because they have no way of comprehending Christianity and because you need them in the fields."[86]

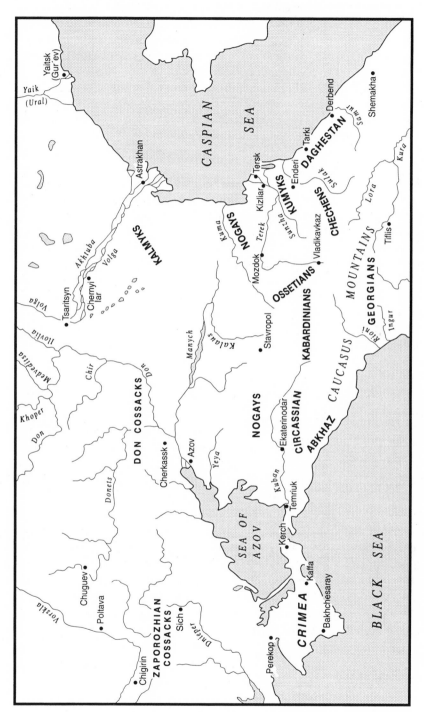

MAP 9. The North Caucasus in the eighteenth century.

Russian policies of providing refuge for fugitives inadvertently contributed to the growing division between the Kabardinian nobles and the commoners. Exploiting such a rift later became central to the administration's policies in the North Caucasus. By promoting a social conflict within the indigenous society, the Russian government sought to weaken the nobles and thus to increase its leverage over the natives. For instance, one of the tasks of the Russian liaison officer residing among the Kabardinians was "to incite the commoners to be loyal to Russia," and when in 1767 more than 10,000 Kabardinian peasants rebelled against the nobles and threatened to flee, the Russian major was sent to convince the rebels to leave their nobles and settle in Russian territory.[87]

At different times, immediate military and strategic considerations compelled the government to resort to a noninterference policy. Thus, in 1778 the Foreign Office rejected as impractical the Astrakhan governor's suggestions to protect the Kabardinian commoners from the abuses of their nobles and to transfer and resettle them along the Siberian fortification line. The Foreign Office advised the governor that "it is outside the interests of this side to consider the nature of the commoners' relation to the nobles," that this would constitute an interference with the Kabardinian right of ownership and would reinforce the suspicions of the Crimea and the Ottoman Porte. The instructions continued: "As for the fact that the commoners may rebel and kill their own nobles, that is even for the better; then there will be fewer Kabardinian nobles, and it will happen by the hands of their people, so that this side could not be blamed."[88]

A few years later, when the Russian government was less concerned about a potential conflict with the Ottoman Porte and keeping up the appearance of fair play, Prince G. A. Potemkin-Tavricheskii instructed the commander of the Russian troops in the Caucasus, General P. S. Potemkin, to reject any requests from the Kabardinian nobles for the return of commoners who had fled to escape oppression. Leaving no doubt about his views on the subject, he added, "I regard the separation of the commoners from the nobles the surest way to secure our frontier."[89]

By the end of the eighteenth century, the government realized that its policy of sowing divisions between the nobles and their people in the frontier regions of the North Caucasus and Kazakhs steppe had become counterproductive. Such policies reduced the government's ability to exercise control over the course of events in native societies already debilitated by civil wars and internal rebellions. Deciding to reverse its policies of playing the native nobles and commoners off against each other, St. Petersburg opted for supporting the interests of the nobles in exchange for their cooperation with the Russian authorities. For the time being, the continuous flow of the natives across the frontier into Russia was reduced, but it did not cease.

COLONIAL CONTEST I: LAW AND ADMINISTRATION

> When you speak of justice with our peasants, the big idea is
> compensation. A cattle keeper or cultivator who loses his whole family has
> lost his whole economic support system. You can kill the man who
> committed genocide, but that's not compensation—that's only fear and
> anger. This is how our peasants think.
>
> —PHILIP GOUREVITCH, *We Wish to Inform You
> That Tomorrow We Will Be Killed with Our Families:
> Stories from Rwanda*

Those natives who crossed the frontier to convert and settle within the imperial boundaries rapidly became subject to Russian law. But numerous native peoples in the frontier area, whom the Russian government officially considered to be its subjects, de facto remained outside of Russia's political control and its legal structure. In the absence of a political concept of autonomy, or a vaguely defined notion of protectorship, emerging slowly in the mid-eighteenth century, how were the Russian authorities to resolve frontier disputes with their purported subjects?

Among many contentious issues, the question of the escape and return of native fugitives was perhaps the most troublesome. Returning such fugitives was only one possible solution, but the Russian authorities resorted to it reluctantly, for the variety of reasons mentioned above. The other, more frequently practiced approach was payment of compensation for each fugitive. In fact, the natives often preferred compensation, which was in accordance with their customary law. Such compensation paid in kind or cash proved to be increasingly attractive with the natives' further dependence on the Russian market.

One of the first demands for compensation from Moscow was presented by the Nogay mirza Urak. In 1536 he asked for a return of a certain mullah Dervish Ali, "who stole horses and fled to you; he was a Muslim and then converted to your faith. Give him back or pay compensation."[90] At various times the government was able to placate the local nobles by ordering its governors on the frontier to pay compensation for fugitives, but as the number of fugitives increased and compensations were paid irregularly, the issue refused to go away and remained the source of numerous conflicts with the native chiefs.

Murder was another case that required compensation and was congruent with the customary law of blood money practiced by most native societies, with the exception of some regions of the Caucasus where blood vendetta was more common. In 1564 a Nogay beg requested that a penalty of 100 rubles be sent to him for the murder of his envoy in Kazan, because "no one can make the dead alive."[91] Whether his request was granted or rebuffed is unknown. Such cases abounded, however, and even the arrest and punishment of the felons in accordance with Russian laws failed to satisfy the local rulers, who continued to demand compensation. In the 1740s, for instance, when three Kalmyks were beaten to death by Russian peasants in a dispute over land, the guilty Russians had their nostrils torn out and were given a life sentence of labor in saltpeter mines. According to Kalmyk law, however, all offenses were punishable by a fine, and the Kalmyk ruler, Donduk-Dashi, expected to receive 50 rubles for each murdered Kalmyk. After being told that the culprits' verdict was worse than a death sentence, he continued to insist on monetary compensation.[92]

The issue of capital punishment clearly underlined the differences between the Russian legal code and native customary law. The indigenous peoples continuously resisted Russian attempts to introduce capital punishment into native law where such a practice did not exist, and the heaviest penalty for murder was a fine paid in a variety of valuable items. When such a fine was not paid, the victimized side had the right to launch a *barimta* (*baranta*), a forcible seizure of herds from those who were guilty of crimes.

In fact, barimta was the most widespread means of retribution for a number of different offenses in the steppe societies. But the Russian frontier authorities, under orders to maintain peace among the various nomadic peoples, were often incapable and unwilling to distinguish between barimta and other raiding activities. With the natives' growing dependence on Russia, the government began to assume responsibility for resolving the judicial disputes not only between the Russians and non-Russians but also among its restless nomadic subjects. For the Russian officials, raiding was all about the theft of horses and other herds, and thus it was a crime that had to be prevented, and those responsible had to be caught and punished.

One such typical confrontation between the Russian and Kazakh notions of justice was recorded in 1746. When some Kazakhs raided the Kalmyks in response to their previous raids, the Kazakh khan, Abulkhayir, was ordered to find those responsible and have their nostrils and ears torn out and their right hands cut off. St. Petersburg insisted that the culprits be punished in accordance with the statutes for robbery in the legal code of 1649. Only vigorous objections from the Kazakhs forced the government to relent and agree on limiting the punishment to lashes with a knout.[93]

The old customs and the new laws continued to collide for a long time after the initial encounters between the natives and Russian authorities. But the Russians would not go away, and the proximity of the Russian forts and settlements, the growing conflicts with the Russian population over grazing lands and fishing sites, and greater dependence on the Russian administration were simply unavoidable.

Increasingly, the native chiefs were prepared to submit themselves to the mediation of the Russian administration. But while putting the natives under the authority of Russian law was always desired, it was not always politically expedient. In 1628, driven to despair, the Nogay mirzas appealed to the Russian government for protection against the Kalmyks, and added that because "they could no longer resolve their disputes in accordance with their Muslim laws," they wished to submit to the tsar's court and Russian laws to help them reconcile their rivalries. Interested in further weakening the Nogays and concerned with the appearance of noninterference, Moscow rejected their plea. But more than a century later, the government did not hesitate to oblige the Kalmyk khan, Donduk-Dashi, who urged the Russian authorities in 1741 to help him compile a new legal code, one that would help to resolve Russo-Kalmyk disputes. When the new code was finally compiled, it plainly reflected the Kalmyks' growing dependence on Russian economy, law, and administration; Russian money could be used to pay fines, corporal punishment was introduced for certain types of theft, and some disputes were to be investigated solely by the Russian authorities.[94]

In the second half of the eighteenth century, with the relative security of Russia's frontiers and its unquestionable military superiority over the neighboring states and peoples in the south, the government attempted anew to affect changes directly within the indigenous societies. The Kalmyks were the first to become the target of this new approach. In 1762, as the government conferred the title of viceroy on a new Kalmyk ruler, it also introduced a change in the Kalmyk institution of *zargo*. Traditionally, a khan's conciliar body consisted of eight zayisangs (members of the lesser nobility) solely from the khan's ulus; now the zargo was to represent the zayisangs elected by all Kalmyk uluses in accordance with their population.

The reconstitution of the zargo was intended to undermine the authority of the Kalmyk khan and to increase the government's leverage over the Kalmyks. But this strategy backfired. The new Russian approach disturbed the traditional balance of power between the khan and the established Kalmyk secular and clerical elite, who were further antagonized by the intrusive Russian policies. Nine years after the reconstitution of the zargo, its members agreed with the khan that Russia's policies threatened the very existence of the Kalmyk people. Shortly after a great majority of Kalmyks had left the Volga in 1771 for their historic homeland in Jungaria, a government decree hastily abolished the zargo among those Kalmyks who remained in the Caspian steppe.[95]

This policy failure among the Kalmyks did not prevent the government from other attempts to remold the indigenous societies and put them under the firmer control of the Russian authorities. Throughout the 1780s in the Kazakh steppe and 1790s in the North Caucasus, the government introduced a new instrument of control, a system of native and frontier courts. Detailed directives came personally from Catherine II, who took a lively interest in "pacifying the wild peoples of Her Empire."

In 1786 the governor-general of Orenburg, Baron Osip Igelstrom, informed Eraly sultan that the empress had decreed that the khan of the Kazakh Lesser Horde, Nuraly, be detained and his title abolished. The Horde was to be divided into three parts, each led by a chief notable elected from among other notables. To resolve frontier disputes, the Frontier Court (*pogranichnyi sud,* later referred to as *divan*) was established in Orenburg. It was to be composed of six Kazakh notables and one sultan, along with six Russian officials. This court was to judge both Kazakhs and Russians. Each of the three parts of the newly divided Lesser Horde was to have its own local court (*rasprava*) to adjudicate Kazakh matters. A reliable Russian or Tatar informer was to be attached to the local courts in the guise of a deputy. All members of the courts were to be paid from the Russian treasury.[96]

The attempts by the Russian government to institute structural changes among the Kazakhs brought familiar results. Russia's reliance on notables and commoners in administering the Kazakhs sharply antagonized the Kazakh nobles and pitted one group against the other. Abolishing the authority of the khan proved to be an extreme step, unpopular with both the nobles and commoners. In 1788, the advice of the local military commander, D. Grankin, was to impose upon the Kazakhs the Russian administrative and military system: dividing the Lesser Horde into four parts similar to Russian counties (*uezd*s) and reconstituting the Frontier Court with only six members: one notable from each part of the Horde, one Russian secretary with a knowledge of Tatar, and one member of the Islamic clergy, a mullah.[97]

The proposed changes pleased no one. A Russian ban on barimta between the Kazakhs and Ural Cossacks and its replacement with the Frontier Courts were resented by both the Kazakh nobles and commoners. In yet another effort to impose the semblance of the Russian political and legal system on the Kazakhs, Igelstrom submitted one more proposal in October 1789. He suggested dividing the Horde into six parts with a local court in each, and establishing one chief administrator of the Horde with the title of khan. This too proved to be unrealistic, unenforceable, and unacceptable to the Kazakh factions.[98]

Eight years later, Baron Igelstrom made his last attempt to bring the Kazakh factions together with a modified proposal to establish a Khan's Council, consisting of six notables representing major clans. When this idea, too, proved to be unfeasible, Igelstrom decided to move closer to the position of the Kazakh nobility, abolishing the Khan's Council and strengthening the authority of the khan appointed by the government.[99]

Throughout the last quarter of the eighteenth century, various attempts by Russian officials to alter the traditional balance of power among the Kazakh authorities by imposing foreign legal and administrative structures proved to be premature. Despite the government's willingness to change the composition of the Frontier Courts or Khan's Council, these very institutions were seen by the Kazakh nobles and notables as too intrusive and undermining their traditional power base. It was not until 1824 that the Kazakhs of the Lesser Horde, no longer capable of resisting the government's plans, found themselves divided into three parts and the position of their khan abolished. Their last khan was brought to Orenburg to reside there with the honorary but meaningless title of First Member of the Frontier Commission.

COLONIAL CONTEST II: LAND

> And by reason of the incursions of the said tartars, the Russes do not plow
> or sow in these parts (though the land is extremely rich). . . .
> It is a thousand times to be lamented, that so rich and noble a countrey,
> situated on the side of the great river Wolga . . .
> should now lye in a manner waste without inhabitants.

—JOHN PERRY, *The State of Russia under the Present Czar*

To the south and southeast of Muscovy lay the vast expanses of the steppe, uncultivated and unsettled. Yet Moscow's initial expansion into the area was driven less by an idea of civilizing "the wild and empty lands" than by strategic, military, and commercial considerations. Throughout the seventeenth century, the granting of newly acquired lands secured behind the military fortification lines was the principal compensation to the Muscovite servitors for their military service. By the eighteenth century, with the expanding Russian frontiers increasingly intruding into the traditional nomadic pastures, the acquisition of new territories needed for the construction of forts, settlements, and cultivation brought the Russian government into direct confrontation with the native population. The Russian government's land policies became a central issue in Russia's colonization of the region.

By the mid-eighteenth century Russia's sprawling forts and Cossack settlements studded the banks of the rivers flowing south into the Caspian and Black seas, while the newly built fortification lines crossed the steppe in an east–west direction. The Russian government was now in a position to control and often dictate the seasonal migratory routes to the nomads. To cross the rivers or pass through the fortification lines, the natives had to seek permission from the Russian authorities, who often used the issue to force the natives' compliance with its various demands.

The gradual loss of pasturelands by the Kalmyks is a typical example of Russian policies in the southern steppe. In 1718, the Tsaritsyn fortification line connected the Volga and Don rivers and effectively locked the Kalmyks into the lower Volga area. The line cut off the summer migration routes of the Kalmyks to the north, and one of the possible escape routes from their traditional foes, the Kuban Nogays. Both the Kalmyks' military fortunes and their economic well-being were now increasingly in the hands of the Russian authorities.

By the late 1760s, the Kalmyks indeed found themselves hemmed in by the Tsaritsyn and Mozdok fortification lines in the north and south, and by the Don and Yaik Cossacks in the west and east. Driven to despair by the continuous loss of their grazing grounds to German colonists and pushed away farther into the arid steppe, the Kalmyks resolved to take a dramatic step—an exodus of the entire people back to Jungaria, the last such mass migration of a nomadic people in the Eurasian steppe.[100]

The expanding fortification lines brought security to the Russian towns and villages vulnerable to the nomadic raids and made it possible to launch a more vigorous colonization of the steppe. In 1763 the government compiled a list of "the lands, which were inside the Russian Empire as well as vacant and suitable for settlement." The provinces chosen for settling were those of Belgorod, Astrakhan, Orenburg, and Tobolsk. In other words, the government resolved to settle and cultivate a huge expanse of the northern fringe of the Eurasian steppe from the Don River in the west to the Irtysh River in the east, lands that were traditional summer pastures of various nomadic peoples and were now considered to be the empire's southern borderlands.[101]

At the core of the land disputes between the Russian government and the nomadic inhabitants of the steppe lay fundamentally different notions of land ownership and its intended usage. As far as the Russian government was concerned, the newly acquired lands were empty spaces belonging to no one. As such these lands had to be appropriated, transformed into a part of the imperial domain, divided, settled, and farmed. For the nomads, on the other hand, the same lands were indispensable pastures in common possession of the ulus or another aggregate nomadic unit.

These divergent attitudes and goals were first clearly articulated in the mid-seventeenth century, during one of the Russo-Kalmyk encounters over the issue. Confronted by Russian demands to vacate the Caspian steppe, the Kalmyk chief, Daichin, insisted that "land and water belonged to God," and that the Kalmyks had merely seized the pastures of the defeated Nogays. A century later, government officials heard similar arguments from the Kazakhs when the government assigned them pastures by decrees, demanding that the Kazakhs obtain permission from the frontier authorities and pay crossing fees. The Kazakhs responded with astonishment: "The grass and water belong to Heaven, and why should we pay any fees?"[102]

The growing number of Russian fisheries and the natives' raids against them remained one of the common sources of contention. In one such case in 1750, the safety of the Russian fishermen became a concern of the government when it considered the complaint of the Astrakhan merchant Aleksei Kurochkin, who had been previously granted fishing rights between the estuaries of the Yaik and Emba rivers. A seemingly simple matter came under the consideration of the Foreign Office when it became known that the Kazakhs had captured Russian fishermen and claimed the area to be their pastureland. The Office recommended that because the benefits to the treasury from these fisheries were small, it was not worth risking Russian lives and antagonizing the Kazakhs. The Office of Commerce agreed and revoked Kurochkin's right to fish there.[103]

Small concessions notwithstanding, by the late eighteenth century the Kazakhs found themselves in a situation similar to that of the Kalmyks. The Orenburg and Siberian fortification lines outlined the most northern boundaries of the Kazakhs' possible migrations. At the same time, to prevent their skirmishes with the Kalmyks, the government forbade the Kazakhs to move westward and instructed the Yaik Cossacks to enforce the ban and prevent the Kazakhs from crossing the Yaik.

Catherine II envisioned the Kazakhs serving as an irregular Russian military and the steppe transformed through the newly built towns, mosques, schools, and trading centers. Islam was to be put in the service of the empire, and her plans included recruiting and paying the loyal mullahs from among the Kazan Tatars, who could encourage the Kazakhs' loyalty and ensure their peaceful intentions. Other Muslims, such as merchants of Bukhara and Tashkent residing in Tobolsk, were exempt from local laws, taxation, or any service, "in order to attract more of them to settle in the Russian Empire and to expand trade with the neighboring peoples."[104]

After all, the government could point to some previous successes in pursuing a policy of pacification of the nomads. Such, for instance, was the case of several Nogay groups who in the mid-seventeenth century asked for Moscow's protection and were allowed to settle and graze their herds near Astrakhan. They became known as the Yurt Tatars, residing in fortified compounds near the city. They were allowed to enter Astrakhan without arms and trade there. Many of them converted to Christianity, their women married Russians, and their men joined the musketeers or became townsmen.[105]

If the experience of the Yurt Tatars could not be easily applied to the Kazakhs, the government's plans for colonization of the Kazakh steppe were even less suitable for another remote part of the empire. Throughout the eighteenth century, the North Caucasus remained a religious frontier separating the Christian and Islamic worlds. Islam had much deeper roots in this region than in the Kazakh steppe, and the local Islamic establishment, supported by the neighboring Islamic states, was not yet prepared for accommodation with the Russian government.

The settlement of the North Caucasus frontier closely mirrored Russia's policies in the region. Initially native fugitives from the Caucasus had been dispersed among the Russian forts and Cossack settlements along the frontier. But the proximity of their new residences to their old villages proved too dangerous, as the war parties organized by the local nobles frequently raided the frontier settlements in order to regain their fugitives. Relying on its experience with the Kalmyk converts, the government decreed in 1750 that the converts had to be moved farther away from the Russian borders and settled together among the Russians, so that they could learn farming and perform military service. Some were dispatched to join the Don and Volga Cossacks, others to become state peasants in the Tambov province. Even the Don and Volga proved to be too close to prevent the converts from fleeing, and other, more remote locations in the Orenburg province and Siberia were suggested.[106]

In 1762, with the frontier further secured, the government decided that the converts should play an important role in settling the region. In its report to Catherine II, the Senate suggested that in order to strengthen the Kizliar region, a new fort should be built for settling the newly converted Ossetians and Kabardinians. Such a fort was to have a church and a priest, who could make journeys into the mountains to evangelize the peoples of the Caucasus. Furthermore, Georgians, Armenians, and other Christian nations (*natsii*) could be invited to establish silk and other industries, and each of these nations should be allowed to settle separately and build their own churches. Catholics, too, were to be settled and given a government loan for the construction of their church. Only Muslims were not allowed to settle there.[107] The imperial Russian frontier was conceived as a Christian one.

The growing presence of Russian towns and forts, settlers and soldiers was rapidly changing the traditional landscape of the region. The physical and ecological changes could not be easily separated from the government's military and political objectives. In 1768, General Potapov ordered the demolition of a dam on one of the Terek's tributaries. The water, which was used by the Kumyks for the irrigation of their fields, now was diverted to surround Fort Kizliar to improve its defenses.[108] The construction of Fort Mozdok in the early 1740s caused bitter complaints from the Kabardinians, who demanded that the fort be razed because "it is being built where we cut wood and graze our cattle. There is no need for this fort because there is no danger to us or Your Majesty."[109] But the government had a different opinion; it maintained that the fort was being built on land that did not belong to the Kabardinians.

By the 1790s, the frontier of the North Caucasus was transformed into a continuous stretch of Russian fortifications connecting the Black and Caspian seas along the Kuban and Terek rivers. The Russian forts and settlements built on the natives' land had a profound and damaging impact on the indigenous population. As the Russian colonization of the region exacerbated the crisis within the indigenous societies, both nobles and commoners were compelled to appeal to the authorities for help in resolving the conflicts between them. In 1783, the Kabardinian nobles submitted a list of their grievances to the "Supreme Commander of the borderlands from the Dnieper River to the Volga," G. A. Potemkin. Most of the complaints were not new: the authorities did not keep their promises, favored Georgians and

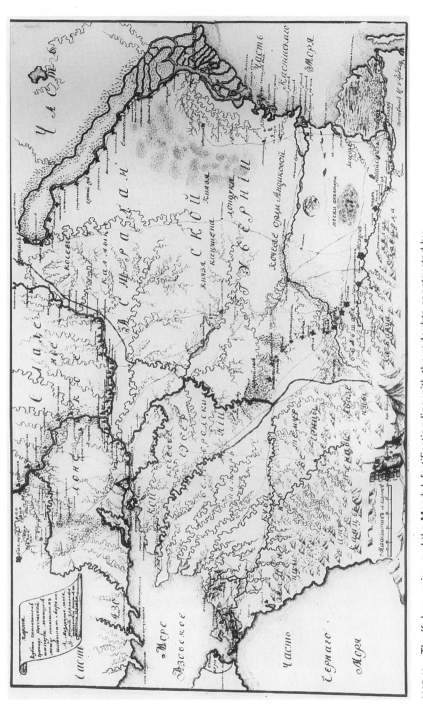

MAP 10.   The Kuban region and the Mozdok fortification line with the redoubts constructed by General Alexander Suvorov (late 1770s). Courtesy of the Central State Archive of the Military History of Russia, Moscow.

Armenians, seized their lands, and did not return their people. The nobles asked to be allowed to graze their horses behind the Mozdok fortification line. Then, in a simultaneous recognition of their own helplessness and the administration's influence, they specifically asked the Russians to order the feuding between the Kabardinian nobles and the commoners stopped. The petition was signed by thirty-six nobles and thirty-eight lesser nobles (*uzdens*) who offered loyalty if their conditions were met.

At the same time, the commoners dispatched deputies to deliver a petition of their own to the Russian authorities. The deputies explained that they were unaware of the contents of the nobles' petition to the authorities and were concerned that the nobles had been plotting against them. They asked for protection from the abuses of their landlords and permission to resettle and farm behind the fortification line "because we do not have enough farming land on this side." The petition was signed by thirty-two deputies, who promised on behalf of all the commoners to obey Russian orders without reservation.[110]

By the 1790s, realizing that its policy of encouraging commoners against their nobles was becoming counterproductive, the government was compelled to take sides. St. Petersburg chose to rely on the native nobility in governing the region and appointed local nobles to the recently organized local and Frontier Courts. Of course, some concessions had to be made, and the nobles were finally allowed to cross the Mozdok fortification line to graze their horses. Caution was not abandoned, however, and the nobles were required to be unarmed and in possession of a special pass (*bilet*) issued by the Russian military commander in the Caucasus.[111]

With the construction of the fortification lines, the natives found themselves dependent on the benevolence of the local authorities, who now controlled access to their traditional pasturelands, forests, fisheries, and, of course, the new markets. General P. S. Potemkin, condemning the exploitation and the harsh conditions of the Kabardinian peasants, believed that the complaints of the local nobles about being constrained and oppressed by the Russian fortifications were a mere excuse: "What they consider oppression is the fact that our army is serving as an impediment to their inhumanity."[112] One can only wonder whether the general held similar views on the plight of the Russian serfs.

The newly acquired lands did not remain vacant for long. Orders came to follow the example of the Novorossiisk province and distribute the lands behind the fortification line. Some officials recommended that lands along the Terek River be used for farming, planting vineyards, and producing silk. Lands around Mozdok were distributed among the Cossacks, settlers from Russia, and fugitives from the Caucasus.[113] In time, the newly acquired lands were completely transformed from pastureland held in common ownership by the natives into farmland owned by individual Russians. What had been a perilous frontier had been decisively turned into an imperial borderland.

Situated on the westernmost periphery of the Eurasian steppe, Russia's frontiers in the south and southeast were similar to those of other states and empires on the edges of the steppe, such as the northern and northwestern frontiers of China and the northern and eastern frontiers of Persia. The intermittent eruptions of the nomadic tribes emerging from the heart of Inner Asia (contemporary Mongolia and northwestern China) to subdue their nomadic rivals and to overwhelm the neighboring states continually threatened the settled communities along the steppe frontiers.

These frontiers remained "soft targets," vulnerable to large-scale nomadic invasion and impossible to defend against small-scale lightning raids. The lessons of the Mongol conquest and its devastating impact upon the entire Eurasian continent were clear: only strong states with a centralized government capable and willing to devote significant resources to the defense of the steppe frontier could prevent similar disasters. By the late eighteenth century, the relentless expansion of the Russian Empire to the south and southeast and of Qing China to the north and northwest brought an end to the long era of nomads' domination of the steppe and their ever-present threat to neighboring states. The steppe was slowly colonized, and its remaining inhabitants were impoverished and pacified by imperial arms.

Russia's continuing expansion southward was both defensive and opportunistic. The southern frontier could not be defended by traditional means of pitched battles between regular armies or by constructing fortifications around towns and cities yet to be built. Conventional peace treaties common among nation-states were meaningless along the southern frontier. Instead, relative peace with the nomads could be purchased only through the delivery of large amounts of gifts and payments to the nomadic elites. When the payments stopped, the nomads readily offered their service to the higher bidder, and a former ally could easily become an adversary.

Even when peace along the steppe frontier was agreed upon, it brought an end only to large-scale invasions. The native elites had a limited ability to exercise control over their politically fragmented societies, and they were often powerless to prevent small-scale raids. Raiding activity was deeply embedded in the social, economic, and political fabric of nomadic society. Compelled to confront the threat of societies organized for raiding, Russia, in turn, emerged as a society organized for continuous war. While application of Russia's growing military, economic, and political power successfully reduced the threat of raids in the eighteenth century, the need to transform pasturelands into agricultural colonies and industrial enterprises kept the government on a confrontational course with its nomadic neighbors. Whether intent on eliminating nomadic raids or settling and cultivating new lands, the government's experiences dictated the same conclusion: the nomadic way of life eventually had to disappear.

For Russia, the road to security along its southern frontier was a long and arduous one. The invasion of the Mongols in the thirteenth century and their subsequent long domination had a devastating impact upon the Russian lands. For two centuries, the Russian princes failed in their various attempts to shake off the crushing burden of Mongol taxation and to achieve political independence. Only by the late fifteenth century did Moscow finally succeed in ending its long subordination to the Mongols. Out of the convulsions of the dissipating Golden Horde, Moscow emerged to rule and unite Russian lands under the authority of the grand prince.[1]

The collapse of the Golden Horde notwithstanding, Moscow's sovereignty was initially little more than rhetorical. Unable to disentangle itself from the complex web of burdensome economic ties with the Golden Horde's numerous successors, Moscow continued to submit a dizzying array of tributes, payments, and taxes to the Crimea, Kazan, and the Nogays. At the time, Moscow found it neither easy nor expedient to extricate itself from the political legacy of the Golden Horde.

Throughout the sixteenth century, the assumption that Moscow was one of the successors to the Golden Horde served both to justify its expansion southward and eastward and to legitimate its conquests. In a remarkable blend, Moscow derived its legitimacy simultaneously from two different traditions: the Christian tradition of Byzantium and the secular political tradition of the Golden Horde. The latter became obsolete only with the ascension to the throne of the Romanov dynasty as the Russian state emerged from the Time of Troubles with a renewed and accentuated Christian identity.

From the sixteenth century onward, Moscow's goals along the steppe frontier were to limit the damage from nomadic raids, channel the nomads' explosive thrusts against Russia's foes, and employ the nomadic cavalry as irregular Russian military. In time, the large nomadic armies proved to be helpless against Russia's muskets and artillery, river boats armed with cannon, and disruptive Cossack raids. By the eighteenth century, the Russian army had dramatically improved its ability to conduct effective campaigns in the steppe. Construction of fortification lines that advanced the supply lines farther south and the deployment of light field cannon had devastating effects on the nomadic armies.

The advancement of fortification lines farther into the steppe had immediate and serious consequences for the steppe societies. Russia's ability to contain the nomadic invasions cut into the traditional source of income for the nomads—booty. Denied "quick and dirty" access to the undifferentiated potluck of goods and human chattel, the nomads grew ever more dependent on access to Russian markets to trade, barter, or otherwise solicit valuable merchandise. Furthermore, the government was now in a position to extend its control over the traditional nomadic pasturelands, thus making vital seasonal migrations dependent on the goodwill of the Russian authorities.

The natives were in no position to match the growing power of the Russian government. Their increasingly inadequate responses were limited to raids, written protestations, and migration and proved unable to stop the heavy machine of Russian colonization: a military bristling with firepower; a bureaucracy armed with scribes, interpreters, and customs officials; colonists vying for land; church clerics intent on saving the natives' souls; and, not least, a corrosive lure of opportunities for a growing number of native runaways.

Even so, Russia's eventual success in expanding and stabilizing its southern frontier came at great human and material cost. One rough calculation may suffice to give an idea of some of the direct expenses incurred by the government along the frontier. In the first half of the seventeenth century alone, the Crimeans received from Moscow 1 million rubles in various forms of tribute and taxes. During the same time, they captured as many as 150,000 to 200,000 Russians.[2] A conservative estimate of 100,000 people redeemed at an average price of 50 rubles per person would require a sum of 5 million rubles. Thus, over a period of fifty years, Moscow poured into the Crimea alone 6 million rubles. By comparison, 1 million rubles spent between 1600 and 1650 could have provided for the construction of four small towns annually. In other words, in the first half of the seventeenth century, Russia was short 1,200 small towns. That Russia was underurbanized in comparison to its Western European neighbors is an undisputed fact, but that this shortage of urban centers may, in no small degree, be related to the nature of Russia's southern frontier is poorly understood.

The numbers of towns and cities not built and fields not plowed would present an even starker illustration of the nation's stunted growth when one considers the full range of costs and resources diverted to the defense of the southern frontier: the lost manpower of those Russians who were captured and sold into slavery; cattle and various valuable items seized as booty; physical damage to villages and towns; presents, ransoms, and other payments to native elites; continuous construction of the new fortification lines (the "Great Wall of Russia"); and maintenance of the garrisons and auxiliary military.[3]

Long after the disappearance of the Mongols, the existence of the southern frontier continued to debilitate the Russian economy in a variety of ways. The hundreds of thousands captured by raiding parties were joined by thousands of Russian runaways, who preferred the freedom and adventure of frontier life to the burdens of daily existence at home. They became Cossacks, the mirror image of their nomadic adversaries, who, like them, chose to live off booty and pillage.

Initially the Russian government had little choice but to tolerate the escape of its people to the frontier. Later it began to encourage and support the Cossacks' raiding activity as the most effective antidote to nomadic forays. But if escape was a safety valve for the Russians, it proved to be a temporary one. In time, the government succeeded in consolidating its control over the frontier and the Cossacks, in a process that led to a series of Cossack revolts, traditionally and mistakenly referred to as "peasant wars." Until the middle of the nineteenth century, the frontier region remained the center of the largest antigovernment uprisings led by Cossacks (the Time of Troubles and the Razin and Pugachev uprisings).

The nature of the steppe frontier defined the very character of Russia's principal economic and social institutions. The government's ability to expand into the new territories in the south and southeast far exceeded its ability to settle and cultivate the new lands. It was not accidental that the vast majority of lands granted by the tsars in exchange for and conditioned by military service (*pomest'e*) were located in the south and southeast, whereas allodial possessions predominated in the western part of Russia.

The steady advance of the Russian frontier into the open spaces continued to attract those seeking opportunities on society's edge. The perennial shortage of labor in Russia prompted the government to enserf the peasants and stop the hemorrhaging of limited labor resources. The fact that serfdom in Russia became legally codified as late as 1649 clearly reflected the expansive nature of Russian frontiers. By contrast, serfdom had largely disappeared from much of Western Europe by the fifteenth century, when European frontiers became consolidated into state boundaries.

Prior to the eighteenth century, Russian expansion in the south was driven by strategic and politico-theological considerations. While numerous sherts between Moscow and various native peoples were, in fact, peace treaties or at best a form of a political protectorate, the government's rhetoric of political theology did not allow articulating reality in these terms. Instead, Moscow hastily declared the newly encountered peoples to be the tsar's subjects and considered the treaties with them to be their unconditional allegiances. By the mid-eighteenth century, the political vocabulary of the Russian government shifted from notions of political theology to the modern European notions of Rationality and Enlightenment. The natives were now viewed as "savages" in need of civilization, and their political status within the empire was defined as "protectorship." In a curious reversal of the Western European experience with "the Other," in Russia the natives were seen first as "unfaithful subjects," and only later as "ignoble savages."

With much of the steppe frontier consolidated by military means, the time had arrived to utilize the economic potential of the recent territorial acquisitions—to settle and colonize the lands. A new imperial consciousness was on display by the 1770s, when new lands in the southwestern region of the empire were given the name "New Russia" (*Novorossiia*), not unlike New England and New Spain in the Americas.

Russia's systematic and persistent expansion proved to be far more successful than that of the neighboring Ottoman and Persian empires. At first, the vast expanses of the steppe, a "no-man's-land" that no state could effectively control, came under Moscow's sway, followed by the incorporation of territories and peoples into the empire of the Russian Christian monarchs. Russia's success can be attributed not only to the unquestionable superiority of its arms, but also to Western methods of colonization. Unlike the Persians, who were content to launch occasional punitive campaigns to compel their putative subjects to submit tribute, or the Ottomans, who only sporadically fortified their frontiers and brought in occasional settlers, the Russian government proceeded in a systematic fashion to incorporate the new territories and peoples into the empire's military, political, economic, and administrative system.

Surely Russian expansion could not have advanced at the same pace without the close cooperation and self-interest of many native nobles. In time, the native elites split into pro- and anti-Russian factions. While the co-optation of local elites was an important part of government policies, Russia also actively engaged in co-opting the native commoners by encouraging their defection and conversion to Orthodox Christianity. The latter policy proved to be a double-edged sword. Initially successful in further dividing the native nobles and commoners, the Russian policy of giving refuge to fugitive commoners and converting them to Christianity antagonized the nobles and served to undermine the government's very policy of securing the loyalty and cooperation of the native population. Realization that such a policy only reinforced the notion of a religious frontier and pushed the

225

native nobles into the arms of the Islamic clergy led to a reversal of the government's traditional policies in the late eighteenth century.

Like its imperial symbol, the double-headed eagle, facing at once west and east, the Russian Empire was deeply wedged between two distinct worlds. Russia's attitudes and policies in the southern and southeastern regions of the empire prove to be significantly different from those in the empire's western realm, where the conquered territories had been already densely settled, cultivated, and populated predominantly by other Christians. In its western borderlands, the government could hardly argue that the local population was in need of Christianity and civilization or rely on policies suitable to relations with the tribal chiefs and their nomadic confederations. Instead it preferred a more traditional alliance with the local elites.

In contrast, the Russian government undertook an active physical transformation of its southern and eastern regions by constructing forts and towns and encouraging Christian agricultural settlements. With equal forcefulness, but less successfully, the government engaged in an early modern form of "social engineering" by attempting to fashion the lifestyle and identity of the steppe inhabitants in its own image of Christian—that is, loyal, enlightened, and civilized—subjects of the empire. And in addition to the traditional policies of "divide and rule" applied to the elite, the Russian policies here often and deliberately favored the indigenous commoners at the expense of the elite, so that the government could more effectively manipulate the mutual hostility between the two groups.

Russia's expansion in the south, long defined and abetted by the lack of state-organized societies, resulting in a political vacuum and porous frontiers, had a dramatic impact upon the native population. The natives' increasing dependence on Russia exacerbated existing political and social cleavages and created new ones within the indigenous societies. Visible economic benefits of cooperation and trade with Russia continued to attract the local elites, whose changing demands and expectations were translated into a rising burden on the commoners. The native societies found themselves further dependent on Russia, as they were increasingly drawn into Russian markets and the latter's political sphere of influence. The results of such integration were the enrichment of the elites, the impoverishment of the commoners, and the growing social and economic differentiation within societies ripe for internal strife.[4]

From the beginning of its expansion in the mid-sixteenth century, Russia's experiences, objectives, attitudes, and policies along the southern frontier were more typical of European expansion in the High Middle Ages than of European colonization of the New World. It was only in the middle of the eighteenth century that various Russian officials consciously began to model Russia's goals and policies on Western Europe's experiences in the New World. Yet unlike medieval Europe, where the frontier regions came under the control of powerful and independent marcher lords, or later European colonial projects in the Americas and Asia, which were predominantly driven by mercantilist interests, Russian expansion in the south throughout the period was articulated by a government motivated first and foremost by geopolitical concerns, and only later by economic and commercial interests.[5]

While the authority of the Crown was formally the basis of the British Empire, the reins of power in the empire were in the hands of the Parliament, private institutions, trading companies, families (such as the founders of Maryland and Pennsylvania), and voluntary associations in charge of propagating Christianity. Consider, for instance, the role of the large British trade companies, the Hudson Bay and East India companies, the latter of which ruled India until 1858, when it finally ceded control of the country to the British government.

The Russian Empire exhibited no such dispersal of power. The only comparable examples in Russian history were two brief periods when charters were granted to the merchant Stroganov family to colonize Siberia in the 1560s and to the Russian-American Company to rule Alaska from 1799 until 1867, the year it was sold to the United States. Even in Spanish America, where the Spanish Crown was in far greater control of colonization than were its European counterparts, the private companies and the church enjoyed significant autonomy. By contrast, Moscow's colonization of the vanquished lands and peoples was emphatically a government enterprise. In this sense, and contrary to the received wisdom, the Russians were "ahead" of the Europeans, who only in the nineteenth century began to rely on the full machinery of the state to incorporate their overseas possessions and to establish a formal rule.

The fact that expansion and colonization in Russia were overwhelmingly undertaken by the government remained one of the most distinct factors separating Russia's colonial experience in the south from that of other European colonial powers before the nineteenth century. It continued to affect the nature of Russian colonialism in more than one way. Contrary to a recent fashion of seeing in almost every colonial encounter a "middle ground," which implies not the dominance of a single culture but the confluence of several equal cultural traditions, it is no wonder that little such middle ground can be found in Russia. The middle ground was indeed practiced where the parties involved had been driven by pragmatic concerns of trading instead of ideological doctrines. Such was the case on the early American frontier, where the Native Americans encountered private merchants and trappers.

In Russia, however, where the process of colonization was chartered and controlled by the government, the authorities had little interest in or tolerance for the middle ground. Even when such a concept was implicitly present, as in the yasak-paying procedures, the government's ideology allowed no room for a middle ground, and the official rhetoric continued to deny the reality on the ground. At different times the Russian government attempted and did create syncretic frontier institutions. But they proved to be short-lived, and it was apparent to both the natives and Russians alike that such institutions were nothing more than barely disguised attempts to put local practices in the service of the Russian imperial authorities.

One would search the Russian colonial landscape in an equally vain hope to find Russia's own Bartolomé de Las Casas or Edmund Burke. If they did exist, their voices were certainly muffled. For to protest the treatment of the natives, either in the name of God, as Las Casas did, or in the name of humanity, as Burke did, meant to question the government and its policies, something that few dared to do directly.[6] Instead one finds plenty of Russian Warren Hastings, corrupt and brutal governor-generals implacable in their righteous superiority toward the native population. It seems that the dominance of the state interests in Russia's colonial endeavors eschewed any possibility of an explicit colonial discourse.

A contiguous, extended, and lasting frontier separating the worlds of Christianity and Islam was another distinctive feature of Russia's colonial experience. From the New World to South Africa, the Europeans encountered numerous polytheists who were easily pushed aside by the settlers. It was only in parts of Asia, most notably in northern India, that the British intruded into the Islamic lands. But neither the British private entrepreneurs nor the government had any intention of settling India with British colonists or actively converting the natives to Christianity.[7] Russia, on the other hand, aspired to combine both features by bringing Christian settlers to predominantly Muslim areas and explicitly encouraging the natives' religious conversion, thus unmistakably magnifying a religious dimension of the colonial conflict.

There was one other place—southeastern Europe—where Christian Europe encountered the Islamic world along a contiguous religious divide. But the dynamics in these borderlands, contested for centuries between the Austro-Hungarian and Ottoman empires, were distinctly different from those in Russia's open steppe frontier. Here two imperial states were divided by a formal border, where the Habsburgs were engaged in a *Reconquista* of sorts, reconquering traditionally Christian lands from Muslim occupation.

While the Russian empire in the southern borderlands was built with a full range of colonial policies toward its various subjects, Russian imperial experience is traditionally set apart from the colonial experience of the Western European empires because of Russia's expansion in contiguous territories. Indeed, Russia's imperial vision was articulated in terms of the universal monarchy and blurred the separation between metropolis and colonial periphery, between the peoples within and outside the imperial boundaries, and between the administrative and legal institutions in the metropolitan areas and colonial periphery. But even though the Russian government refused to conceive of Russia as a colonial empire, its attitudes, objectives, and strategies in the southern borderlands were fundamentally no different from those of the Western European empires in their overseas possessions.

Russia's initial colonization of the steppe may be best described as "an organic colonialism," that is, colonialism determined largely by its defensive needs to secure and stabilize the empire's southern borderlands. It was not until the nineteenth century, when the steppe had finally been conquered and the nomads subdued, that Russia's further expansion into the Caucasus and Central Asia began to look like a classic example of western colonialism driven to conquest and domination by utilitarian concerns.

Even then, in contrast to the Western European societies, which in time developed a political vocabulary and institutions to deal with the multidimensional economic, political, and legal certainties of their empires, the Russian government continued to deny the complex reality of its multiethnic and multireligious empire and proceeded to maintain its image as an indivisible empire-nation. The government's sole response to the increasingly complex imperial challenges was its continuing emphasis on centralization and homogenization.

The colonial legacy of the Russian empire, never articulated and even less resolved, was inherited by the new Soviet regime in 1917. In the following seventy-four years, the Soviet government was confronted with similarly conflicting if somewhat different goals and dilemmas. The extent to which the Soviet government succeeded in resolving them is arguable, but at least it was able to realize both the importance and the complexity of the ethno-national-religious composition of the Soviet Union and to formulate its objectives in a yet another imperial project known as "nationality policies."

The same terms often had different meanings in different Turko-Mongol societies and at different times. I therefore chose to define the terms below as they are used only in the context of this book.

amanat   a hostage surrendered to the Russian authorities by a non-Christian people

bahadur (*bogatyr*)   an honorary title of a distinguished warrior among the Turkic peoples

barimta   a customary law among the nomads, whereby a victimized party has the right of forcible seizure of an offender's herds or other property in order to recover a debt or to revenge an insult

beg (*bek, bii*)   the chief ruler among the Nogays; among most Turko-Mongol peoples it was a title of the highest non-Chinggisid nobles

bobyl   a landless state peasant; here specifically an unregistered Tatar, Chuvash, or Mari migrant working on Bashkir lands in the eighteenth century

chetverik   a measure equal to one-eighth of a chetvert, about one pood or thirty-five pounds

chetvert   a measure of grain equal to about eight poods or 277 pounds in the eighteenth century *deti boiarskie*   the Muscovite servitors of the middle rank

diak   a head of a government office in Muscovy

divan   a khan's advisory council among the Turkic peoples

kabak   a village in the North Caucasus

kalgay   an heir apparent in the Crimea

kazak (better known as *Cossack*)   originally fugitives from the Turko-Mongol societies, organized in small independent bands living entirely off booty and pillage

keikuvat   the third in line of succession among the Nogays

khan   a member of the Chinggis dynasty and a supreme ruler of a Turko-Mongol people

mirza   a member of the nobility among the Turkic peoples

mufti   the officially appointed highest authority among the ulema

mukhtar   a headman, a notable among the Kazakhs who was in charge of about one hundred tents

mullah   a senior member of the ulema

nureddin   an heir apparent among the Nogays; the third in line of succession in the Crimea

oglan   a member of a ruling house among the Turko-Mongols, a Chinggisid prince

pasha   a title of an Ottoman military governor

shamkhal   a chief ruler among the Kumyks in the North Caucasus

shert'   a written document stipulating conditions of peace between Moscow and a Turko-Mongol people

tarkhan   a privilege of tax exemption granted to a distinguished member of the Turko-Mongol society

tayiji   a nobleman, a member of the ruling dynasty among the Oirats and Mongols

tayishi   a nobleman, a member of the ruling dynasty among the Kalmyks

tepter   a registered Tatar, Chuvash, or Mari migrant working on Bashkir lands

toibuga   the fourth in line of succession among the Nogays

ulema   the official interpreters of the Islamic law, members of the religious-judicial hierarchy *ulus*   an appanage consisting of people and herds, or a people in general among the Turko-Mongol peoples

utsmii   a chief ruler of the Kaitags (Dargins) in present-day Daghestan

uzden   a lesser noble among the Kumyks and other Turkic peoples of the Caucasus

voevoda   a title of a Russian military governor

yasak   a tribute or tax paid by non-Christian peoples

yurt   an appanage, territory, land; more specifically, a nomadic tent

zargo (*jargo* among the Kazakhs)   a khan's advisory council among the Kalmyks

zayisang   a member of the lesser nobility among the Kalmyks

LIST OF ABBREVIATIONS

AI	Akty istoricheskie, sobrannye i izdannye Arkheograficheskoi komissiei
AOGA	Astrakhanskii oblastnoi gosudarstvennyi arkhiv
AVMF	Arkhiv Voenno-Morskogo Flota
AVPRI	Arkhiv vneshnei politiki Rossiiskoi imperii
ChOIDR	Chteniia v imperatorskom obshchestve istorii i drevnostei rossiiskikh pri Moskovskom universitete
DAI	Dopolneniia k aktam istoricheskim, sobrannye i izdannye Arkheograficheskoi komissiei
DRV	Drevniaia Rossiiskaia Vivliofika
GAOO	Gosudarstvennyi Arkhiv Orenburgskoi Oblasti
HJAS	Harvard Journal of Asiatic Studies
HUS	Harvard Ukrainian Studies
PDRV	Prodolzhenie drevnei rossiiskoi vivliofiki
PSPR	Polnoe sobranie postanovlenii i rasporiazhenii po vedomstvu pravoslavnogo ispovedaniia Rossiiskoi imperii

PSPREP	Polnoe sobranie postanovlenii i rasporiazhenii po vedomstvu pravoslavnogo ispovedaniia Rossiiskoi imperii. Tsarstvovanie Elizavety Petrovny
PSZ	Polnoe sobranie zakonov Rossiiskoi imperii
RGADA	Rossiiskii gosudarstvennyi arkhiv drevnikh aktov
RIB	Russkaia istoricheskaia biblioteka
SIRIO	Sbornik Imperatorskogo Russkogo Istoricheskogo Obshchestva
TsGARK	Tsentral'nyi gosudarstvennyi arkhiv Respubliki Kalmykiia
VIA	Tsentral'nyi gosudarstvennyi voenno-istoricheskii arkhiv

Introduction

1. Edward L. Keenan, "Reply," *Russian Review* 46, no. 2 (1987), p. 200.

2. A short summary based on literature exemplifying such an approach is by Denis J. B. Shaw, "Southern Frontiers of Muscovy, 1550–1700" in J. H. Bater and R. A. French, eds., *Studies in Russian Historical Geography* (London: Academic Press, 1983), vol. 1, pp. 117–42.

3. For an informative discussion of these issues see Robert Bartlett, *The Making of Europe: Conquest, Colonization and Cultural Change, 950–1350* (Princeton: Princeton University Press, 1993) and Angus MacKay, *Spain in the Middle Ages: From Frontier to Empire, 1000–1500* (New York: St. Martin's Press, 1977).

4. This apt description of Spain is equally applicable to Russia; see Thomas Babington Macaulay, "Ranke's History of the Popes," in *Critical Historical Essays,* 2 vols. (London: J. M. Dent and Sons, 1907), vol. 2, p. 50.

5. Such was the view of all major Russian historians in the eighteenth and nineteenth centuries: N. M. Karamzin, Prince M. M. Shcherbatov, S. M. Solov'ev, and V. O. Kliuchevskii.

1. The Sociology of the Frontier

1. *Rossiiskii gosudarstvennyi arkhiv drevnikh aktov* (hereafter *RGADA*), *Dela po guberniiam,* F. 248, op. 3, *Dela po Astrakhanskoi gubernii,* 1720–21, kn. 94, ll. 55–56.

2. *RGADA,* F. 248, op. 126, *Dela i prigovory Pravitel'stvuiushchego Senata po Orenburgskoi gubernii,* no. 135, l. 91.

3. For a detailed discussion of social and political organization of the various Turko-Mongol nomadic societies, see two classic studies: Anatoly Khazanov, *Nomads and the Outside World* (Cambridge: Cambridge University Press, 1985), and Thomas J. Barfield, *The Perilous Frontier: Nomadic Empires and China* (Cambridge, Mass.: Basil Blackwell, 1989).

4. B. A.-B. Kochekaev, *Nogaisko-russkie otnosheniia v 15–18 vv.* (Alma-Ata: Nauka Kazakhskoi SSR, 1988), pp. 24–27; R. G. Kuzeev, *Narody Srednego Povolzhia i Iuzhnogo Urala* (Moscow: Nauka, 1992), pp. 70–78; *Nogaitsy: Istoriko-geograficheskii ocherk*, ed. I. K. Kalmykov et al. (Cherkessk: Stavropol'skoe kn. izd-vo, 1988), pp. 18–22; V. M. Zhirmunskii, *Tiurkskii geroicheskii epos* (Leningrad: Nauka, 1974), pp. 412–14; Yuri Bregel, "Tribal Tradition and Dynastic History: The Early Rulers of the Qongrats according to Munis," *Asian and African Studies* 16 (1982), p. 386.

5. Sigizmund Herberstein, *Zapiski o Moskovskikh delakh*, trans. A. I. Malein (St. Petersburg: Izd. A. S. Suvorina, 1908), p. 157.

6. *Prodolzhenie drevnei rossiiskoi vivliofiki* (hereafter *PDRV*), 11 vols. (St. Petersburg: Imper. Akademiia Nauk, 1786–1801); repr., *Slavic Printings and Reprintings* 251, ed. C. H. van Schooneveld. (The Hague: Mouton, 1970), vol. 8, pp. 264–65; vol. 9, pp. 17, 249–50.

7. *PDRV*, vol. 11, pp. 233–36, 271–98; "Akty vremeni Lzhedmitriia 1-go (1603–1606), Nogaiskie dela," ed. N. V. Rozhdenstvenskii, in *Chteniia v imperatorskom obshchestve istorii i drevnostei rossiskikh pri Moskovskom universitete: Sbornik* (hereafter *ChOIDR*) (Moscow, 1845–1918), vol. 264, pt. 1 (1918), p. 110; Kochekaev, *Nogaisko-russkie otnosheniia*, pp. 38–40; Zhirmunskii, *Tiurkskii*, p. 414; *PDRV*, vol. 8 pp. 269–77; vol. 9, pp. 37–39.

8. Kochekaev, *Nogaisko-russkie otnosheniia*, pp. 42–45. For example, in 1580 the Nogay beg, Urus, canceled his plans to attack Muscovy after a majority of "the Nogay mirzas and the best people" advised him against the campaign (*RGADA*, Nogaiskie dela no. 9, ll. 156–57).

9. M. Khudiakov, *Ocherki po istorii Kazanskogo khanstva* (Kazan: Gos. izd-vo, 1923, repr. 1990), pp. 43–45, 72–83; Halil Inalcik, "Giray," in *Islam Ansiklopedisi* (Istanbul: Milli Egitim Basimevi, 1948), vol. 4, pp. 783–85.

10. V. V. Vel'iaminov-Zernov, *Issledovanie o Kasimovskikh tsariakh i tsarevichakh*, 4 vols. (St. Petersburg: Imp Akademiia nauk, 1863–87), vol. 2, pp. 410–48; V. E. Syroechkovskii, "Muhammed-Gerai i ego vassaly," in *Uchenye zapiski MGU*, no. 61 (1940), pp. 28–39; *Sbornik Imperatorskogo Russkogo Istoricheskogo Obshchestva* (hereafter *SIRIO*), 148 vols. (St. Petersburg, 1867–1916), vol. 95, no. 2, pp. 39–40.

11. Khudiakov, *Ocherki*, pp. 190–95, 198–209; Edward L. Keenan, *Muscovy and Kazan, 1445–1552: A Study in Steppe Politics* (Ph.D. diss., Harvard University, 1965), pp. 89–97: Azade-Ayse Rorlich, *The Volga Tatars: A Profile in National Resilience* (Stanford: Hoover Institution Press, 1986), pp. 28–30.

12. *Istoriia Kazakhskoi SSR*, 5 vols. (Alma-Ata: "Nauka" Kazakhskoi SSR, 1977–81), vol. 2, pp. 244–45; Zhirmunskii, *Tiurkskii*, pp. 119–54.

13. Ibid., vol. 2, pp. 176–81, 248–51, 264–73; *Istoriia Uzbekskoi SSR*, 4 vols. (Tashkent: Fan, 1967–68), vol. 1, pp. 504–7.

14. Michael Khodarkovsky, *Where Two Worlds Met: The Russian State and the Kalmyk Nomads, 1600–1771* (Ithaca: Cornell University Press, 1992), pp. 9–14, 33–40. For the most thorough discussion of the social and political organization of the Kalmyk

society see Dittmar Schorkowitz, *Die soziale und politische Organisation bei den Kalmücken (Oiraten) und Prozesse der Akkulturation vom 17. Jahrhundert bis zur Mitte des 19. Jahrhunderts* (Frankfurt am Main: Peter Lang, 1992).

15. *PDRV,* vol. 7, p. 244.

16. I. Ia. Zlatkin, *Istoriia Dzhungarskogo khanstva, 1635–1758,* 2nd ed. (Moscow: Nauka, 1983), pp. 19–43; Khodarkovsky, *Where Two Worlds Met,* pp. 5–8.

17. Ethnically and linguistically, Daghestan was and remains one of the most diverse regions on earth. One may observe with no great surprise that the ethnic hierarchies of the past survived both the Soviet and post-Soviet periods only to be called ethnopolitics today. For instance, the region of central Daghestan with the border town of Khasaviurt has been a residence for Kumyks, Avars, Chechens, and other smaller ethnic groups for centuries. Traditionally the Kumyks had been a dominant group, and when in 1997 the Avar, not the Kumyk, was elected to head the local administration, ethnic violence followed (*Nezavisimaia gazeta,* May 13, 1997).

18. V. K. Gardanov, *Obshchestvennyi stroi Adygskikh narodov (18–pervaia polovina 19 v.)* (Moscow: Nauka, 1967), pp. 180–206; *Istoriia narodov Severnogo Kavkaza s drevneishikh vremen do kontsa 18 v.,* ed. B. B. Piotrovskii (Moscow: Nauka, 1988), pp. 283–98.

19. *Kabardino-russkie otnosheniia: Dokumenty i materialy,* 2 vols. (Moscow: AN SSSR, 1957), vol. 2, no. 256, p. 364. The first Russian report of the various Chechen clans was made in 1587, when the Russian envoys on the way to Georgia passed through the highlands and mentioned the Michkiz, Indili, and Shubut clans; see *Snosheniia Rossii s Kavkazom: Materialy izvlechennye iz Moskovskogo Ministerstva Inostrannykh del, 1578–1613,* comp. S. L. Belokurov (Moscow: Univ. tip., 1889), no. 4, p. 33. The word "Chechen" as an ethnonym is first encountered in 1708; see *Polnoe sobranie zakonov Rossiiskoi imperii: Sobranie pervoe* (hereafter *PSZ*), 45 vols. (St. Petersburg, 1830), vol. 4, p. 421. It is found on the Russian map of 1719 (*Kabardino-russkie,* vol. 1, p. 289); see also U. Iaudaev, "Chechenskoe plemia," in *Sbornik svedenii o kavkazskikh gortsakh,* 10 vols. (Tiflis, 1868–81), vol. 6, p. 3.

20. Guillaume le Vasseur, Sieur de Beauplan, *A Description of Ukraine,* trans. and ed. Andrew Pernal and Dennis Essar (Cambridge, Mass.: Harvard Ukrainian Research Institute, 1993), p. 48; Khodarkovsky, *Where Two Worlds Met,* pp. 142–43.

21. *SIRIO,* vol. 41, no. 43, p. 196; no. 72, p. 354; vol. 95, no. 38, p. 706; *PDRV,* vol. 9, pp. 100–108.

22. *PDRV,* vol. 10, p. 102.

23. *SIRIO,* vol. 41, no. 68, p. 333.

24. A. A. Novosel'skii, *Bor'ba Moskovskogo gosudarstva s tatarami v pervoi polovine 17 veka* (Moscow-Leningrad: AN SSSR, 1948), p. 211. For the specific military tactics of the Crimean Tatars, see Beauplan, *A Description of Ukraine,* pp. 48–61, and L. J. D. Collins, "The Military Organization of the Crimean Tatars during the 16th and 17th Centuries," in V. J. Parry and M. E. Yapp, eds., *War, Technology and Society in the Middle East* (London: Oxford University Press, 1975), pp. 257–76.

25. *SIRIO,* vol. 41, no. 66, p. 324; vol. 95, no. 16, p. 292; Khodarkovsky, *Where Two Worlds Met,* pp. 30–31.

26. *SIRIO,* vol. 95, no. 25, p. 441.

27. *Polnoe sobranie russkikh letopisei: Patriarshaia ili Nikonovskaia letopis'* (hereafter *Nikonovskaia*) (Moscow: Nauka, 1965), vol. 13, p. 65; *SIRIO,* vol. 95, no. 38, p. 706.

28. *SIRIO,* vol. 41, no. 72, p. 361; no. 78, p. 381; vol. 95, no. 2, pp. 19–21.

29. *PDRV*, vol. 9, pp. 101–11.

30. Ibid., p. 267.

31. Khodarkovsky, *Where Two Worlds Met*, p. 132; *Kazakhsko-russkie otnosheniia v 16–18 vekakh: Sbornik dokumentov i materialov* (Alma-Ata: AN Kazakhskoi SSR, 1961), no. 33, p. 86.

32. *SIRIO*, vol. 41, no. 72, p. 360; *Opisanie gosudarstvennago arkhiva starykh del,* comp. P. I. Ivanov (Moscow: Tip. S. Selivanskogo, 1850), p. 258; Norman Davies, *God's Playground: A History of Poland,* 2 vols. (New York: Columbia University Press, 1982), vol. 1, pp. 139–41.

33. Novosel'skii, *Bor'ba*, p. 436.

34. *Materialy po istorii Uzbekskoi, Tadzhikskoi i Turkmenskoi SSR*. Vol. 1: *Torgovlia s Moskovskim gosudarstvom i mezhdunarodnoe polozhenie Srednei Azii v 16–17 vv.* (Leningrad: AN SSSR, 1932), pp. 386–97.

35. *SIRIO*, vol. 95, no. 23, p. 408.

36. Khudiakov, *Ocherki*, pp. 136–37.

37. Novosel'skii, *Bor'ba*, p. 238.

38. *The Muscovite Law Code (Ulozhenie) of 1649,* Part 1: *Text and Translation,* trans. and ed. Richard Hellie (Irvine, Calif.: Charles Schlacks Jr., 1988), ch. 8, pp. 17–18; *Rossiiskaia Akademiia Nauk. Arkhiv,* F. 1714, op. 1, *Novosel'skii, A. A.,* no. 66, l. 123. For a brief time in the 1660s, Moscow instituted a separate administrative office (Polonianichnyi Prikaz), whose sole responsibility was ransoming the Russians from captivity in the Crimea, Central Asia, and elsewhere. In the 1670s the office ceased to exist, and its functions were absorbed by other government offices.

39. *The Muscovite Law Code (Ulozhenie) of 1649,* ch. 19, art. 33, p. 159; ch. 20, art. 34, p. 172.

40. *SIRIO*, vol. 95, no. 16, pp. 292–93.

41. *PDRV*, vol. 8, p. 284.

42. Ibid., pp. 64–65; S. M. Solov'ev, *Istoriia Rossii s drevneishikh vremen,* 15 vols. (Moscow: Izd. sotsial'no-ekonomicheskoi literatury, 1959–1966), vol. 3, pp. 413–15, 444.

43. Alan Fisher, "The Ottoman Crimea in the Sixteenth Century," *Harvard Ukrainian Studies* (hereafter *HUS*), no. 2 (1981), pp. 141–42.

44. Halil Inalcik, "The Customs Registers of Caffa, 1487–1490," in Victor Ostapchuk, ed., *Sources and Studies on the Ottoman Black Sea,* vol. 1 (Cambridge, Mass.: Harvard University Press, 1996), pp. 93, 145–46; Halil Inalcik and Donald Quataert, eds., *An Economic and Social History of the Ottoman Empire, 1300–1914* (Cambridge: Cambridge University Press, 1994), pp. 283–85.

45. Peter F. Sugar, "The Ottoman 'Professional Prisoner' on the Western Borders of the Empire in the Sixteenth and Seventeenth Centuries," *Etudes Balkaniques* 7, no. 2 (1971), pp. 82–91, as quoted in Mark Stein, *Seventeenth-Century Ottoman Forts and Garrisons on the Habsburg Frontier* (Ph.D. diss., University of Chicago, 2000), ch. 1.

46. *SIRIO*, vol. 95, no. 16, p. 292; *RGADA*, F. 123, *Krymskie dela,* kn. 13, l. 57; *Materialy po istorii Uzbekskoi, Tadzhikskoi i Turkmenskoi SSR,* vol. 1, pp. 386–97.

47. *PDRV*, vol. 10, pp. 168–189, 260; *RGADA*, F. 127, op. 1, *Nogaiskie dela,* kn. 9, ll. 73, 79–85, 143–44, 177 ob.; no. 10, l. 123. In 1634 Polish and Lithuanian prisoners were allowed to depart for home freely; see A. G. Man'kov, *Ulozhenie 1649 goda: Kodeks feodal'nogo prava Rossii* (Leningrad: Nauka, 1980), p. 117.

48. *PDRV,* vol. 10, pp. 124–32; *RGADA,* F. 89, *Turetskie dela,* kn. 3, ll. 114–15, 260.

49. *RGADA,* F. 127, op. 1, *Nogaiskie dela,* kn. 10, ll. 3 ob., 87, 88, 93, 120–21, 140.

50. *Rossiiskaia Akademiia Nauk. Arkhiv,* F. 1714, op. 1, *Novosel'skii, A. A.,* no. 66, l. 169; Khodarkovsky, *Where Two Worlds Met,* pp. 159–61; *Kazakhsko-russkie otnosheniia v 16–18 vekakh,* no. 88, p. 209.

51. *Kazakhsko-russkie otnosheniia v 16–18 vekakh,* no. 33, p. 64; no. 76, pp. 181, 184; no. 88, pp. 209, 211. In 1722 Russia's envoy to Bukhara, Flori Beneveni, reported even larger numbers of Russian captives in the region: one thousand Russian captives in Bukhara, two thousand in Samarkand and among the Uzbeks, 1,500 in Khiva and the Arals, and an unknown number in Balkh and in Astarabad in Persia; see A. N. Popov, "Snosheniia Rossii s Khivoiu i Bukharoiu pri Petre Velikom: Prilozheniia," *Zapiski Imperatorskogo russkogo geograficheskogo obshchestva* 9 (1853), p. 377.

52. *Mezhdunarodnye otnosheniia v Tsentral'noi Azii: 17–18 vv. Dokumenty i materialy,* 2 vols. (Moscow: Nauka, 1989), vol. 1, no. 3, pp. 43–44. For instance, custom did not prevent the Kazakhs from releasing Oirat captives without a ransom upon the Oirats' demand. Insistence on the force of custom was rather an indication of the Kazakhs' independent status vis-à-vis Russia and the strong attraction of ransom, even if it threatened to provoke Russia's ire.

53. *SIRIO,* vol. 95, no. 21, p. 358.

54. *PDRV,* vol. 8, pp. 270–72; *SIRIO,* vol. 95, no. 21, p. 378.

55. *Kazakhsko-russkie otnosheniia v 16–18 vekakh,* no. 224, pp. 570–71; *PSZ,* vol. 14, no. 10,654, pp. 677–78; vol. 20, no. 14,489, p. 402; vol. 22, no. 16,534, p. 839. For more on the topic of non-Christians' escape and migration to Russia, see ch. 5.

56. Ibid., no. 255, p. 573.

57. *PDRV,* vol. 9, p. 103.

58. Ibid., vol. 8, pp. 219, 222–23, 249, 289, 293, 301, 322; vol. 9, pp. 1, 16, 36, 72, 79, 90, 105, 152, 189, 218, 238, 296, 301; vol. 10, pp. 14, 89, 153, 210, 212; vol. 11, pp. 1, 94–96; *RGADA,* F. 119, op. 1, *Kalmytskie dela,* d. 8, l. 2; Khodarkovsky, *Where Two Worlds Met,* p. 127. A Russian contemporary claimed that in the mid–seventeenth century between thirty and fifty thousand horses were brought for sale in Moscow annually; see Grigorii Kotoshikhin, *O Rossii v tsarstvovanie Alekseia Mikhailovicha,* 4th ed. (St. Petersburg: Tip. glavnogo upravleniia udelov, 1906), p. 92; see also M. V. Fekhner, *Torgovlia russkogo gosudarstva so stranami vostoka v 15 veke* (Moscow, 1956), p. 19.

59. *RGADA,* F. 127, op. 1, *Nogaiskie dela,* kn. 9, ll. 16–22. Diaks Andrei Shchelkalov and his brother Vasilii had a long and distinguished career within the Muscovite Foreign Office; see *D'iaki i pod'iachie posol'skogo prikaza v 16 veke: Spravochnik,* comp. V. I. Savva (Moscow: Institut istorii SSSR, 1983).

60. *PDRV,* vol. 8, pp. 25–26, vol. 9, pp. 280–82; Khodarkovsky, *Where Two Worlds Met,* pp. 26–27; *PSZ,* vol. 3, no. 1585, p. 313.

61. *SIRIO,* vol. 41, no. 28, pp. 106–7; no. 43, p. 196; no. 58, pp. 268–69; no. 63, p. 296; no. 80, pp, 391–98; no. 81, pp. 399–413; no. 97, p. 515; vol. 95, no. 2, pp. 22–30; no. 37, p. 673; no. 38, pp. 680–88. For the Ottoman trade in the Black Sea, see *An Economic and Social History of the Ottoman Empire,* pp. 275–314.

62. *Pamiatniki diplomaticheskikh i torgovykh snoshenii Moskovskoi Rusi s Persiei,* ed. N. I. Veselovskii, 3 vols. (St. Petersburg, 1890–98), vol. 3, pp. 633–34; I. K. Kirilov, *Tsvetushchee sostoianie vserossiiskogo gosudarstva* (composed in 1727) (Moscow: Nauka,

1977), p. 230. For the prices of various items in seventeenth-century Russia, see Richard Hellie, *The Economy and Material Culture of Russia, 1600–1725* (Chicago: University of Chicago Press, 1999). On the growing dominance of the Russian trade in the Black Sea, see Idris Bostan, "Rusya'nin Karadeniz'de Ticarete Bashlamasi ve Osmanli Imperatorlugu (1700–1787)," *Türk Tarih Kurumu, Belleten* 59 (1995), pp. 353–94.

63. Khodarkovsky, *Where Two Worlds Met*, pp. 157–61.

64. *Kazakhsko-russkie otnosheniia v 16–18 vekakh*, no. 38, p. 96; V. V. Dorofeev, *Nad Uralom-rekoi* (Cheliabinsk: Iuzho-Ural'skoe knizh. izd., 1988), pp. 5–52. For more details see ch. 5.

65. *Kazakhsko-russkie otnosheniia v 16–18 vekakh*, no. 225, p. 576; no. 246, p. 630; vol. 2, no. 27, p. 57. Edward Keenan employed the same pertinent metaphor in his "Muscovy and Kazan: Some Introductory Remarks on the Patterns of Steppe Diplomacy," *Slavic Review* 26, no. 4 (1967), pp. 548–58.

66. *Kazakhsko-russkie otnosheniia v 16–18 vekakh*, no. 37, p. 89; no. 170, pp. 439–40; *Kazakhsko-russkie otnosheniia v 18–19 vekakh: Sbornik dokumentov i materialov* (Alma-Ata: Nauka, 1964), no. 83, pp. 143–44.

67. Halil Inalcik, "The Khan and the Tribal Aristocracy: The Crimean Khanate under Sahib Giray I," *HUS* 3/4 (1979–80), pt. 1, pp. 445–66.

68. N. N. Pal'mov, *Etiudy po istorii privolzhskikh kalmykov 17 i 18 veka*, 5 vols. (Astrakhan: Tip. Kalmoblitizdata, 1926–32), vols. 3–4, pp. 289–90.

69. *Kazakhsko-russkie otnosheniia v 16–18 vekakh*, no. 152, p. 394; no. 225, pp. 579–80; no. 269, pp. 686–87; *Kazakhsko-russkie otnosheniia v 18–19 vekakh*, no. 57, p. 106. A Russian military officer among the Kazakhs, Nikolai Rychkov, observed in 1771 that the heads of the Kazakh large families and clans had more influence than a khan; see *Dnevnye zapiski puteshestviia Kapitana Nikolaia Rychkova v kirgis-kaisatskoi stepi, 1771 god* (St. Petersburg: Imp. Akademiia Nauk, 1772), pp. 23–24.

70. Vel'iaminov-Zernov, *Issledovanie*, vol. 3, pp. 183, 317–18.

71. Khodarkovsky, *Where Two Worlds Met*, pp. 126–27, 143–44.

72. Ibid., pp. 194–95.

73. *Kazakhsko-russkie otnosheniia v 16–18 vekakh*, no. 153, p. 401.

74. Ibid., no. 152, p. 394; no. 225, pp. 580–83; no. 269, pp. 686–87.

75. Ibid., no. 225, p. 580.

76. Ibid., no. 165, p. 419; no. 167, pp. 432–33.

77. *PSZ*, vol. 23, no. 17,080, pp. 569–74. Such a ritual was already used in the 1740s; see *Kazakhsko-russkie otnosheniia v 16–18 vekakh*, no. 175, pp. 444–46.

78. *Snosheniia Rossii s Kavkazom*, no. 12, p. 208.

79. *SIRIO*, vol. 41, no. 19, p. 69.

80. *RGADA*, F. 127, op. 1, *Nogaiskie dela*, kn. 9, 1579g., pp. 95–96.

81. *PDRV*, vol. 8, pp. 265–67; Khodarkovsky, *Where Two Worlds Met*, pp. 98, 113, 145–46.

82. *PDRV*, vol. 8, pp. 102–3, 233, 269.

83. Ibid., vol. 8, pp. 316–17. For more on this issue, see the section "Ideology through Diplomacy."

84. Ibid., vol. 9, p. 17.

85. *Akty istoricheskie, sobrannye i izdannye Arkheograficheskoi komissiei* (hereafter *AI*), 5 vols. (St. Petersburg, 1841–43), vol. 1, no. 160, p. 291.

86. *Rossiiskaia Akademiia Nauk. Arkhiv,* F. 1714, op. 1, *Novosel'skii, A. A.,* no. 66, l. 105.

87. *Snosheniia Rossii s Kavkazom,* no. 6, p. 53–62. A similar appeal was issued by the Armenian bishop Martin asking for protection of the Armenians in Derbent, who claimed to have been forced to convert to Islam; see *Tsentral'nyi gosudarstvennyi voenno-istoricheskii arkhiv* (hereafter *VIA*), F. VUA, d. 18,472, l. 3. Both Georgians and Armenians continued to look toward Russia for protection; see Ronald Grigor Suny, *The Making of the Georgian Nation* (Bloomington: Indiana University Press, 1988), pp. 56–59.

88. *Snosheniia Rossii s Kavkazom,* no. 12, p. 203. Another appeal from the sham-khal to the sultan came more than one hundred years later, after the Russian con-quest of Azov in 1696, the most significant Ottoman fortress in the region. The shamkhal asked for Ottoman troops, cannon, and munitions in order to dislodge the Russians from their newly built fort at Tatartüp on the Terek River in Kabarda. The sultan dispatched a force, but far smaller than requested. Unable to reach Kabarda, this force was then stationed at the recently built Ottoman fort of Achu in the estuary of the Kuban River; see Silahtar Mehmet Aga Findiklili, *Nusretname,* ed. Ismet Parmaksizoglu, 2 vols. (Istanbul, 1962–66), vol. 1, pp. 323–24. In the 1750s, unable to count on the sultan, the shamkhal appealed for protection to both the Persians and Russians at the same time; see P. G. Butkov, *Materialy dlia novoi istorii Kavkaza, s 1722 po 1803 god,* 3 vols. (St. Petersburg, 1869), vol. 1, p. 254. In the 1770–80s, facing a Russo-Georgian alliance, the rulers of Daghestan and Azerbaijan again appealed to Istanbul for help; see *Bashbakanlik Arshivi* (Istanbul, Hatti Hümayun Tasnifi), nos. 73, 94; *Osmanli Devleti ile Azerbaycan Türk Hanliklari Arasindaki Münasa-betlere dair Arshiv Belgeleri,* vol. 1 (1578–1914) (Ankara, 1992), pp. 62–93. Similar concerns were raised by the Nogays in the wake of Moscow's expansion in the Volga region (*PDRV,* vol. 9, p. 267).

89. *Kabardino-russkie otnosheniia,* vol. 1, no. 6, pp. 14–15; no. 12, pp. 23–25; *Snosheniia Rossii s Kavkazom,* no. 33, p. 572.

90. *Russko-dagestanskie otnosheniia 17–pervoi chetverti 18 vv.: Dokumenty i materialy* (Makhachkala: Dagestankoe kn. izd, 1958), no. 79, p. 174.

91. *RGADA,* F. 123, *Krymskie dela,* kn. 13, 1567g.; Prince Mikhail Shcherbatov, *Istoriia Rossiiskaia,* 11 vols. (St. Petersburg: Imp. Akademiia Nauk, 17—), vol. 5, pt. 2, p. 54.

92. *Kazakhsko-russkie otnosheniia v 16–18 vekakh,* no. 88, p. 211; Khodarkovsky, *Where Two Worlds Met,* pp. 182, 193. *Snosheniia Rossii s Kavkazom,* no. 4, pp. 26–27, 37. In 1775 a Russian official in Astrakhan suggested that under the pretext of faith and reconstruction of the destroyed churches, the Russian government should begin settling the town of Tatartüp, a strategic location close to Georgia, which would allow for better control of Kabarda; see *Kabardino-russkie otnosheniia,* vol. 2, no. 220, p. 314.

93. *Russko-dagestanskie otnosheniia,* no. 131, pp. 261–62.

94. *RGADA,* F. 248, op. 113, d. 1257, l. 14 ob.

95. *VIA,* F. 52, op. 1, d. 350, pt. 4; d. 72, pt. 1, l. 1.

96. Ibid., d. 72, pt. 1, l. 197, 203 ob.

97. *Kabardino-russkie otnosheniia,* vol. 2, no. 119, p. 161.

98. Findiklili, *Nusretname,* vol. 2, p. 247. Despite this victory, the Kabardinians were forced to resume the payments of slave tribute shortly thereafter. Russia's inability to protect them from Crimean predations was often bemoaned by the Kabardinian nobles; see *Astrakhanskii oblastnoi gosudarstvennyi arkhiv* (hereafter

AOGA), F. 394, op. 2; *Astrakhanskaia gubernskaia kantseliariia*, d. 12, ll. 100–103. In 1755 they again refused to provide the slaves to the Crimea; see *Tsentral'nyi derzhavnyi istorychnyi arkhiv Ukrainy v misti Kjivi*, F. 59, op. 1, d. 2668, l. 6.

99. *Snosheniia Rossii s Kavkazom*, no. 20, p. 305. On conversion to Christianity see chapter 4.

100. *Kabardino-russkie otnosheniia*, vol. 2, no. 256, pp. 360, 362.

101. *Kazakhsko-russkie otnosheniia v 18–19 vekakh*, no. 70, pp. 129–30; *Dnevnye zapiski puteshestviia Kapitana Nikolaia Rychkova*, p. 26.

102. *PSZ*, vol. 22, no. 16,292, pp. 493–95; no. 16,400, pp. 604–6. Throughout the 1780s the government constructed two mosques in the towns of Troitsk and Orenburg. However, neither the new mosques nor the Islamic school built in Orenburg were successful in attracting the Kazakhs. The school had on average one or two pupils a year, some of whom died from measles and other illnesses; see A. Dobrosmyslov, "Zaboty imperatritsy Ekateriny II o prosveshchenii kirgizov," *Trudy Orenburgskoi uchenoi arkhivnoi komissii* no. 9 (1902), pp. 51–63.

103. Danil' D. Azamatov, "Russian Administration and Islam in Bashkiriia (18th–19th Centuries)," in Michael Kemper, Anke von Kügelgen, and Dmitriy Yermakov, eds., *Muslim Culture in Russia and Central Asia from the 18th to the Early 20th Centuries* (Berlin: Klaus Schwarz Verlag, 1996), pp. 100–111; Allen J. Frank, *Islamic Historiography and "Bulghar" Identity among the Tatars and Bashkirs of Russia* (Leiden: Brill, 1998), pp. 35–38.

104. M. P. Viatkin, *Batyr Srym* (Moscow and Leningrad: AN SSSR, 1947), pp. 274–87.

105. Charles Halperin suggested that the Muscovite "ideology of silence" on the frontier was necessary in order to reconcile religious antagonisms with the pragmatic issues of coexistence; see his "The Ideology of Silence: Prejudice and Pragmatism on the Medieval Religious Frontier," *Comparative Studies in Society and History* 26, no. 4 (1984), pp. 442–66. For a discussion of the Muscovite royal titles see Marc Szeftel, "The Title of the Muscovite Monarch Up to the End of the Seventeenth Century," *Canadian-American Slavic Studies* 13, nos. 1–2 (1979), pp. 59–81. The most recent discussion of the Russian court ceremonies and titles is in Richard Wortman, *Scenarios of Power: Myth and Ceremony in Russian Monarchy*, vol. 1 (Princeton: Princeton University Press, 1995), pp. 22–41. On diplomatics in the Muslim world, see *Encyclopaedia of Islam*, new edition (Leiden: E. J. Brill, 1965 ff.), vol. 2, pp. 301–16; for Mongol diplomatics, M. A. Usmanov, *Zhalovannye akty Dzhuchieva ulusa, 14–16 vv.* (Kazan: Kazanskii Universitet, 1979); and for Ottoman and Crimean diplomatics, Jan Reychman and Ananiasz Zajaczkowski, *Handbook of the Ottoman-Turkish Diplomatics* (The Hague: Mouton, 1968).

106. The idea of the Muscovite princes as heirs to the Chinggisid rulers of the Golden Horde was first developed by one of the founders of the "Eurasian" school, Prince E. Trubetskoi, in *Nasledie Chingiskhana* (Berlin, 1925). Various aspects of this idea were further discussed by George Vernadsky in *A History of Russia*, 6th rev. ed. (New Haven: Yale University Press, 1969), and Michael Cherniavsky in "Khan or Basileus: An Aspect of Russian Mediaeval Political Theory," *Journal of the History of Ideas* 20, no. 4 (1959), pp. 459–76. Moscow clearly displayed its attitude toward Rome during its negotiations with the pope's Jesuit envoy, Antonio Possevino, in 1582. Possevino strongly objected when the Russians referred to the pope as if he were an ordinary priest. He exhorted them that the emperor and other rulers

considered the pope a representative of God and the teacher of all Christians; see Antonio Possevino, S.J., *The Moscovia*, trans. Hugh F. Graham (Pittsburgh: University of Pittsburgh Press, 1977), pp. 128–29, 173. On the idea of Moscow as the New Israel see Daniel B. Rowland, "The Third Rome or the New Israel?" *Russian Review* 55, no. 4 (1996), pp. 591–614.

107. Solov'ev, *Istoriia*, vol. 3, p. 515. Jaroslaw Pelenski argued convincingly that Moscow's claims to the Kievan Rus were largely motivated by the necessity to assert and legitimize its right over the Kievan lands vis-à-vis Poland-Lithuania; see "The Origins of the Official Muscovite Claims to the 'Kievan Inheritance,'" *HUS* 1, no. 1 (1977), pp. 29–52.

108. Possevino, *The Moscovia*, pp. 135–36.

109. *SIRIO*, vol. 41, no. 1, pp. 1–2. In general, the envoy was told to agree to Mengli Giray's conditions only after he had bargained on every issue and exhausted every excuse.

110. Ibid., vol. 95, no. 7, p. 113.

111. *Rossiiskaia Akademiia Nauk. Arkhiv,* F. 1714, op. 1, *Novosel'skii, A. A.*, no. 66, l. 21; *SIRIO*, vol. 41, no. 50, pp. 231–36; no. 58, p. 264.

112. *PDRV,* vol. 7, p. 309. On honor and its central place in early modern Russian society, see Nancy Schields Kollmann, *By Honor Bound: State and Society in Early Modern Russia* (Ithaca: Cornell University Press, 1999).

113. "Akty vremeni Lzhedmitriia 1-go (1603–1606), Nogaiskie dela," ed. N. V. Rozhdenstvenskii, in *ChOIDR*, vol. 264, pt. 1 (1918), pp. 119–20.

114. Khodarkovsky, *Where Two Worlds Met*, p. 69.

115. *Russko-dagestanskie otnosheniia*, no. 17, pp. 64–65.

116. *PDRV,* vol. 10, pp. 210–11; vol. 11, pp. 206–7; *RGADA, Nogaiske dela*, kn. 9, p. 24.

117. *RGADA,* F. 127, op. 1, *Nogaiskie dela*, kn. 9, pp. 151–52.

118. Ibid., kn. 10, pp. 3–6, 24–25.

119. *SIRIO*, vol. 95, no. 16, pp. 269–70.

120. Ibid., vol. 41, no. 1, pp. 5–7; vol. 95, no. 7, pp. 118–23.

121. S. V. Bakhrushin, "Ostiatskie i vogul'skie kniazhestva v 16 i 17 vv.," in *Nauchnye trudy,* 4 vols. (Moscow, 1952–59), vol. 3, pt. 2, p. 152; *SIRIO*, vol. 95, no. 36, p. 666. In the sixteenth century, a copy of the Quran was kept in the Kremlin for the Tatars and other Muslims to be sworn on it (Keenan, "Muscovy and Kazan," p. 553).

122. Possevino, *The Moscovia*, p. 57.

123. *RGADA,* F. 123, *Krymskie dela*, kn. 15, l. 396; see also kn. 9, ll. 2, 30.

124. *PDRV,* vol. 8, p. 82. In 1537 Ivan IV was addressed as the "white kniaz" and later the "white tsar" (p. 32). The meaning of the title "white tsar" has been a subject of some speculation. I subscribe to a view that it was used to refer to a ruler in charge of the western territories of the former Chinggis Empire ("the right wing"), and thus a successor to the khans of the Golden Horde; see M. G. Safargaliev, "Raspad Zolotoi Ordy," *Uchenye Zapiski Mordovskogo gosudarstvennogo universiteta* 11 (1960), p. 15; V. P. Iudin, "Ordy: Belaia, Siniaia, Seraia, Zolotaia," in *Kazakhstan, Sredniaia i Tsentral'naia Aziia v 16–18 vv.* (Alma-Ata: "Nauka" Kazakhskoi SSR, 1983), pp. 120–26; V. V. Trepavlov, *Gosudarstvennyi stroi Mongol'skoi imperii 13 v* (Moscow: Vostochnaia literatura, 1993), pp. 86–93.

125. *PDRV*, vol. 8, pp. 316–17.

126. *RGADA*, F. 127, op. 1, *Nogaiskie dela*, kn. 10, p. 87.

127. *Istoricheskoe opisanie drevnego Rossiiskogo muzeia pod nazvaniem masterskoi i Oruzheinoi palaty* (Moscow: Tip. Mosk. Univ., 1807), pp. 18–26.

2. Frontier Concepts and Policies in Muscovy

1. Michael Khodarkovsky, "From Frontier to Empire: The Concept of the Frontier in Russia, Sixteenth-Eighteenth Centuries," *Russian History, The Frontier in Russian History* 19, nos. 1–4 (1992), p. 115.

2. *Slovar' russkogo iazyka 11–17 vv.* (Moscow: Nauka, 1982), vol. 9, p. 65.

3. I. I. Sreznevskii, *Materialy dlia slovaria drevne-russkogo iazyka po pis'mennym pamiatnikam,* 4 vols. (St. Petersburg: Tip. Imp. AN, 1912), repr. ed. (Moscow: Nauka, 1989), vol. 1, pt. 1, p. 584; vol. 3, pt. 1, pp. 179–80; *Dukhovnye i dogovornye gramoty velikikh kniazei 14–16 vv.,* no. 23, p. 62.

4. *Drevniaia rossiiskaia vivliofika* (hereafter *DRV*), comp. Nikolai Novikov, 2nd ed., 22 vols. (Moscow: Tip. kompanii tipograficheskoi, 1788–1791); repr., *Slavic Printings and Reprintings* 250/1, ed. C. H. van Schooneveld (The Hague: Mouton, 1970), vol. 5, p. 50; *Slovar' russkogo iazyka 11–17 vv.,* vol. 4, p. 123. This was also true in the east, where Russia confronted Qing China. The word *granitsa* is found in the text of the Nerchinsk treaty signed in 1689 by Russian and Chinese officials; see *Russko-kitaiskie otnosheniia v 17 veke: Materialy i dokumenty,* 2 vols. (Moscow: Nauka, 1972), vol. 2, pp. 656–59.

5. *Slovar' russkogo iazyka 11–17 vv.,* vol. 8, p. 8; *Sbornik dokumentov po istorii Buriatii 17 v.,* pp. 336–37.

6. *Sbornik dokumentov po istorii Buriatii 17 v.,* comp. G. N. Rumiantsev and S. B. Okun' (Ulan-Ude: BNII, 1960), p. 360.

7. Ibid., p. 203.

8. Ibid., p. 205.

9. *AI*, vol. 4, p. 473.

10. Cf. Daniel Nordman, *Frontières de France: de l'espace au territoire, XVI–XIX siècle* (Paris: Gallimard, 1998), pp. 31–39.

11. For a discussion of these and other frontier terms, see Daniel Power, "Frontiers: Terms, Concepts, and the Historians of Medieval and Early Modern Europe," in Daniel Power and Naomi Standen, eds., *Frontiers in Question: Eurasian Borderlands, 700–1700* (London: Macmillan, 1999), pp. 1–13.

12. Lucien Febvre, *A Geographical Introduction to History* (New York: Alfred Knopf, 1929), pp. 297–300; Anthony Pagden, *Lords of All the World: Ideologies of Empire in Spain, Britain and France, c. 1500–c. 1800* (New Haven: Yale University Press, 1995), p. 107; Peter Sahlins, *Boundaries: The Making of France and Spain in the Pyrenees* (Berkeley: University of California, 1989); Nordman, *Frontières de France,* pp. 63–66.

13. As quoted in Mark Bassin, "Turner, Solov'ev, and the 'Frontier Hypothesis': The Nationalist Signification of Open Spaces," *Journal of Modern History* 65, no. 3 (1993), p. 492.

14. *PDRV*, vol. 8, p. 74; *SIRIO*, vol. 41, no. 101, p. 553; vol. 95, no. 1, p. 18. In an attempt to establish direct ties with Istanbul bypassing the Crimea, Vasilii III sug-

gested that the Muscovite delegation depart from Riazan and the Ottoman from Azov. But because the raids by the Astrakhan kazaks made it unsafe to meet in the middle, Vasilii proposed that both parties meet closer to the Muscovite frontier, along the Khoper and Medveditsa rivers (*SIRIO*, vol. 95, no. 38, pp. 688–89).

15. Vel'iaminov-Zernov, *Issledovaniie*, vol. 3, p. 23; *Slovar' russkogo iazyka 11–17 vv.*, vol. 5. p. 294. In 1679 all frontier towns were classified into Siberian, "Ponizovye" (the towns along the middle Volga River), and "Ukrainnye" (the towns along the southern frontier) (*DRV*, vol. 15, pp. 233–41). For a list of specific southern frontier towns in the sixteenth and seventeenth centuries, see Georgii Saatchian, "Russkoe Pole," *Rodina*, no. 2 (1996), p. 50.

16. *PDRV*, vol. 8, p. 74.

17. *SIRIO*, vol. 41, no. 39, p. 172; no. 100, p. 539; vol. 95, no. 10, pp. 152–56.

18. "Akty vremeni Lzhedmitriia 1-go," pp. 105–9.

19. Bernard Lewis, *The Muslim Discovery of Europe* (New York: W. W. Norton, 1982), p. 206; Khodarkovsky, *Where Two Worlds Met*, p. 66.

20. N. A. Kazakova, *Russko-livonskie i russko-ganzeiskie otnosheniia: Konets 14-nachalo 16 v.* (Leningrad: Nauka, 1975), pp. 188–94.

21. *SIRIO*, vol. 95, no. 16, pp. 271, 287.

22. *PDRV*, vol. 10, pp. 20–21.

23. *Snosheniia Rossii s Kavkazom*, no. 10, p. 79; no. 12, p. 112.

24. *RGADA*, F. 127, op. 1, *Nogaiskie dela*, d. 2, 1616g., l. 6.

25. *Kazakhsko-russkie otnosheniia v 16–18 vv.*, no. 33, pp. 53–54.

26. Ibid., no. 250, pp. 639–41.

27. To ensure that the oath of allegiance was genuine, the Muscovite authorities persisted in finding out whether the shert' was *priamaia*, that is, performed in accordance with the customs of a given people. See S. V. Bakhrushin, "Iasak v Sibiri v 17 v.," in *Nauchnye trudy*, vol. 3, pt. 2, pp. 65–66; see also his "Ocherki po istorii Krasnoiarskogo uezda v 17 v.," in *Nauchnye trudy*, vol. 4, p. 47.

28. Bakhrushin, "Ostiatskie i vogul'skie," vol. 3, pt. 2, p. 152.

29. Ibid.; "Vologodsko-permskaia letopis'," in *Polnoe sobranie russkikh letopisei* (Moscow and Leningrad, 1959), vol. 26, p. 277.

30. N. P. Shastina, "Pis'ma Lubsan taidzhi v Moskvu," in *Filologiia i istoriia mongol'skikh narodov* (Moscow: Izd-vo vostochnoi literatury, 1958), pp. 279–81; *RGADA*, F. 119, op. 1, *Kalmytskie dela*, d. 3, l. 6; E. I. Kychanov, *Povestvovanie ob oiratskom Galdane Boshoktu-Khane* (Novosibirsk: Nauka, 1980), p. 53. For more on the issue of translation see the section "Translating or Colonizing?" later in this chapter.

31. Vasilii Bakunin, "Opisanie istorii kalmytskogo naroda," *Krasnyi arkhiv: Istoricheskii zhurnal* 3 (1939), pp. 214–15. For more on the Kalmyks and the issue of political status, see Khodarkovsky, *Where Two Worlds Met*, pp. 67–73, 131–32.

32. *Kabardino-russkie otnosheniia*, vol. 1, no. 165, p. 264.

33. *Russko-dagestanskie otnosheniia 17–pervoi poloviny 18 vv.*, no. 96, pp. 224–25.

34. *RGADA*, F. 248, op. 113, *Opis' del Sekretnoi Ekspeditsii Senata*, d. 1257, l. 14 ob.

35. *Russko-ossetinskie otnosheniia v 18 veke, 1742–62*, vol. 1, comp. M. M. Bliev (Ordzhonikidze: Izd-vo "IR," 1976), no. 53, p. 121; nos. 56, 57, pp. 123–27.

36. *Kazanskii Universitet: Rukopisnyi otdel*, no. 4865; *Akty sobrannye Kavkazskoi Arkheograficheskoi komissiei*, vols. 1–12 (Tiflis, 1866–83), vol. 1, p. 91. On patronage,

see Ernest Gellner, "Patrons and Clients," in Ernest Gellner and John Waterbury, eds., *Patrons and Clients in Mediterranean Societies* (London: Duckworth, 1977), pp. 1–6; on the idea of kunak in the Caucasus, see M. O. Kosven, *Etnografiia i istoriia Kavkaza* (Moscow: Vostochnaia literatura, 1961), pp. 126–29.

37. *Kazakhsko-russkie otnosheniia v 16–18 vv.*, vol. 2, no. 70, p. 125.

38. *Snosheniia Rossii s Kavkazom*, no. 19, p. 305.

39. Ibid., no. 10, p. 77; *Kabardino-russkie*, vol. 1, no. 78, p. 167.

40. Bakhrushin, "Ocherki," 47. In its instructions to the military governors of Kazan in 1649, the government specified that hostages were to be taken from those with established authority, wealth, and large families (*"krepki, vladetel'ny i semianisty"*); see V. D. Dmitriev, "'Tsarskie' nakazy Kazanskim voevodam 17 veka," in *Istoriia i kul'tura Chuvashskoi ASSR: Sbornik statei* (Cheboksary, 1974), vol. 3, pp. 293–94.

41. *Snosheniia Rossii s Kavkazom*, no. 6, p. 58.

42. *Russko-mongol'skie otnosheniia 1607–1636*, no. 4, pp. 28–29; S. K. Bogoiavlenskii, "Materialy po istorii kalmykov v pervoi polovine 17 veka," *Istoricheskie zapiski* 5 (1939), p. 73; P. S. Preobrazhenskaia, "Iz istorii russko-kalmytskikh otnoshenii v 50–60kh godakh 17 veka," *Zapiski Kalmytskogo nauchno-issledovatel'skogo instituta iazyka, literatury i iskusstva* 1 (1960), p. 66.

43. *Snosheniia Rossii s Kavkazom*, no. 10, p. 77.

44. Ibid., no. 11, pp. 142–43.

45. Preobrazhenskaia, "Iz istorii," pp. 66–67.

46. Bakhrushin, "Ocherki," pp. 48–49.

47. *Kabardino-russkie*, vol. 1, no. 129, pp. 200–202.

48. Bakhrushin, "Ocherki," p. 47; see also his "Iasak," pp. 66–67. In 1743, during the Kazakh khan Abulkhayir's visit to the Russian town of Orsk, some of his people died there from being fed rotten rye bread; see *Kazakhsko-russkie otnosheniia v 16–18vv*, no. 109, pp. 281–82.

49. *Kabardino-russkie*, vol. 1, nos. 137, 139, pp. 209–12; vol. 2, nos. 186–87, pp. 276–77.

50. RGADA, F. 248, op. 3, *Dela po Orenburgskoi komissii i Ufimskoi provintsii za 1742–43gg.*, kn. 147, l. 14; *Kazakhsko-russkie otnosheniia v 16–18vv*, no. 96, p. 248; no. 109, p. 282; no. 175, pp. 444–46.

51. *Kazakhsko-russkie otnosheniia v 16–18vv*, nos. 94–95, pp. 222–29.

52. Ibid., no. 119, p. 302.

53. Ibid., no. 255, pp. 578–79.

54. Viatkin, *Batyr Srym*, p. 227.

55. *Kabardino-russkie otnosheniia*, vol. 2, no. 220, p. 316.

56. *Kazakhsko-russkie otnosheniia v 16–18vv*, no. 114, pp. 292–94; no. 119, pp. 302–7. The Kazakh khan Nuraly could not hide his astonishment at the sight of his son dressed in Russian military uniform and speaking fluent Russian (ibid., no. 256, p. 654).

57. *Sbornik dokumentov po istorii Buriatii 17 v.*, p. 360; Bakhrushin, "Ocherki," p. 97; *PSZ*, vol. 3, no. 1594, p. 367; no. 1670, p. 534.

58. *PDRV*, vol. 10, pp. 67; vol. 11, p. 86. Thirty years later, the Nogay beg Urus objected to the Muscovite intrusion into the region of the Ufa and Samara rivers, where he collected yasak from the Bashkirs; see V. V. Trepavlov, *Nogai v Bashkirii, 15–17 vv.: Kniazheskie rody nogaiskogo proiskhozhdeniia* (Ufa, 1997), pp. 12–14.

59. For more on taxation among the Mongols, see two seminal articles: H. F. Schurmann, "Mongolian Tributary Practices of the Thirteenth Century," *Harvard Journal of Asiatic Studies* (hereafter *HJAS*) 19 (1956), pp. 304–89, and John Masson Smith, Jr., "Mongol and Nomadic "Taxation," *HJAS* 30 (1970), pp. 46–85. See also I. P. Ermolaev, *Srednee Povolzh'e vo vtoroĭ polovine 16–17 vv.* (Kazan: Kazanskii Universitet, 1982), pp. 72–74; Andreas Kappeler, *Russlands erste Nationalitäten: Das Zarenreich und die Völker der Mittleren Wolga vom 16 bis 19 Jahrhundert* (Cologne: Böhlau Verlag, 1982), pp. 102–3. The most recent discussion of the yasak in Siberia is in Yuri Slezkine, *Arctic Mirrors: Russia and the Small Peoples of the North* (Ithaca: Cornell University Press, 1994), pp. 20–32, 60–71.

60. *Kazakhsko-russkie otnosheniia v 16–18vv*, nos. 26, 30, 92, pp. 37, 43, 218.

61. Ibid., no. 210, p. 539.

62. Bakhrushin, "Iasak," p. 71.

63. Ibid., pp. 71–72; *Kolonial'naia politika Moskovskogo gosudarstva v Iakutii v 17 veke*, ed. Ia. P. Al'kor and B. D. Grekov (Leningrad: Institut narodov Severa, 1936), no. 191, pp. 239–40.

64. Bakhrushin, "Iasak," pp. 72–73; Bakhrushin, "Ocherki," pp. 55–56; *Kolonial'naia*, no. 40, pp. 92–93.

65. *Kolonial'naia*, no. 17, p. 25; no. 45, pp. 98–99.

66. Bakhrushin, "Iasak," pp. 74–75; *Kolonial'naia*, no. 43, p. 96; no. 44, p. 98.

67. *Istoriia Iakutskoi ASSR*, 3 vols. (Moscow: AN SSSR, 1957), vol. 2, p. 139.

68. Richard White makes a similar observation of the exchange network between the French and the Algonquians in the eighteenth-century America, where trade and gift exchanges could no longer be disentangled; see *The Middle Ground: Indians, Empires, and Republics in the Great Lakes Region, 1650–1815* (Cambridge: Cambridge University Press, 1991), p. 141.

69. *Dukhovnye i dogovornye gramoty velikikh i udel'nykh kniazei 14–16 vv.*, no. 5, p. 20; no. 10, p. 30; no. 12, p. 36; no. 19, p. 53.

70. Ibid., no. 101, pp. 417, 419.

71. Some of Moscow's competitors in the steppe politics used a more explicit terminology. For instance, the Polish kings referred to their payments to the Crimeans as *yergeld* (from German *Jahrgeld*) and the Ottoman sultans as *yillik;* both terms literally meant annuity.

72. *SIRIO*, vol. 41, no. 1, pp. 2–3.

73. Solov'ev, *Istoriia*, vol. 4, pp. 266–67.

74. "Kaznu v Krym prodolzhat' prisylat' s pribyl'iu," *Rossiiskaia Akademiia Nauk. Arkhiv*, F. 1714, op. 1, *Novosel'skii, A. A.*, no. 66, l. 144.

75. *Arkhiv Voenno-Morskogo Flota* (St. Petersburg) (hereafter *AVMF*), F. 233, op. 1, *Kantseliariia grafa Apraksina*, no. 222, ll. 116–19.

76. *SIRIO*, vol. 95, d. 16, pp. 273, 279; vol. 41, no. 48, pp. 219–20; *PDRV*, vol. 7, pp. 300–302, 321.

77. *SIRIO*, vol. 41, no. 43, p. 196; no. 46, p. 211; *PDRV*, vol. 11, p. 27.

78. *SIRIO*, vol. 41, no. 87, p. 446; vol. 95, no. 10, pp. 169–70; no. 16, pp. 298–300.

79. Ibid., vol. 41, no. 64, p. 310; vol. 95, no. 19, p. 340; no. 21, p. 358.

80. Ibid., no. 68, pp. 330–32.

81. *PDRV*, vol. 9, p. 86; vol. 10, p. 54; Novosel'skii, *Bor'ba*, p. 96.

82. *PDRV*, vol. 7, pp. 233–37; vol. 8, pp. 249–51; vol. 9, pp. 265–66.

83. Ibid., vol. 11, pp. 17, 30–32, 156–67; *RGADA*, F. 127, op. 1, *Nogaiskie dela*, kn. 10, 1582g., pp. 131–32.

84. *PDRV*, vol. 8, p. 184.

85. Foreign observers of the early-eighteenth-century Russia described the government payments to the Kalmyks as "subsidies"—Friedrich Christian Weber, *The Present State of Russia*, 2 vols. (London, 1723), vol. 1, p. 52—or "annual pension"—John Perry, *The State of Russia under the Present Tsar* (London, 1716), p. 85.

86. *Russko-dagestanskie otnosheniia 17–pervoi chetverti 18 veka: Dokumenty i materialy* (Makhachkala: Dagestanskoe knizhnoe izd., 1958), no. 96, pp. 223–25.

87. *Kazakhsko-russkie otnosheniia v 16–18vv*, no. 168, p. 437.

88. On the issue of translation as a colonization of consciousness, see Vicente L. Rafael, *Contracting Colonialism: Translation and Christian Conversion in Tagalog Society under Early Spanish Rule* (Ithaca: Cornell University Press, 1988); Jean and John Comaroff, *Of Revelation and Revolution: Christianity, Colonization and Consciousness in South Africa*, vol. 1 (Chicago: University of Chicago Press, 1991); Tsvetan Todorov, *The Conquest of America* (New York: Harper Perennial, 1984). For an overview of the issue in pre-fourteenth-century Asia, see Denis Sinor, "Interpreters in Medieval Inner Asia," *Asian and African Studies, Journal of Israel Oriental Society* 16 (1982), pp. 293–320.

89. The difference between the two categories was underscored in the traditional phrase which accompanied the document "interpreted by an interpreter," or "translated by a translator" (*tolmachil tolmach, perevodil perevodchik*); see *Tsentral'nyi gosudarstvennyi arkhiv Respubliki Kalmykiia* (hereafter *TsGARK*), F. 36, op. 1, d. 9, l. 6.

90. *Snosheniia Rossii s Kavkazom*, no. 10, p. 77.

91. *RGADA*, F. 138, op. 1, *Dela o Posol'skom prikaze i sluzhivskikh vrem*, d. 15, ll. 2–4.

92. Possevino, *The Moscovia*, p. 52.

93. *RGADA*, F. 138, op. 1, d. 1, ll. 1–7. In the early seventeenth century, Tsar Boris Godunov expanded the *Kazanskii dvorets* to include the administration of Astrakhan, Siberia, and all the towns along the southern frontier.

94. Ibid., dela 11, 13; *Kazanskii Universitet: Rukopisnyi otdel*, no. 4393, l. 1 ob., roll 348; no. 108; l. 2, roll 373, no. 154. Note that Richard Hellie, whose data encompass annuities and wages for a period from 1614 to 1725 throughout Muscovy, has significantly lower annuities: thirty-six rubles for translators and fifteen for interpreters (Hellie, *The Economy*, pp. 419, 421). While the competence, volume, and variety of translations were steadily improving throughout the seventeenth century, the translated literary texts were exclusively from Western languages into Russian; see I. M. Kudriavtsev, "'Izdatel'skaia deiatel'nost' Posol'skogo prikaza (k istorii russkoi rukopisnoi knigi vo vtoroi polovine 17 veka)," *Kniga: issledovaniia i materialy. Sbornik* 8 (1963), pp. 179–244; *Istoriia russkoi perevodnoi khudozhestvennoi literatury*, ed. Iurii Levin, 2 vols., vol. 1: *Drevniaia Rus': 18 vek* (St. Petersburg: "Dmitrii Bulanin," 1995), pp. 63–72.

95. *Snosheniia Rossii s Kavkazom*, no. 19, pp. 297–99.

96. Khodarkovsky, *Where Two Worlds Met*, p. 65.

97. *SIRIO*, vol. 41, no. 64, pp. 307–8.

98. Bakunin, "Opisanie," *Krasnyi arkhiv* 3 (1939), pp. 214–15.

99. Possevino, *The Moscovia,* p. 72; *SIRIO,* vol. 95, no. 4, pp. 81–82; *Kazakhsko-russkie otnosheniia v 18–19 vekakh,* no. 29, p. 68.

100. *RGADA,* F. 127, op. 1, *Nogaiskie dela,* kn. 9, l. 20; *PDRV,* vol. 9, pp. 280–82; *Kazakhsko-russkie otnosheniia v 18–19 vekakh,* no. 83, p. 146.

101. When a mission of the Muscovite interpreter, Semen Trofimov, dispatched to Kabarda in 1638 had been deemed a success, his annuity was raised from three to fourteen rubles (*RGADA,* F. 115, *Kabardinskie, cheikesskie i diugie dela,* op. 1. d. 6, ll. 3–7).

102. *PDRV,* vol. 10, pp. 138–39; *SIRIO,* vol. 41, no. 22, pp. 130–31; vol. 95, no. 38, pp. 692–93.

103. *Polnoe sobranie postanovlenii i rasporiazhenii po vedomstvu pravoslavnogo ispo-vedaniia Rossiiskoi imperii,* 19 vols. (St. Petersburg, 1869–1915), vol. 5 [1725–27], no. 1777, p. 355 (hereafter *PSPR*).

104. Michael Khodarkovsky, "'Not by Word Alone': Missionary Policies and Religious Conversion in Early Modern Russia," *Comparative Studies in Society and History* 38, no. 2 (1996), p. 282.

105. Ibid., pp. 283, 287; V. N. Vitevskii, *I. I. Nepliuev i Orenburgskii krai v prezhnem ego sostave do 1758g.,* 3 vols. (Kazan: Tip. V. M. Kliuchnikova, 1897), vol. 3, p. 833.

3. Taming the "Wild Steppe"

1. *SIRIO,* vol. 41, no. 1, p. 4. Such a frontier, separating the lands of the Russian princes from the lands of the Golden Horde, already existed in the thirteenth century; see V. L. Egorov, *Istoricheskaia geografiia Zolotoi Ordy v 13–14 vv.* (Moscow: Nauka, 1985), pp. 232–33.

2. *SIRIO,* vol. 41, no. 2, p. 11.

3. Ibid., vol. 41, no. 5, pp. 17–19.

4. Such is the standard postulate in Russian and Soviet historiography. See K. B. Bazilevich, *Vneshniaia politika Russkogo tsentralizovannogo gosudarstva: vtoraia polovina 15 veka* (Moscow: Moskovskii universitet, 1952), pp. 168–69; A. L. Khoroshkevich, *Russkoe gosudarstvo v sisteme mezhdunarodnykh otnoshenii kontsa 15-nachala 16 v* (Moscow: Nauka, 1980), p. 171. Historians of Russia in the West correctly questioned such an interpretation but did not show why it was wrong. See George Vernadsky, *Russia at the Dawn of the Modern Age* (New Haven: Yale University Press, 1959), p. 77; Keenan, "Muscovy and Kazan: Some Introductory Remarks," p. 549; Charles J. Halperin, *Russia and the Golden Horde* (Bloomington: Indiana University Press, 1985), pp. 70–72; Janet Martin, *Medieval Russia, 980–1584* (Cambridge: Cambridge University Press, 1995), pp. 317–18, 386–87. Most recently, Donald Ostrowski argued convincingly that "the stand on the Ugra" was fashioned into a pivotal event in Russian history by the church ideologues; see Ostrowski, *Muscovy and the Mongols: Cross-Cultural Influences on the Steppe Frontier, 1304–1589* (Cambridge: Cambridge University Press, 1998), pp. 164–68.

5. Solov'ev, *Istoriia,* vol. 3, pp. 81–82. Charles Halperin traces the time of the emerging Muscovite claims to political "liberation" from the Golden Horde to the middle of the sixteenth century and the origins of the phrase "the Tatar Yoke" to the seventeenth century; see his *The Tatar Yoke* (Columbus, Ohio: Slavica Press, 1986), pp. 149–66.

6. *SIRIO*, vol. 41, no. 6, p. 25.

7. For arguments against the yarlik authenticity see Keenan, *Muscovy and Kazan, 1445–1552,* pp. 72–77, and his "The Yarlik of Axmed-Khan to Ivan III: A New Reading," *International Journal of Slavic Linguistics and Poetics* 11 (1967), pp. 32–47.

8. Solov'ev, *Istoriia,* vol. 3, p. 77.

9. A similar turn of events occurred in 1472, when Ahmad's army suddenly retreated; see Solov'ev, *Istoriia,* vol. 3, pp. 75–76.

10. Solov'ev, *Istoriia,* vol. 3, p. 361, n. 123.

11. *SIRIO*, vol. 41, no. 44, p. 199. Abak khan was a member of the Sheybani branch of the Chinggisid dynasty and was based in Tiumen, the center of the western Siberian part of the Golden Horde; see Abul-Ghazi Bahadur Khan, *Rodoslovnoe drevo tiurkov,* trans. G. S. Sablukov (Kazan: Tip. Imp. Universiteta, 1906), p. 156.

12. Solov'ev, *Istoriia,* vol. 3, p. 82; V. M. Zhirmunskii, *Tiurkskii geroicheskii epos* (Leningrad: Nauka, 1974), p. 438. Yet Ivan did not quite trust his Nogay ally, who could have exaggerated the news in order to receive greater presents. Ivan instructed his envoy to the Crimea to seek confirmation of Ahmad's death and to maintain the alliance with Mengli Giray against Ahmad khan's sons (*SIRIO*, vol. 41, no. 6, p. 27).

13. *PDRV,* vol. 8, p. 178. The assassination of Ahmad khan is usually attributed to Abak khan or Yamgurchi mirza (Bazilevich, *Vneshniaia,* pp. 167–68).

14. *SIRIO*, vol. 41, no. 13, p. 51; no. 14, p. 52.

15. Vel'iaminov-Zernov, *Issledovanie,* vol. 1, pp. 97–126; Bazilevich, *Vneshniaia,* pp. 108–12; B. D. Grekov and A. Iu. Iakubovskii, *Zolotaia Orda i ee padenie* (Moscow-Leningrad: AN SSSR, 1950), pp. 423–25. In 1486 it was reported that the sons of Ahmad khan were going to attack Mengli Giray, only if they were convinced that the Ottomans would not help him (*SIRIO*, vol. 41, no. 14, p. 53).

16. G. A. Fedorov-Davydov, *Obshchestvennyi stroi Zolotoi Ordy* (Moscow: Moskovskii Universitet, 1973), pp. 166–67; Kochekaev, *Nogaisko-russkie,* pp. 50–52.

17. *SIRIO*, vol. 41, no. 3, p. 14.

18. Vel'iaminov-Zernov, *Issledovanie,* vol. 1, pp. 13–28. Keenan observes correctly that Kasimov must have been given to Kasim upon agreement between Vasilii II and Ulug Muhammed (*Muscovy and Kazan, 1445–1552,* p. 397). The role of Kasimov in the Muscovite-Crimean relations under Ivan III is discussed by Janet Martin, "Muscovite Frontier Policy: The Case of the Khanate of Kasimov," *Russian History, The Frontier in Russian History* 19 (1992), nos. 1–4, pp. 169–79.

19. *SIRIO*, vol. 41, no. 1, p. 5; no. 4, p. 15; no. 13, pp. 45–46. Vel'iaminov-Zernov incorrectly believed that Nur Devlet became the Kasimov khan only in 1486. In fact, this happened in 1478 or 1479; see Vel'iaminov-Zernov, *Issledovanie,* vol. 1, p. 90; *SIRIO*, vol. 41, no. 5, p. 17.

20. *SIRIO*, vol. 41, no. 35, p. 151.

21. Khudiakov, *Ocherki,* pp. 25–43. Edward Keenan's unpublished dissertation *Muscovy and Kazan, 1445–1552* remains an indisputably brilliant account and analysis of events leading to Moscow's conquest of Kazan in 1552.

22. *SIRIO*, vol. 41, no. 16, p. 59; no. 18, pp. 61–62; Khudiakov, *Ocherki,* pp. 45–48.

23. *SIRIO* vol. 41, no. 19, p. 69.

24. Ibid., no. 19, p. 68; no. 20, p. 74.

25. Ibid., no. 19, p. 63; no. 21, pp. 75–76.

26. Ibid., no. 27, p. 98; no. 29, p. 110; Vel'iaminov-Zernov, *Issledovanie*, vol. 1, p. 144.

27. *SIRIO*, vol. 41, no. 23, pp. 81–82, 85.

28. Ibid., no. 23, p. 83; no. 25, p. 90.

29. Mengli sent a similar appeal to Muhammed Amin in Kazan (ibid., no. 28, pp. 105–9; no. 29, p. 110).

30. Ibid., no. 32, p. 122; nos. 28–31, pp. 104–20.

31. Ibid., no. 28, p. 109; no. 31, pp. 119–20.

32. Ibid., no. 33, p. 133; no. 40, pp. 180–82; no. 44, p. 199. In 1491 Musa harbored several fugitive mirzas from Yamgurchi. He then sent a cryptic message to Ivan suggesting that they could come and serve him in Moscow. Ivan showed a considerable zeal in making sure they did join his service (ibid., no. 33, pp. 130–31).

33. Ibid., no. 33, p. 132.

34. Ibid., no. 39, p. 172; no. 41, pp. 189–92. When his plea to Mengli Giray failed, the Polish king sent his envoy directly to the Ottoman sultan and promised to pay a large sum in gold ducats if Mengli were convinced to remove his kazaks from Belgorod. Shortly thereafter, the sultan sent orders to Mengli to this effect (ibid., no. 46, p. 209).

35. Ibid., no. 45, p. 202; no. 46, p. 211; no. 48, p. 222. Kashtanov believes that the choice of Zvenigorod was prompted by Ivan's intention to secure his hold on this region and neutralize similar claims by other princes; see S. M. Kashtanov, *Sotsial'no-politicheskaia istoriia Rossii kontsa 15–pervoi poloviny 16 v* (Moscow: Nauka, 1967), p. 73.

36. *SIRIO*, vol. 41, no. 51, pp. 236–37; Khudiakov, *Ocherki*, pp. 52–53, 59; Janet Martin, "The Tiumen' Khanates' Encounters with Muscovy, 1481–1505," in C. Lemercier-Quelguejay et al., eds., *Passé Turco-Tatar, Présent Soviétique* (Paris: Editions Peeters, 1986), pp. 82–86.

37. *SIRIO*, vol. 41, no. 56, p. 255; no. 58, p. 263; no. 59, pp. 277–79; no. 64, pp. 321–24.

38. Ibid., no. 64, pp. 301–2; no. 68, pp. 330–32; no. 72, pp. 354, 360.

39. Ibid., no. 72, pp. 354–59; no. 74, pp. 367–68; no. 78, pp. 378–79; no. 82, pp. 413–16. For a distinction between the arquebusiers and musketeers, see Richard Hellie, *Enserfment and Military Change in Muscovy* (Chicago: University of Chicago Press), pp. 160–63.

40. *SIRIO*, vol. 41, no. 83, pp. 416–22; no. 87, p. 444. The focus of one lengthy essay was to correct the previous erroneous assumptions and to show that the Great Horde did not vanish but, in fact, was annexed by Mengli Giray. See Leslie Collins, "On the Alleged 'Destruction' of the Great Horde in 1502," in A. Bryer and M. Ursinus, eds., *Manzikert to Lepanto: The Byzantine World and the Turks, 1071–1575* (Amsterdam: Adolf M. Hakkert, 1991); pp. 361–400.

41. *SIRIO*, vol. 41, no. 85, p. 433; no. 86, p. 435.

42. Ibid., no. 87, pp. 445, 450, 451; no. 90, p. 474.

43. Ibid., no. 95, pp. 505–11; no. 96, p. 516; no. 98, pp. 520–23, 534.

44. Relevant documents for the years 1505–8 are unavailable. See *SIRIO*, vol. 95, no. 2, pp. 19–21.

45. In 1508 the Nogay Sheidiak mirza assured Vasilii's envoys that Moscow had nothing to fear from the seventeen sons of the deceased Musa mirza and that the

Nogays' main concerns were trade with Moscow and safety from the Cossack raids (ibid., vol. 95, no. 1, pp. 11–15; no. 4, pp. 70–72, 79–80).

46. Ibid., no. 3, pp. 60–69. Peace with Poland was concluded on October 8, 1508; see *The Cambridge History of Poland to 1696*, ed. W. F. Reddaway et al. (Cambridge: Cambridge University Press, 1950), p. 302.

47. *SIRIO*, vol. 41, no. 79, p. 390; no. 89, p. 468; no. 90, pp. 474–76; no. 93, pp. 490, 495; Khudiakov, *Ocherki*, pp. 53–58.

48. *SIRIO*, vol. 41, no. 81, pp. 412–13; no. 88, pp. 461, 463.

49. Ibid., vol. 95, no. 2, p. 42.

50. Vasilii's mistrust of Abdullatif was obvious. A few years later he allowed Abdullatif's mother, Nur Sultan, to come to visit her son in Moscow, as long as he remained under Moscow's watchful eye (ibid., no. 6, pp. 100–101).

51. Ibid., no. 2, pp. 42, 48–51; no. 3, p. 54; Kashtanov, *Sotsial'no-politicheskaia*, pp. 246–47; Khudiakov, *Ocherki*, pp. 69–70.

52. *SIRIO*, vol. 95, no. 3, pp. 54–59, 68; no. 4, pp. 74–75, 81–82.

53. Ibid., vol. 95, no. 7, pp. 113, 118–23; *The Cambridge History of Poland*, pp. 303–4; Jaroslaw Pelenski, "The Emergence of the Muscovite Claims to the Byzantine-Kievan 'Imperial Inheritance,'" *HUS*, no. 7 (1983), p. 531. A recent visit to Moscow by an embassy of the Holy Roman Emperor Maximilian and the emperor's acknowledgment of Vasilii's title of tsar further confirmed the rising status of Moscow.

54. *SIRIO*, vol. 95, no. 10, pp. 153–55, 158, 160.

55. Ibid., no. 10, pp. 146–77. Solov'ev wrongly believed that Muhammed Giray used this title only when addressing the Riazan prince (Solov'ev, *Istoriia*, vol. 3, p. 248).

56. *SIRIO*, vol. 95, no. 10, pp. 167–70.

57. Ibid., no. 6, p. 97; no. 7, p. 108; no. 10, p. 151, no. 11, p. 186, no. 12, pp. 195–96, 209–13, 222–23; *Nikonovskaia*, p. 15; Khudiakov, *Ocherki*, pp. 71, 82.

58. *SIRIO*, vol. 95, no. 13, pp. 229–35.

59. Ibid., no. 16, p. 271.

60. Ibid., no. 16, pp. 277, 282.

61. Ibid., no. 16, p. 285.

62. Ibid., no. 16, pp. 287, 296–98. The Nogays were divided. Chagir mirza with twelve other Nogay mirzas came to the Crimea to seek help against his brother Shigim. Fearful, Shigim mirza also sent his envoy to the Crimea to offer his sister in marriage to Muhammed Giray and an alliance against Astrakhan. He had earlier seized thirty thousand people of his brother Chagir mirza and now was afraid that they would leave him if he were attacked by the Crimeans (ibid., no. 9, p. 144; no. 16, pp. 310–11).

63. Ibid., no. 17, pp. 316–33; no. 21, pp. 358–65.

64. Ibid., no. 14, p. 251; no. 21, pp. 377–78; no. 22, p. 386; no. 24, p. 419. See also Vel'iaminov-Zernov, *Issledovanie*, vol. 1, pp. 217–46.

65. *SIRIO*, vol. 95, no. 22, pp. 388–89.

66. Ibid., no. 23, p. 408; no. 24, pp. 430–31.

67. Ibid., no. 29, pp. 497, 502.

68. Ibid., no. 28, pp. 481, 488; no. 30, pp. 513, 520.

69. Ibid., no. 31, pp. 549–50; no. 33, pp. 594–98.

70. Ibid., no. 34, p. 609; no. 35, pp. 619–24; no. 36, p. 636; Syroechkovskii, "Muhammed-Gerai," pp. 53–57.

71. *SIRIO*, vol. 95, no. 36, pp. 635–41.

72. Vasilii's justification for installing Shah Ali in Kazan was to insist that such was the wish of the Kazan people. In fact, only a pro-Moscow faction, which at the time was a minority in Kazan, might have wished this. See ibid., no. 36, p. 661; Khudiakov, *Ocherki*, p. 77; Syroechkovskii, "Muhammed-Gerai," p. 53.

73. *SIRIO*, vol. 95, no. 37, pp. 670–71; no. 38, p. 679.

74. Ibid., no. 37, p. 673; no. 38, pp. 680, 684–88.

75. Ibid., no. 38, p. 696. An English translation of this letter is in Jaroslaw Pelenski, *Russia and Kazan: Conquest and Imperial Ideology (1438–1560s)* (The Hague: Mouton, 1974), p. 70. Shortly thereafter, Vasilii would claim Kazan as his patrimony (ibid., p. 76). (Pelenski suggested incorrectly that Ivan III was already "investing" the khans of Kazan. There is no evidence of any investiture by Moscow before 1519, when Shah Ali was sworn to be a khan; ibid., p. 31.)

76. In 1521 it was reported that the Ottoman sultan Süleyman sent the Crimean khan no annuity (ulüfe) and no standard (sancak)-investiture; see *SIRIO*, vol. 95, no. 38, p. 678.

77. Ibid., no. 37, pp. 668–69; no. 38, pp. 675, 679.

78. Khudiakov, *Ocherki*, pp. 76–81; Pelenski, *Russia and Kazan*, pp. 34–35; *SIRIO*, vol. 95, no. 38, p. 706.

79. His original name was Khuday-Kul. After Kazan's fall to Moscow in 1487, he was brought to Moscow together with his brother, the khan of Kazan, Ali, and other relatives. While Ali together with his mother and brother perished in exile, Khuday-Kul was released from captivity, converted to Orthodoxy in 1505, and was married to the sister of Vasilii III, Evdokiia (Khudiakov, *Ocherki*, pp. 47–48).

80. Solov'ev, *Istoriia*, vol. 3, pp. 265–67.

81. Herberstein, *Zapiski o Moskovitskikh delakh*, p. 163; V. D. Smirnov, *Krymskoe khanstvo pod verkhovenstvom Ottomanskoi Porty do nachala 18 veka* (St. Petersburg: Tip. A. S. Suvorina 1887), p. 392; Syroechkovskii, "Muhammed-Gerai," p. 57; Zhirmunskii, *Tiurkskii*, pp. 442–43; Pelenskii, *Russia and Kazan*, p. 35.

82. Khudiakov, *Ocherki*, pp. 86–87.

83. Ibid., pp. 86–98; Solov'ev, *Istoriia*, vol. 3, pp. 69–72; Pelenski, *Russia and Kazan*, pp. 36–40.

84. At the same time his brother, Mamay continued to support his deposed son-in-law, Safa Giray, and in 1533 the Nogays led by Safa Giray together with Crimean troops plundered the Riazan province; see *PDRV*, vol. 7, pp. 225–32; *Nikonovskaia*, pp. 65, 69–71; Zhirmunskii, *Tiurkskii*, p. 430.

85. Ibid., pp. 238–42, 250; Shcherbatov, *Istoriia Rossiiskaia*, vol. 5, pt. 1, supplements, p. 489.

86. *PDRV*, vol. 7, pp. 244–45, 249–51; Zhirmunskii, *Tiurkskii*, p. 445.

87. *PDRV*, vol. 7, pp. 259–65.

88. Ibid., pp. 274–76, 286–94.

89. Ibid., pp. 319–22, 337–42.

90. Ibid., pp. 348; vol. 8, pp. 24–25, 32, 35–36, 54–56.

91. Smirnov, *Krymskoe khanstvo*, p. 416; Özalp Gökbilgin, *1532–77 Yillari Arasinda Kirim Hanligi'nin Siyasi Durumu* (Ankara: Sevinc Matbaasi, 1973), pp. 19–29. An account of the same event in contemporary Russian sources emphasized the piety and the strength of the Muscovite troops; see Solov'ev, *Istoriia*, vol. 3, pp. 444–47.

92. *Nikonovskaia,* pp. 128–29; *Gosudarstvennyi arkhiv Rossii 16 stoletiia: Opyt rekonstruktsii,* prepared by A. A. Zimin (Moscow: Insititut Istorii AN SSSR, 1978), pp. 299–300; *PDRV,* vol. 8, pp. 86–93.

93. *PDRV,* vol. 8, pp. 82–84, 97–105.

94. Ibid., pp. 114–126, 132–33.

95. Ibid., pp. 141, 144–45, 174–75, 183.

96. Ibid., pp. 155–6, 205, 207–210, 214–18, 276.

97. Ibid., pp. 269–77.

98. Ibid., pp. 263–67.

99. Khudiakov, *Ocherki,* pp. 136–38; Halil Inalcik, "The Khan and the Tribal Aristocracy," pp. 464–66; *PDRV,* vol. 8, p. 325.

100. *PDRV,* vol. 8, pp. 170, 172, 201, 264–65.

101. Ibid., pp. 227–29, 305.

102. Ibid., pp. 239, 240, 279, 286.

103. Ibid., p. 303.

104. Ibid., pp. 310–12; Pelenski, *Russia and Kazan,* pp. 88–91.

105. *PDRV,* vol. 8, pp. 316–17.

106. Ibid., pp. 313–21; Khudiakov, *Ocherki,* pp. 138–42.

107. *PDRV,* vol. 9, pp. 1–3, 37–39.

108. Ibid., vol. 8, pp. 329–36; vol. 9, pp. 4–15, 37–39.

109. Ibid., vol. 9, pp. 60–65.

110. Ibid., pp. 64–66, 80, 81.

111. Ibid., pp. 100–108.

112. Ibid., pp. 103, 105.

113. Ibid., pp. 118–20.

114. Ibid., p. 130.

115. Ibid., pp. 122–26, 152–56.

116. Ibid., pp. 169–75.

117. Ibid., pp. 163–68. According to Richard Hellie's calculations, ten *kad'* of honey amounted to almost one ton.

118. Ibid., pp. 184, 189–91, 208–21.

119. Ibid., pp. 226–42; Solov'ev, *Istoriia,* vol. 3, pp. 486–87.

120. *PDRV,* vol. 9, pp. 240–60.

121. Ibid., pp. 286–312.

122. Ibid., pp. 261–68.

123. Ibid., pp. 265, 268, 271, 285; Zhirmunskii, *Tiurkskii,* p. 472.

124. *PDRV,* vol. 9, p. 283; vol. 10, pp. 9–17.

125. Ibid., vol. 10, pp. 20–21, 26–34, 53–54, 67–69, 93–94.

126. Ibid., pp. 58–65, 75–86.

127. Ibid., pp. 124–32, 140–43, 180, 252, 260.

128. Ibid., pp. 181, 194, 195, 205, 210, 220, 277, 287.

129. Ibid., pp. 318–19.

130. Ibid., vol. 11, pp. 42–62.

131. *RGADA,* F. 123, *Krymskie dela,* kn. 13, l. 57, 66 ob., 67, 71 ob., 82, 83; Solov'ev, *Istoriia,* vol. 3, pp. 599, 602; E. I. Kusheva, "Politika russkogo gosudarstva na Severnom Kavkaze v 1552–1572gg.," *Istoricheskie zapiski* 34 (1950), pp. 279–80; Novosel'skii, *Bor'ba,* pp. 23–27; P. A. Sadikov, "Pokhod tatar i turok na Astrakhan v 1569 g.,"

Istoricheskie zapiski 22 (1947), pp. 143–50. While Tin Ahmed beg was ready to assist the Crimea, some of the mirzas chose to help Astrakhan (*PDRV*, vol. 11, p. 203).

132. Solov'ev, *Istoriia*, vol. 3, pp. 602–4; Halil Inalcik, "Osmanli-Rus Rekabetinin Menshei ve Don-Volga Kanali Teshebbüsü (1569)," *Türk Tarih Kurumu, Belleten*, no. 46 (1948), pp. 342–402; A. N. Kurat, "The Turkish Expedition to Astrakhan in 1569 and the Problem of the Don-Volga Canal," *Slavonic and East European Review* 40 (1961), pp. 7–23; Alexander Bennigsen, "L'Expédition turque contre Astrakhan en 1569, d'après les Registres des 'Affaires importantes' des Archives ottomanes," in *Cahiers du Monde Russe et Soviétique* 8, no. 3 (1967), pp. 427–46. The linking of the Volga and Don rivers had to wait until the 1950s, when the Soviet government oversaw construction of the canal.

133. *Kabardino-russkie*, vol. 1, no. 10, p. 20; no. 13, p. 26; no. 16, pp. 27–29; *Puteshestviia russkikh poslov 16–17 vv.: Stateinye spiski* (Moscow-Leningrad: AN SSSR, 1954), p. 76.

134. Solov'ev, *Istoriia*, bk. 3, pp. 606–10; Novosel'skii, *Bor'ba*, pp. 28–32. In 1579 Ivan referred to Kazan as his patrimony (*votchina*); see *RGADA*, F. 127, op. 1, *Nogaiskie dela*, kn. 9, p. 73.

135. *PDRV*, vol. 11, pp. 77–78, 86–119; *D'iaki i pod'iachie posol'skogo prikaza v 16 veke*, pp. 137–148. In 1570 Andrei Vasil'evich was charged with treason and is presumed to have been executed. Whether there were indeed grounds for such a charge, whether they were connected to the above offer, or whether the diak became one of the victims of Ivan IV's paranoia is unknown.

136. Ibid., pp. 176–185, 233–36. Besides these payments, Urus demanded that presents be sent to his four wives, several younger brothers, nine sons, and eight daughters.

137. Ibid., pp. 195, 202–5, 226, 264.

138. Ibid., pp. 271–302.

139. *RGADA*, F. 127, op. 1, *Nogaiskie dela*, kn. 9, pp. 24–25, 50–54.

140. Ibid., pp. 86, 87, 95, 96.

141. Ibid., pp. 151–53, 156–60, 163.

142. Ibid., kn. 9, pp. 186, 268, 276; kn. 10, pp. 3–6.

143. Ibid., kn. 10, pp. 22–25.

144. Ibid., pp. 48, 61–64; Novosel'skii, *Bor'ba*, pp. 31–32.

145. *RGADA*, F. 127, op. 1, *Nogaiskie dela*, kn. 10, pp. 87, 88, 93. The Nogay embassy was reported to have visited Bukhara, where the Nogays' "pledge of allegiance" was welcomed; see Audrey Bruton, *The Bukharans: A Dynastic, Diplomatic and Commercial History, 1550–1702* (New York: St. Martin's Press, 1997), pp. 39, 41.

146. *RGADA*, F. 127, op. 1, *Nogaiskie dela*, kn. 10, pp. 87, 88, 93, 120–21, 140.

147. Ibid., pp. 140, 143, 195, 196, 205–7, 247, 266.

148. Khudiakov, *Ocherki*, pp. 166–67; Novosel'skii, *Bor'ba*, pp. 34–35, 44.

149. Smirnov, *Krymskoe khanstvo*, pp. 441–43; Novosel'skii, *Bor'ba*, p. 35.

150. Novosel'skii, *Bor'ba*, pp. 36–37.

151. Ibid., p. 37.

152. Ibid., pp. 38–40; "Akty vremeni Lzhedmitriia 1-go," p. 110.

153. Solov'ev, *Istoriia*, vol. 4, pp. 265–66.

154. Novosel'skii, *Bor'ba*, p. 44. For the summary of the frontier defense in the late sixteenth and early seventeenth centuries, see Hellie, *Enserfment*, pp. 175–80.

4. From Steppe Frontier to Imperial Borderlands

1. "Akty vremeni Lzhedmitriia," pp. 105–9, 136, 139–42.
2. Novosel'skii, *Bor'ba*, pp. 60–65, 68, 89; Khodarkovsky, *Where Two Worlds Met*, p. 77.
3. Novosel'skii, *Bor'ba*, pp. 91–93.
4. Ibid., pp. 95–97.
5. Ibid., pp. 138–39.
6. Ibid., pp. 140–41; Khodarkovsky, *Where Two Worlds Met*, p. 78.
7. Khodarkovsky, *Where Two Worlds Met*, p. 80.
8. Novosel'skii, *Bor'ba*, pp. 142–45.
9. Ibid., pp. 148–49.
10. Ibid., p. 227; Khodarkovsky, *Where Two Worlds Met*, pp. 80–82.
11. Throughout the eighteenth century the Nogays' fortunes changed more than once. Most of them became the subjects of the Crimea, but in the late 1750s they rose in arms against the Crimean khan. After Russia's annexation of the Crimea and Kuban region in the 1780s, the Nogays found themselves within the borders of the Russian Empire and resisted Russian plans to relocate them into the middle Volga area. Finally, dispersed and forcefully resettled within Russia's southern borderlands, tens of thousands of the Nogays availed themselves of an opportunity to immigrate to the Ottoman Empire in the early 1860s. For more details, see Kochekaev, *Nogaisko-russkie otnosheniia*, pp. 191–260; Barbara Kellner-Heinkele, *Aus den Aufzeichnungen des Said Giray Sultan: Eine zeitgenössische Quelle zur Geschichte des Chanats der Krim um die Mitte des 18. Jarhhunderts* (Freiburg im Breslau: Klaus Schwarz Verlag, 1975), pp. 149–83; Khodarkovsky, *Where Two Worlds Met*, pp. 202–28.
12. Novosel'skii, *Bor'ba*, pp. 237–38, 296.
13. *Rossiiskaia Akademiia Nauk. Arkhiv*, F. 1714, op. 1, *Novosel'skii, A. A.*, no. 66, l. 144. The Crimea's other concern was Moscow's active encouragement of the closer cooperation between the Don and Tersk Cossacks (ibid., ll. 56, 60–61). For the effectiveness of the Cossack naval raids against the Crimea see Victor Ostapchuk "Five Documents from the Topkapi Palace Archive on the Ottoman Defense of the Black Sea against the Cossacks (1639)," *Journal of Turkish Studies* 11 (1987), pp. 49–104.
14. Novosel'skii, *Bor'ba*, pp. 305–7; Hellie, *Enserfment*, pp. 128–31; Brian Davies, "The Recovery of Fugitive Peasants from Muscovy's Southern Frontier: The Case of Kozlov, 1636–40," *Russian History, The Frontier in Russian History* 19 (1992), nos. 1–4, pp. 29–56; Valerie A. Kivelson, *Autocracy in the Provinces: The Muscovite Gentry and Political Culture in the Seventeenth Century* (Stanford: Stanford University Press, 1996), p. 251.
15. On the evolution of the fortification lines see A. I. Iakovlev, *Zasechnaia cherta Moskovskogo gosudarstva v 17 veke* (Moscow: Tip. I Lisnera, 1916); V. P. Zagorovskii, *Belgorodskaia cherta* (Voronezh: Voronezhskii Universitet, 1969); A. V. Nikitin, "Oboronitel'nye sooruzheniia zasechnoi cherty 16–17 vv.," *Materialy i issledovaniia po arkheologii SSSR* 44 (1955), pp. 116–213; Novosel'skii, *Bor'ba*, pp. 293–96. For works in English which discuss the situation and fortifications in the south see Brian Davies, *The Role of the Town Governors in the Defense and Military Colonization of Muscovy's Southern Frontier: The Case of Kozlov, 1635–38*, 2 vols. (Ph.D. diss., University of Chicago, 1983); Richard Hellie, *Enserfment*, pp. 174–80; Carol Belkin Stevens, *Soldiers on the Steppe: Army Reform and Social Change in Early Modern Russia* (DeKalb: Northern Illinois University Press, 1995), pp. 19–36.

16. *AOGA*, F. 1010, op. 1, *Astrakhanskaia prikaznaia izba*, d. 7, ll. 1–5.

17. Khodarkovsky, *Where Two Worlds Met*, pp. 83–87. Readers interested in a more detailed history of the Kalmyks in the seventeenth century are referred to chapters 3 and 4 of my earlier book.

18. Ibid., pp. 248–50.

19. *RGADA*, F. 119, op. 1, *Kalmytskie dela*, d. 3, ll. 6–7.

20. Ibid., no. 4, ll. 1–10. *Rossiiskaia Akademiia Nauk. Arkhiv.* F. 1714, op. 1, *Novosel'skii, A. A.*, no. 66, l. 68. G. A. Sanin, *Otnosheniiia Rossii i Ukrainy s Krymskim khanstvom v seredine 17 veka* (Moscow: Nauka, 1987), pp. 59–62.

21. *Rossiiskaia Akademiia Nauk. Arkhiv.* F. 1714, op. 1, *Novosel'skii, A. A.*, no. 66, ll. 130–37; Michael Khodarkovsky, "The Stepan Razin Uprising: Was It a 'Peasant War'?" *Jahrbücher für Geschichte Osteuropas* 42, no. 1 (1994), pp. 7–10.

22. Khodarkovsky, *Where Two Worlds Met*, pp. 90–99.

23. Ibid., pp. 105–33.

24. Ibid., 151.

25. *RGADA*, F. 115, op. 1, *Kabardinskie, cherkesskie i drugie dela*, d. 3, 1719g., ll. 3–4.

26. Khodarkovsky, *Where Two Worlds Met*, pp. 163–66.

27. Ibid., pp. 176–88. Governor Volynskii described Cheren-Donduk as stupid and vain but saw no alternative to appointing him khan (*AVMF*, F. 233, op. 1, no. 228, ll. 120–23).

28. Ibid., pp. 198–212. The title of khan had been restored in 1731 (see ch. 1).

29. *TsGARK*, F. 27, op. 2, *Astrakhanskaia kontora kalmytskikh i tatarskikh del*, d. 5, l. 7.

30. *Gosudarstvennyi Arkhiv Orenburgskoi Oblasti (hereafter GAOO)*, Orenburg, F. 3, *Orenburgskaia gubernskaia kantseliariia*, d. 118, ll. 1–4, 153, 242–45; d. 119, ll. 116–17, 389–95; d. 120, ll. 8–11, 34–35, 386–88; *Kazanskii Universitet: Rukopisnyi otdel*, no. 4876; *TsGARK*, F. 35, op. 1, *Kalmytskaia ekspeditisiia pri Astrakhanskoi gubernskoi kantseliariii*, d. 6.; Khodarkovsky, *Where Two Worlds Met*, pp. 224–35; M. M. Batmaev, *Kalmyki v 17–18 vekakh: Sobytiia, liudi, byt* (Elista: Kalmytskoe knizhnoe izd-vo, 1993), pp. 354–65.

31. *GAOO*, F. 3 d. 121, l. 232; *Arkhiv vneshnei politiki Rossiiskoi imperii* (hereafter *AVPRI*), Moscow, F. 119, op. 119/2, *Kalmytskie dela*, 1769–76gg., kn. 33, ll. 76–81.

32. Pal'mov, *Etiudy*, vol. 5, "Dela zemel'nye," p. 36. At the time, Panin, with the title of *Oberhofmeister*, was in charge of various foreign and internal affairs; see David L. Ransel, *The Politics of Catherinian Russia: The Panin Party* (New Haven: Yale University Press, 1975), pp. 201–2.

33. In 1761 the government considered removing the Kalmyks from the jurisdiction of the Foreign Office and placing them under the jurisdiction of the Senate; see *AVPRI*, F. 119, op. 119/2, *Kalmytskie dela*, 1761g., d.7.

34. Batmaev, *Kalmyki*, pp. 366–69; *Ocherki istorii Kalmytskoi*, pp. 221–23, 236.

35. Pal'mov, *Etiudy*, vol. 5, p. 6.

36. "Rasporiazheniia ob upravlenii Kalmytskim narodom," *Zhurnal Ministerstva Vnutrennikh Del* 15, no. 1 (1835), pp. 1–XXXVI; *Ocherki istorii Kalmytskoi*, pp. 242–43; L. S. Burchinova, "Kalmykiia v sisteme gosudarstvennogo upravleniia Rossii," in *Dobrovol'noe vkhozhdenie Kalmytskogo naroda v sostav Rossii: Istoricheskie korni i znachenie* (Elista, 1985), pp. 51–52.

37. *RGADA*, F. 127, op. 1, *Nogaiskie dela*, kn. 9, ll. 36–37; kn. 10, ll. 7, 22; *PDRV*, vol. 11, p. 186. A detailed but tendentious discussion of the Russo-Kazakh relations can be found in V. Ia. Basin, *Rossiia i kazakhskie khanstva v 16–18 vv.* (Alma-Ata: "Nauka"

Kazakhskoi SSR, 1971). For the most competent and sophisticated discussion see N. G. Apollova, *Ekonomicheskie i politicheskie sviazi Kazakhstana s Rossiei v 18–nachale 19 v* (Moscow: AN SSSR, 1960). Martha Brill Olcott uncritically follows the standard Soviet edition of *Istoriia Kazakhskoi SSR*, 2 vols. (Alma-Ata: AN Kazakhskoi SSR, 1957) in her monograph *The Kazakhs* (Stanford: Hoover Institution Press, 1987), pp. 24–30.

38. *Kazakhsko-russkie otnosheniia v 16–18 vv.*, no. 1, pp. 3–5.

39. Ibid., p. 9; Vel'iaminov-Zernov, *Issledovaniia*, vol. 2, pp. 393–99; *Istoriia Sibiri*, ed. A. P. Okladnikov, 5 vols. (Leningrad: Nauka, 1968), vol. 2, p. 35–36; Abul-Ghazi, *Rodoslovnoe drevo tiurkov*, p. 156. Muscovite officials were likely to be aware of the crucial role Tevekkel played in helping Abdulla khan II of Bukhara (1557–98) get rid of his rivals. In 1582 Tevekkel brought Abdulla the severed heads of his foremost rivals. See "Sharaf-Name-i-Shahi," in S. K. Ibragimov et al., eds., *Materialy po istorii kazakhskikh khanstv 15–18 vekov* (Alma-Ata: Nauka Kazakhskoi SSR, 1969), p. 311. For a brief discussion of Central Asian politics in the late sixteenth century see *Istoriia Uzbekskoi SSR*, 2 vols. (Tashkent: AN Uzbekskoi SSR, 1955–57), vol. 1, pp. 406–8; Burton, *The Bukharans*, pp. 90–98.

40. *Mezhdunarodnye otnosheniia v Tsentral'noi Azii*, vol. 1, no. 2, p. 40.

41. In addition to Yasy, Tashkent was also spared destruction by the Oirats because it submitted to them and offered to pay tribute. See ibid., no. 3, p. 43; no. 23, p. 82; no. 30, p. 103, no. 73, pp. 212–14; "Ta'rikh-i Kipchaki," in *Materialy po istorii kazakhskikh khanstv 15–18 vekov*, pp. 395–97; *Istoriia Kazakhskoi SSR*, 5 vols. (Alma-Ata: "Nauka" Kazakhskoi SSR, 1979), vol. 2, pp. 286–89.

42. *Kazakhsko-russkie otnosheniia v 16–18 vv.*, no. 12, pp. 14–15; no. 13, p. 16; no. 19, pp. 22–25; *Istoriia Kazakhskoi SSR*, vol. 2, pp. 295–96. The most detailed account of Russian trade with Bukhara prior to the eighteenth century is found in Burton, *The Bukharans*, pp. 460–501.

43. Khodarkovsky, *Where Two Worlds Met*, pp. 157–61; *Kazakhsko-russkie otnosheniia v 16–18 vv.*, no. 24, p. 31.

44. *Kazakhsko-russkie otnosheniia v 16–18 vv.*, nos. 14, 15, pp. 16–18; no. 16, 19–20; no. 22, pp. 28–29.

45. Ibid., no. 19, p. 22; *Istoriia Kazakhskoi SSR*, vol. 3, pp. 17–18; "Ta'rikh-i Amniia," in *Materialy po istorii Kazakhskikh khanstv 15–18 vv.*, pp. 486–87; Popov, "Snosheniia Rossii s Khivoiu i Bukharoiu pri Petre Velikom. Prilozheniia," pp. 379–80.

46. *Istoriia Kazakhskoi SSR*, vol. 3, p. 19–20; *Istoriia Uzbeskoi SSR*, vol. 1, pp. 416–17; Chokan Valikhanov, "Ablai," in *Sobranie sochinenii*, 5 vols. (Alma-Ata: Kazakhskaia Sovetskaia Entsiklopediia, 1985), vol. 4, pp. 111–12.

47. Khodarkovsky, *Where Two Worlds Met*, pp. 151, 185–89.

48. *Kazakhsko-russkie otnosheniia v 16–18 vv.*, no. 38, p. 92; no. 50, p. 107.

49. Ibid., no. 19, p. 24; nos. 25–29, pp. 35–41.

50. Ibid., no. 33, pp. 49, 53–54.

51. Ibid., pp. 54–61.

52. Ibid., pp. 62–67, 79, 81.

53. Ibid., pp. 73–85.

54. Ibid., no. 40, pp. 95–96; no. 43, pp. 99–101.

55. *Materialy po istorii Rossii: Sbornik ukazov i drugikh dokumentov, kasaiushchikhsia upravleniia i ustroistva Orenburgskogo kraia*, 2 vols., comp. A. I. Dobromyslov (Oren-

burg: Tip. Sachkova, 1900), vol. 1, 1734 god, pp. 1–50. For a chronology of the first two decades of Orenburg's history and the region's geography, see P. I. Rychkov, *Istoriia Orenburgskaia (1730–1750)* (Orenburg, 1896), and his "Topografiia Orenburgskoi gubernii," in *Orenburgskie stepi v trudakh P. I. Rychkova, E. A. Eversmana, S. S. Neustroeva* (Moscow: Izd-vo geograficheskoi lit., 1949), pp. 41–204. Alton S. Donnelly discusses the founding of Orenburg and its impact on the Bashkirs in his *The Russian Conquest of Bashkiria, 1552–1740: A Case Study in Imperialism* (New Haven: Yale University Press, 1968). The story below, however, is different in both substance and interpretation from Donnelly's.

56. *Materialy po istorii Rossii,* pp. 1, 19, 37–49.

57. Ibid., pp. 50–56; *Kazakhsko-russkie otnosheniia v 16–18 vv.,* no. 51, pp. 115–16.

58. *Materialy po istorii Rossii,* pp. 20–21; *Materialy po istorii Bashkirskoi ASSR,* ch. 1 (1936), pp. 56–57; Donnelly, *The Russian Conquest,* pp. 82–95. To prevent the danger of emerging of "a clever rebel, like Stepan Razin" among the Bashkirs, the regional commander, General Rumiantsev, recommended in 1736 a set of draconian measures to crush the Bashkirs' rebellious spirit. Its recommendations included a prohibition on marriage among the Bashkirs without permission from the governor of Kazan, and an imposition of a tax of one horse per wedding if the governor's permission was obtained; see *RGADA,* F. 248, op. 126, *Dela i prigovory Pravitel'stvuiushchego Senata po Orenburgskoi gubernii,* d. 135, ll. 77–90.

59. *Kazakhsko-russkie otnosheniia v 16–18 vv.,* no. 59, p. 123.

60. Ibid., nos. 61, 62, pp. 125–26; no. 68, p. 132.

61. Ibid., nos. 75–76, pp. 175–77.

62. Ibid., no. 76, pp. 178–80, 182.

63. Ibid., no. 76, pp. 183–84.

64. Ibid., no. 81, p. 189.

65. Apollova, *Ekonomicheskie,* pp. 113–30.

66. *Kazakhsko-russkie otnosheniia v 16–18 vv.,* no. 87, p. 203; no. 88, p. 210.

67. Ibid., no. 83, pp. 193–94; no. 86, p. 202; no. 88, p. 212.

68. Ibid., no. 88, pp. 211–12.

69. Ibid., no. 84, p. 197; no. 85, pp. 198–200.

70. Ibid., nos. 93–96, pp. 220–237; *Mezhdunarodnye otnosheniia v Tsentral'noi Azii,* vol. 1, no. 125, pp. 304–5.

71. *Kazakhsko-russkie otnosheniia v 16–18 vv.,* no. 96, pp. 237–48; no. 98, pp. 254–58; no. 108, pp. 276–81.

72. Ibid., no. 96, pp. 248, 250; no. 104, p. 268; no. 106, pp. 273–75; no. 108, p. 276.

73. Ibid., no. 96, p. 248; no. 105, pp. 269–72; no. 109, pp. 281–82; no. 113, pp. 290–92.

74. Ibid., no. 114, pp. 292–94; no. 119, pp. 302–7.

75. Ibid., no. 135, pp. 341–48.

76. Ibid., nos. 139, 142, 144, 149–51.

77. Ibid., no. 152, pp. 392–95; no. 153, pp. 397–98; no. 165, p. 424; no. 166, p. 425; *GAOO,* F. 3 op. 1, d. 18, ll. 194–203.

78. *Kazakhsko-russkie otnosheniia v 16–18 vv.,* no. 152, pp. 394–95; no. 153, p. 401; nos. 154–56, pp. 404–8. Bupay, wishing to see her son Nuraly as heir to her late husband, denounced Barak as unreliable and more interested in alliance with the Oirats and Volga Kalmyks than with Russia (*GAOO,* F. 3 op. 1, d. 18, ll. 31, 129).

79. *Kazakhsko-russkie otnosheniia v 16–18 vv.,* no. 165, pp. 419–20; no. 166, pp. 425–32; no. 167, pp. 432–38; no. 168, p. 437; no. 175, pp. 444–46.

80. Ibid., no. 178, pp. 451; no. 190, pp. 493–97; no. 191, pp. 497–98.

81. Ibid., no. 190, p. 496; no. 196, pp. 510–11; no. 197, pp. 515–17.

82. Ibid., no. 210, p. 539.

83. Ibid., no. 210, p. 540.

84. Ibid, nos. 206–7, pp. 533–36; nos. 211–14, pp. 540–48.

85. I. Ia. Zlatkin, *Istoriia Dzhungarskogo khanstva, 1635–1758,* 2d ed. (Moscow: Nauka, 1983), pp. 290–302; Barfield, *The Perilous Frontier,* pp. 292–94.

86. V. N. Vitevskii, *I. I. Nepliuev i Orenburgskii krai,* vol. 3, p. 900; *Kazakhsko-russkie otnosheniia v 16–18 vv.,* no. 219, pp. 553–54. In March 1758 Empress Elizabeth instructed Nuraly khan to attack the Chinese; see *Kazanskii Universitet: Rukopisnyi otdel,* no. 4866.

87. *Kazakhsko-russkie otnosheniia v 16–18 vv.,* no. 225, p. 572.

88. Ibid., pp. 575–77.

89. Ibid., pp. 578–90.

90. Ibid., no. 246, pp. 630–32.

91. Ibid., no. 250, pp. 639–41; no. 256, pp. 653–54, 658.

92. Ibid., no. 261, pp. 669–74; no. 263, p. 677; no. 267, p. 683; no. 276, p. 702.

93. For details, see the first section of this chapter.

94. *Kazakhsko-russkie otnosheniia v 18–19 vv.,* nos. 1–4, pp. 3–14.

95. Ibid., nos. 9–13, pp. 18–25. Cf. the similar behavior of the Kalmyks during the Razin uprising in the 1670s and numerous other examples.

96. Ibid., nos. 25–26, pp. 50–54; no. 27, p. 60; no. 32, p. 74; *Istoriia Kazakhskoi SSR,* vol. 1 (1957), pp. 272–79.

97. *Kazakhsko-russkie otnosheniia v 18–19 vv.,* no. 27, pp. 54–62; no. 32, p. 74.

98. Ibid., no. 34, p. 76; *Istoriia Kazakhskoi SSR,* vol. 3 (1979), p. 105.

99. *Istoriia Kazakhskoi SSR,* vol. 1 (1957), p. 278; Viatkin, *Batyr Srym,* pp. 195–98.

100. *Istoriia Kazakhskoi SSR,* vol. 1 (1957), pp. 282–83.

101. Viatkin, *Batyr Srym,* pp. 193–205.

102. *PSZ,* vol. 22, no. 15,991, pp. 142–44; no. 16,292, pp. 493–95; no. 16,400, pp. 604–6; see also ch. 4.

103. For Igelstrom's experience in the Crimea, see Alan W. Fisher, *The Crimean Tatars* (Stanford: Hoover Institution Press, 1978), pp. 71–78.

104. *Kazakhsko-russkie otnosheniia v 18–19 vv.,* nos. 62–64, pp. 114–16; no. 66, pp. 118–21; no. 70, p. 126.

105. Viatkin, *Batyr Srym,* pp. 240–41; Apollova, *Ekonomicheskie,* p. 249.

106. *GAOO,* F. 5, op. 1, d. 44, ll. 5, 86.

107. *Kazakhsko-russkie otnosheniia v 18–19 vv.,* no. 70, pp. 125–32. The mufti, Muhammedjan Khusainov, remained the head of the Muslim Spiritual Assembly from 1789 to 1824; see Michael Kemper, *Sufis und Gelehrte in Tatarien und Baschkirien, 1789–1889* (Berlin: Klaus Schwarz Verlag, 1998), pp. 50–66.

108. Viatkin, *Batyr Srym,* pp. 242–45; *Materialy po istorii Kazakhskoi SSR (1785–1828),* vol. 4 (Moscow-Leningrad: AN SSSR, 1940), no. 15, pp. 74–76.

109. Viatkin, *Batyr Srym,* pp. 271–86.

110. Ibid., pp. 305–7; *Kazakhsko-russkie otnosheniia v 18–19 vv.,* no. 74, p. 134; no. 78, p. 137; *Istoriia Kazakhskoi SSR,* vol. 3 (1979), pp. 122–23.

111. Viatkin, *Batyr Srym*, pp. 311, 317–20.

112. *Kazakhsko-russkie otnosheniia v 18–19 vv.*, nos. 81–83, pp. 139–48.

113. Viatkin, *Batyr Srym*, pp. 325–31.

114. Ibid., pp. 336–40.

115. Ibid., pp. 346–57; *Kazanskii Universitet: Rukopisnyi otdel*, nos. 4867–72.

116. Viatkin, *Batyr Srym*, pp. 366–67; *Kazakhsko-russkie otnosheniia v 18–19 vv.*, no. 127, pp. 217–21; *Istoriia Kazakhskoi SSR*, vol. 3, pp. 156–62, 167–69.

5. Concepts and Policies in the Imperial Borderlands

1. The word "wild" was then mostly used to designate uncultivated lands to be distributed to the tsar's servitors; see *Slovar' russkogo iazyka 11–17 vv.* 16 (1990), p. 206. For eschatological images of the steppe nomads in pre-Mongol Rus, see Leonid Chekin, "The Godless Ishmaelites: The Image of the Steppe in Eleven-Thirteenth Centuries Rus'," in *Russian History, The Frontier in Russian History* 19, nos. 1–4 (1992), pp. 9–28.

2. *SIRIO*, vol. 41, no. 1, pp. 6–8; no. 14, p. 248; *Stepennaia kniga*, 2 vols. (Moscow: Tip. Imp. Univ., 1775) vol. 2, p. 248; *PDRV*, vol. 8, p. 195.

3. S. V. Chicherina, *O privolzhskikh inorodtsakh i sovremennom znachenii sistemy N. I. Il'minskogo* (St. Petersburg: Elektro-Tip. N. Ia. Stoikovoi, 1906), p. 4; Priest S. Bagin, *Ob otpadenii v magometanstvo kreshchennykh inorodtsev Kazanskoi eparkhii i o prichinakh etogo iavleniia* (Kazan: Tsentral'naia tip., 1910), p. 4; Paul Werth, "Big Candles and 'Internal Conversion': The Mari Animist Reformation and Its Russian Appropriations," in Robert P. Geraci and Michael Khodarkovsky, eds., *Of Religion and Empire: Missions, Conversion, and Tolerance in Tsarist Russia* (Ithaca: Cornell University Press, 2001), pp. 161–62; *Snosheniia Rossii s Kavkazom*, p. 305; *Kabardino-russkie*, vol. 2, no. 255, p. 362.

4. RGADA, F. 248, op. 113, *Opis' del Sekretnoi Ekspeditsii Senata*, d. 181, l. 20; *Kazakhsko-russkie otnosheniia v 16–18 vv.*, pp. 74, 81, 96, 138.

5. A. S. Pushkin, *Istoriia Pugachevskogo bunta*, ed. P. A. Efremov (St. Petersburg: Izdanie Ia. A. Isakova, 1881), p. 10.

6. Michael Khodarkovsky, "'Ignoble Savages and Unfaithful Subjects': Constructing Non-Christian Identities in Early Modern Russia," in Daniel R. Brower and Edward J. Lazzerini, eds., *Russia's Orient: Imperial Borderlands and Peoples, 1700–1917* (Bloomington: Indiana University Press, 1997), p. 10; *Kazakhsko-russkie otnosheniia v 16–18 vv.*, no. 246, pp. 630–32.

7. *Kazakhsko-russkie otnosheniia v 16–18 vv.*, no. 37, p. 90.

8. *Kabardino-russkie otnosheniia*, vol. 2, no. 199, p. 276.

9. *PSZ*, vol. 22, no. 16,292, pp. 492, 495; no. 16,400, p. 604.

10. *Kabardino-russkie otnosheniia*, vol. 2, no. 256, p. 364.

11. During the Razin uprising, the Don Cossacks described to the investigating Russian officials a man who came to them with a letter and invited them to join the rebels of the Shatsk district as follows: he "had the mug of a Cheremis" (*a v mordu Cheremis*); see *Krest'ianskaia voina pod predvoditel'stvom Stepana Razina: Sbornik dokumentov*, 4 vols. (Moscow, 1954), vol. 2, pt. 1, no. 155, p. 183. The closest term to "race" was *priroda* (lit. origin, descent), such as *po prirode, prirody Bashkirskoi*, or *Kalmytskoi*. For a fascinating discussion of some of these issues, see Yuri Slezkine, "Naturalists

versus Nations: Eighteenth-Century Russian Scholars Confront Ethnic Diversity," in Brower and Lazzerini, eds., *Russia's Orient*, pp. 27–57.

12. Prince Mikhail Shcherbatov, "Statistika v razsuzhdenii Rossii," in *ChOIDR*, bk. 3, pt. 11 (1859), p. 46.

13. *RGADA*, F. 1274, op. 1, d. 211, 1775g., l. 1; *Kabardino-russkie otnosheniia*, vol. 2, no. 164, pp. 218–19. The separation of the terms *natsiia* and *narod* was not always consistent. For instance, in her letter to the Kazakh khan Julbars in 1738, the Empress Anne used the word "nation" in referring to "the khans of other nations"; see *Kazakhsko-russkie otnosheniia v 16–18 vv.*, no. 66, p. 129.

14. On missions in Russia see most recently Geraci and Khodarkovsky, eds., *Of Religion and Empire*.

15. Epifanii, *Zhitie Sviatogo Stefana, episkopa Permskogo* (St. Petersburg: Tip. Imp. AN, 1897), pp. 24–74.

16. *PDRV*, vol. 5, p. 242.

17. Khodarkovsky, "Not by Word Alone," p. 273.

18. *PDRV*, vol. 10, pp. 318–19.

19. *Akty, sobrannye v bibliotekakh i arkhivakh Rossiiskoi Imperii Arkheograficheskoi ekspeditsieiu Imp. Akademii Nauk.*, 4 vols. (St. Petersburg: Tip. II otd. Imp. Kantseliarii, 1836), vol. 1, no. 358, pp. 436–39.

20. Smirnov, *Krymskoe khanstvo*, p. 565.

21. I. T. Pososhkov, *Zaveshchanie otecheskoe*, ed. E. M. Prilezhaev (St. Petersburg: Sinodal'naia tip., 1893), p. 323. Pososhkov further urged the government to send missionaries to the Kamchatka Peninsula in the Far East, "for if the Catholics find out, they will send their mission" (ibid., p. 327).

22. *Pis'ma i bumagi imperatora Petra Velikogo*, 12 vols. (St. Petersburg and Moscow, 1887–1977), vol. 1, note to no. 227, pp. 694–95.

23. *RGADA*, F. 248, op. 3, *Kantseliariia Senata. Dela po Azovskoi gubernii*, 1713–18gg., kn. 96, ll. 808–9; *PSZ*, vol. 2, no. 867, pp. 312–13; *PSZ*, vol. 5, no. 2734, pp. 66–67; no. 2990, p. 163; *Dokumenty i materialy po istorii Mordovskoi*, vol. 1, pt. 2, no. 79, pp. 398–99.

24. *PSPR*, vol. 2 (1722), no. 713, p. 400; no. 888, p. 578. Peter I's decree of 1718 ordered non-Christians assigned to work in shipbuilding industries while exempting Russian peasants from this hard labor. Numerous complaints from non-Christians went unanswered, and conversion remained the only way to avoid this onerous duty; see ibid., vol. 3 (1746–52) (St. Petersburg, 1912), no. 1233, pp. 387–92. Tax exemptions upon conversion were offered as early as 1681; see *PSZ*, vol. 2, no. 867, p. 313; *DAI*, vol. 8, no. 89, pp. 310–11.

25. One of the most striking accounts came from the Kazan metropolitan Sil'vestr in 1729. He reported that 170 years after their conversion to Christianity, the "old converts" (*starokreshchennye*) continued to reside in their old villages far from the churches, remaining wholly ignorant of the Russian language and Christian laws; see "Luka Konashevich, Episkop Kazanskii," *Pravoslavnyi Sobesednik* (October 1858), pp. 234–37.

26. *PSZ*, vol. 11, no. 8236, pp. 248–56; Mozharovskii, "Izlozhenie," pp. 61–62; Efim Malov, "O novokreshchennykh shkolakh v 18 veke," *Pravoslavnoe obozrenie* 26 (July 1868), pp. 354–57.

27. "Luka Konashevich," p. 233.

28. *Polnoe sobranie postanovlenii i rasporiazhenii po vedomstvu pravoslavnogo ispovedaniia Rossiiskoi imperii: Tsarstvovanie Elizavety Petrovny*, 4 vols. (St. Petersburg, 1899–1912), vol. 2 (1744–45), no. 662, pp. 143–45 (hereafter *PSPREP*). Separating converts from non-Christians was seen as another important way of securing the success of the mission. In 1740 the Senate decreed the appointment of a trustworthy person who would supervise the resettlement of converts and not take bribes; see "Luka Konashevich," pp. 464–65.

29. *PSZ*, vol. 14, no. 10,597, p. 608.

30. *PSPREP*, vol. 1 (1741–43) (St. Petersburg, 1899), no. 17, pp. 21–22; no. 70, p. 85; vol. 3 (1746–52) (St. Petersburg, 1912), no. 1007, pp. 83–85; no. 1115, pp. 200–202; vol. 4 (1753–62) (St. Petersburg, 1912), no. 1735, pp. 497–98; *PSZ*, vol. 11, no. 8349, pp. 369–70.

31. This was a time when a status of the Christians within the Ottoman Empire became a growing concern among the European states. In response, the Ottomans raised the issue of a status of the Muslims within the Russian Empire.

32. *PSPREP*, vol. 3 (1746–52), no. 1174, pp. 283–85; no. 1193, pp. 310–13.

33. *Istoriia Tatarii v materialakh*, pp. 190–91. The numbers seem to be grossly inconsistent. In the early 1740s converts in the region were reported to have numbered 13,322 out of a total non-Christian population of 285,464; see "Luka Konashevich," p. 233.

34. During the Razin uprising the non-Christian gentry chose to join the rebels; see Khodarkovsky, "The Stepan Razin Uprising: Was It a 'Peasant War'?" pp. 13–17. During the Pugachev uprising, the non-Christians again turned their rage against church officials, murdering 132 of them in the Kazan region alone; see Mozharovskii, "Izlozhenie," p. 98.

35. *RGADA*, F. 248, op. 113, no. 257, l. 5.

36. "Luka Konashevich," pp. 239–40, 469–70; *PSPREP*, vol. 4 (1753–62) (St. Petersburg, 1912), no. 1550, p. 291.

37. *Polnoe sobranie postanovlenii i rasporiazhenii po vedomstvu pravoslavnogo ispovedaniia Rossiiskoi imperii: Tsarstvovanie Ekateriny Alekseevny*, 3 vols. (St. Petersburg, 1910–15), vol. 1 (1762–72), no. 176, pp. 217–18.

38. The recognition of religious differences among its own subjects did not prevent Russia from seeing itself as a protector of all Orthodox Christians. Thus, four years after the conquest of the Crimea in 1774, the Russian government insisted on expatriation of all Christians who lived in the Crimea. More than thirty-one thousand of these Christians were reluctantly delivered to the Russians by the Crimean khan; see Solov'ev, *Istoriia*, vol. 15, p. 235. One particular provision, which eventually led to recognizing Russia's right to be a protector of Orthodox Christians within the Ottoman Empire, was negotiated in the 1774 treaty of Küchük-Kaynarja. This provision of the treaty later served as Russia's justification for laying imperial claims to much of the European territory under the Ottoman dominion; see John T. Alexander, *Catherine the Great: Life and Legend* (New York: Oxford University Press, 1989), p. 141.

39. *SIRIO*, vol. 32, no. 76, pp. 541–44.

40. Ibid., vol. 147, pp. 221–22; vol. 115, pp. 379–80.

41. Ibid., vol. 115, pp. 311–12, 319–28.

42. Ibid., vol. 115, pp. 353–56, 421–24, 448.

43. Bagin, *Ob otpadenii v magometanstvo kreshchennykh inorodtsev*, p. 4.

44. Shcherbatov, "Statistika," p. 64.

45. Mozharovskii, "Izlozhenie," p. 107.

46. *AI*, vol. 2, no. 43, pp. 56–57; *Opisanie gosudarstvennogo arkhiva starykh del*, pp. 253–66.

47. *PSPREP*, vol. 2 (1744–45), no. 651, pp. 123–28; no. 805, pp. 310–13.

48. *PSPR*, vol. 5 (1725–1727), no. 1846, pp. 416–18; no. 1908, pp. 487–88.

49. *Kabardino-russkie otnosheniia*, vol. 2, no. 256, pp. 360, 362.

50. Ibid., vol. 2, no. 116, pp. 147–48; no. 221, p. 318. Moscow's earliest and even more fantastic claim to the North Caucasus is found in the 1554 instructions to the Muscovite envoys departing for Poland. When they were asked why Moscow claimed the Circassians as its subjects, they were to reply that the Circassians were fugitives from Riazan and therefore Moscow's old subjects; see Solov'ev, *Istoriia Rossii*, vol. 3, p. 515. Fifty years later, Tsar Fedor repeated such claims in his letter to the Ottoman sultan. He explained that the new Russian forts had been built in the Caucasus because "from eternity the Kabardinian princes, the Circassian princes of the Highlands, and the shamkhal were our subjects in the Riazan region and then they fled from Riazan and settled in the mountains; then the Circassians and the Kabardinians petitioned our father, Tsar Ivan, to submit to him and became his subjects"; see *Kabardino-russkie otnosheniia*, vol. 1, no. 43, p. 71.

51. B. F. Pfaf, "Materialy po istorii osetin," in *Sbornik svedenii o kavkazskikh gortsakh*, vol. 5, p. 95.

52. For more on the Nakshbandi order, which originated in the region of Bukhara in Central Asia in the fourteenth century and became one of the most influential orders of the Sufi Islam, see "Nakshbandiyya," in C. E. Bosworth et al., eds., *The Encyclopaedia of Islam*, new ed. (Leiden, 1992), vol. 7, pp. 933–39. On the Mansur uprising, see A. Bennigsen, "Un Mouvement populaire au Caucase au XVIII siècle: la 'Guerre Sainte' du *sheikh* Mansur (1785–1791), page mal connue et controversée des relations russo-turques," *Cahiers du Monde Russe et Soviétique* 5, no. 2 (1964), pp. 159–205.

53. Khodarkovsky, *Where Two Worlds Met*, p. 230; Aleksei Levshin, *Opisanie Kirgiz-Kazach'ikh ili Kirgiz-Kaisakskikh ord i stepei*, 3 parts (St. Petersburg: Tip. Karla Kraia, 1832), pt. 3, p. 3.

54. Several classic studies are D. I. Bagalei, *Ocherki iz istorii kolonizatsii stepnoi okrainy Moskovskogo gosudarstva* (Moscow: Universitetskaia tip., 1887); G. I. Peretiatkovich, *Povolzh'e v 15 i 16 vv. (Ocherki iz istorii kraia i ego kolonizatsii)* (Moscow, 1877), and his *Povolzh'e v 17 i nachale 18 veka. (Ocherki iz istorii kolonizatsii kraia)* (Odessa, 1882); M. K. Liubavskii, *Obzor istorii russkoi kolonizatsii s drevneishikh vremen i do XX veka.*, ed. A. Ia. Degtiarev (Moscow: Moskovskii Universitet, 1996).

55. Kappeler, *Russlands erste Nationalitäten*, p. 261.

56. *RGADA*, F. 248, op. 113, d. 257, ll. 1–15; *Materialy po istorii Rossii: Sbornik ukazov i drugikh dokumentov*, vol. 1, p. 21.

57. *RGADA*, F. 248, op. 126, *Dela i prigovory Pravitel'stvuiushchego Senata po Astrakhanskoi gubernii*, d. 90, l. 13; Khodarkovsky, *Where Two Worlds Met*.

58. Of course, aristocratic diaspora was typical of medieval Europe; see Robert Bartlett, *The Making of Europe*, pp. 24–59.

59. *SIRIO*, vol. 41, no. 27, p. 100; no. 34, p. 144, no. 79, pp. 384–86.

60. Ibid., vol. 41, no. 3, p. 14; no. 6, p. 28; vol. 95, no. 38, pp. 692–93; *PDRV*, vol. 8, pp. 4–5.

61. Vel'iaminov-Zernov, *Issledovanie*, vol. 1, p. 28.

62. *SIRIO*, vol. 41, no. 4, p. 15; no. 5, p. 17; no. 33, pp. 130–31.

63. For more on Abdullatif, see ch. 3; Khodarkovsky, *Where Two Worlds Met*, p. 102.

64. *SIRIO*, vol. 95, no. 1, pp. 14–15, no. 2, p. 37.

65. The last khan of Kazan, Yadyger, converted in 1553 and took the Christian name of Simeon. Utemish Giray, taken from Kazan to Moscow as a child, was given the name of Aleksandr upon his conversion; see *Rodoslovnaia kniga kniazei i dvorian Rossiiskikh i vyezzhikh*, 2 vols. (Moscow: Universitetskaia tip. Novikova, 1787), pp. 24–27; "Pravlenie tsaria Ivana Vasil'evicha," in *DRV*, vol. 17, p. 173.

66. A list of prominent converts and their land grants can be found in *RIB*, vol. 8, no. 39, pp. 278–84, and in *ChOIDR* 191 (1899), no. 4, pt. 5, pp. 5–8. A long list of valuable items granted to the Kabardinian princes upon their conversion included golden crosses, sable furs and hats, caftans, silks, and numerous other items; see *Kabardino-russkie otnosheniia*, vol. 1, no. 46, p. 75; no. 120, pp. 173–75.

67. A daughter of Tsar Aleksei was promised in marriage to the Kasimov prince Seyid-Burkhan upon his conversion; see Vel'iaminov-Zernov, *Issledovanie*, vol. 3, p. 200. Cf. the names of the commanders in Tsar Boris' campaign against the Crimea in 1598; see Shcherbatov, *Istoriia Rossiiskaia*, vol. 7, pt. 1, p. 23. From the early seventeenth century, the Kabardinian dynasty of Cherkasskii princes was extremely important in implementing Russian policies in the North Caucasus; see *Kabardino-russkie otnosheniia*, vol. 1, no. 46, pp. 73–75.

68. The son of the Siberian khan Kuchum, Abulkhayir, was the first of his dynasty to convert in 1591. Although his son was known as Vasilii Abulgairovich, his grandson's name, Roman Vasil'eveich, could no longer be distinguished from a native Russian name; see Vel'iaminov-Zernov, *Issledovanie*, vol. 3, pp. 54–55.

69. In 1686 the tsar decreed that the dynasties of the ruler of Imeretia in the Caucasus and the princes of Siberia and Kasimov were to be entered into the Genealogical Book of the Russian nobility; see Vel'iaminov-Zernov, *Issledovanie*, vol. 4, p. 144.

70. *Kazakhsko-russkie otnosheniia v 16–18 vv.*, no. 43, pp. 99–101; no. 56, p. 120–21; no. 59, pp. 122–23; no. 147, p. 373; no. 225, p. 589.

71. *Kabardino-russkie otnosheniia*, vol. 1, pp. 5–13; V. V. Dorofeev, *Nad Uralom-rekoi* (Cheliabinsk: Iuzhno-Ural'skoe izd-vo, 1988), pp. 6–8; Khodarkovsky, *Where Two Worlds Met*, p. 226.

72. *Kabardino-russkie otnosheniia*, vol. 2, no. 165, pp. 221–22.

73. Contrast this with the annuity of five thousand rubles given to Russia's brief regent, Ernst-Johann Biren (Biron), upon his exile to Tobolsk in 1741.

74. *PDRV*, vol. 9, pp. 308–12; vol. 10, p. 72; vol. 11, pp. 100–101.

75. *Snosheniia Rossii s Kavkazom*, p. 371.

76. *RGADA*, F. 248, op. 126, *Dela i prigovory Pravitel'stvuishchego Senata po Astrakhanskoi gubernii, 1716–1722 gg.*, d. 90, l. 10; *PSZ*, vol. 3, no. 1585, p. 311; Khodarkovsky, *Where Two Worlds Met*, pp. 106–7, 112, 132, 180–82, 203, 205–6. On Christianity among the Kalmyks, see K. Kostenkov, "O rasprostranenii khristianstva u kalmykov," *Zhurnal Ministerstva Narodnogo Prosveshcheniia* 144 (August 1869), pp. 103–59, and more recently G. Sh. Dordzhieva, "Politika samoderzhaviia i pravoslavnaia missiia sredi kalmykov (konets 17 v.–1771 g.)," in *Kul'tura i byt Kalmykov (Etnograficheskie*

issledovaniia) (Elista, 1977), pp. 17–39. It was more difficult for the government to secure the return of the Kalmyks who fled to join the Don Cossacks; see *AVMF,* F. 233, op. 1, d. 12, ll. 79–81.

77. The Kalmyk khan Ayuki submitted numerous requests to the Astrakhan governor to release his people; see *TsGARK,* F. 36, op. 1, *Sostoiashchii pri kalmytskikh delakh pri Astrakhanskom gubernatore,* d. 9, ll. 7, 55; *PSZ,* vol. 20, no. 14,489, p. 402; Khodarkovsky, "Not by Word Alone," pp. 267–93; *Russko-dagestanskie otnosheniia 17-pervoi poloviny 18 vv.,* no. 80, p. 177; no. 84, p. 180.

78. *RGADA,* F. 248, op. 126, *Dela i prigovory Pravitel'stvuiushchego Senata po Oren-burgskoi gubernii,* d. 135, 1735–37gg., l. 78; Vitevskii, *Nepliuev,* p. 439; Khodarkovsky, *Where Two Worlds Met,* pp. 208–9.

79. *PSZ,* vol. 16, no. 11,886, p. 321.

80. *AOGA,* F. 1010, op. 1, *Astrakhanskaia prikaznaia izba,* d. 5, l. 1–2; *PSPREP,* vol. 2 (1744–45) (St. Petersburg, 1907), no. 933, p. 448; *PSPR,* vol. 6 (1727–30) (St. Petersburg, 1889), no. 2214, pp. 313–16.

81. *RGADA,* F 248, op. 113, d. 1412, l. 6; *Kazakhsko-russkie otnosheniia v 16–18 vv.,* no. 224, pp. 570–71.

82. *AVPRI,* F. 119, op. 5, *Kalmytskie dela,* 1755g., d. 17, ll. 17–20.

83. *Kabardino-russkie otnosheniia,* vol. 2, nos. 98–99, pp. 122–24; no. 124, pp. 167–68; no. 212, p. 298. For the earliest accounts chronicling Russian expansion in the Caucasus see S. M. Bronevskii, *Istoricheskie vypiski o snosheniiakh Rossii s Persiei, Gruziei i voobshche s gorskimi narodami, v Kavkaze obitaiushchimi, so vremen Ivana Vasil'evicha do nyne,* ed. I. K. Pavlova (St. Petersburg: Peterburgskoe Vostokovedenie, 1996); Butkov, *Materialy dlia novoi istorii Kavkaza, s 1722 po 1803 god;* and Michael Khodarkovsky, "Of Christianity, Enlightenment, and Colonialism: Russia in the North Caucasus, 1500–1800," *Journal of Modern History* 71, no. 2 (1999), pp. 394–430.

84. *Kazakhsko-russkie otnosheniia,* vol. 2, no. 175, p. 236; no. 212, pp. 298–99.

85. Ibid., vol. 2, no. 202, pp. 282–84.

86. Ibid., vol. 2, no. 213, p. 302.

87. Ibid., vol. 2, nos. 194–95, pp. 269–73; no. 212, p. 298.

88. Ibid., vol. 2, no. 227, p. 331; no. 223, p. 321.

89. *VIA,* F.52, op. 1, d. 286, pt. 3, ll. 8–10; *Kabardino-russkie otnosheniia,* vol. 2, no. 251, p. 355.

90. *PDRV,* vol. 8, pp. 11–12.

91. Ibid., vol. 11, pp. 100–101.

92. Nil Popov, *V. N. Tatishchev i ego vremia* (Moscow: Tip. V. Gracheva, 1861), pp. 339–40. Pal'mov cites several other such cases; see Pal'mov, *Etiudy,* vol. 2, pp. 128, 139, 142.

93. *RGADA,* F. 248, op. 113, d. 181, ll. 4–13, 23, 38; *Kazakhsko-russkie otnosheniia v 16–18 vv.,* no. 155, p. 406; Viatkin, *Batyr Srym,* p. 320. A year before the decree from the Empress Elizabeth instructed the Kalmyk khan, Donduk-Dashi, to punish the Kalmyks in the same manner; see Khodarkovsky, *Where Two Worlds Met,* pp. 45, 166, 222. The issue of barimta remained no less pertinent in the nineteenth century; see Virginia Martin, "Barimta: Nomadic Custom, Imperial Crime," in Brower and Laz-zerini, eds., *Russia's Orient,* pp. 249–70.

94. Novosel'skii, *Bor'ba,* pp. 148–49; Khodarkovsky, *Where Two Worlds Met,* pp. 43–44, 214.

95. Khodarkovsky, *Where Two Worlds Met,* pp. 44–45, 225, 230–32.

96. *PSZ,* vol. 22, no. 15,991, pp. 142–44; no. 16,292, pp. 493–95; no. 16,400, pp. 604–6; *Istoriia Kazakhskoi SSR,* vol. 3 (1979), pp. 118–120; *Kazakhsko-russkie otnosheniia v 18–19 vv.,* no. 66, p. 120; Viatkin, *Batyr Srym,* p. 225. For more on the Frontier Courts, see ch. 4.

97. *GAOO,* F. 5, op. 1, 1788g., d. 22, ll. 35–71; *Kazakhsko-russkie otnosheniia v 18–19 vv.,* no. 70, pp. 129–30.

98. Viatkin, *Batyr Srym,* pp. 242–45.

99. Ibid., pp. 346–57. For more details see ch. 4.

100. Khodarkovsky, *Where Two Worlds Met,* pp. 163, 182–85, 230. For a discussion of Russia's military and political expansion along the southern frontier in the eighteenth century, see John P. LeDonne, *The Russian Empire and the World, 1700–1917* (Oxford: Oxford University Press, 1997), pp. 89–154.

101. *AVMF,* F. 212, op. 1, no. 33, l. 161.

102. Khodarkovsky, *Where Two Worlds Met,* p. 249; *Kazakhsko-russkie otnosheniia v 16–18 vv.,* no. 228, p. 596; *Istoriia Kazakhskoi SSR,* vol. 1 (1957), pp. 282–83.

103. *Kazakhsko-russkie otnosheniia v 16–18 vv.,* d. 199, pp. 525–26. The Kalmyks confronted the same issue; see Khodarkovsky, *Where Two Worlds Met,* pp. 217, 224, 227.

104. *PSZ,* vol. 22, no. 16,292, pp. 493–95; no. 16,400, pp. 604–6; no. 16,593, pp. 951–52.

105. *Rossiiskaia Akademiia Nauk. Arkhiv,* F. 1714, op. 1, *Novosel'skii, A. A,* no. 66, l. 51.

106. *Kabardino-russkie otnosheniia,* vol. 2, no. 125, pp. 168–69. For a brief description of the military settlements in the North Caucasus, see John P. LeDonne, *Ruling Russia: Politics and Absolutism in the Age of Absolutism, 1762–1796* (Princeton: Princeton University Press, 1984), pp. 294–97.

107. *RGADA,* F. 248, op. 113, d. 1257, ll. 1, 19, 20; *AVPRI,* F. 118, op. 1, *Kizliarskie i Mozdokskie dela,* d. 1; *Kabardino-russkie otnosheniia,* vol. 2, no. 164, pp. 218–19. Of course, reality was always somewhat different from the ideal, and a shortage of settlers and resources compelled the government not only to bring thousands of serfs and state peasants but also to encourage some Tatars and Kalmyks to settle the region; see *PSZ,* vol. 22, no. 16,194, pp. 388–92; Pal'mov, *Etiudy,* vol. 5, p. 6.

108. I. A. Gol'denshtedt, *Geograficheskoe i statisticheskoe opisanie Gruzii i Kavkaza* (St. Petersburg, 1809), p. 4.

109. *Kabardino-russkie otnosheniia,* vol. 2, no. 99, p. 123.

110. *VIA,* F. 52, op. 1, d. 286, pt. 3, ll. 20–25; *AVPRI, Kabardinskie dela,* F. 115, op. 4, d. 2.

111. *VIA,* F. 52, op. 1, d. 567, l. 42; *AVPRI, Ingushkie dela,* F. 114, op. 1.

112. *Kabardino-russkie otnosheniia,* vol. 2, no. 256, p. 361.

113. Ibid., nos. 188–89, pp. 255–59; no. 251, p. 355; *Don i Stepnoe Predkavkaz'e, 18–pervaia polovina 19 v. Zaselenie i khoziaistvo* (Rostov-na-Donu, 1977), p. 61.

Conclusion

1. The issue of the Mongol impact on Russia has been thoroughly politicized in Russian historiography. Most Russian and Soviet historians attributed Russia's backwardness vis-à-vis the West to the Mongol "yoke." Some Western historians argued that Mongol impact was short-lived and largely benign with an implication that the causes of Russian backwardness had to be looked for within Russian society proper.

For a balanced view of the issue see Charles J. Halperin, "Russia in the Mongol Empire in Comparative Perspective," *Harvard Journal of Asiatic Studies* 43, no. 1 (1983), pp. 239–61, and recently Ostrowski, *Muscovy and the Mongols,* pp. 36–132.

2. Novosel'skii, *Bor'ba,* pp. 434–42.

3. For instance, the construction cost of the fortification line in the Kozlov district in the 1630s was estimated at five hundred rubles per kilometer. This was a conservative estimate, and it did not take into account large and numerous indirect costs; see Zagorovskii, *Belgorodskaia cherta,* p. 89; Davies, *The Role of the Town Governors,* vol. 2, pp. 490–509. The construction of the Tsaritsyn fortification line in 1718 was another example of the government's priorities. Despite long-existing plans for the construction of a canal connecting the Volga and Don rivers, the government chose to build in its place a fortified line, which effectively sealed off a route often used for nomadic incursions. The formidable nature of these defenses made a lasting impression on contemporaries. By 1777 the Tsaritsyn line was no longer necessary, and its garrisons were moved farther south to the newly built fortification lines in the North Caucasus. Despite the large expenditures, the commitment of resources and military personnel, and the transitory nature of such fortification lines, security and military concerns remained the government's top priority. The construction of the Volga-Don canal, which was planned and undertaken many times, had to wait until the 1950s.

4. No less significant were the natives' high death rates from exposure to measles, syphilis, and tuberculosis. This issue has attracted no attention from scholars of Russia and still awaits serious investigation. Sporadic archival evidence indicates, however, that the spread of diseases must have been as detrimental to various indigenous populations as that in the better documented case of the Native Americans.

5. Robert Bartlett and Angus MacKay, eds., *Medieval Frontier Societies* (Oxford: Oxford University Press, 1989). Consider also the following remark by the nineteenth-century French political scientist Emile Boutmy. He concluded that America was not so much a democracy but a huge commercial company for the discovery, cultivation, and capitalization of its enormous territory: "The United States are primarily a commercial society . . . and only secondarily a nation"; see William Cronon, *Nature's Metropolis* (New York: W. W. Norton, 1991), p. 53.

6. Those who attempted to question Russian policies and suggest an alternative were discouraged from doing so. One characteristic example was that of Khan-Giray, a native of the Caucasus and an officer in the Russian military. In 1836 he submitted his manuscript "Zapiski o Cherkessii" for approval of government officials. The manuscript was placed among the classified documents and was under review by senior Russian officials for four years until Emperor Nicholas I personally found its publication "inconvenient." The manuscript was kept secret and remained buried in the archives until finally discovered in the 1950s. It remains unpublished. See M. O. Kosven, *Etnografiia i istoriia Kavkaza* (Moscow: Vostochnaia literatura, 1961), pp. 196–98; *Khan-Girei. Izbrannye proizvedeniia* (Nal'chik: "El'brus," 1974), pp. 15–18.

7. There is an important distinction between a settler colony (Australia) and a nonsettler one (India); see Patrick Wolfe, "History and Imperialism: A Century of Theory, from Marx to Postcolonialism," *American Historical Review* 102, no. 2 (1997), pp. 418–19.

BIBLIOGRAPHY

Archival Sources

Arkhiv vneshnei politiki Rossiiskoi imperii (AVPRI), Moscow
F. 114, op. 1, *Ingushskie dela*, d. 1
F. 115, op. 4, *Kabardinskie dela*, d. 2
F. 118, op. 1, *Kizliarskie i Mozdokskie dela*, d. 1
F. 119, op. 2, *Kalmytskie dela*, 1761g., d. 7; 1769–76gg., kn. 33
F. 119, op. 5, *Kalmytskie dela*, 1755g., d. 17

Arkhiv Voenno-Morskogo Flota (AVMF), Petersburg
F. 212, op. 1, d. 33
F. 233, op. 1, *Kantseliariia grafa Apraksina*, dela 12, 222, 228

Astrakhanskii oblastnoi gosudarstvennyi arkhiv (AOGA), Astrakhan
F. 394, op. 2, *Astrakhanskaia gubernskaia kantseliariia*, d. 12
F. 1010, op. 1, *Astrakhanskaia prikaznaia izba*, dela 5, 7

Bashbakanlik Arshivi, Istanbul
Hatti Hümayun Tasnifi, nos. 73, 94

Gosudarstvennyi arkhiv Orenburgskoi Oblasti (GAOO), Orenburg
F. 3, op. 1, *Orenburgskaia gubernskaia kantseliariia*, dela 18, 118–21
F. 5, op. 1, d. 22, 1788g.; d. 44, 1791–92gg.

Kazanskii Universitet. Rukopisnyi otdel, Kazan, Tatarstan
Nos. 4393, 4866–72, 4876

Rossiiskaia Akademiia Nauk. Arkhiv, Moscow
F. 1714, op. 1, *Novosel'skii, Aleksei Andreevich,* d. 66, *Russko-krymskie otnosheniia v 17 veke*

Rossiiskii gosudarstvennyi arkhiv drevnikh aktov (RGADA), Moscow
F. 89, *Posol'skii prikaz. Turetskie dela,* kn. 3
F. 115, op. 1, *Posol'skii prikaz. Kabardinskie, cherkesskie i drugie dela,* dela 3, 6
F. 119, op. 1, *Posol'skii prikaz. Kalmytskie dela,* dela 3, 4, 8
F. 123, *Posol'skii prikaz. Krymskie dela,* knigi 9, 13, 15
F. 127, op. 1, *Posol'skii prikaz. Nogaiskie dela,* knigi 9, 10; d. 2
F. 138, op. 1, *Dela o Posol'skom prikaze i sluzhivshikh v nem,* dela 1, 15
F. 248, op. 3, *Kantseliariia Senata. Dela po Azovskoi gubernii, 1713–18gg.,* kn. 96
F. 248, op. 3 *Senat. Dela po guberniiam. Dela po Astrakhanskoi gubernii, 1720–21,* kn. 94
F. 248, op. 3. *Senat. Dela po guberniiam. Dela po Orenburgskoi komissii i Ufimskoi provintsii za 1742–43gg.,* kn. 147
F. 248, op. 113, *Opis' del Sekretnoi Ekspeditsii Senata,* dela 181, 257, 1257, 1412
F. 248, op. 126, *Dela i prigovory Pravitel'stvuiushchego Senata po Astrakhanskoi gubernii,* 1716–22gg., d. 90
F. 248, op. 126, *Dela i prigovory Pravitel'stvuiushchego Senata po Orenburgskoi gubernii,* d. 135, 1735–37gg.
F. 1274, op. 1, d. 211, 1775g.

Tsentral'nyi derzhavnyi istorychnyi arkhiv Ukrainy v misti Kjivi, Kiev, Ukraine
F. 59, op. 1, d. 2668

Tsentral'nyi gosudarstvennyi arkhiv Respubliki Kalmykiia (TsGARK), Elista, Kalmyk Republic
F. 27, op. 2, *Astrakhanskaia kontora kalmytskikh i tatarskikh del,* d. 5
F. 35, op. 1, *Kalmytskaia ekspeditisiia pri Astrakhanskoi gubernskoi kantseliariii,* d. 6
F. 36, op. 1, *Sostoiashchii pri kalmytskikh delakh pri Astrakhanskom gubernatore,* dela 7, 9

Tsentral'nyi gosudarstvennyi voenno-istoricheskii arkhiv Rossiskoi Federatsii (VIA), Moscow
F. 52, op. 1, d. 286, pt. 3
F. 52, op. 1, d. 567; d. 350, pt. 4; d. 72, pt. 1
F. VUA, d. 18,472

Primary Sources

Abul-Ghazi Bahadur Khan. *Rodoslovnoe drevo tiurkov.* Edited and translated by G. S. Sablukov. Kazan: Tip. Imp. Universiteta, 1914.
Akty istoricheskie, sobrannye i izdannye Arkheograficheskoi komissiei. 5 vols. St. Petersburg, 1841–43.
Akty, sobrannye Kavkazskoi Arkheograficheskoi komissiei. Vols. 1–12. Tiflis, 1866–83.
Akty, sobrannye v bibliotekakh i arkhivakh Rossiiskoi Imperii Arkheograficheskoi Ekspeditsieiu Imp. Akademii Nauk. 4 vols. St. Petersburg: Tip. II otd. Imp. Kantseliarii, 1836.

Beauplan, Guillaume le Vasseur, Sieur de. *A Description of Ukraine.* Edited and translated by Andrew Pernal and Dennis Essar. Cambridge, Mass.: Harvard Ukrainian Research Institute, 1993.

Bronevskii, S. M. *Istoricheskie vypiski o snosheniiakh Rossii s Persiei, Gruziei i voobshche s gorskimi narodami, v Kavkaze obitaiushchimi, so vremen Ivana Vasil'evicha do nyne.* Edited by I. K. Pavlova. St. Petersburg: Peterburgskoe Vostokovedenie, 1996.

Cook, John, M.D. *Voyages and Travels through the Russian Empire, Tartary, and Part of the Kingdom of Persia.* 2 vols. Edinburgh, 1770. Reprint, ed. A. L. Fullerton, Newtonville, Mass.: Oriental Research Partners, 1997.

Dnevnye zapiski puteshestviia Kapitana Nikolaia Rychkova v kirgis-kaisatskoi stepi, 1771 god. St. Petersburg: Imp. Akademiia Nauk, 1772.

Dokumenty i materialy po istorii Mordovskoi ASSR. 3 vols. Saransk, 1939–51.

Dopolneniia k aktam istoricheskim, sobrannye i izdannye Arkheograficheskoi komissiei. 12 vols. St. Petersburg, 1846–75.

Drevniaia rossiiskaia vivliofika. Compiled by Nikolai Novikov. 2nd ed. 22 vols. Moscow: Tip. kompanii tipograficheskoi, 1788–1791. Reprint, ed. C. H. van Schooneveld, *Slavic Printings and Reprintings,* 250/1. The Hague-Paris: Mouton, 1970.

Dukhovnye i dogovornye gramoty velikikh i udel'nykh kniazei 14–16 vv. Edited by L. V. Cherepnin. Moscow-Leningrad: AN SSSR, 1950.

Epifanii. *Zhitie Sviatogo Stefana, episkopa Permskogo.* St. Petersburg: Tip. Imp. AN, 1897.

Findiklili, Silahtar Mehmet Aga. *Nusretname.* 2 vols. Edited by Ismet Parmaksizoglu. Istanbul, 1962–66.

Gosudarstvennyi arkhiv Rossii 16 stoletiia: Opyt rekonstruktsii. Prepared by A. A. Zimin. Moscow: Institut Istorii AN SSSR, 1978.

Herberstein, Sigizmund. *Zapiski o Moskovitskikh delakh.* St. Petersburg: Tip. A. S. Suvorin, 1908.

Istoriia Tatarii v materialakh i dokumentakh. Moscow: Gos. sots-ekon. izd., 1937.

Kabardino-russkie otnosheniia v 16–18 vv.: Dokumenty i materialy. 2 vols. Moscow: AN SSSR, 1957.

Kazakhsko-russkie otnosheniia v 16–18 vekakh: Sbornik dokumentov i materialov. Alma-Ata: AN Kazakhskoi SSR, 1961.

Kazakhsko-russkie otnosheniia v 18–19 vekakh: Sbornik dokumentov i materialov. Alma-Ata: Nauka, 1964.

Kirilov, I. K. *Tsvetushchee sostoianie vserossiiskogo gosudarstva.* Moscow: Nauka, 1977. Written in 1727.

Kolonial'naia politika Moskovskogo gosudarstva v Iakutii v 17 veke. Edited by Ia. P. Al'kor and B. D. Grekov. Leningrad: Institut narodov Severa, 1936.

Kotoshikhin, Grigorii. *O Rossii v tsarstvovanie Alekseia Mikhailovicha.* 4th ed. St. Petersburg: Tip. glavnogo upravleniia udelov, 1906.

Krest'ianskaia voina pod predvoditel'stvom Stepana Razina: Sbornik dokumentov. 4 vols. Moscow, 1954.

Materialy po istorii Bashkirskoi ASSR. Vol. 1: *Bashkirskie vosstaniia v 17 i pervoi polovine 18 vekov.* Moscow and Leningrad: Izd-vo AN SSSR, 1936.

Materialy po istorii Kazakhskoi SSR (1785–1828). Vol. 4. Moscow-Leningrad: AN SSSR, 1940.

Materialy po istorii Rossii: Sbornik ukazov i drugikh dokumentov, kasaiushchikhsia upravleniia i ustroistva Orenburgskogo kraia. Compiled by A. I. Dobromyslov. 2 vols. Orenburg: Tip. Sachkova, 1900.

Materialy po istorii Uzbekskoi, Tadzhikskoi i Turkmenskoi SSR. Vol. 1: *Torgovlia s Moskovskim gosudarstvom i mezhdunarodnoe polozhenie Srednei Azii v 16–17 vv.* Leningrad: AN SSSR, 1932.

Mezhdunarodnye otnosheniia v Tsentral'noi Azii. 17–18 vv.: Dokumenty i materialy. 2 vols. Moscow: Nauka, 1989.

The Muscovite Law Code (Ulozhenie) of 1649. Part 1: *Text and Translation.* Edited and translated by Richard Hellie. Irvine, Calif.: Charles Schlacks, Jr., 1988.

Opisanie gosudarstvennogo arkhiva starykh del. Compiled by P. I. Ivanov. Moscow: Tip. S. Selivanskogo, 1850.

Osmanli Devleti ile Azerbaycan Türk Hanliklari Arasindaki Münasabetlere dair Arshiv Belgeleri. Vol. 1 (1578–1914). Ankara, 1992.

Pamiatniki diplomaticheskikh i torgovykh snoshenii Moskovskoi Rusi s Persiei. Edited by N. I. Veselovskii. 3 vols. St. Petersburg, 1890–98.

Patriarshaia ili Nikonovskaia letopis'. In *Polnoe sobranie russkikh letopisei.* Vol. 13. Moscow: Nauka, 1965.

Perry, John. *The State of Russia under the Present Tsar.* London, 1716.

Pis'ma i bumagi imperatora Petra Velikogo. 12 vols. St. Petersburg and Moscow, 1887–1977.

Polnoe sobranie postanovlenii i rasporiazhenii po vedomstvu pravoslavnogo ispovedaniia Rossiiskoi imperii. 19 vols. St. Petersburg, 1869–1915.

Polnoe sobranie zakonov Rossiiskoi imperii: Sobranie pervoe. 45 vols. St. Petersburg, 1830.

Popov, A. N. "Snosheniia Rossii s Khivoiu i Bukharoiu pri Petre Velikom. Prilozheniia." *Zapiski Imperatorskogo russkogo geograficheskogo obshchestva* 9 (1853), pp. 237–424.

Pososhkov, I. T. *Zaveshchanie otecheskoe.* Edited by E. M. Prilezhaev. St. Petersburg: Sinodal'naia tip., 1893.

Possevino, Antonio, S. J. *The Moscovia.* Translated by Hugh F. Graham. Pittsburgh: University of Pittsburgh, 1977.

Prodolzhenie drevnei rossiiskoi vivliofiki. 11 vols. St. Petersburg: Imper. Akademiia Nauk, 1786–1801. Reprint, ed. C. H. van Schooneveld, *Slavic Printings and Reprintings,* 251. The Hague-Paris: Mouton, 1970.

Puteshestviia russkikh poslov 16–17 vv.: Stateinye spiski. Moscow-Leningrad: AN SSSR, 1954.

"Rasporiazheniia ob upravlenii Kalmytskim narodom." *Zhurnal Ministerstva Vnutrennikh Del* 15, no. 1 (1835), pp. I–XXXVI.

Rodoslovnaia kniga kniazei i dvorian Rossiiskikh i vyezzhikh. 2 vols. Moscow: Universitetskaia tip. Novikova, 1787.

Rozhdenstvenskii, N. V., ed. "Akty vremeni Lzhedmitriia 1-go (1603–1606), Nogaiskie dela." In *Chteniia v imperatorskom obshchestve istrorii i drevnostei rossiiskikh pri Moskovskom universitete: Sbornik,* vol. 264, pt. 1 (1918). Moscow, 1845–1918.

Russkaia istoricheskaia biblioteka. 39 vols. St. Petersburg and Leningrad, 1872–1927.

Russko-dagestanskie otnosheniia 17-pervoi chetverti 18 vv.: Dokumenty i materialy. Makhachkala: Dagestankoe kn. izd-vo, 1958.

Russko-kitaiskie otnosheniia v 17 veke: Materialy i dokumenty. 2 vols. Moscow: Nauka, 1972.

Russko-mongol'skie otnosheniia 1607–1636: Sbornik dokumentov. Moscow: Izd-vo vostoch-noi literatury, 1959.

Russko-ossetinskie otnosheniia v 18 veke, 1742–62. Vol. 1. Ordzhonikidze: Izd-vo "IR," 1976.

Rychkov, P. I. *Istoriia Orenburgskaia (1730–1750).* Orenburg, 1896.

———. "Topografiia Orenburgskoi gubernii." In *Orenburgskie stepi v trudakh P. I. Rychkova, E. A. Eversmana, S. S. Neustroeva,* pp. 41–204. Moscow: Izd-vo geo-graficheskoi lit., 1949.

Sbornik dokumentov po istorii Buriatii 17 v. Compiled by G. N. Rumiantsev and S. B. Okun'. Ulan-Ude: BNII, 1960.

Sbornik Imperatorskogo Russkogo Istoricheskogo Obshchestva. 148 vols. St. Petersburg, 1867–1916.

"Sharaf-Name-i-Shahi." In S. K. Ibragimov et al., eds., *Materialy po istorii kazakhskikh khanstv 15–18 vekov,* pp. 237–312. Alma-Ata: Nauka Kazakhskoi SSR, 1969.

Shcherbatov, Mikhail, kniaz'. *Istoriia Rossiiskaia.* 11 vols. St. Petersburg: Imp. Akad-emiia Nauk, 17—.

———. "Statistika v razsuzhdenii Rossii." In *ChOIDR,* book 3, pt. 11 (1859), pp. 46–92.

Slovar' russkogo iazyka 11–17 vv. Moscow: Nauka, 1978ff.

Snosheniia Rossii s Kavkazom. Materialy izvlechennye iz Moskovskogo Ministerstva Inostran-nykh del, 1578–1613. Compiled by S. L. Belokurov. Moscow: Universitetskaia tip., 1889.

Sreznevskii, I. I. *Materialy dlia slovaria drevne-russkogo iazyka po pis'mennym pamiat-nikam.* 4 vols. St. Petersburg: Tip. Imp. AN, 1912. Reprint, Moscow: Nauka, 1989.

Stepennaia kniga. 2 vols. Moscow: Tip. Imp. Universiteta, 1775.

"Ta'rikh-i Amniia." In S. K. Ibragimov et al., eds., *Materialy po istorii Kazakhskikh khanstv 15–18 vekov,* pp. 476–92. Alma-Ata: Nauka Kazakhskoi SSR, 1969.

"Ta'rikh-i Kipchaki." In S. K. Ibragimov et al., eds., *Materialy po istorii kazakhskikh khanstv 15–18 vekov,* pp. 386–97. Alma-Ata: Nauka Kazakhskoi SSR, 1969.

Vologodsko-permskaia letopis'. In *Polnoe sobranie russkikh letopisei,* vol. 26. Moscow-Len-ingrad: Nauka, 1959.

Weber, Friedrich Christian. *The Present State of Russia.* 2 vols. London, 1723.

Secondary Sources

Alexander, John T. *Catherine the Great: Life and Legend.* New York: Oxford University Press, 1989.

Algar, Hamid. "Nakshbandiyya." In C. E. Bosworth et al., eds., *The Encyclopaedia of Islam,* vol. 7, pp. 933–39. New Edition. Leiden, 1992.

Apollova, N. G. *Ekonomicheskie i politicheskie sviazi Kazakhstana s Rossiei v 18-nachale 19 v.* Moscow: AN SSSR, 1960.

Azamatov, Danil' D. "Russian Administration and Islam in Bashkiriia (18th–19th Centuries)." In Michael Kemper, Anke von Kügelgen, and Dmitriy Yermakov, eds., *Muslim Culture in Russia and Central Asia from the 18th to the Early 20th Centu-ries,* pp. 91–111. Berlin: Klaus Schwarz Verlag, 1996.

Bagalei, D. I. *Ocherki iz istorii kolonizatsii stepnoi okrainy Moskovskogo gosudarstva.* Mos-cow: Universitetskaia Tip., 1887.

Bagin, S., priest. *Ob otpadenii v magometanstvo kreshchennykh inorodtsev Kazanskoi eparkhii i o prichinakh etogo iavleniia.* Kazan: Tsentral'naia Tip., 1910.

Bakhrushin, S. V. "Iasak v Sibiri v 17 v." In *Nauchnye trudy,* vol. 3, pt. 2, pp. 49–85. Moscow: AN SSSR, 1952–59.

———. "Ocherki po istorii Krasnoiarskogo uezda v 17 v." In *Nauchnye trudy,* vol. 4, pp. 7–192.

———. "Ostiatskie i vogul'skie kniazhestva v 16 i 17 vv." In *Nauchnye trudy,* vol. 3, pt. 2, pp. 86–152.

Bakunin, Vasilii. "Opisanie istorii kalmytskogo naroda." *Krasnyi arkhiv: Istoricheskii zhurnal* no. 3 (1939), pp. 189–254.

Barfield, Thomas J. *The Perilous Frontier: Nomadic Empires and China.* Cambridge, Mass.: Basil Blackwell, 1989.

Bartlett, Robert. *The Making of Europe: Conquest, Colonization and Cultural Change, 950–1350.* Princeton: Princeton University Press, 1993.

Bartlett, Robert, and Angus MacKay, eds. *Medieval Frontier Societies.* Oxford: Oxford University Press, 1989.

Basin, V. Ia. *Rossiia i kazakhskie khanstva v 16–18 vv.* Alma-Ata: "Nauka" Kazakhskoi SSR, 1971.

Bassin, Mark. "Turner, Solov'ev, and the 'Frontier Hypothesis': The Nationalist Signification of Open Spaces." *Journal of Modern History* 65, no. 3 (1993), pp. 473–511.

Batmaev, M. M. *Kalmyki v 17–18 vekakh: Sobytiia, liudi, byt.* Elista: Kalmytskoe knizhnoe izd-vo, 1993.

Bazilevich, K. B. *Vneshniaia politika Russkogo tsentralizovannogo gosudarstva: Vtoraia polovina 15 veka.* Moscow: Moskovskii Universitet, 1952.

Bennigsen, Alexander. "L'Expédition turque contre Astrakhan en 1569, d'après les Registres des 'Affaires importantes' des Archives ottomanes." *Cahiers du Monde Russe et Soviétique* 8, no. 3 (1967), pp. 427–46.

———. "Un mouvement populaire au Caucase au XVIII siècle: La 'Guerre Sainte' du *sheikh* Mansur (1785–1791), page mal connue et controversée des relations russo-turques." *Cahiers du Monde Russe et Soviétique* 5, no. 2 (1964), pp. 159–205.

Bogoiavlenskii, S. K. "Materialy po istorii kalmykov v pervoi polovine 17 veka." *Istoricheskie zapiski* no. 5 (1939), pp. 48–101.

Bostan, Idris. "Rusya'nin Karadeniz'de Ticarete Bashlamasi ve Osmanli Imperatorlugu (1700–1787)." *Türk Tarih Kurumu, Belleten* 159 (1995), pp. 353–94.

Bregel, Yuri. "Tribal Tradition and Dynastic History: The Early Rulers of the Qongrats According to Munis." *Asian and African Studies* 16 (1982), pp. 386–401.

Burchinova, L. S. "Kalmykiia v sisteme gosudarstvennogo upravleniia Rossii." In *Dobrovol'noe vkhozhdenie Kalmytskogo naroda v sostav Rossii: Istoricheskie korni i znachenie,* pp. 48–56. Elista, 1985.

Burton, Audrey. *The Bukharans: A Dynastic, Diplomatic and Commercial History, 1550–1702.* New York: St. Martin's Press, 1997.

Butkov, P. G. *Materialy dlia novoi istorii Kavkaza, s 1722 po 1803 god.* 3 vols. St. Petersburg, 1869.

Chekin, Leonid. "The Godless Ishmaelites: The Image of the Steppe in Eleven–Thirteenth Centuries Rus." *Russian History, The Frontier in Russian History* 19, nos. 1–4 (1992), pp. 9–28.

Cherniavsky, Michael. "Khan or Basileus: An Aspect of Russian Mediaeval Political Theory." *Journal of the History of Ideas* 20, no. 4 (1959), pp. 459–76.

Chicherina, S. V. *O privolzhskikh inorodtsakh i sovremennom znachenii sistemy N. I. Il'minskogo.* St. Petersburg: Elektro-Tip. N. Ia. Stoikovoi, 1906.

Collins, L. J. D. "The Military Organization of the Crimean Tatars during the 16th and 17th Centuries." In V. J. Parry and M. E. Yapp, eds., *War, Technology and Society in the Middle East,* pp. 257–76. London: Oxford University Press, 1975.

———. "On the Alleged 'Destruction' of the Great Horde in 1502." In A. Bryer and M. Ursinus, eds., *Manzikert to Lepanto: The Byzantine World and the Turks, 1071–1575,* pp. 361–400. Amsterdam: Adolf M. Hakkert, 1991.

Comaroff, Jean, and John Comaroff. *Of Revelation and Revolution: Christianity, Colonization and Consciousness in South Africa.* Vol. 1. Chicago: University of Chicago Press, 1991.

Cronon, William. *Nature's Metropolis.* New York: W. W. Norton, 1991.

Davies, Brian. "The Recovery of Fugitive Peasants from Muscovy's Southern Frontier: The Case of Kozlov, 1636–40." *Russian History, The Frontier in Russian History* 19, nos. 1–4 (1992), pp. 29–56.

———. *The Role of the Town Governors in the Defense and Military Colonization of Muscovy's Southern Frontier: The Case of Kozlov, 1635–38.* 2 vols. Ph.D. dissertation, University of Chicago, 1983.

Davies, Norman. *God's Playground: A History of Poland.* 2 vols. New York: Columbia University Press, 1982.

D'iaki i pod'iachie posol'skogo prikaza v 16 veke. Spravochnik. Compiled by V. I. Savva. Moscow: Institut istorii SSSR, 1983.

Dmitriev, V. D. "'Tsarskie' nakazy Kazanskim voevodam 17 veka." In *Istoriia i kul'tura Chuvashskoi ASSR: Sbornik statei,* vol. 3, pp. 293–324. Cheboksary, 1974.

Dobrosmyslov, A. "Zaboty imperatritsy Ekateriny II o prosveshchenii kirgizov." *Trudy Orenburgskoi uchenoi arkhivnoi komissii* no. 9 (1902), pp. 51–63.

Don i Stepnoe Predkavkaz'e, 18-pervaia polovina 19 v: Zaselenie i khoziaistvo. Rostov-na-Donu: Izd. Rostovskogo Universiteta, 1977.

Donnelly, Alton S. *The Russian Conquest of Bashkiria, 1552–1740: A Case Study in Imperialism.* New Haven: Yale University Press, 1968.

Dordzhieva, G. Sh. "Politika samoderzhaviia i pravoslavnaia missiia sredi kalmykov (konets 17 v.–1771 g.)." In *Kul'tura i byt Kalmykov (Etnograficheskie issledovaniia).* Elista, 1977.

Dorofeev, V. V. *Nad Uralom-rekoi.* Cheliabinsk: Iuzho-Ural'skoe knizh. izd., 1988.

Egorov, V. L. *Istoricheskaia geografiia Zolotoi Ordy v 13–14 vv.* Moscow: Nauka, 1985.

Ermolaev, I. P. *Srednee Povolzh'e vo vtoroi polovine 16–17 vv.* Kazan: Kazanskii Universitet, 1982.

Febvre, Lucien. *A Geographical Introduction to History.* New York: Alfred Knopf, 1929.

Fedorov-Davydov, G. A. *Obshchestvennyi stroi Zolotoi Ordy.* Moscow: Moskovskii Universitet, 1973.

Fekhner, M. V. *Torgovlia russkogo gosudarstva so stranami vostoka v 15 veke.* Moscow: Nauka, 1956.

Fisher, Alan W. *The Crimean Tatars.* Stanford: Hoover Institution Press, 1978.

———. "The Ottoman Crimea in the Sixteenth Century." *Harvard Ukrainian Studies* 5, no. 2 (1981), pp. 141–42.

Frank, Allen J. *Islamic Historiography and "Bulghar" Identity among the Tatars and Bashkirs of Russia*. Leiden: Brill, 1998.

Gardanov, V. K. *Obshchestvennyi stroi Adygskikh narodov (18–pervaia polovina 19 v.)* Moscow: Nauka, 1967.

Gellner, Ernest. "Patrons and Clients." In Ernest Gellner and John Waterbury, eds., *Patrons and Clients in Mediterranean Societies*, pp. 1–18. London: Duckworth, 1977.

Geraci, Robert, and Michael Khodarkovsky, eds. *Of Religion and Empire: Missions, Conversion and Tolerance in Tsarist Russia*. Ithaca: Cornell University Press, 2001.

Gökbilgin, Özalp. *1532–77 Yillari Arasinda Kirim Hanligi'nin Siyasi Durumu*. Ankara: Sevinc Matbaasi, 1973.

Gol'denshtedt, I. A. *Geograficheskoe i statisticheskoe opisanie Gruzii i Kavkaza*. St. Petersburg, 1809.

Grekov, B. D., and A. Iu. Iakubovskii. *Zolotaia Orda i ee padenie*. Moscow and Leningrad: AN SSSR, 1950.

Halperin, Charles J. "The Ideology of Silence: Prejudice and Pragmatism on the Medieval Religious Frontier." *Comparative Studies in Society and History* 26, no. 4 (1984), pp. 442–66.

———. *Russia and the Golden Horde: The Mongol Impact on Medieval Russian History*. Bloomington: Indiana University Press, 1985.

———. "Russia in the Mongol Empire in Comparative Perspective." *Harvard Journal of Asiatic Studies* 43, no. 1 (1983), pp. 239–61.

———. *The Tatar Yoke*. Columbus, Ohio: Slavica Press, 1986.

Hellie, Richard. *The Economy and Material Culture of Russia, 1600–1725*. Chicago: University of Chicago Press, 1999.

———. *Enserfment and Military Change in Muscovy*. Chicago: University of Chicago Press, 1971.

Iakovlev, A. I. *Zasechnaia cherta Moskovskogo gosudarstva v 17 veke*. Moscow: Tip. I. Lisnera, 1916.

Iaudaev, U. "Chechenskoe plemia." In *Sbornik svedenii o kavkazskikh gortsakh*, vol. 6, pp. 2–14. Tiflis, 1868–81.

Inalcik, Halil. "The Customs Registers of Caffa, 1487–1490." In Victor Ostapchuk, ed., *Sources and Studies on the Ottoman Black Sea*. Cambridge, Mass.: Harvard University Press, 1996.

———. "Giray." In *Islam Ansiklopedisi*, vol. 4, pp. 783–85. Istanbul: Milli Egitim Basimevi, 1948.

———. "The Khan and the Tribal Aristocracy: The Crimean Khanate under Sahib Giray I." *Harvard Ukrainian Studies* 3–4 (1979–80), pt. 1, pp. 445–66.

———. "Osmanli-Rus Rekabetinin Menshei ve Don-Volga Kanali Teshebbüsü (1569)." *Türk Tarih Kurumu, Belleten*, no. 46 (1948), pp. 342–402.

———. and Donald Quataert, eds. *An Economic and Social History of the Ottoman Empire, 1300–1914*. Cambridge: Cambridge University Press, 1994.

Istoricheskoe opisanie drevnego Rossiiskogo muzeia pod nazvaniem masterskoi i Oruzheinoi palaty. Moscow: Tip. Moskovskogo Universiteta, 1807.

Istoriia Iakutskoi ASSR. 3 vols. Moscow: AN SSSR, 1957.

Istoriia Kazakhskoi SSR. 2 vols. Alma-Ata: AN Kazakhskoi SSR, 1957.

Istoriia Kazakhskoi SSR. 5 vols. Alma-Ata: "Nauka" Kazakhskoi SSR, 1977–81.

Istoriia narodov Severnogo Kavkaza s drevneishikh vremen do kontsa 18 v. Edited by B. B. Piotrovskii. Moscow: Nauka, 1988.

Istoriia russkoi perevodnoi khudozhestvennoi literatury. 2 vols. Edited by Iurii Levin. Vol. I: *Drevniaia Rus': 18 vek.* St. Petersburg: "Dmitrii Bulanin," 1995.

Istoriia Sibiri. 5 vols. Edited by A. P. Okladnikov. Leningrad: Nauka, 1968.

Istoriia Uzbekskoi SSR. 4 vols. Tashkent: Fan, 1967–68.

Iudin, V. P. "Ordy: Belaia, Siniaia, Seraia, Zolotaia." In *Kazakhstan, Sredniaia i Tsentral'naia Aziia v 16–18 vv.,* pp. 106–64. Alma-Ata: "Nauka" Kazakhskoi SSR, 1983.

Kappeler, Andreas. *Russlands erste Nationalitäten: Das Zarenreich und die Völker der Mittleren Wolga vom 16 bis 19 Jahrhundert.* Cologne: Böhlau Verlag, 1982.

Kashtanov, S. M. *Sotsial'no-politicheskaia istoriia Rossii kontsa 15–pervoi poloviny 16 v.* Moscow: Nauka, 1967.

Kazakova, N. A. *Russko-livonskie i russko-ganzeiskie otnosheniia. Konets 14–nachalo 16 v.* Leningrad: Nauka, 1975.

Keenan, Edward L. *Muscovy and Kazan, 1445–1552: A Study in Steppe Politics.* Ph.D. dissertation, Harvard University, 1965.

———. "Muscovy and Kazan: Some Introductory Remarks on the Patterns of Steppe Diplomacy." *Slavic Review* 26, no. 4 (1967), pp. 548–58.

———. "Reply." *Russian Review* 46, no. 2 (1987), pp. 198–212.

———. "The Yarlik of Axmed-Khan to Ivan III: A New Reading." *International Journal of Slavic Linguistics and Poetics* 11 (1967), pp. 32–47.

Kellner-Heinkele, Barbara. *Aus den Aufzeichnungen des Said Giray Sultan: Eine zeitgenössische Quelle zur Geschichte des Chanats der Krim um die Mitte des 18. Jarhhunderts.* Freiburg im Breslau: Klaus Schwarz Verlag, 1975.

Kemper, Michael. *Sufis und Gelehrte in Tatarien und Baschkirien, 1789–1889.* Berlin: Klaus Schwarz Verlag, 1998.

Khazanov, Anatoly. *Nomads and the Outside World.* Cambridge: Cambridge University Press, 1985.

Khodarkovsky, Michael. "From Frontier to Empire: The Concept of the Frontier in Russia, Sixteenth-Eighteenth Centuries." *Russian History, The Frontier in Russian History* 19, nos. 1–4 (1992), pp. 115–28.

———. "Ignoble Savages and Unfaithful Subjects": Constructing Non-Christian Identities in Early Modern Russia." In Daniel R. Brower and Edward J. Lazzerini, eds., *Russia's Orient: Imperial Borderlands and Peoples, 1700–1917,* pp. 9–26. Bloomington: Indiana University Press, 1997.

———. "'Not by Word Alone:' Missionary Policies and Religious Conversion in Early Modern Russia." *Comparative Studies in Society and History* 38, no. 2 (1996), pp. 267–93.

———. "Of Christianity, Enlightenment, and Colonialism: Russia in the North Caucasus, 1500–1800." *Journal of Modern History* 71, no. 2 (1999), pp. 394–430.

———. "The Stepan Razin Uprising: Was It a 'Peasant War'?" *Jahrbücher für Geschichte Osteuropas* 42, no. 1 (1994), pp. 1–19.

———. *Where Two Worlds Met: The Russian State and the Kalmyk Nomads, 1600–1771.* Ithaca: Cornell University Press, 1992.

Khoroshkevich, A. L. *Russkoe gosudarstvo v sisteme mezhdunarodnykh otnoshenii kontsa 15–nachala 16 v.* Moscow: Nauka, 1980.

Khudiakov, M. *Ocherki po istorii Kazanskogo khanstva.* Kazan: Gos. izd-vo, 1923. Reprint, Kazan, 1990.

Kivelson, Valerie A. *Autocracy in the Provinces: The Muscovite Gentry and Political Culture in the Seventeenth Century.* Stanford: Stanford University Press, 1996.

Kochekaev, B. A.-B. *Nogaisko-russkie otnosheniia v 15–18 vv.* Alma-Ata: Nauka Kazakhskoi SSR, 1988.

Kollmann Schields, Nancy. *By Honor Bound: State and Society in Early Modern Russia.* Ithaca: Cornell University Press, 1999.

Kostenkov, K. "O rasprostranenii khristianstva u kalmykov." *Zhurnal Ministerstva Narodnogo Prosveshcheniia* 144 (August 1869), pp. 103–59.

Kosven, M. O. *Etnografiia i istoriia Kavkaza.* Moscow: Vostochnaia literatura, 1961.

Kudriavtsev, I. M. "Izdatel'skaia' deiatel'nost' Posol'skogo prikaza (k istorii russkoi rukopisnoi knigi vo vtoroi polovine 17 veka)." *Kniga: issledovaniia i materialy. Sbornik* 8 (1963), pp. 179–244.

Kurat, A. N. "The Turkish Expedition to Astrakhan in 1569 and the Problem of the Don-Volga Canal." *Slavonic and East European Review* 40 (1961), pp. 7–23.

Kusheva, E. I. "Politika russkogo gosudarstva na Severnom Kavkaza v 1552–1572gg." *Istoricheskie zapiski* 34 (1950), pp. 236–87.

Kuzeev, R. G. *Narody Srednego Povolzhia i Iuzhnogo Urala.* Moscow: Nauka, 1992.

Kychanov, E. I. *Povestvovanie ob oiratskom Galdane Boshoktu-Khane.* Novosibirsk: Nauka, 1980.

LeDonne, John P. *Ruling Russia: Politics and Absolutism in the Age of Absolutism, 1762–1796.* Princeton: Princeton University Press, 1984.

———. *The Russian Empire and the World, 1700–1917.* Oxford: Oxford University Press, 1997.

Levshin, Aleksei. *Opisanie Kirgiz-Kazach'ikh ili Kirgiz-Kaisakskikh ord i stepei.* 3 parts. St. Petersburg: Tip. Karla Kraia, 1832.

Lewis, Bernard. *The Muslim Discovery of Europe.* New York: W. W. Norton, 1982.

Liubavskii, M. K. *Obzor istorii russkoi kolonizatsii s drevneishikh vremen i do XX veka.* Edited by A. Ia. Degtiarev. Moscow: Moskovskii Universitet, 1996.

Macaulay, Thomas Babington. "Ranke's History of the Popes." In *Critical Historical Essays.* 2 vols. London: J. M. Dent and Sons, 1907.

MacKay, Angus. *Spain in the Middle Ages: From Frontier to Empire, 1000–1500.* New York: St. Martin's Press, 1977.

Malov, Efim. "O novokreshchennykh shkolakh v 18 veke." *Pravoslavnoe obozrenie* 26 (July 1868), pp. 354–97.

Man'kov, A. G. *Ulozhenie 1649 goda: Kodeks feodal'nogo prava Rossii.* Leningrad: Nauka, 1980.

Martin, Janet. *Medieval Russia, 980–1584.* Cambridge: Cambridge University Press, 1995.

———. "Muscovite Frontier Policy: The Case of the Khanate of Kasimov." *Russian History, The Frontier in Russian History* 19, nos. 1–4 (1992), pp. 169–79.

———. "The Tiumen' Khanates' Encounters with Muscovy, 1481–1505." In C. Lemercier-Quelguejay et al., eds., *Passé Turco-Tatar: Présent Soviétique,* pp. 78–96. Paris: Editions Peeters, 1986.

Martin, Virginia. "Barimta: Nomadic Custom, Imperial Crime." In Daniel R. Brower and Edward J. Lazzerini, eds., *Russia's Orient: Imperial Borderlands and Peoples,* pp. 249–70. Bloomington: Indiana University Press, 1997.

Mozharovskii, Apollon. "Izlozhenie khoda missionerskogo dela po prosveshcheniiu inorodtsev s 1552 po 1867 goda." *ChOIDR* 1 (January–March 1880), pp. 1–237.

Nikitin, A. V. "Oboronitel'nye sooruzheniia zasechnoi cherty 16–17 vv." *Materialy i issledovaniia po arkheologii SSSR* 44 (1955), pp. 116–213.

Nogaitsy: Istoriko-geograficheskii ocherk. Edited by I. K. Kalmykov et al. Cherkessk: Stavropol'skoe kn. izd-vo, 1988.

Nordman, Daniel. *Frontières de France: de l'espace au territoire, XVI–XIX siècle.* Paris: Gallimard, 1998.

Novosel'skii, A. A. *Bor'ba Moskovskogo gosudarstva s tatarami v pervoi polovine 17 veka.* Moscow-Leningrad: AN SSSR, 1948.

Ocherki istorii Kalmytskoi ASSR. Vol. 1. Moscow: Nauka, 1967.

Olcott, Martha Brill. *The Kazakhs.* Stanford: Hoover Institution Press, 1987.

Ostapchuk, Victor. "Five Documents from the Topkapi Palace Archive on the Ottoman Defense of the Black Sea against the Cossacks (1639)." *Journal of Turkish Studies* 11 (1987), pp. 49–104.

Ostrowski, Donald. *Muscovy and the Mongols: Cross-Cultural Influences on the Steppe Frontier, 1304–1589.* Cambridge: Cambridge University Press, 1998.

Pagden, Anthony. *Lords of All the World: Ideologies of Empire in Spain, Britain and France, c. 1500–c. 1800.* New Haven: Yale University Press, 1995.

Pal'mov, N. N. *Etiudy po istorii privolzhskikh kalmykov 17 i 18 veka.* 5 vols. Astrakhan: Tip. Kalmoblitizdata, 1926–32.

Pelenski, Jaroslaw. "The Emergence of the Muscovite Claims to the Byzantine-Kievan 'Imperial Inheritance.'" *Harvard Ukrainian Studies* 7 (1983), pp. 520–31.

———. "The Origins of the Official Muscovite Claims to the 'Kievan Inheritance.'" *Harvard Ukrainian Studies* 1, no. 1 (1977), pp. 29–52.

———. *Russia and Kazan: Conquest and Imperial Ideology (1438–1560s).* The Hague: Mouton, 1974.

Pfaf, B. F. "Materialy po istorii osetin." *Sbornik svedenii o kavkazskikh gortsakh* 5 (1871), pp. 95–132.

Popov, Nil. *V. N. Tatishchev i ego vremia.* Moscow: Tip. V. Gracheva, 1861.

Power, Daniel. "Frontiers: Terms, Concepts, and the Historians of Medieval and Early Modern Europe." In Daniel Power and Naomi Standen, eds., *Frontiers in Question: Eurasian Borderlands, 700–1700,* pp. 1–13. London: Macmillan, 1999.

"Pravlenie tsaria Ivana Vasil'evicha." In *DRV,* vol. 17, pp. 108–77.

Preobrazhenskaia, P. S. "Iz istorii russko-kalmytskikh otnoshenii v 50–60kh godakh 17 veka." *Zapiski Kalmytskogo nauchno-issledovatel'skogo instituta iazyka, literatury i iskusstva* no. 1 (1960), pp. 49–84.

Pushkin, A. S. *Istoriia Pugachevskogo bunta.* Edited by P. A. Efremov. St. Petersburg: Izdanie Ia. A. Isakova, 1881.

Rafael, Vicente L. *Contracting Colonialism: Translation and Christian Conversion in Tagalog Society under Early Spanish Rule.* Ithaca: Cornell University Press, 1988.

Ransel, David L. *The Politics of Catherinian Russia: The Panin Party.* New Haven: Yale University Press, 1975.

Reddaway, W. F., et al., eds. *The Cambridge History of Poland to 1696.* Cambridge: Cambridge University Press, 1950.

Reychman, Jan, and Ananiasz Zajaczkowski. *The Handbook of the Ottoman-Turkish Diplomatics.* The Hague-Paris: Mouton: 1968.

Rorlich, Azade-Ayse. *The Volga Tatars: A Profile in National Resilience.* Stanford: Hoover Institution Press, 1986.

Rowland, Daniel B. "The Third Rome or the New Israel?" *Russian Review* 55, no. 4 (1996), pp. 591–614.

Saatchian, Georgii. "Russkoe Pole." *Rodina* no. 2 (1996), pp. 48–50.

Sadikov, P. A. "Pokhod tatar i turok na Astrakhan v 1569 g." *Istoricheskie zapiski* no. 22 (1947), pp. 132–66.

Safargaliev, M. G. *Raspad Zolotoi Ordy* in *Uchenye zapiski Mordovskogo gosudarstvennogo universiteta* 11 (1960), pp. 1–98.

Sahlins, Peter. *Boundaries: The Making of France and Spain in the Pyrenees.* Berkeley: University of California Press, 1989.

Sanin, G. A. *Otnosheniia Rossii i Ukrainy s Krymskim khanstvom v seredine 17 veka.* Moscow: Nauka, 1987.

Schorkowitz, Dittmar. *Die soziale und politische Organisation bei den Kalmücken (Oiraten) und Prozesse der Akkulturation vom 17. Jahrhundert bis zur Mitte des 19. Jahrhunderts.* Frankfurt am Main: Peter Lang, 1992.

Schurmann, H. F. "Mongolian Tributary Practices of the Thirteenth Century." *Harvard Journal of Asiatic Studies* 19 (1956), pp. 304–89.

Shastina, N. P. "Pis'ma Lubsan taidzhi v Moskvu." In *Filologiia i istoriia mongol'skikh narodov,* pp. 275–88. Moscow: Izd-vo vostochnoi literatury, 1958.

Shaw, Dennis J. B. "Southern Frontiers of Muscovy, 1550–1700." In J. H. Bater and R. A. French, eds., *Studies in Russian Historical Geography,* vol. 1, pp. 117–42. London: Academic Press, 1983.

Sinor, Denis. "Interpreters in Medieval Inner Asia." *Asian and African Studies, Journal of Israel Oriental Society* 16 (1982), pp. 293–320.

Slezkine, Yuri. *Arctic Mirrors: Russia and the Small Peoples of the North.* Ithaca: Cornell University Press, 1994.

————. "Naturalists versus Nations: Eighteenth-Century Russian Scholars Confront Ethnic Diversity." In Daniel R. Brower and Edward J. Lazzerini, eds., *Russia's Orient: Imperial Borderlands and Peoples, 1700–1917,* pp. 27–57. Bloomington: Indiana University Press, 1997.

Smirnov, V. D. *Krymskoe khanstvo pod verkhovenstvom Ottomanskoi Porty do nachala 18 veka.* St. Petersburg: Tip. A. S. Suvorina 1887.

Smith, John Masson, Jr. "Mongol and Nomadic Taxation." *Harvard Journal of Asiatic Studies,* 30 (1970), pp. 46–85.

Solov'ev, S. M. *Istoriia Rossii s drevneishikh vremen.* 15 vols. Moscow: Izd. sotsial'no-ekonomicheskoi literatury, 1959–66.

Stein, Mark. *Seventeenth-Century Ottoman Forts and Garrisons on the Habsburg Frontier.* Ph.D. dissertation, University of Chicago, 2000.

Stevens, Carol Belkin. *Soldiers on the Steppe: Army Reform and Social Change in Early Modern Russia.* DeKalb: Northern Illinois University Press, 1995.

Sugar, Peter F. "The Ottoman 'Professional Prisoner' on the Western Borders of the Empire in the Sixteenth and Seventeenth Centuries." *Etudes Balkaniques* 7, no. 2 (1971), pp. 82–91.

Suny, Ronald Grigor. *The Making of the Georgian Nation.* Bloomington: Indiana University Press, 1988.

Syroechkovskii, V. E. "Muhammed-Gerai i ego vassaly." *Uchenye zapiski MGU* 61 (1940), pp. 1–71.

Szeftel, Marc. "The Title of the Muscovite Monarch Up to the End of the Seventeenth Century." *Canadian-American Slavic Studies* 13, nos. 1–2 (1979), pp. 59–81.

Todorov, Tsvetan. *The Conquest of America*. New York: Harper Perennial, 1984.

Trepavlov, V. V. *Gosudarstvennyi stroi Mongol'skoi imperii 13 v.* Moscow: Vostochnaia literatura, 1993.

———. *Nogai v Bashkirii, 15–17 vv. Kniazheskie rody nogaiskogo proiskhozhdeniia*. Ufa, 1997.

Trubetskoi, Prince E. *Nasledie Chingiskhana*. Berlin, 1925.

Usmanov, M. A. *Zhalovannye akty Dzhuchieva ulusa, 14–16 vv.* Kazan: Kazanskii Universitet, 1979.

Valikhanov, Chokan. "Ablai." In *Sobranie sochinenii*, vol. 4, pp. 111–16. Alma-Ata: Kazakhskaia Sovetskaia Entsiklopediia, 1985.

Vel'iaminov-Zernov, V. V. *Issledovanie o Kasimovskikh tsariakh i tsarevichakh*. 4 vols. St. Petersburg: Imp Akademiia nauk, 1863–87.

Vernadsky, George. *A History of Russia*. 6th rev. ed. New Haven: Yale University Press, 1969.

———. *Russia at the Dawn of the Modern Age*. New Haven: Yale University Press, 1959.

Viatkin, M. P. *Batyr Srym*. Moscow and Leningrad: AN SSSR, 1947.

Vitevskii, V. N. *I. I. Nepliuev i Orenburgskii krai v prezhnem ego sostave do 1758g.* 3 vols. Kazan: Tip. V. M. Kliuchnikova, 1897.

White, Richard. *The Middle Ground: Indians, Empires, and Republics in the Great Lakes Region, 1650–1815*. Cambridge: Cambridge University Press, 1991.

Whittaker, Cynthia Hyla. "The Idea of Autocracy among Eighteenth-Century Russian Historians." In Jane Burbank and David L. Ransel, eds., *Imperial Russia: New Histories for the Empire*, pp. 32–59. Bloomington: Indiana University Press, 1998.

Wolfe, Patrick. "History and Imperialism: A Century of Theory, from Marx to Postcolonialism." *American Historical Review* 102, no. 2 (1997), pp. 388–420.

Wortman, Richard. *Scenarios of Power: Myth and Ceremony in Russian Monarchy*. Vol. 1. Princeton: Princeton University Press, 1995.

Zagorovskii, V. P. *Belgorodskaia cherta*. Voronezh: Voronezhskii Universitet, 1969.

Zhirmunskii, V. M. *Tiurkskii geroicheskii epos*. Leningrad: Nauka, 1974.

Zlatkin, I. Ia. *Istoriia Dzhungarskogo khanstva, 1635–1758*. 2nd ed. Moscow: Nauka, 1983.

Page references in italics refer to illustrations.

MICHAEL KHODARKOVSKY

is Associate Professor of History at Loyola University of Chicago. He is author of *Where Two Worlds Met: The Russian State and the Kalmyk Nomads, 1600-1771* and co-editor (with Robert Geraci) of *Of Religion and Empire: Missions, Conversion, and Tolerance in Tsarist Russia.*